ALSO BY JACQUELINE SIMENAUER

(with Anthony Pietropinto)
Beyond the Male Myth

SINGLES:
THE NEW
Americans

Jacqueline Simenauer and David Carroll

Simon and Schuster | New York

For my mother
Tillie Himelstein
who gave me courage

For my husband
Peter
and daughter
Tara
who give me happiness

SIMON AND SCHUSTER and colophon are trademarks of Simon & Schuster.
Designed by Irving Perkins Associates
Manufactured in the United States of America
1 2 3 4 5 6 7 8 9 10

Library of Congress Cataloging in Publication Data

Simenauer, Jacqueline.
  Singles: the new Americans.
  1. Single people—United States. 2. Social
surveys—United States. I. Carroll, David,
1942–   . II. Title.
HQ800.4.U6S54   305   81–23293
ISBN 0-671-25052-3   AACR2

Contents

Introduction
Singles in America

This book is written in an effort to fill an important gap, that of a definitive and nationally representative study revealing how single men and women in America conduct their private lives.

There have been, it is true, a number of volumes written on the subject of single life. But all of these are either first-person narratives, psychological overviews, or the "how-to-cope" variety of self-help book.

This work represents something quite different. It is not a book based on the personal views of the authors, but on an objective, scientifically designed survey of the social, psychological, and sexual aspects of single life, described by *singles themselves*.

This book is the first nationwide representative survey of singles ever done in the United States.

Thus if you are a single, if you are contemplating becoming single, or if you are a happily married person curious to know what those on the other side of matrimony are up to, in any case there is something here to pique your curiosity and feed your thought.

THE NEW AMERICANS

Approximately one out of every three adults in the United States, some fifty million people between the ages of twenty and fifty-five, are single. The post–World War II baby crop has matured with a vengeance, and an unprecedented number have chosen to wait longer before marrying, are obtaining divorces more frequently, or have decided to remain permanently uncommitted. Quick remarriage after divorce is becoming a thing of the past. Since 1970 the number of people who live alone has jumped from eleven million to 17.8 million according to 1980 Census Bureau statistics, and this accounts for almost a quarter of all American households. (In 1978 almost a fifth of all home-buyers were unmarried.)

Such statistics go on for pages. The message behind them is simple: The single population in America is on the increase.

We set out to establish a kind of psychosexual portrait of this growing population. We asked singles where they meet, what attracts and repels them during these first encounters. We asked about dating games and dating fears and pleasures, about sexual values and ploys, about the ups and downs people pass through in the first year of divorce. We probed for details concerning the pros and cons of cohabitation, of living by oneself, of being a single parent, of homosexuality, bisexuality, celibacy, virginity. We asked singles why they are single— whether it is by choice or by circumstance. Terms such as "loneliness," "promiscuity," "job satisfaction," "rejection," "personal growth," "physical fear," "guilt," "economic fulfillment," "friendship," "inadequacy," and "freedom" crop up frequently throughout the study. We attempted to sort out these responses and sketch a clear picture of the way singles perceive their situation. We questioned singles on their greatest problems and their most profound gratifications. Is single life the desperate, lonely affair we often hear described? Is it a giddy, unending orgy? We asked subjects what motivates them to stay single, what motivates them to remarry. How do the respondents compare single life with married life? Which do they ultimately prefer? Why? What advice would they give to those who are considering divorce; to those who are thinking of becoming single again?

On a broader plane we attempted to understand the state of being single as a *social and sociological* institution. Is the unmarried state in America a fad? Is it a trend? Will *all of us* at some future date be singles? Will singleness continue to proliferate, or will the swing of the pendulum reestablish the primacy of marriage? Do most singles view singleness as a permanent lifestyle to be pursued for its own sake? Or do they see it as a temporary condition, a transitionary period before or between marriages? And what, in fact, do they feel about marriage in general?

How, we asked, have such social movements as feminism affected the interplay between singles? Surely men have experienced the effects of this new movement in one way, women in another. Single life also varies in relation to socioeconomic class, educational and occupational background, age, and gender. Which group has the best time of it, which the worst? How do singles themselves see the future of their mode of life in America?

Responses to these and many more questions were often unexpected, seldom prosaic. Our sampling of singles represents a wide spectrum of personalities and world views ranging from the conservative, old-line, highly moral and traditional approach to life and love, through the laissez-faire "do your own thing" attitude, to the libertine and ultra-libertine porn-magazine, centerfold approach.

Though singles, perhaps surprisingly, generally tend toward a conservative rather than a radical bias, their ultimate attitude is difficult to pinpoint, since many singles are both more conservative *and* more experimental than ever before. (See, for example, the woman who praises the virtues of matrimony but believes in open marriage; or the single man who believes it is his prerogative to ask a woman out on the first date and her prerogative to ask on all the rest.)

While new and sometimes highly unconventional social modes are being tested, old modes are still treasured by a majority of singles, albeit in a somewhat altered form. And sometimes both attitudes are held side by side by the same individual. Often, in fact, we find singles torn between the traditional and modern, with many of them attempting to reconcile these unfamiliar companions in unusual ways.

HOW THIS BOOK WAS WRITTEN

This book was conceived more than three years ago. Though both authors had previously been involved in projects of magnitude (see Pietropinto and Simenauer, *Beyond the Male Myth*), neither realized just how much time, labor, expense, and thought this particular enterprise would ultimately demand.

First, the authors had to devise the questions—not an easy task as anyone who has ever tried to put together an impartial survey will know. In compiling such a questionnaire, each question must count one hundred percent; each of the six or seven possible answers must be designed to represent a separate finding in and of itself. The art of survey-writing is the art of putting as much as possible into as little space as is imaginable.

After a number of consultations with psychiatrists, psychologists, and sociologists; after several pretests with singles; after nine months of revision and restructuring, MARC—Marketing and Research Counselors, Inc.—one of the ten largest survey companies in the country, was selected to handle the study. They immediately spotted possible complications. Questions that probe psychological and sexual experience are invariably controversial. Would the questions be too personal? (Our fears were increased when we learned that two states [Utah and Virginia] would not allow MARC's field people to administer the questionnaire.) MARC had never administered a survey along these lines. Would their field people be able to handle this kind of sensitive material?

When the test results came in, a five-hundred-page computer printout plus thousands of handwritten essay replies, we breathed a sigh of relief. Not only had MARC's field people done their job well, not only had the respondents been generous with their time and private thoughts, but those questioned had not hesitated to give thorough answers to the essay questions as well, many of which turned out to be small masterpieces of drama, intrigue, and comedy.

And then the book had to be written. Information had to be pondered, sifted, collated, and organized endlessly. Meeting followed meeting. Then more notes, more ideas. Fifty psychiatrists and psychologists from across the country were consulted by phone and in person. They were presented with findings from the survey, always in their field of expertise, and were asked for professional analysis. Separate interviews were carried on with singles and with individuals connected with the singles world. This material would serve as a complement to the survey information. Concurrently, the authors pored through thousands of essay-questions, coming up with the most informative and intriguing responses from the lot. Slowly the work took shape. It was over two years in writing. In the end a kind of socio-psychological monolith emerged, a compendium of data covering practically every aspect of single life. This book is the result.

THE SURVEY IS REPRESENTATIVE

Before beginning this book, certain facts should be understood concerning the survey itself. The survey is the very heart of the book, its *raison d'etre,* and all other material included herein is designed as analysis, clarification, or addendum to its findings.

There are several ways to construct a survey. The group of people who walk down a certain street in a certain town may be asked for opinions on a particular subject. The results of these interviews may then be published as a survey. It is a survey all right, but a nonrepresentative one. The people included are all from a single geographical area, and are thus not indicative of the population distribution as a whole. They may be from all walks of life, education levels, all races, ages, all socioeconomic levels—or they may not. There is no way of telling. And if in fact there is a preponderance of people in, say, their twenties or thirties, or if most of the respondents are men, or if the majority of testees happen to come from a section of the community that holds a particular prejudice on the subject of the survey, then the objectivity will be even further skewed. A survey of this kind is a hit-or-miss affair even if it includes many thousands or even hundreds of thousands of replies. It is in no way *representative* of the entire nation.

To be representative, a survey must be mathematically designed by people familiar with population statistics. It must represent the whole country as reflected in the census figures. This means that a certain number of people should be interviewed in this state, a certain number in that state, the exact figure determined by previously established population ratios. Further, it means that testees who answer questions must be selected from a calculated cross section of socioeconomic, educational, occupational, and age levels throughout the country.

In other words, to be representative, a study must exhibit a kind of mini-model of the nation as a whole, a microcosm of society. In our survey we tested three thousand people. Because our study is representative, our findings would have remained virtually the same had we sampled three hundred thousand people. Or three million. To put it another way, if we learn that 50 percent of single male testees feel this way about a particular issue, we are saying, by extrapolation, that 50 percent of *all* single male Americans feel the same way about this issue.

HOW THE TEST WAS CONDUCTED

Three thousand men and women in 36 of our most populous states, 57 major cities, and 275 metropolitan areas participated in the survey. Respondents ranged in age from twenty to fifty-five. Some were new to single life, some old; some had married once, twice, or even three and four times, others had never been married at all.

Approximately 250 of MARC's field personnel were dispatched to hundreds of locations across the nation to find suitable respondents and administer our multiple-choice questionnaire containing fifty-five questions (each with six or seven possible answers) plus the essay questions. The individuals tested were asked to reveal in detail certain vital statistics concerning their marital status (married once, twice, never, and so on), type of sexual partners preferred, income, education, living arrangements, length of time single, age, occupation, and race. These were broken down as follows:

1. Marital status
   a. Never married
   b. Divorced once
   c. Divorced twice or more
   d. Widowed

2. Type of sexual partner preferred
   a. I prefer members of my own sex/I am bisexual
   b. I prefer members of the opposite sex
   c. I am celibate

3. Type of living arrangement
   a. Live with a member of the opposite sex
   b. Live with a member of the same sex
   c. Live alone
   d. Live with family
   e. Live with a group

4. Length of time you have been single
   a. Two years or less
   b. Three to five years
   c. Six to nine years
   d. Ten to thirty years
   e. All my life

5. Your age
   a. 20 to 24
   b. 25 to 34
   c. 35 to 44
   d. 45 to 55

6. Extent of education
   a. High school or less
   b. High school graduate
   c. Some college
   d. College graduate and more
   e. Postgraduate

7. **Annual income***
   a. Under $13,000
   b. $13,000 but under $18,000
   c. $18,000 but under $23,000
   d. $23,000 but under $28,000
   e. $28,000 but under $33,000
   f. $33,000 but under $43,000
   g. $43,000 and over

8. *Your occupation*
   Professional (Doctors, lawyers, engineers, stockbrokers, journalists, etc.)
   Managerial (Company officers, managers, proprietors, executives, etc.)
   Other white collar
   Blue collar
   Clerical (Including bookkeepers, secretaries, stenographers, telephone operators, etc.)
   Student
   Laborer
   Other (*specify*)

9. *Race*
   a. White
   b. Black
   c. Other†

The questionnaire was administered to singles in colleges, singles bars, singles apartment complexes, singles clubs, self-help groups, office buildings, discotheques, restaurants, recreation areas and centers, health and tennis clubs, places of work, community centers, Parents

* These statistics have been adjusted proportionately upward since the time of the original survey, in ratio to inflationary increases. Although our "high income group" is called "$23,000 and over" it actually encompasses a large group of people making considerably more than $23,000 a year. Approximately one-third of this group has an income of $33,-000 and over, and 10% of this "$23,000 and over" group has an income of over $43,000 a year.
† It should be pointed out that mention of racial subgroups vis-à-vis single life is intentionally kept to a minimum. The reason for this is not simply because the racial question is a sensitive one, but that in seeking single testees, MARC's field people discovered that black singles and white singles do not ordinarily mingle at the same spots. As a result, the number of single black people actually interviewed is well below the national average, registering at a false 4 percent; this means that any statistics concerning black or other racial minorities derived from these findings are not representative.

Without Partners chapters, and many other locations. All respondents were guaranteed complete anonymity as to name and address.

In addition, to learn what single people experience physically and emotionally during the initial stages of divorce, a separate two-page survey was designed to be answered exclusively by divorced singles. A separate section of the book is devoted to these unique findings.

Mounds of statistical material accumulated on the test sites. These were then returned to the testing company's main offices where they were fed into computers, the final printout providing not only the percentages for each question, but a complete breakdown of how testees in each of the subgroups responded.

For example, when we asked "Why are you single?" we not only learned that X percent of men and X percent of women are single because, as one answer states, "I like the lifestyle," but further, that X percent of *never married* men who *went to college, make more than twenty-three thousand dollars a year,* and *live alone* like the single lifestyle, as compared with, say, X percent of *twice-married, high school-educated* male *blue-collar workers.* Or, as another example, that X percent of *lesbian women over thirty-four years of age* who *live with their families* claim to "like the lifestyle," while another X percent of *once-divorced college women* in their early *twenties* are single because (as stated in a different answer) "I haven't found the right person to marry." As can be seen, the possibilities for comparison and combination are very large.

PROFILES AND BONUS FINDINGS

In order to take advantage of the subgroup findings without bogging down the text, two separate devices are used throughout the book. The first is titled "Profiles." These are portraits of men and women based on a combination of subgroup findings. For instance, included in Chapter 1 is a profile of the kind of woman one would be likely to meet at a singles bar. We arrived at this profile by consulting the subgroup findings to Question 1 ("Where do you meet most of the men/women you date?"), taking the highest percentage under each subgroup category (in this case women who specifically meet a majority of the men they date in bars), and combining them into a composite portrait. A picture of this person is thus assembled that includes her age, occupation, educational level, income, whether she lives at home, and so forth. There are many such profiles throughout the book, chosen both for their factual and for their inherent interest.

The second device is called "Bonus Findings." Bonus Findings are boxed-off sections of findings that, though of lesser importance, are nonetheless significant or curious enough to be included. They are found in most chapters of the book, and can be studied for their interesting secondary revelations or passed over quickly, according to the reader's taste. A sample Bonus Findings looks like this:

BONUS FINDINGS
- Forty percent of widowed men say they are single because they like the lifestyle. Only 4 percent of men divorced once feel the same way.
- The longer a man is single, the more likely he is to feel that he's unmarried because he hasn't met the right woman.
- Over half of men who have been divorced once say they plan to marry again, and that they like being married.
- Almost two-thirds of once-divorced women say that they like being married and will marry again if given the opportunity.
- High income–earning women tend to prefer the single life more than low income–earning women. Nine percent of women making thirteen thousand dollars or less say they want to be single, whereas 16 percent of women making over twenty-three thousand dollars say the same.

THE QUESTIONNAIRES

Two questionnaires were printed, one for men, one for women. Although many of the questions were the same for both sexes, some were not. A sample question looks like this:

1. *Where do you meet* most *of the men/women you date?*
  a. Through friends
  b. At social gatherings
  c. At bars, discos, nightclubs, etc.
  d. At singles functions

e. At work
f. Through personal ads in newspapers, magazines
g. Don't know

The questions are loosely organized to coincide with the chapter arrangements—which are in turn arranged to approximate the sequence in which single people meet, date, fall in love, settle down, and so forth. In other words, the chapters themselves follow the chronology that most singles go through in their social and romantic lives.

Before beginning, we would like to acknowledge help from the following people:

To Tim Prior of MARC for aid and attention beyond the call of duty; to the fifty or more professionals who gave their time and intellect to make this a better book; to Dr. Peter Stein, in recognition of his helpful critique; to Evelyn Tute, for her help and devotion; to Arnold Lyslo and Sarah Hollbrook, for their gift; to Anthony Pietropinto, M.D., for his insight and creativity; to the test subjects, and to those whom we personally interviewed, who opened their hearts as well as their minds; to Dan Green, for putting us on the right track; and to John Herman, for keeping us there; and lastly, to our mates, Hannah and Peter—so patient these many years!

Chapter 1

Meeting ||||

How and Where Singles Get Together

In this chapter on "Meeting" we ask:

1. Where do you meet most of the men/women you date?

2. How and where do you meet men/women, and how do you attract the men/women you want to meet? Is it difficult or easy to meet men/women today?

3. What sort of experiences resulted from meeting men at bars?

4. How often do women respond favorably to your attempts to pick them up in casual situations—at bars, parks, beaches, etc.?

5. What is the biggest obstacle to picking up a woman?

6. If an attractive opportunity presented itself, would you allow a man to pick you up?

7. Have you ever placed or answered personal advertisements in romantic or sexually oriented periodicals? If so, describe your more interesting experiences. What did you indulge in and with whom? Would you recommend the practice? If you never answered such ads, have you considered it? What stopped you? What do you imagine such experiences would be like?

8. List in order of importance the qualities that turn you on to a single man:

   1. Money, status and position

   2. Sense of humor

   3. Intelligence, perceptivity

   4. Physical attractiveness

   5. Skill as a lover

   6. Integrity, sensitivity, kindness, understanding

   7. Common interests, talents, backgrounds

9. What sort of man/woman turns you off and what sort of man/woman turns you on? How does the kind of man/woman that turns you on act, think, and speak?

10. Describe how you look to others (rate your own appearance).

11. What part does physical appearance play in your selection of a mate? Would you reject or become involved with a person on the grounds of looks alone? Why or why not?

12. Which of the two listed items most turns you off in a woman?

13. Which of the two listed items most turns you off in a man?

With many of the old rules concerning the sexes changing, there are opportunities for contact open to unmarried people today that were undreamed of a century ago—such opportunities as introduction clubs, nationwide singles groups, mechanical-electronic intermediaries, advertisements in the newspaper. How many singles avail themselves of the new dating "technology," the computer fix-ups and television introductions? Has the pickup achieved respectability? How many still find their romantic companions through the traditional methods of introduction and family contact? What do singles say about singles bars? About an encounter weekend, or a matchmaker's office? What kinds of people does one meet through these means? How often are such meetings successful? Do singles recommend them? And, perhaps most importantly, what are the attributes that singles search for in each other during these meetings? Our first question to respondents asked:

1. **Where do you meet most of the** | **Men** | **Women***
men/women you date?

	Men	Women*
a. Through friends	30%	36%
b. At social gatherings	22%	18%
c. At bars (discos, nightclubs, etc.)	24%	18%
d. At singles functions	14%	18%
e. At work	10%	9%
f. Through personal ads in news-papers, magazines	1%	—
g. Don't know	1%	2%

* Here and throughout, percentage totals that add up to materially more than 100 percent are due to multiple responses. Since numbers are rounded off, totals will often not equal exactly 100 percent.

Most singles meet in a relatively traditional way. Approximately a third meet through friends, another 30 percent at social gatherings or during work hours. This accounts for over 60 percent of the subjects.

From another standpoint, however, this means that almost 40 percent of respondents meet in a *non-traditional* manner, at bars and at singles functions in particular. This is a rather large number.

Major Finding: *Almost 40 percent of single men and women make their initial romantic contact at bars or single functions.*

Considering that fifty years ago introductions were made almost exclusively through family contacts, work, school, conventional social gatherings, and close friends, this finding shows what a major change has taken place in the way men and women meet. It also suggests that bars, introduction groups, singles functions, and the like, formerly considered barely legitimate, have recently become more or less acceptable. Even though the curse may not be entirely removed from such "introductionless" meeting practices, the pressures to meet are often so great that singles engage in them anyway.

BONUS FINDINGS

- The man who has been divorced once is equally at home meeting women in all the places mentioned above—at bars, through friends, at social gatherings. Men who have been divorced twice or more, however, have a predilection for singles bars—one third of divorced men meet most of the women they date there.
- The woman who is most likely to meet the men she dates through friends has never been married, lives with a roommate of the same sex (perhaps in a dormitory or shared apartment), and has a college degree.
- Though fewer than 10 percent of women meet their dates at work, those who do meet them on the job are likely to have been divorced at least once, to be in their early twenties, and to live alone, work in a white-collar situation, and have some college education.
- College students have the best chance of meeting partners through their friends. Professional people have the least chance.
- Among very successful career women, 40 percent claim friends are the best source of introduction, while one out of four will meet men at singles functions or at singles bars. Successful career women have a greater tendency to meet their partners through work than any of the other groups.
- One out of every ten men at singles bars is a financially successful bachelor.

THE SINGLES BAR

From our standpoint, any bar that caters to a romantically inclined mixed crowd is a singles bar. The findings indicate that *one out of four* men and almost *one out of five* women meet most of their mates at singles bars. This represents a sizable portion of singles in America, confirming the belief that mixed bars can no longer be ignored as major social centers for the sexes.

Who goes to singles bars? Whom is one likely to meet there? The following composite profile, compiled from the questionnaires, gives some clues:

PROFILE: What type of man is one most likely to meet at a singles bar?

PROFILE SUMMARY: The "average" male at a singles bar is a blue-collar, middle- to lower-middle-income person. He holds a high school diploma but probably never attended college. (At a bar, a woman is twice as likely to meet a man who has only a high school degree as one who graduated from college.) He is probably younger than thirty-five. (The mean age for unmarried men who frequent singles bars is between twenty-five and thirty-four.) Most likely he has been divorced twice and has remained unmarried more than three years. He makes between thirteen thousand and twenty-three thousand dollars a year.

PROFILE: What type of woman is one most likely to meet at a singles bar?

PROFILE SUMMARY: The majority of women are young. Less than 10 percent of women over forty-five years of age report frequenting singles bars. (So much for the notion of singles bars being hangouts for older, desperate women.) While the largest percentage of women in bars have been divorced twice or more, the second largest group have never been married. Thus many female bar-goers are what have been called "lifers," people who have been single all their lives. This cognomen includes both the "old maid" and the "professional single," women who can't get married and women who won't get married. After the never-marrieds, the largest number of women at bars have been single for two years or less. Thus the typical mixed bar is fairly evenly populated with never married and recently divorced women. Educationally, most women hold high school diplomas but never attended college. They earn under thirteen thousand dollars a year, placing them in the lowest economic level of the survey. Mostly they work at blue-collar jobs.

Mixed bars are not fertile soil for fortune hunters. Men who make more than twenty-three thousand dollars a year prefer meeting women through friends or work, and only 10 percent of women with a comparable salary go to singles bars at all.

At the same time, though the majority of singles bars cater to a lower-income clientele, others—enough to constitute a visible minority—attract the affluent and the aspiring. This becomes evident in the answers to our first essay question.

2. How and where do you meet men/women, and how do you attract the men/women you want to meet? Is it difficult or easy to meet men/women today?

The following extracts are taken from the answers of the more affluent respondents:

Man, Phoenix, AZ: My job lets me afford literally any place I want to go to meet women, yet I meet most of the ones I date at bars. Most bars in my area are populated with both sexes. It's convenient and if the bar is pleasant it's an all right way to meet.

Woman, Manhattan, NY: I'm in my late twenties and believe it or not I've been going to singles bars to meet men since I was eighteen. Especially since my new promotion and new salary grade (which is very good for someone my age), I find that I have very little time for a social life. The bars are convenient to where I live, I'm not scared to go, and it's been working for me.

Man, Boston, MA: While, because of my profession (I have a good law practice) I feel I have to be careful as to where I go to meet women, I find that certain bars cater to the type of women I like, and are perfectly respectable. Most of these women come to bars to meet men, not just to drink, which is fine with me. A bar is a sexually oriented place and is all about social intercourse (and the other kind of intercourse as well).

Most Singles Speak Critically of Singles Bars

Most respondents speak critically of singles bars. About 75 percent of references to bars in the essays are pejorative:

Woman, Los Angeles, CA: I meet most of my men in bars, alas! I just don't know where else to go to meet them. Even the best of these places are sleazy but I feel trapped. I've tried dating services but they are worse. At least in a bar you can nurse your drink and mind your own business.

Woman, Manhattan, NY: The men I meet at singles bars are mostly out for sex. Everybody is so superficial there. No one has anything to them, just scarecrows. They're all like the ticky-tack people. There are a lot of guys from New Jersey dressing up in suits they can't afford who are really just dumb clods from nowhere. The whole scene is a big phony act.

Woman, Washington, DC: All the men want is sex. It's so discouraging. I used to go to bars to have a good time until I realized I *wasn't* having a good time or meeting anyone very nice. The only reason most men were being nice to me (when they were) was just to get me into bed.

The scenario at singles bars is well defined and even ritualistic, and newcomers are quickly put through their paces. The men are here mostly for sex, the women to meet men:

Man, Chicago, IL: I go to bars for one reason mostly, to meet horny ladies. I meet plenty of them there. The setup is perfect but you have to have some balls to go up and talk to them.

Woman, San Francisco, CA: The whole bar thing is a game. You both pretend you're not there to meet each other and of course you are. The man has to go through this phony line talking about his work and his political beliefs, mumbo-jumbo, mumbo-jumbo. The female listens attentively as if something serious and real were being said. She bats her eyelashes and waits for him to invite her home. This is why I've stopped going so much to bars. I feel I've exhausted the possibilities.

Man, Portland, OR: Inside these places there are two types of guys, the regular who every night gets the best barstools and the pick of the best girls. They seem to talk the loudest and know everyone. The outsiders, the shmoes, what about them? Most of the latter are feigning amusement or disinterest or a mixture of both these things. Also an additional helping of embarrassment, insecurity and—you got it—a big hardon, their tongues are hanging out.

The basic ground rule is that anyone can come up to anyone—but anyone can walk away from anyone too, and the manner in which this is done is at the discretion of the rejector. Respondent after respondent decried the boorishness they encountered at singles bars:

Woman, Brooklyn, NY: I've never felt so rejected and alone as I've felt at bars. A person at a bar is a piece of meat on the rack and the men look you over and don't even care if they insult you by staring at you. Some men make comments at you. This is not a nice place to be.

"Piece of meat on the rack" and similar phrases are used in a number of essays. One respondent says: "Bars are okay for the insensitive, but the meatrack is for the insensitive only." A woman comments: "I can't stand the meat-on-the-rack attitude of people at bars; it's like a butcher shop." Another: "At a bar I am just a side of beef swinging up there for the inspection of all the males present." Even a man mentions: "I sometimes feel like something on display for sale at a singles bar."

Respondents also dwell on the "body language" that goes on at a bar:

Woman, Houston, TX: There is a certain language of meeting at these places which I haven't been able to understand and which no one has explained to me. And really, the bars scare me because I believe that the men do not get a true opinion of my character due to the fact that they meet me in a bar. I can't figure out what they want there. People seem to be signaling each other some way.

Dr. Norma Southworth and Dr. Robert Camargo of New York City have studied the body language of the singles bar. Their findings indicate that in a singles bar, traditional sex roles are highlighted and even exaggerated by body signals and messages. Women who take the role of initiator are less successful at meeting men than those who allow themselves to be approached. Moreover, women must demonstrate their willingness for contact through the traditional language of body cues: touching, smiling, preening, staring. Men, on the other hand, are expected to show their attention by eye-to-eye contact, leaning in a woman's direction, and aggressive physical confrontation. Success at the singles bar, according to Southworth and Camargo, demands that traditional sex roles be maintained. Anyone visiting the singles bar must learn this silent code before success can be achieved.

Several essays give credence to Southworth and Camargo's thesis:

Woman, Atlanta, GA: In my experience trying to meet men at bars I have been sadly disappointed. Don't expect that male stereotypes have changed much. When I made several "moves" on attractive men they didn't care to respond. They want to be the ones in charge. For this reason I've found bars to be lousy spots for really meeting "enlightened" men.

Man, Philadelphia, PA: A singles bar is a big game. Women play coy and men play macho. Women look at men with a come-hither glance. Men go over and sometimes get shot down because the women are just prick-teasers. The women give you the come-on with smiling looks. It's like a kid's game. The sex roles are so fixed and laughable. Everybody knows why they're there but the truth of it has to be hidden in "body language."

Woman, New Orleans, LA: I sometimes go to singles bars to meet men, and since I have had plenty of experience in how to get to know men I find attractive, I can make my way around pretty well. The men there don't like women very much. They aren't very nice to them, but occasionally you'll find a nice guy. You have to know how to tell the drips from the good guys by the way they come on to you.

Apropos of the common claim that men look down on women in singles bars, Dr. Shirley Zussman, President of the American Association of Sex Educators, Counselors and Therapists, tells us that the problem is due to the male notion that a woman's mere presence at a bar is tantamount to an admission of her promiscuity. This supposition brings out a kind of aggressivity in men that they might not demonstrate in more conventional surroundings. "I think," says Dr. Zussman, "a stamp is attached to singles bars. If a man doesn't make overtures to a woman there, she feels very undesirable and he feels unmasculine. But if he does, then the woman believes that all the man wants is sex. It's a no-win situation for both parties."

Not all respondents are so bleak on the subject of singles bars. About a fifth of those who mention them do so in a positive way:

Woman, Seattle, WA: For a few years I have met most men I know in a bar downtown. I go there several times a week. I just love the bartender there. He knows what I drink and he gives me every third free on the house. Sometimes they have raffles there or "Sadie Hawkins" night when the women talk first to the men. Most of the guys who come in are fun and easy to talk to.

Man, Baltimore, MD: Of all the places singles bars are the easiest to find women in. For this reason I recommend them. The quality isn't always great. You have to separate the wheat from the tares but isn't life like that anyway? What's the difference from meeting at a bar or a party, disco, etc.? The difference is that the people there have come to meet *you* and *you* them.

Singles bars are by no means exclusively valued as places to make romantic contact. "Bars are just great places to go and relax," writes a respondent, "simply a good place to be at home and meet your friends." When respondents speak positively of single bars, they are often referring to a neighborhood bar. "Singles bars are good for meeting if they're in your neighborhood," writes a woman. "Then everyone knows you and you're a familiar face, you feel at ease." We often hear bars described as "home away from home," or a place "to forget your troubles."
In the essays, we frequently encounter such phrases as "It's a surprise to me to see who might be coming in that door each night."

Woman, Akron, OH: I meet men at the bars which are located in my neighborhood. I know many of the men there already and I feel pretty safe with them. It's a surprise for me to see who might be coming in the door each night and that keeps me coming back regularly each night—though I can't get away from feeling a little cheap because I am here.

One woman from Miami sums up a predominant attitude: "The foundation, walls, and floors of the bar I go to are built of the same material: Hope."

Some Respondents Report Getting Hooked on Singles Bars

A number of subjects indicate a kind of addiction to the singles bar. They don't necessarily like singles bars, they don't really want to be there, but loneliness drives them on:

Woman, Jersey City, NJ: It has been six years now since I first started going to a singles bar. I have not enjoyed bar-going and have frequently been embarrassed by the kind of men I meet there. The men are often "wolves" and on the make. The problem with me is I can't find any other place besides this bar where I can go, and I am so used to going there every night that I don't think I could change if I wanted to. I am between the devil and the deep blue sea.

One of the singles we spoke with is a woman from New York, Pamela L. An attractive and articulate woman, she freely admits to a passion for her singles bar on the Upper West Side of New York City. "I came to this bar a few years ago by accident," she tells us. "It was during the time when the film *Looking for Mr. Goodbar* was scaring every woman out of bars. One of my best girlfriends had just met a great guy at this bar, and the two of them invited me to come along as a third." The first evening Pamela met a man who, in her words, was "a little dull but vigorous and very available." She had a brief affair with him and then came back for more. Soon she became a regular.

"I've talked to loads of men in this place. Some are great, some—most you'd say—aren't so hot. A few turn out to be what you want, or at least seem that way for a while. I'm stuck on this place now."

Is Pamela an addict of singles bars? "I don't like that word very much," she told us. "It doesn't make me feel very good about myself. I like the bar and go there a lot. If that's an addiction, then I'm an addict. You don't have to play games here. It cuts through the red tape. At any time you could meet this really super man. That's what it's all about. Some Lone Ranger who'll ride in and sweep me off to Never Never Land. It *does* happen, you know."

To John-Harvey, a soft-spoken lawyer from a large western city, there is no question that his frequent visits to singles bars represent a compulsion. "I went to the same bar for three straight years. Every night, three years! I met so many women in that place! Whew! Sometimes I brought them home or they went home with me, it didn't matter. Just score, score, score! That was the name of the game."

In his years of single life John-Harvey had several unusual encounters. "Once I took a woman back to my house and it turned out she was a man—'she' started getting five-o'clock shadow when we were making out. That made me puke but I went back to the same place anyway, on the next night, believe it or not. It was the only place I knew where I wouldn't feel alone at night.

"After this incident another thing happened. There was this girl named Janice who I picked up at the bar because I was sorry for her, and who latched onto me. The next morning I couldn't get her to leave my apartment. She begged to stay just for the day. She kept saying she had nowhere to go. I was sad about what she said and so I let her hang around. Mistake! The next day it was the same thing, nowhere to go, all alone, blah, blah, blah. I realized she wasn't *going* to leave unless I threw her out. I had a sicky on my hands. I tried to reason with her but it didn't work, so I finally picked her up and carried her out the door. Okay? As soon as I did that she starts hollering 'Rape! Rape!' In my hallway she kicked me in the groin and kept screaming 'Rape!' at the top of her lungs. What a scene! The cops got involved—someone called them. The neighbors got up a petition to have me evicted.

"After that I got the message. Finally. I never went back to the bar, but, you know, I really had to fight the temptation several times. It was almost like trying to stop smoking. Within a year I was married to my present wife."

Many reports mention the topic of *safety* at the singles bar. Wherever members of the opposite sex go for public rendezvous, there will of course be the possibility of trouble, especially for women. Our next question reveals the extent to which female bar-goers can expect difficulties.

3. **(Women's questionnaire)** *Have any of the following experiences ever resulted from your meeting with a man at a bar?* **(Circle answers that apply.)**

	Women
a. Physical abuse	5%
b. Verbal or psychological abuse	16%
c. Perverse sexual demands	7%
d. Robbery	2%
e. Acquired venereal disease	2%
f. Rape	3%
g. Was conned out of money or property	3%
h. Abduction	—
i. Other	2%

Major Finding: Forty percent of single women have suffered some kind of physical or mental abuse at a singles bar.

BONUS FINDINGS

- Women divorced twice or more suffered five times as much *physical abuse* at bars as women divorced only once.
- Women who are living with men suffered more *verbal and psychological abuse* at bars than women living alone or with their family.
- Practically twice as many women living with men claim they've had *perverse sexual demands* made upon them at bars than women who live alone. Ten percent of women in their early twenties claim the same, though fewer than 2 percent of women over forty-five report suffering perverse demands.
- Two percent of women divorced once report being *raped* following an encounter at a singles bar—as compared with 8 percent of women divorced twice or more.
- Women who have been married twice or more have been *robbed* four times more frequently by a contact made at a bar than women never married. Women who have been divorced twice were *conned out of money or property* at a bar more than twice as commonly as those who were never married.
- The younger a woman is, the more likely she is to encounter *perverse sexual demands* at a bar. The older she is, the more likely she is to be robbed.

If we add the percentages of women who have had difficulty, the number surpasses a third of our sample. More than *one out of every three* women who go to singles bars have had some kind of incident at a bar, ranging from the unpleasant to the life-threatening. Several essay questions describe these difficulties. Two women elaborate on the details of run-ins:

Woman, Jersey City, NJ: I was picked up at a bar by a cute looking guy who looked like your model type. I went to his house with him. It was a really nice modern apartment filled with swanky furniture and pillows all over the floor. There were mirrors on the walls. It was like a place built for intimacy. Everything was fine between us at first and I was very excited by the whole thing. We kissed and hugged and he seemed fine to me. Then he got up all of a sudden and went into the bathroom. He was in there a long time and finally came out naked. No preparations or anything. I was a bit taken back. He barked at me to take off my clothes. It was like Dr. Jekyll and Mr. Hyde. I did and he put his hands on my throat. This was very frightening and I've never had anything like that happen before. I asked him what he was going to do and he said that depended on me, that I better do everything he said. Then he made me put his penis in my mouth, and when it was in he started pulling my ears and my hair and hitting the top of my head very hard. If I cried out he shouted at me to shut up and continue. After I had done this for him for about ten minutes he threw me onto the floor and fell on me. It was very rough. Later on I had some black-and-blue marks, though nothing serious. I sometimes wonder what he would have done if I'd refused him. After it was all over he started telling me how sorry he was if he'd hurt me, and how he hoped I was okay. He even asked for my phone number! I gave him a wrong number and got out of there as fast as I could. The whole thing was awful!

The second description is briefer and more bizarre:

Woman, Winston-Salem, NC: This man and I left the bar and drove along the highway supposedly heading to his home. After a ways he turned to me and asked me if I'd been getting "my kicks." I didn't know what he was talking about. Then he stopped the car in the middle of nowhere and got out and went over to the side. He leaned against the car and stuck out his rear end. He told me to kick him. At first I thought he was kidding but he was very serious about it, I could tell from the way he acted. To make a long story short, I did what he told me to because I was scared, and kicked him a number of times until he seemed to have an orgasm. Then he drove me home without a word.

Of all the single women who frequent singles bars, we learn from our subgroup findings that the one who has the roughest time of it there is the educated, high-wage-earning career woman. She suffers *three times* as much physical abuse as other women, is robbed *twice* as often, raped almost *three times* as often, and acquires venereal disease with far more frequency than all others. She also admits to being conned out of money at *double* the average rate.

Why are career women more subject to abuse? According to Dr. Elayne Kahn, a psychologist in private practice in New York City who counsels many singles, "Educated high-earning women have a very high expectation rate when they go to bars. They feel themselves to be the cream of the crop and expect to be treated accordingly. But at a bar the men mostly view the women as sex objects. Such a woman goes to the bar to meet a man, while the man goes to find a sex partner. She goes home with him and he demands his brand of sex—why else was she there, he thinks. The woman takes this as an offense or attack, and perhaps an incident occurs, whereas a less attractive, more seasoned woman in the same situation would know the rules of the game and not take the man's advances in such a manner. Also, a high-wage-earning woman is often better-looking than the rest because she can afford to make herself look good. She becomes a kind of target at bars. Certain men go there looking for her type, the attractive, well-groomed woman, knowing they can get something out of her. And they do.

"Men *do* see women differently at bars," claims Dr. Kahn. "Women go expecting to be treated as equals. They see themselves that way. But men don't. It's a breakdown of communications. The men expect the women to be looser. Men tell me this, that they look at women differrently in bars than anywhere else. Women are naive that way. They don't perceive the way they are perceived."

THE PICKUP

Another means by which single people get acquainted is the pickup.

For a large number of men, problems concerning pickups linger with the persistence of an unanswered question. Many men who have wished to meet women this way but have been intimidated, or who have tried and failed, or even who have tried and occasionally succeeded still wonder if there is some kind of secret formula necessary for making a successful pickup.

Meanwhile, women are equally unclear about how men feel toward women who get picked up. For men and women alike, the pickup remains a vexing enigma:

Man, Burlington, VT: Several of my friends meet all their chicks by picking them up. They walk up and in a couple of minutes have a conversation going. I don't know how they do it. Whenever I try it doesn't work well.

Man, Oklahoma City, OK: I've met a few women by pickups but this is a hard way to do it. I found that after a couple of attempts that blew up in my face I got gun-shy and stopped trying. I'd like women to know what it's like to be a man sometime and have to be the aggressor. I read in books on being single how women are open to being picked up but I sure haven't found that to be the case.

4. (Men's questionnaire) *How often do women respond favorably to your attempts to pick them up in casual situations—at bars, parks, beaches, etc.?*

Almost two thirds of single men report that they have tried to meet women by means of pickups. Of that group, one third have had good success, reporting that the majority of women respond to their attempts.

The youngest of our survey, the twenty- to twenty-four-year-olds, report the best results. As men grow older their success dips a bit, perhaps because women of their corresponding age group have become more cautious. Surprisingly perhaps, the survey also shows that the high-income professional is most likely to engage in pickups. Men in the lower-income bracket make far fewer attempts.

Finally, only a tiny proportion report that *every* woman says "yes" to their attempts. On the other hand, the consensus among American single men is that women *will* allow themselves to be picked up—only 5% said women *almost never* respond to their appeals.

5. (Men's questionnaire) *What is the biggest obstacle to picking up a woman?*

	Men
a. The woman seems unapproachable	24%
b. The man can't get up the nerve	24%
c. There is no obstacle; it's simple	19%
d. Most women are too respectable to be picked up	7%
e. It's difficult for a man to think of what to say	17%
f. Women are too frightened	8%
g. Don't know	3%

Two categories count for almost half of the responses.

1. The woman seems unapproachable (24 percent)
2. The man can't get up the nerve (24 percent)

Add to this:

3. Women are too respectable (7 percent)
4. It's difficult to think of what to say (17 percent)

BONUS FINDINGS

• Financially successful bachelors claim to be the most successful in picking up women. Forty percent of men in the highest income bracket—more than any other income group—say that a majority of women respond successfully to their attempts to pick them up.
• Widowed men hardly ever try to pick up women— two thirds of them claim they rarely make the attempt.
• The longer a man has been single the more apt he is to make an effort to pick up a woman.

Almost three quarters of single men check reasons based on fear and rebuff. Only 19 percent claim there's no obstacle to picking up women. Smaller numbers believe women are frightened.

Are these fears real? Do women slap men in the face during a pickup? Or is this a holdover from a Jean Harlow movie? '

6. (Women's questionnaire) *If an attractive opportunity presented itself, would you allow a man to pick you up?*

Major Finding: *Almost three quarters of the women we surveyed said they would definitely be willing to let a man pick them up.*

Of this group, 48 percent said they would allow themselves to be picked up if the man was equally appealing.

Seventeen percent said they would agree to a pickup only if they were in a daring mood.

Seven percent were emphatic enough on the subject to say *Certainly, the old values have to change.*

Slightly more than a quarter report having qualms about it. Of these some are too frightened; some think it morally wrong; some are worried about what others might think or about feeling cheapened in the process.

A few interesting secondary findings also emerge.

1. *Divorced women and pickups*—Women who have been divorced twice are the most vocal about changing the old values.
2. *Age and willingness to be picked up*—There are few differences in attitude among female age groups concerning the question of the pickup. However, almost twice the number of women over thirty-five assert that the old values have to change.
3. *Education level*—Professional women and those with a college degree are somewhat more liberal concerning the pickup than blue-collar workers and women with high school degrees only. Eighteen percent of college graduates say they would allow themselves to be picked up if in a daring mood. Only 13 percent of blue-collar workers agree.

From these findings a composite profile emerges:

PROFILE: What type of woman is most likely to allow herself to be picked up?

PROFILE SUMMARY: She is between the ages of twenty-five and thirty-four and has never been married. She probably attended college but chances are she did not finish. She is in the high-wage-earning bracket, lives alone, holds a white-collar job.

PROFILE: What type of woman is least likely to allow herself to be picked up?

PROFILE SUMMARY: This woman is young, probably in her early twenties. She lives with her family, works at a professional job, and has most likely been divorced once (or perhaps widowed at an early age). She holds a college degree.

Very young women, women still in college or those singlemindedly concentrating on their careers, are the least eager to be picked up. Most compliant is the woman who earns a good salary and holds a secure job. She is generally at an age—twenty-five to thirty-four—when she feels at home in the social whirl but hasn't yet been whirled too thoroughly. She is, in other words, successful and confident enough to be called a woman of the world, one who knows where she's headed and what she wants; one self-assured enough to meet without the formality of an official go-between and to take the chance inherent in a pickup.

Thus, a majority of single women are willing to entertain the possibility of being picked up—but only to entertain the idea, not to embrace it enthusiastically.

"There are many unconscious inhibitions in women," says Dr. Kahn. "They *think* they would like to be picked up but don't necessarily *let* themselves, and they are very judgmental when the time comes. Basically, though, I've found that men don't make the effort enough. Women would be more responsive if the men made more attempts."

Major Finding: Most women are willing to be picked up—but only if the time, the place, and the man all meet their particular standards.

In their essay responses, women mention several provisos that may account for the discrepancy between the obstacles facing men and the willingness of women. These are:

1. That the woman be in the right mood

Woman, Chicago, IL: Sure I'll get picked up if I feel in the mood for it. If things have been going my way that day or if I'm horny and want a date for the weekend, why not? Times get bad sometimes and then some horny guy hitting on me is the last thing I want to hear about. I'm like that.

Woman, Winston-Salem, NC: Occasionally I meet men at bars or at book stores, bus stops, etc. or at singles bars. I have to feel like it if I give them my number. I only go to bars to meet men when I'm in "the mood."

Woman, Tacoma, WA: How and when and where do I meet men? I do not set myself up to vamp men and I don't think of ways to attract men. It just happens if I'm in the mood, usually by a chance meeting. He says "Hi," I say either "goodbye" or "hi" back and things are off to the races.

2. That the man be appealing

Woman, Washington, DC: Whether or not I let myself be "picked up" is mostly dependent on whether or not the guy really turns me on. I'd say that I meet about a fifth of the men I know by happenstance meetings here and there.

Woman, Pittsburgh, PA:

Meet through pickups.

Only if the guy is a groove.

No idiots need apply.

Should have long blonde curly hair and be cute as hell.

Should be anxious to have a fun time. Not just sex but well-rounded and full days and nights.

Pickups are the best if you're brave enough. Just look back at the guy when he looks at you—a smile is sure to let him know you're interested. If he hesitates smile again—he'll come, wagging his tail.

3. That the place where the pickup occurs be agreeable

Woman, Chicago, IL: Where I meet is as critical as *how* I meet. The place should be a romantic kind of place with the proper lights, setting, some wine and music like a nice bar populated by friendly people from the neighborhood. The same guy who turned me on in a nice place like this might turn me off if he just came up on the street and started talking to me.

Though more single women than ever before are willing to meet men without introductions, they remain sharply discriminating about the style of the meeting. The how and where of the pickup are only slightly less important than the who. There is even a kind of hierarchy of acceptability among locales for pickups. A rough outline might look as follows:

ACCEPTABLE

Established singles meeting places, such as singles bars, dances, discos, parties, singles functions, invitational social affairs, health clubs, cruises, cultural affairs, any social meeting place or event.

SOMEWHAT ACCEPTABLE

"Friendly" public places, such as parks, the beach; such public gatherings as rock concerts or open-air festivals, street or country fairs, amusement parks; sporting places, such as roller-skating rinks, bowling alleys, tennis courts, running paths, libraries, dog-walking areas, museums, art galleries; long trips on trains or planes; political rallies.

MARGINALLY ACCEPTABLE

Neutral public places, such as supermarkets, bookstores, restaurants, department stores, buses or subways, airports, any public city transportation, depots, movie theaters.

GENERALLY UNACCEPTABLE

Potentially dangerous or highly anonymous places, such as on the street, cruising cars, phone calls from strange men introducing themselves, strange proposals by letters, etc.

Though this list is far from exhaustive, and though pickups do succeed on the streets and do not at places where they are supposed to, the outline is more or less representative. Most of the essays on the subject agree that the place where the pickup is attempted weighs heavily in the chance of success.

Woman, Toledo, OH: I would hook up with an interesting man if the place and the guy were right. If a nice man comes up to me in a supermarket and starts a conversation I'm not going to slap him in his face. But if some guy tries to stop me on the street with a phony-baloney bit about how sexy I am, that's not for me.

Woman, Kansas City, MO: I find it easy to meet men and I will find them in places around, but only in certain places—not sitting next to someone in a movie theater or in the lobby of a hotel. That's for hookers. That would make me feel loose. Even at a laundromat. I want to meet a man in a place like a bar, at a party, at the house of a friend.

Woman, Toledo, OH: There's a difference in my book between a pickup and a meeting. When I think of a pickup I think of some sleazy scene with a yechy man pawing me at a bar. If a neatly dressed, clean man comes up to me in an open place and is friendly and nice, I will be nice back.

At the same time, men often seem bewildered about what it is women want from them during a pickup:

Man, Denver, CO: Some of the women I meet are in bars. I come up and start talking to them but half the time they don't seem to understand what I'm talking about or be interested. For a while I tried to pick up girls at your standard places. I would go up to someone that looked good and ask for her address and phone number. I finally gave up because the ones I got to meet this way were usually not first-raters and the others didn't respond well.

Man, Grand Rapids, MI: Since the time I was in high school in Cleveland as a young man I have been absolutely nonplussed over the prospect of meeting women. When I was younger I tried meeting them by just saying "Hello," but that got me nowhere fast. Freud once said, "The greatest mystery to me is what it is a woman wants." I agree with Mr. Freud. I'm not unattractive and am reasonably well-spoken. Once in Bermuda I saw a beautiful redhead on the beach who I flipped over. I got up my courage and walked up to her. I introduced myself but she didn't say a word. I stood there with egg on my face for a few minutes waiting for something to happen. What *did* happen was that she stood up—and was about six foot two, at least three inches higher than me. She never said a word, just stood up. That kind of sums up my experience at trying to meet girls.

While we are on the general topic of pickups, here are some other remarks made by men:

"If you want to get to know women, better strike while the iron is hot. He who hesitates is lost. You have to talk to them immediately and not be shy. Women sense when a man is shy; they take it for lack of self-confidence, and most women don't like that."

"Picking up women is the best way to meet because you are in control, and you choose the woman who looks best to you. If she walks away you've lost nothing in the attempt."

"Meet when you want. Just be cool. Women like men who seem together and on top of things. They *want* you to come up to them. They're as anxious as men but have been trained to hide their feelings."

The notion of hesitation and loss often appears in conjunction with the pickup:

Man, Chicago, IL: I rarely bother with formal kinds of ways to meet women. Dances turn me off and I'm lousy at disco. I own a shirt that says "Disco Sucks." My attitude is "When you see what you want, go after it." Like if I see a woman who pleases me in a bus or store, I know that the chemistry is right. Why else would I be attracted? If I don't make my move then, the opportunity is lost forever, and chances are I'll never see her again.

Some women say that when they are interested in meeting a man they let him know it by means of direct or indirect signaling. A few of the methods mentioned:

"I move over in the general direction of a man, get close to him so he can talk to me."

"I make eye-contact for a few seconds longer than I usually would. I don't blink during this time."

"I try to tell him with my body language that I'm interested; a smile or the way I sit."

"I send out good vibrations."

"I act very friendly when he speaks to me, smile a lot, and touch him now and then gently on the wrist or arm. I keep my gaze locked into his."

"Just being feminine and womanish does it. I sometimes feel like a magnet that can attract men by sending out waves to them. Yes, they feel them."

"Sometimes you can flirt with your eyes. Movements, the way you walk across the room. A quick glance at the man you're interested in, then looking away, then another quick glance."

Men describe this symbolic language in their own phrases:

"Eye-contact is the way I meet the women I like. I let them know everything from the way I look at them."

"I broadcast my manhood. It comes out of my genitals and the woman I'm sending it to usually gets the picture. I set up a two-way receiving and sending station."

"If there's a woman I like I try to concentrate all my energy and thoughts on her. Visualization exercises: I picture myself holding her naked, and kissing her. I keep this thought in mind as I look at her."

"I smile and look as pleasant and attractive as possible while I do. I ease slowly over in her direction. I keep an eye on the way she reacts to this, to see if she's looking receptive or at least aware of my approach."

The pickup story as shown here remains an ambiguous one at best. For those who have had a bashful time of it, the situation is the high school hop revisited: The boys on the far side of the gym and the girls on the near, all scanning each other with secret longing. Each is as eager as the other to get together; but somewhere in the gap things go wrong. The man's approach is too rushed, too tongue-tied, or not forthcoming at all. The woman is self-conscious, over-choosy, cautious. At the delicate moment, toes are stepped on or nerve lost. Messages go undeciphered or wrongly translated. Men and women push away while they are pulled together, each paralyzed by a similar fear of rejection. Often the intensity of this fear propels them into the very failure they dreaded.

However, not all men and women are ill-at-ease with pickups, and many feel at home in this situation. Though respondents may complain about painful details or the inherent dangers, few condemn the practice entirely. This indicates that a broad change in the relationships between the sexes has taken place over the past years. Because of the lack of legitimate means of meeting and the recent explosion of the singles population, this once-taboo act is gradually becoming more widespread and admissible—generally, we say, and with many qualifications—depending on the place, the manner, the woman and man.

PERSONAL ADVERTISEMENTS

Personal "get-acquainted" ads fall into three categories. First are the kind explicitly demanding sex. Often the requests are on the fringe of the socially acceptable, or they involve various alternate forms of sexuality.

Next come ads that ask for a nice guy/gal who, besides being caring, intelligent, kind to animals, and so forth, is willing to "explore fantasies" or "make a commitment to hedonism"; i.e., he or she must be immediately sexually available as well as personable and attractive.

Third are the requests made for companionship and possible permanent relationships. No direct sexual strings are attached.

The advertisements in the first two categories are ordinarily placed in sexually oriented magazines and newspapers. Those in the third can be found in a wide range of popular periodicals and journals.

The way the ads work is simple. A man or woman sends in a request plus a check. He or she is assigned a reference number, which will be featured when the ad is published. Readers then answer the ad by number, and wait for a response. After several weeks the periodical forwards an envelope full of these unopened replies to the advertiser, and the advertiser answers the letters at her or his own discretion. Occasionally for a fee a paper or magazine will publish names and addresses (usually code names and box numbers), and the correspondence is carried on directly.

Opinions on the value, quality, and safety of personal ads are sharply divided. Our essay question asks

7. Have you ever placed or answered personal advertisements in romantic or sexually oriented periodicals? If so, describe your more interesting experiences. What did you indulge in and with whom? Would you recommend the practice? If you never answered such ads, have you considered it? What stopped you? What do you imagine such experiences would be like?

Major Finding: Most singles have never placed or answered personal advertisements. A surprising number have considered it.

Checking back to our question on where and how singles meet, we see that personal ads account for no more than 1 percent of meetings for men, and almost none for women. This is a pretty slim figure, and it comes as no shock that only a tiny number of essay subjects have tried the classifieds at all. It seems significant, however, that so many have at one time or another thought about it.

Woman, Phoenix, AZ: I've never answered such ads, though I admit there are times I've thought about it. But I was afraid I might get into a situation where I couldn't handle it. I imagine these experiences are very erotic.

Woman, Manhattan, NY: When I want to titillate myself and have sexual fantasies I imagine I just wrote a letter to a man who wanted to meet a beautiful woman full of life, love and spirit. I imagine him to be extremely handsome, wealthy, and dynamite as a lover, all the things a woman's heart is made for. Of course, I would never write such a letter, just imagine it.

Woman, Nashville, TN: I have not answered such ads, but have thought of it. A friend of mine tries to talk me into it. She met a highly intelligent lawyer that way but later found out, through his admittance, that his sexual activities were a direct characteristic of his sexual identity crisis. He only enjoyed oral sex in that he was not sure if he wanted to indulge in heterosexual or homosexual activities.

Man, Little Rock, AR: I haven't. But I might if I had the availability of such ads in ass-backwards Arkansas.

The question of personal ads often triggers deep emotional reactions. Sometimes these reactions are in the form of fantasy, sometimes in the form of outrage and disgust. Some respondents, for instance, make no distinction between hardcore pornographic offerings and the straightforward lonely-hearts variety:

Man, Los Angeles, CA: This kind of advertising is vulgar and demeaning to love and romance! It stinks! You should be ashamed for bringing it to peoples' attention.

Woman, Detroit, MI: You've got to be kidding. I've not "indulged" because it sounds tacky and low-class. I think the type of person you'd meet placing a personal ad should be arrested and castrated. They're mostly the creeps responsible for rape of women.

More commonly, respondents eschew the personal ads for the reasons one might suspect: fear, distaste, distrust:

Woman, Chillicothe, OH: If someone has to advertise in papers, that could mean they can't meet people through legitimate channels. So something's probably wrong with them. Maybe it's just a good fast way of getting into someone's house. They can do anything they please with the helpless victim.

Woman, Tampa, FL: No, no, I would never consider answering such ads. I'm afraid of being raped or killed by a looney! The man who I answered would know I was desperate (or think that) and would think he could easily take advantage of me.

Woman, Des Moines, IA: I have never placed any ad or answered any. The reason why is because I am very beautiful, lovely, desirable, and well-shapen, and have beautiful nipples like diamond points on the end of my breasts. All the men want and need me.

The small group that *did* answer the ads have both praise *and* some wild-and-woolly stories:

Man, Omaha, NB: "I replied to an ad that intrigued me, placed by a girl who *sounded* like she had the same interests. When I received a reply I called her and tried to set up a date. She was very strange, too secretive and elusive. Finally we set up a common meeting place. I couldn't (wasn't allowed) to come to her house. Then she never showed up. The next day she called saying she lied about her age. She had been divorced twice, her father disowned her, and not to call her. *I would not recommend it.* I'd like to see and talk with the person I'm going out with and cut through the bullshit.

Man, Marina Del Rey, CA: Yes, I have answered personal advertisements in sexually oriented literature on many occasions. The experience has always been very exciting sexually and I have engaged in a variety of sexual practices with the women involved. These have included oral sex, anal sex, regular intercourse, and group sex.

Man, Hartford, CT: I have answered ads in the past and perhaps will in the future. Generally I find these people to be very low class or prostitutes. Sex to me is as necessary as eating, sleeping, working. I would recommend it just as I support the case for prostitution as an alternative to rape. The contacts I have had included oral sex; mutual bathing; use of aids such as vibrators, jelly, whipped cream. I personally have not tried bondage, discipline, golden showers—they do not look appealing to me.

Man, Jacksonville, MS: Yes, it was just real quick sex. Both members were satisfied and that's one thing that counts.

Several respondents report the kind of Bacchanalias that many suppose might result from answering these advertisements.

Man, Miami, FL: Whee! I met two sisters through an ad in *Hustler* magazine. Two fantastic women, great in bed. We met at a bar and had a few drinks to size each other up. Then they moved very close to me, one on either side and began stroking my legs. Well, needless to say my penis was like steel as they kept it up (so to speak) until after a while we went back to my place. First Jackie went down on me and then Joanie humped my leg until she came. They switched positions. We went at it all night. Great, I recommend it. Jackie and Joanie and I still have great sex and are all good friends.

Woman, Fort Worth, TX: I answered one ad in good faith. It didn't mention any particular sexual requirements and the man sounded good. Well, it turned out he was deep into group sex. Somehow I liked him and let myself get talked into it. We went to one of his friend's houses and there were about ten or twelve people there standing around self-consciously. Nobody seemed to know what to do, though from what I could tell they had met before like this. Most, it turned out, had met through answering requests in a certain magazine, like me. Then one tall blonde woman just all of a sudden took off her clothes and everyone else started doing it too. The whole thing was cold and humorless, and I was very embarrassed. Everyone solemnly rubbed baby oil over themselves and we formed a self-conscious pile of bodies. Arms and legs and genitalia were everywhere, and the smell of bodies. It felt like I was part of a big, sweaty, silly animal. To this day I'm not sure who was doing what to me but somehow I ended up on the floor making "love" to a short, redheaded man who breathed very fast. The pile had broken up and people were paired off in corners. The thing I remember most was how *quiet* it was. I expected moans and groans but no one one seemed to make a sound. The redheaded man had an orgasm (I guess) and then a woman was hugging me. This was too much. I got up quickly, gathered what I could find of my clothes, and left without anyone paying any attention (apparently I was not the first person to leave one of these sessions abruptly). Certainly the experience was interesting. I'm a writer and all experience is important. But when I look back on it it was a waste of time. The word that best describes it is *empty.* After that, *dull.*

Finally, one experience recorded by a male respondent is on the harrowing side:

Man, Van Nuys, CA: I answered one ad in an underground newspaper. I was given a phone number to call. The voice on the phone sounded nice. Maybe too nice when I think about it now. It turned out her "house" was a hotel. We met on a street corner and went there. She unlocked the door to the room, acting sexy and so forth. I figured she was a hooker and that I'd bargain with her when we got inside. Once inside a man came out of the bathroom with a knife. He asked me for my wallet. Then they locked me in the bathroom and took off. That was my experience answering a sexually oriented advertisement.

The Verdict on Personal Ads

One must use special discernment when placing or answering ads in the hardcore sexual market. A percentage of ads are for straight-out prostitution, while S&M personals almost always involve some form of sexual deviation. Such ads are frequently placed by highly neurotic or unstable individuals, respondents frequently tell us, or by those with a high tolerance for enduring the physical pain of others. Not all are like this, of course, and probably not many, but enough to warrant a caution.

The quality of applicants in the personals is consistently criticized by our respondents. Words like "boring," "unintelligent," "ordinary," and "strange" crop up. According to *The Challenge of Being Single* by Marie Edwards and Eleanor Hoover, an interview with the publisher of *Singles Register* revealed that most ads draw about 40 replies. One divorcee attracted as many as 168. And yet we learn from Hoover and Edwards' own survey material that respondents report only *4 or 5* turn out to be "highly desirable."

Dr. Robert Sollod, Associate Professor of Psychology at Cleveland State University, director of the professional program in psychology at Cleveland State, and psychologist in private practice in Cleveland, has definite feelings about the pros and cons of the personals: "In a strange way the personals bring back some of the mystery of romance. They represent the unknown. They appeal to a kind of voyeuristic curiosity in us. Who is going to write back, and what will he or she say? Who's out there? What are they all really doing? I'm afraid there's more titillation than substance involved, however. To me, the ads seem potentially more exploitative and sadistic than any other element of the singles scenes. The personals remind me of the casting couch—impersonal, for sex only, exploitative . . ."

Our last essay in this section sums up several of the reasons why, despite the availability, such a small number of singles answer or place personal ads:

Man, Milwaukee, WI: Yes, of course I've thought about it. Who wouldn't think about it? Here are women offering themselves sexually, or at least offering themselves in some way. For people with kinky tastes it's very appealing. I've been tempted myself. I have a rather specialized sexual taste of my own which I won't mention here, and it's not so easy to get women to go along with it. So I am indeed tempted.

Why don't I? Let me count the ways. First, because I might get ripped off. Second, because I might meet some super weirdo. Third, because I might get a disease. Fourth, because anyone who advertises just can't be too much in demand, especially a woman. (I mean, men have a hard time pursuing, but if you're a good-looking chick why should you have trouble?) Fifth, because I would be embarrassed at such a meeting, and would feel there is something inadequate in me that causes me to answer the ad. Sixth, the girl would be embarrassed and the whole meeting would be awkward. Seventh, *anyone* could show up, and how do you get rid of her if she's a dog? Eighth, something in my conscience just tells me it's not so cool. Enough said?

MATCHMAKERS AND SINGLES FUNCTIONS

Fourteen percent of men and 18 percent of women—almost one out of five singles—meet most of their dates through singles organizations. These organizations are both profit and nonprofit agencies that specialize in helping singles meet other singles. They are mentioned so frequently in the essays that there can be little doubt such organizations have come into their own.

These organizations fall broadly into two categories: matchmakers and scene-setters:

Matchmaker—The matchmaker provides men and women with direct introductions. The matching is done under the protection of personal screening, of locating the "precisely right" mate for the customer's personality. The process can work by a number of methods, some of them technological and mechanical, others direct and personal. Computer dating, questionnaire matching, and the human matchmaker are the best known.

Scene-Setters—These are the impresarios of the dating industry. Their stock-in-trade is providing a comfortable atmosphere in which singles can easily get acquainted. The scene-setter rarely arranges introductions. "It" (the scene-setter is usually an organization) provides the opportunity, often at a social situation such as a cocktail party, dance, discussion group, or sporting event. The single must then do the rest.

In the essays that follow, both varieties of organization are mentioned:

Man, Urbana, IL: I meet some women through dating services. Though I was turned off over this at first I took a chance and things came up all right. I paid $50.00 and, after a personal interview, was given ten names of women who were supposed to be my type. My first date was a red-headed girl, short, well-built, who was pure TNT. We were in the sack the first night and she couldn't please me enough, really sweet. The other dates I had were dull though. Personally I'd recommend this way.

Woman, Key West, FL: I am a cashier (hourly wage) at a singles club (150 members) so I see things firsthand. The most positive experience is that you meet a variety of people. It's on the up and up, and the people are mostly eager and cleancut. I recommend selected groups. Marriage and long-term bonding frequently occur in my organization. The most negative things are the obviously bitter and overtly shy persons who nobody talks to. They are rejected and resent not having "fun" when it's all their own fault.

Man, Houston, TX: My one sojourn into paid dating was a place called Unmarrieds, Inc. (or something like that). I felt ridiculous doing it but was needful enough to do it anyway. I met a group of nice women. Most were as apologetic as I was about meeting in this way. One finds that after the first few minutes you forget the manner in which you've met and it becomes like any other date.

What types of people go to singles functions? Calvis Ruston runs a small private dating service in a southern Texas city. Ruston claims that "I get every imaginable type coming in here, not just your middle class but all kinds from bricklayers to presidents of companies. Single people are a needy bunch in my experience. Every level of society too."

John Raymond, head of Club World in Beverly Hills, is of the same opinion: "We have people from age twenty-five to fifty-five. All kinds. On the one hand, a *Fortune* Five Hundred type, another a carpet salesman. There's no one single type."

Still, according to our survey there definitely *is* a *singles-function type*. The following profiles are based on composite percentages from Question 1:

PROFILE: What kind of man is one most likely to meet at a singles function?

> PROFILE SUMMARY: This man has been divorced twice or more and lives alone. He's been single from three to nine

years, is between the ages of forty-five and fifty-five, and is
a high-salaried, college-educated professional.

PROFILE: What kind of woman is one most likely to meet at a singles
function?

PROFILE SUMMARY: She has been divorced at least once and
perhaps twice. She lives alone, has a high school diploma
or less, holds a white-collar job. She is between the ages of
forty-five and fifty-five.

The average single function-goer comes mainly from the older age
brackets. While a third of all women who go to singles functions are
forty-five or older, fewer than 3 percent are in their early twenties; a
similar ratio exists among the men. From age twenty-five to thirty-four
interest picks up for both sexes, but only for approximately one out of
ten. Singles groups, it can be stated, attract an older crowd.

According to our data, one out of five male single function-goers is a
high-wage earner. Interviews with several managers and owners of
dating services bear this out. "Most men who come in here are comfortable financially," says Les Brand, a matchmaker from Cleveland.
A matchmaker from New York City, Rae Laefer, tells us: "Some
women have money also. I have one woman on Sutton Place who can't
drive but keeps a car in the garage of her apartment building just in
case a man doesn't have his own and wants to borrow one. She pays a
hundred and thirty-five dollars a month just to garage it. And they
have to afford my fee too. But don't worry, a lot of your older women
get their fee back five times in dinners."

Thus the composite portrait of the male single-function type: He's
been married several times (often has children), may be fairly well off
financially, is usually in his forties and fifties, and tends to hold a prestigious job. This image presents a different picture from, say, the typical young "swinger" often thought to predominate at singles functions.
Why older? Why more financially secure, and with multiple marriages?

According to Dr. Sollod, people in their forties and fifties are often
isolated from romantic contacts by the heavy demands of their jobs.
"We're divided into so many firms, institutions, groups," he comments,
"that people in successful, busy situations don't get much chance to
meet. Their lives are tied up with their careers. When they need a date

they have to go somewhere where it's instantly available—like a singles function.

"Also, people who have careers and who are older have done plenty of dating by now, and may no longer feel idealistic about love, or believe that destiny is going to drop a perfect mate in their lap. Instead of relying on fate, they understand the practicalities—you have to go out and do it yourself. Older, successful people know that the same attitude that has helped them succeed at their jobs helps on other fronts too—making yourself available to those who can help you get what you want."

THE MATCHMAKERS

Let's take a closer look at both varieties of singles organizations. First the matchmaker. At one time he or she was the only professional source of such meetings in town, the local middleman/woman who egged clients into willing and sometimes semi-willing alliances. Today there are many variations on this ancient profession, some of them aided by the machine. Not all, however, have totally broken from the past, and in some cities there are still old-fashioned "marriage brokers" who specialize in bringing singles together.

Woman, Chicago, IL: I go to a matchmaker. Not to be mixed up with a dating service. A dating service gives you a list and you never know who you're going to be stuck with. A matchmaker starts with one person at a time and lets you get to know him. I want to know about his problems and his life. This way I can take it a step at a time. I am introduced to the man I am to meet in the office of the matchmaker. It is very informal and convenient for both of us. The people are well screened, and there are never any crazies. I go out with him for some time and really get to know him that way, so I strongly recommend this method. It is old fashioned and safe.

Man, Manhattan, NY: I have used the services of a personal marriage broker in New York City. She arranged introductions in her office and made certain that the women she introduced me to were the kind I would like. I was surprised to find that these women were of a higher quality than I'd met at singles groups or even through my friends. On the whole they were attractive, well-spoken women. The matchmaker

costs quite a lot of money, about three hundred dollars for five introductions.

Several respondents speak of computer dating operations where, for
a fee ranging from twenty-five to fifteen hundred dollars, the organization provides an interview, a battery of questionnaires and psychological testing programs, a computer through which this information is
processed, and a final printout matching the customer's card with similar data cards. Reports of computer dating from our respondents are
mixed:

Man, Akron, OH: The most positive experience I had was through a
computer dating comany in my home town. I paid a lot of money but
the names I got were all nice persons and I feel I got my money's
worth—especially since I ended up marrying one of the females on the
list. We're in the process of divorce now, but that's not the computer's
fault. I'm thinking of using the same company again, so here I go!

Woman, Baton Rouge, LA: I once put my name on a computer dating
service and lost $500 in the experience. The business ripped me off and
didn't give me a date, and escaped with personal facts about myself,
including nude pictures. It was an unpleasant experience. Don't do it.

Some compatibility services feature technical gimmickry. Astro-
dating matches people according to their zodiacal birth signs and stel-
lar affinities. Record dating makes tape cassettes of the customer's
voice and plays them to interested parties. Television dating is a rather
expensive approach where parties view one another on closed-circuit
video setups. All these methods perform essentially the same function,
gathering information about customers' personalities and matching
them up statistically for compatibility. As for the value and advisabil-
ity of pursuing these methods, that depends on the company and the
person involved. If anything, reports tend to be on the dubious side:

Woman, St. Louis, MO: When I lived in Cincinnati I had several bad
experiences with a dating bureau that charged me a lot of money and
then provided only a few dates, most of whom were jerks. So all I
would say here is that you should watch out for these kinds of ripoffs.

Man, Detroit, MI: Several times back in New York I used a video dating service which was not great but not a ripoff either. Expensive! Met

several girls but not worth the price. Also, computer dating, but never followed through. Best way to meet girls is the old way, just introduce yourself. The hell with the middleman.

THE SCENE-SETTERS

John Raymond is founder of the American Sexual Freedom Movement in Southern California and its offspring, Club World. "I incorporated my idea of sexual freedom into a moneymaking plan," he tells us. "I packaged sex and singles-matchmaking as a financial venture, a sort of IBM corporation, with bright-eyed and bushy-tailed reps, nice offices, earth tones, all that."

Using modern marketing techniques and computer hardware, Raymond's enterprise today has offices in three major cities, selling romantic opportunities for singles. "We invite people in for an interview," he explains, "and discuss what it is they're interested in. If they want to enroll, it's a certain fee for lifetime membership, plus an annual renewal fee. There are two aspects to the program. First is the Club Directory, which everyone receives. People can read about others in it, contact them, and meet on a one-to-one basis. Each member has to send in his résumé and appear in the Directory. Then we have activities, parties, discussion groups, weekend tours, workshops, seminars. We have a full-time director of member services. We also maintain a corporate penthouse in Manhattan where we hold some of our activities, and places in Florida and Beverly Hills."

Raymond's operation is typical of the larger scene-setting organizations. Central offices are established in major cities; bulletins and "yearbooks" are issued to members giving names and addresses; large amounts of money are spent on advertising and promotion. Within the setup itself a number of recreational opportunities are offered—sporting events, group discussions, theater parties, restaurant trips, and so forth. In the long run the basic service provided is contact and legitimacy: Singles are brought together and given the opportunity to meet. It's up to them to do the rest.

We received several essays from respondents who had used these clubs. As usual, some were enthusiastic, some were not.

Woman, Newton, MA: Meeting men has been fairly easy because I now go to a regular group that arranges outings to football games, holds tennis matches and fashion shows, and lots of interesting activities, the kind you would go to *even* if you didn't want to meet someone. We have regular skiing parties on Saturdays not far out of Boston and those are the best of all places to meet other people. This has filled a gap in my life, and not only men but women that I have met there have become my friends.

Man, Baltimore, MD: I went to a singles "club" organization thinking that it was going to be a kind of sex party, and instead I found a lot of middle-class people like myself. Most of them were about as lonely as I am. In looks the women were slightly above average without too many glamour girls. The men were lawyers, businessmen, the kind of men I went to college with on the whole. It was really just like any other social gathering, so I have gone back several times. When I got over the initial embarrassment of just being there it was fine, and I would recommend it as a good place to meet other people.

Woman, Pittsburgh, PA: Once I paid an annual joining fee to partake of a so-called "singles club," and to this day I feel I wasted my money, as the quality of the people was terrible, the so-called "activities" were a joke (one outing into the mountains for a day canceled when everyone showed up and waited for two hours for a host who never showed up and who never even excused himself). I never got the feeling the officials of the club gave a darn about me. They just wanted my money. The services they provided were way below par.

Woman, Philadelphia, PA: Singles organizations are big industries now in our country. I was curious so I investigated. I wanted to know whether they are ripoffs or places where you can really meet caring men. To tell you the truth, I'm still not sure what they are. I paid a six-month initiation fee and was allowed to partake in two social functions each week. The functions were all low-spending kinds of numbers. Like, they would have an outing at a restaurant, or a museum. These are places where you don't have to pay. At the museum *we* had to pay the admission at the door. In other words, the organization itself was kind of shifty and shadowy, and I certainly didn't feel I could trust them. The kind of people that came, however, were a different story. This amazed me. They were on the whole rather well-to-do people, the women in really chic clothes and a lot of the men looking like they worked for E. F. Hutton or IBM. There were a few weirdos in the crowd, but not many, and a few blue-collar types who seemed mainly out of place. Of course I ended up with the blue-collar guy because I felt sorry for him. We went home together and he tried to jump me, and I wiggled away, virtuous as always, and got home as fast as I could and tried to digest the whole experience. Basically it's really just a lot of isolated people trying to reach out, and experimenting with just about anything including paying for it. The people are certainly not different from anywhere else. I for myself don't think I will ever go back to this organization or any others like it, but I could see where it would be okay for certain people.

On the darker side are the not infrequent accusations that singles functions are unsavory and exploitative. Some essayists indicate that those in attendance are usually "on the make" or "on the prowl"; Law-of-the-jungle type metaphors abound. The men are "wolves," the women hungry "vultures." Everyone is "on the hunt" or "sniffing around" for "game." Attending women use their physical attractions as "bait." Men go "on the attack" with their phony lines, and so forth.

Woman, San Francisco, CA: I utilized a paid dating club only once. The first activity I went to had about 300 people standing around a large ballroom in a downtown hotel. The first thing I noticed is that the men feel no qualms about looking you over from head to foot as if they were thinking of eating you for dinner. It's being on display. It's sexy in a way because everyone knows why everyone else is there, but it's just this sexuality that gets in the way. It's on everybody's mind and it kind of engulfs the place and turns it into a barnyard. I'm not a prude—but I felt very much like some kind of animal at this place to prey and be preyed upon.

Wildest of all scene-setters, according to respondents, are the singles resorts:

Woman, Nashville, TN: At [name deleted] resort in Martinique everyone goes off with everyone. It's a crazy scene. And watch out for those instructors! I had a wild time and returned thoroughly exhausted and satisfied.

A few respondents describe their experiences at resorts in orgiastic terms. One description is of a veritable Saturnalia.

Woman, Boston, MA: The resort I went to was on an island in the Caribbean for only single people. There was a lot of mixing and sexual

activity. The instructors were all gigolo types. I never did see them in-
struct anyone except in. . . . You had the feeling they were like male
whores and were there for the takers. Sometimes at night the beach
would be covered with bodies. It was, to be plain, an orgy. The last
night all the wraps were off. The instructors, the men, the women,
some of the waitresses and waiters took a midnight swim and it ended
up in a love-making session that was what I imagine a sex club would
be like. It went on till morning. I would recommend such a place only
for those who go in for such things.

More reserved are the resort hotels that specialize in weekend
events:

Woman, Newark, NJ: I had a weekend at a hotel in the Catskills. Much
to my surprise there were lots of nice-looking guys. However, I felt out
of place. I hate the small talk and the type of kidding around and jok-
ing in weekend singles events. As with all singles functions, the usual
check-it-out atmosphere goes with it. I lacked the confidence and felt
unattractive during the weekend, and felt I'd wasted $100. However,
everyone else seemed to really enjoy it, and there were lots of interesting activities.

Woman, Manhattan, NY: I've had several skirmishes at resorts in the
Pocono regions. It was the same thing as usual with single frenzy, lots
of guys and gals standing around sizing each other up. Small talk. Sex.
Lots of things to do and keep busy with. Tennis, swimming, lotto,
skin-diving instruction. If you don't want to be part of the singles scene
you can just go for the fun of the featured activities. Nothing great but
okay, I suppose.

Still other kinds of scene-setters specialize in culture and sophisticated enticements: singles gourmet dining clubs, singles theater discussion groups, singles backgammon and wine-tasting groups. Here in
theory the onus of frequenting a singles gathering is offset by the fact
that all are gathered in the name of art.

Woman, Manhattan, NY: I'm not sure whether you could really call my
group a "singles" group. What it basically is is a group of unmarried
men and women who get together twice a month to listen to poetry
readings, discuss literature and sometimes chip in to hire a guest professor or speaker on some branch of modern and traditional literature.

It is a nice place to get together. We do it at different members' apartments each meeting, and everyone shares expenses.

Sports gatherings are also popular. There are singles clubs for tennis players, bowlers, skiers, just about every popular sport imaginable. Having an alternate purpose for being at these gatherings, respondents report, eases that "on the spot" feeling.

Woman, Pittsburgh, PA: I belong to a tennis club that caters to unmarried people. The nice thing about it is that it's not really a singles organization kind of thing but a place where one can come to play tennis and also to meet other people if you wish. There are no pressures.

Man, Manhattan, NY: I belong to a health club in downtown New York. When I went to look the place over the advertising stressed pretty girls in tights and all that kind of stuff. The place is mixed with men and women, but the athletic program there is for real, and most people are not there to meet girls or boys but to work out. They have yoga lessons, Nautilus equipment, work-out rooms, a pool, steam baths. Sometimes you meet women there but usually there are more men than women anyway. I don't know if you'd call this a singles spot or not.

Most innocent of the singles organizations are the church groups. These are not exclusively for believers, though religious people tend to favor them over the more secular gatherings. As one born-again Christian remarked in an essay: "If you've got to do the singles thing why not do it for Jesus?" Of all respondents who attend singles organizations, those who frequent church groups are the most enthusiastic:

Woman, Nashville, TN: I have attended church groups which were very nice. I met many nice men but they were as scared of me as I of them (why *is* she divorced, they ask themselves). The men treated me as a Christian man should, not forward or aggressive as I found in clubs and bars. I would recommend church groups if you are wanting a Christian man and not just a one-night stand.

Man, Oklahoma City, OK: The only singles organizations I have or would attend are at my church. Here you *know* you'll meet nice girls who have the same belief as yourself. There's always plenty to do, and our church sponsors lots of exciting events every month like concerts, lectures, hayrides in the summer, picnics and general fun things. I really suggest doing this for any good Christian man or woman.

The list of different scene-setters goes on, and feelings over their value are mixed. Most people judge them as just one more alternative, no better or worse than others. Those who praise them commonly do so because they gather available singles for the agreed-upon purpose of getting acquainted. In this sense they are direct, no-nonsense experiences, with much of the pretending done away with. The negative part is a correlate of the first: the "meat market" atmosphere, which many respondents claim no amount of cultural trimmings can disguise.

"You'll want to consult a matchmaker if you like to avoid risk," Dr. Sollod tells us, "if the idea of conquest or winning another person through some kind of drama, power, charisma, intelligence, or wit doesn't appeal to you. People of this type would rather do it in a more structured way—where they aren't on the line all the time to prove themselves. If it doesn't work out for them, they haven't risked much."

The person who wishes to avoid risk, however, is not necessarily at a disadvantage. "Say you're a man in your fifties," says Dr. Sollod. "You're not as handsome as you once were, but you're very successful and have many assets a woman might enjoy. How are you going to advertise yourself? You can't just walk up to a woman and start telling her all your accomplishments and so forth, and you probably don't want to. For you, a dating service may be perfect. It will push your good features for you and will let others know your strong points without your having to tell them."

There are others who prefer their action fast. "Some people feel matchmakers are too boring. They'd rather go right into the thick of things. And for them the scene-setters are best. At a singles function you can see fifty people at a glance, can quickly pick the two or three who are the most attractive and go after them. It's a much faster technique. Obviously you can't do this with a matchmaker."

How can one decide for oneself concerning the relative merits of matchmakers and scene-setters? Don't become too analytical about it, Dr. Sollod warns. "Don't tell yourself you need this kind of function because of some neurosis or other. Take it simply from the standpoint of your motives and abilities, what you need and what you can do. Define what you really want. Are you interested in a lot of sex? Or do you want a deeper relationship? Be clear about this. Are you interested in the chase? In a boisterous good time? In falling in love?

"Second thing, if you decide to go to a singles function find one that caters to the crowd of people you prefer. Religious, ethnic, or even socio-economic single groups are good this way."

And finally: "It's necessary once you get involved with singles activities to set yourself reasonable goals." The point is to take it slowly. "Enjoy the process, whether it's a singles function, or a bar, or whatever. Try not to feel you're on the line and have to perform. The ways to negotiate single functions have to be learned just like anything else. Don't put ridiculous demands on yourself. Just relax and let yourself get the most out of them you can."

THE FIRST MEETING: WHAT ATTRACTS SINGLES TO EACH OTHER?

What is it that causes one person to be attracted to another? Though oceans of ink have been spilled over this question, and while we have no pretensions to supplying the definitive answer, indications offered by survey respondents help toward an understanding of this mystery. Singles were queried on the issue. In the first question, we presented respondents with a list of positive qualities and asked them to tell us how important each was in terms of initial attractive power. Here are the alternatives offered and the choices made:

a. Money, status and position

Fewer than 10 percent of men claim that *money, status, and position* are *very important* factors in attracting them to a particular woman. Only 17 percent say these are even *somewhat important.* Over a third of men (37 percent) say they don't care one way or the other, while another 30 percent flatly state that these are *unimportant* to them. Six percent say they *don't know.*

Among women, only 15 percent give money a *very important* rank in their priorities. Forty percent say it is *somewhat important,* about a quarter don't care, and 15 percent deem it *unimportant.* Five percent *don't know.*

These responses belie the notion that American singles care primarily for wealth and power. They also discount the supposition that single women are mainly searching for a man with substantial income and influence. Responses to the following essay question, which we will quote through the remainder of this chapter, provide commentary on *money, power,* and so on, and their ability—or lack thereof—to attract.

BONUS FINDINGS

- Only 8 percent of women who are widowed say money, status, and position are very important attractions. Widows in general are the least impressed by a man's financial assets.
- Men who have never been married and who have lived alone for twenty to thirty years place a higher premium on money than do those who have been married at least once. The more times a man has been married, the less important a woman's money and status are to him. Those who have never been married are four times as likely as widowed men to consider money and so on important.
- Women earning high salaries place a greater premium on money than do those in the middle and lower income brackets, while with men it is the opposite—the more money they have, the less they look for money or expect it in a woman.
- Blue-collar men and women rank a partner's financial assets as very important more commonly than do professional men and women.

---

9. What sort of man/woman turns you off and what sort of man/woman turns you on? How does the kind of man/woman that turns you on act, think, and speak?

Woman, Washington, DC: There are many things that are important to me as a turn-on—looks, how well-spoken and neat a man is, how well he knows his way around town. His intelligence, and of course his integrity as a person. I do not like men who boast a lot, and men especially who have money and hold it over your head. "Hi, Baby. I'm rich. You should kiss my toes, therefore." That attitude. Men who are in positions of importance often act that way and that gets to be bothersome and a turn-off. Rich men are nice as long as they are humble about their money and don't expect you to act a certain way towards them just because they *have* money. A lot of men I go out with who have money think they can buy me a night out and then I owe them a roll in the hay in return. I have been given presents by loaded guys and they have literally looked at me as if to say: "Well?" Presents with strings attached are no presents. I am most turned on by an honest, wholesome, well-meaning and decent man. Period.

Man, Chicago, IL: Since this is anonymous, I can tell you honestly what turns me *off* is a woman who is really up there, big job, big salary. I work with a lot of these women (and I have a good position myself) but they seem to be completely disinterested in getting married and having children. I'm not against a woman having her own life, but I prefer women who are more family-oriented. Maybe that sounds chauvinistic, but what turns me *on* is a woman who doesn't continually talk about her job on a date, what she is doing, what she is making, etc. I like women who pay attention to me (and believe me I do the same for them). Women who don't continually talk about the stock market (I used to live with a woman who was a broker), a woman who looks for the same things I do (marriage, kids and home). Maybe being in your thirties labels you "old-fashioned" but that's the kind of woman I want, and I have difficulty in getting turned on by today's hyper career gal. She leaves me cold.

Woman, Manhattan, NY: I learned from my early dating experiences that I had to be careful of falling in love with a man because of his prominence or his power or, of course, his money. A woman can fall for a guy who is in this position very easily without realizing that's why it's happening. Money can make you lie to yourself very easy. Whenever I am turned on by a man who is very wealthy and secure I must ask myself: Am I turned on to *him* or am I turned on to his power and money? That question has saved me several unfortunate involvements, though it is hard to be honest with yourself about such matters sometimes.

"At an earlier date," explains Dr. Leslie Faerstein, therapist in private practice in New York City and formerly of the staff of Columbia Presbyterian Medical Center in New York City, "a woman derived much of her personality and identity from whom she married and where her husband stood in the community. Today I think this is different, primarily because single women are now earning their *own* money. This means a man's money no longer defines a woman's identity, and money for many women is no longer something they look for initially in a new man. What we're seeing is a new breed of woman, one who is getting married much later, putting off having children, establishing her career first. These women are looking for men who are as intelligent and capable as they are, and who offer something first on an emotional level, rather than on a financial one. This woman doesn't need the man for money, status, and position as before—because she already has her own."

b. Sense of Humor

On the list of most important attractions—above physical appearance, above intelligence, above money or expertise in the bedroom, above all priorities but one—comes *sense of humor*. Among singles of all ages there is little variation of opinion on this issue, and in fact more than 85 percent of women and 80 percent of men claim sense of humor to be a *very important* or at least a *somewhat important* attraction.

BONUS FINDINGS

- Only 6 percent of men and 4 percent of women state that sense of humor is *not* important at all as a source of attraction.
- Women who are bisexual or homosexual place less premium on sense of humor than do heterosexual women.
- By a slight margin, the older a man gets, the less important he judges sense of humor to be in a woman. Women react basically the same way—as she gets older, a woman's demands for humor in a man are likely to decrease somewhat.
- When respondents were categorized by their living arrangements, we found that celibate men place by far the *least* premium on sense of humor. Men who live with a female partner place the *greatest* premium on it.
- Widowed men are the most uncertain of the subjects concerning the importance of humor in a mate. Exactly a third of all widowed men claim they *do not know* how important humor in a woman is for them.

The importance of sense of humor is expressed explicitly in these essays:

Man, Cleveland, OH: Different things turn me on in different women. It's not like there is this one thing I am always looking for that will throw the magic switch. The point is that a woman's personality is really the basis where it all starts. If she has a good personality, knows how to laugh, be witty, *take* a joke (very important, that last one), and make one without blushing (even off-color once in a while; the age of priss is past) this can be attractive. A woman should not act "broad" but should have a kind of sparkle about her person. Her laugh should be light and feminine, like bells tinkling in the wind, like water trickling down a spout on its way to the sea, like bird-song and wren-whistle. A woman's grace is what a man sees first—her aplomb, her manner in the world. She must not take herself too seriously. She *must* know how to laugh at life, and herself, and at *you* even if you act like a fool. At all of us, this great human comedy that comes and goes so briefly without leaving as much trace as that made by a ship's wake upon the water. Woman is a complicated species, but so is man. Until they both learn that life is a bubble and that we stand on its brim, and that when it pops the sound it makes will be cosmic laughter—until then I guess we'll all just sit around and do a lot of crying.

Woman, Albuquerque, NM: A man who is funny is important. Life can be dull. I like a man who knows how to bring me out of the blues with his jokes and sense of humor. That's important. I like a man who knows lots of great jokes. Who knows his way around good restaurants or fine eating establishments. He has a *savoir faire* to the way he behaves. He can make me feel that I'm a great girl.

Man, Grand Rapids, MI: A woman who laughs all the time gets on my nerves. A woman who knows how and when to laugh though is a great turn-on for me. A woman who's not afraid to let herself go and to laugh at a good funny movie, or a comedian on television, or even a dirty joke. Knowing how to laugh is one of the most important things in the world.

Woman, Burlington, VT: Men who take themselves so seriously are a bore. Stuffy, non-humorous men are pills. I've known them aplenty and it's like trying to get blood from a stone. When I'm with a man who is casual, free, easy about himself, and who can kid with me, others, himself, he makes me feel like I can trust him and believe in him. It inspires a sense of belief and relaxation.

A woman of some perceptivity writes:

Woman, Queens, NY: Another turn on is that a man know how to make me laugh. For me a sense of humor is a brand of intelligence and intuition. We both look at each other in between the laughter and know exactly what we're thinking, feeling, wanting, hoping and loving. It's the ultimate unspoken togetherness, laughing together. Laughter between a man and a woman has a way of lifting us both out of our little spaces and joining us together for one precious moment of communication.

"Sense of humor," claims Dr. Faerstein, "is not just the ability to deliver a joke or a funny story. It includes the person's entire personality. It's a whole attitude about life, about the other person, about oneself. There is often a basic kind of intelligence that goes along with a good sense of humor, which is valued as much as the humor itself. Sometimes I think that if a man has a good sense of humor this means he is secure, relaxed about life, and not uptight. For women it may mean she is witty, urbane. It implies intelligence, cleverness, a whole panorama of attractive features other than just the humor itself.

"Humor represents a person's attitude toward life, the home he or she was brought up in, the basic personality. Very controlled or very controlling people would probably not have a good sense of humor since they would be afraid to relax and let go. They would lose control (there is always a big element of control in a humorless type of person); they would be afraid to let any piece of themselves show, any weakness. This is why a lack of sense of humor is so unattractive: because it indicates a boring, defensive, manipulating and controlling personality."

c. Intelligence, Perceptivity

More than half of single women (52 percent) rate *intelligence and perceptivity* in a man as being *very important* attractions. A third (33 percent) say they are *somewhat important.* Only 7 percent admit that they don't care one way or the other, and 4 percent claim they are *not important* at all. Four percent say they *don't know.*

Almost two fifths (39 percent) of men feel that *intelligence and per ceptivity* are *very important* to them. Another third (36 percent) feel they are *somewhat important,* and 11 percent say they don't care one way or the other. Six percent say these are *not important.* Eight percent answer they *don't know.*

Intelligence and perceptivity are frequently mentioned in essay answers, especially by respondents who treasure the same qualities in themselves:

Man, Boston, MA: Since I am a creature of education and learning, I must ask that a woman have at least a few basic credentials in that department too. Imagine how difficult it would be to want to discuss matters you believe in and read about, and to get a blank look in return. There is nothing that turns me off faster than a woman without any ideas, ideals, and general savvy about the world.

BONUS FINDINGS

- Fifty-six percent of professional men say intelligence and perceptivity are important to them—compared to only 29 percent of blue-collar men.
- Only about a third of bisexual or lesbian women feel intelligence and perceptivity are important attractions. Three times as many bisexuals and lesbians (as compared to heterosexual women) say they don't care one way or the other about these qualities, and five times as many say they are unimportant. Male homosexuals, however, show no dramatic differences in this valuation as compared to heterosexuals.
- Intelligence and perceptivity are most important to the highly educated men and women, least important to the man and woman who have attended high school only.
- The more times a man has been married, the less importance he places on intelligence. Widowed men are only about half as likely to demand intelligence as men who have never married.
- Men and women who have been single all their lives are much more likely to demand intelligence and perceptivity from a mate than are those who have been single for less than two years.

Woman, Sacramento, CA: It is a man's whole being that turns me on first and last and in between. I don't care what he looks like, how much money he has in the bank—I do care about the quality of his thoughts. His mind and what goes on inside it. I have come to value intelligence over the past few years, and I look for it in first contact with a new man I have just met. It shines through in his sense of humor, his wit, his perspective on the world, and the way his eyes penetrate when they look at you.

"For many younger people today, sex is just a part of life," remarks Dr. Jonathan Weiss, psychologist in private practice and clinical Assistant Professor, Department of Psychiatry, at New York Hospital, Cornell University Medical Center, New York City. "Their primary aim is no longer sex but other qualities, such as *intelligence.* People are better educated today, doing more meaningful work—they want someone they can talk to, not just sleep with. Women are looking for a bright, understanding man. Men are looking for a woman who can give them intellectual support, not just someone they can take for granted who is home raising the kids. They want a partner now, not just a sex mate."

"Women today want someone with whom they can have an equal exchange," claims Dr. Faerstein. "Someone they can talk to, who will listen, and who will make an honest attempt to see their side of things. Of course intelligence in this case doesn't just mean a college degree. It means a kind of innate brightness. I think intelligence here means a kind of basic understanding, willingness to exchange and experience the other person's opinion. In fact that's what single people of both sexes are looking for more and more."

d. Physical Attractiveness

Less than a third of men (29 percent) say that *physical attractiveness* in a woman is a *very important* attraction. Almost half (46 percent) feel it is only *somewhat important.* Twelve percent don't care one way or the other, and 6 percent say it doesn't matter at all. Seven percent *don't know.*

Only 17 percent of single women find *physical attractiveness* to be *very important.* Almost half (46 percent) feel it is just *somewhat important.* A quarter say it doesn't matter one way or the other, and 9 percent report it's *not important* at all. Four percent *don't know.*

Findings here are a bit surprising. In our society there is an acknowledged emphasis placed on physical appearance. Yet in our survey, physical appearance rates rather low compared with other choices. Looks are important, singles tell us, but not *that* important. "Among women," remarks Dr. Faerstein, "unless a man is really gross looking, his looks are not going to count against him. Men say things like 'My God, that's a really beautiful woman.' But I don't usually hear women talking about men in that way. Usually they discuss men more in terms of personality, like 'He's a great guy,' that kind of thing. Men don't always understand this. Because they place such importance on appearance themselves, they naturally assume women do the same, and as a result they may spend hours in the bathroom trying to make them-

selves look good just because they think that's what women really
want. Sometimes you see a beautiful woman with a man who is not so
nice-looking, and the comment will be, 'Oh, he must be great in bed,'
or 'He must be doing something I don't know about.' People don't realize that a *man who can fulfill a woman's emotional needs* is more desirable than a perfect physical specimen who has no feelings.

BONUS FINDINGS

- Among women living with a man, almost twice the
  number (as compared with those who live alone) feel
  physical attractiveness is very important.
- Only a quarter of all widowers (24 percent) feel attractiveness is very important. Only 30 percent feel it
  is somewhat important. Among widows an extremely
  low 7 percent rank appearance as very important.
- The older a woman gets, the less emphasis she
  places on physical attractiveness in a man. Among
  men there is no large difference at any particular
  age—older and younger men have approximately
  the same attitudes toward the importance of looks.
- Lesbian and bisexual women tend to be less concerned with a partner's looks than do heterosexual
  women. Homosexual men are more concerned with
  looks in partners than the average heterosexual, but
  not to a great extent (28 percent of heterosexuals
  say looks are very important, as compared to 33
  percent of gays).

"The only time physical appearance is really important for a woman, and to an extent for men too, is the first impression. Even here,
however, you are not dealing with dazzling beauty but with things like
cleanliness, good grooming, and basic things like that. These things are
the physical bottom line, and once you get past judging them there are
many other qualities that are more important than looks."

"It's very possible," adds Dr. Weiss, "That we are seeing the emer-
gence of a new breed of singles. I think a shift is on today toward a
more conservative value system wherein people realize that they've lost
touch with fundamentals and that they have been involved too long
with superficial conventions, such as what kind of car a person drives
or how good-looking someone is. Somehow these concerns are not
nearly as satisfying as they used to be. People are looking deeper now
for something to give them a sense of direction and a feeling of mean-

ingfulness. They are looking past physical appearance and trying to get to a person's essential qualities. Physical appearance has dominated the scene for a long time, but I believe it is weakening as a social mode and that more significant values are gaining greater acceptance."

Concerning looks as a source of attraction, two other questions provided further information. The first of these, a multiple-choice question, examines one's self-image—the attitude toward one's *own* physical appearance.

10. *Describe how you look to others (pick one of the following).*

Men	Women
a. Extremely handsome	Very beautiful
b. Very attractive	Very attractive
c. Attractive	Pretty
d. Average good looks	Average good looks
e. Interesting looking	Interesting looking
f. Plain	Plain
g. Uncertain	Uncertain
h. Don't know	Don't know

Here are the responses. First, *men:*

- Five percent of single men feel they are *extremely handsome.*
- Nine percent think they are *very attractive.*
- Twenty-eight percent feel they are *attractive.*
- Thirty-three percent feel they have *average good looks.*
- Eleven percent say they are *interesting looking.*
- Six percent feel they are *plain.*
- Seven percent are *uncertain.*
- One percent *don't know.*

And *women:*

- Three percent of single women feel they are *very beautiful.*
- Twelve percent feel they are *very attractive.*
- Thirteen percent characterize themselves as *pretty.*
- Forty-seven percent say they have *average good looks.*

- Twelve percent say they are *interesting looking.*
- Four percent say they are *plain.*
- Eight percent are *uncertain.*
- One percent *don't know.*

BONUS FINDINGS

- Not a *single* widowed man viewed himself as extremely handsome.
- Men who are bisexuals or homosexuals more frequently say they are extremely handsome than do men who are heterosexual (12 percent as compared to 5 percent). The same is true among women: Bisexual and homosexual women are fifteen times more likely to view themselves as very beautiful than are heterosexual women (31 percent versus 2 percent).
- Men and women who have never married are several times more prone to view themselves as extremely attractive or very attractive than are those who have been married at least once.
- The more education a man has, the more he views himself as attractive in general. Only 6 percent of high-school-educated men call themselves very attractive, as compared to 15 percent of college graduates. The same proportion holds true with women.
- Twenty percent of high-income-earning women view themselves as extremely attractive—versus half that number (10 percent) of women making less than thirteen thousand dollars a year.

High-salaried, college-educated professionals more often view themselves as good-looking than do blue-collar, low-income men and women with a lower level of education. There is a definite correlation between personal success and physical self-image.

"Basically," remarks Dr. Weiss, "the issue is self-esteem rather than objective self-appraisal. There *is* no one standard of good looks. I tell this to my women patients who are so concerned with their appearance. I tell them to look at the man who loves his wife and who thinks she's the most beautiful woman in the world—while no one else knows what he sees in her. If you like yourself, you will probably like your appearance too. It's that simple. And you'll act that way toward the world."

"People view themselves as good-looking *especially* if they have a lot of drive and aspiration," adds Dr. Faerstein. "Those who are going on with their education, pursuing higher levels, who are self-confident and self-contained, would generally feel better about their whole selves, inside and out. If you are a professional woman you think of dressing professionally, looking good. You think of yourself as a professional person with all that this implies. Naturally you'll have a better physical self-image than you would if you saw yourself trapped in a miserable job or position. It's all very subjective and dependent on your mood and circumstance of the time."

The second question was an essay.

11. What part does physical appearance play in your selection of a mate? Would you reject or become involved with a person on the grounds of looks alone? Why or why not?

The most common response agrees with Dr. Faerstein's point that looks have their greatest attractive power *during the first few moments* of meeting. After that even the handsomest and the prettiest are on their own:

Man, Toledo, OH: Looks mean a whole lot—for the first five minutes. Then everything else takes over. Then the beauty reveals itself as skin deep or really deep.

Man, Memphis, TN: Physical appearance certainly plays a good part in my first "hit" on a woman, but after that it stops being so important. It has very little to do with my "selection of a mate" if by a mate you mean someone who I am committed to over a period of time. Looks don't help you when you're down. When you have a problem and need your woman to help you out. Looks don't teach you anything about human nature, and usually women who are very good looking are stuck up. Looks can't make love. Looks can't earn love from someone else either. Looks can sometimes be a drawback because people expect so much from you if you're really good looking, and wherever you go you're the focus of attention. What I'm saying is that looks not only don't make for a good person but looks in themselves can be problematical and cause the beautiful person more problems than they are willing to put up with.

Woman, Grand Rapids, MI: While looks can be important for that first impression, such an impression is usually not long lasting. After a while I start to get to know the person and like him for his sense of humor, his warmth, his intelligence, his acceptance of me. None of these things can be accurately foretold by looks. I don't believe I would become involved with a person for looks alone. Attracted at first, yes, but not involved.

A majority of essays agree with what we have just heard: "Appearance," states a respondent, "is nature's way of bringing men and women together. After they're together the personality takes over."

When looks are stressed in the essays it is most often men who do the stressing.

Man, Providence, RI: It is a large part of selection of a mate to me because I find it a heck of a lot easier to fall in love with a beautiful body rather than a woman with a so-so body. I feel a woman with a good body makes for a better lover. She's more experienced. If a woman takes time at her make-up and her appearance I know she's a woman who likes men, cares about herself.

Man, Omaha, NB: I might reject a person on the basis of looks and would need someone who definitely has something going for them physically. Why? If I'm involved with someone, I'm going to spend a great deal of time looking at her (or, very occasionally, him). I wouldn't want to live with someone I don't like to look at. Perhaps it's socially conditioned, and more than likely it's unfair, but I know what makes me unhappy and have to act accordingly. I have had sex with people I find unattractive, but the sexual element usually withers away and the relationship turns into a friendship.

Woman, Philadelphia, PA: In a one-night stand for "sex for the sake of sex" I might be attracted to a man because of his hairy chest, etc. If I want to be turned on sexually I want to be turned on by a good looking guy. But that's just for something fast. Usually I judge a man by his nature and behavior.

Others state that looks are a key factor only if a person is exaggeratedly *unattractive*. Obesity is the number-one turn-off:

Woman, San Diego, CA: "I wouldn't reject a man on the grounds of looks alone unless he was really ugly. If a man is absolutely obese and horrible looking then no, I wouldn't think of going out with him."

Woman, Marina Del Rey, CA: I went out with a fat man once and told him he'd have to lose weight if we were to go out again. That man then lost 60 pounds in order to date me. He was 243 then, and I found myself embarrassed being in his presence. His weight loss has changed both our lives sexually, emotionally and physically because he is now a good-looking man with his self-respect back. We plan to get married soon. I have made him promise to keep his weight down, and told him that if he doesn't I will get a divorce.

Some men and women have a built-in distrust of the spectacularly attractive single:

Man, Albuquerque, NM: Mostly all really good looking girls are jerks. They never had to work for anything in their lives—the men just come up to them as a matter of course. They have no character. Look at your typical beautiful model, she's empty looking.

Man, Toledo, OH: My first wife was a very attractive woman. She was too attractive. I feel she spent all her time on her looks and clothes. She was a good dresser and had an excellent figure. After we'd been married the very thing that attracted me, her good looks, began to get me—she was always making herself pretty, but for who? Not for me anymore. I began to imagine she was having affairs. She started going out by herself looking like a million. She was having affairs I learned—by the cartload. The guys couldn't resist that tall figure and long blonde hair down to her ass. She'd wear low-cut blouses and kind of seemed all helpless and willing to other men, even married ones. Her body started to drive me nuts. She'd come home and start to tell me about the affairs she was having. . . . I don't want to go on with this.

Man, Brooklyn, NY: Sometimes I ask myself why? Why do I have to have a good looking woman? What's so important about it? I tell myself that usually they're the ones with the least on the ball. They're the ones who have had to make the least effort and have gotten the biggest results from life. They haven't had to try. They usually have a dull and poor personality. Did you ever wonder where the term "dumb blonde" comes from? It's from the fact that a good looking, sexy babe needs nothing else but her body to get along in the world. A woman like this is boring and conceited.

One respondent wrote a poignant mini-drama concerning the conflicts that surround physical appearance.

Man, Boston, MA: When I was very young I believed like all other very young men that the way a girl *looks* is the most important thing in the world. I always chased the best lookers in my college class, and, to tell the truth, had a reputation as a bit of an "ass man." Later when I was on my own I wouldn't look at a woman unless she was something else. Being what people call "handsome" myself, I have never had trouble attracting girls. Then, when I was twenty-nine and still single I became engaged to a very beautiful girl named Gloria. Gloria was a peasant at heart though she came from a good family. She had a peasant's beauty like Sophia Loren. She was dark with an incredible figure and perfect legs. I was ready to marry Gloria and she seemed like the one. It was then that I met Mary. Mary was almost funny looking you'd say, not exactly ugly but very plain. She was cute but ordinary. Some of her friends said she looked like Charlie Chaplin because she was short, dark and sometimes wore silly bowties. Anyway, Mary was a terrific girl. A great personality, great sense of humor. She could pull me out of the dumps. She was smart, had been Phi Beta Kappa at Boston University. She helped me with my work and could cook. She could hold a wonderful conversation and sometimes we talked all night. She was many things, even great in bed. Perhaps I should say she was all the things Gloria wasn't. The trouble was *she wasn't pretty.* I'd look at her sometimes and wish her skin was smoother or that her nose wasn't so snubbed. After going out with both girls for some time (Mary on the sly—Gloria would have killed me) I came to a crossroad point. I chose Gloria, mostly because she turned me on so much physically. And I want to tell you that I regretted it ever since. My marriage with Gloria didn't last two years. I got tired of her physical looks after six months, and she even started to look a bit ugly to me. When we separated I went looking for Mary. I learned she was married to another man and living in Cape Cod. She was expecting a child. I think that decision I made ruined my life up to this point.

e. Skill as a Lover

Only 28 percent of men feel that a woman's sexual skill is a *very important* attraction. Thirty-seven percent feel it is *somewhat important* to them. Sixteen percent *don't care one way or the other,* and 12 percent say *it doesn't matter at all.* Eight percent *don't know.*

Among women fewer than one third (30 percent) rate a man's skill as a lover as *very important.* Thirty-seven percent say it is *somewhat important.* Seventeen percent *don't care,* and 12 percent say it is *unimportant.* Five percent *don't know.*

BONUS FINDINGS

• Very few widowed men (17 percent) think a woman's skill as a lover is very important, and even fewer widowed women (12 percent) rate it very important in a man.

• Men and women who have only a high school education, are more likely to call skill as a lover a very important attraction.

• A woman presently living with a man is likely to rate skill as a lover as much more important than is a woman living alone.

• Over a quarter of bisexual and lesbian women claim skill as a lover to be important to them.

Sexual ability ranks among the lowest on the list of priorities. This judgment holds true across the social groups, though there are some interesting variations. For instance, between the ages of twenty and twenty-four, men are not overly concerned with a woman's skill as a lover. Between twenty-five and thirty-four their expectations increase, presumably keeping up with increased sexual activities. For the next years—the late thirties and early forties—good sexual performance will be at the greatest premium for men; when they reach middle age it gradually becomes less important again.

Women's assessment of sex describes a similar curve but tends to peak earlier in the age cycle. In the early twenties sex is as low in importance as it will ever be for women. During the middle twenties and early thirties interest takes a sizable turn upward, then levels off. Finally sex takes a drastic dip in the late thirties and continues to head downward in the forties and fifties. Thus for singles of both sexes the graph describing sexual interest starts low in the early years, moves dramatically upward in young adulthood, and declines in middle age.

f. Common Interests, Talents, Backgrounds

Only one quarter of single men feel that *common interests* and so on are a *very important* attraction, ranking this alternative among the lowest on the list. Forty percent, however, do say it is *somewhat important,* while 15 percent feel it is neither important nor unimportant, and 11 percent state it is *not important* at all. Nine percent *don't know.*

With women, 32 percent feel it is *very important.* Forty-three percent think it is *somewhat important.* Thirteen percent say they don't care, and 7 percent state it is *unimportant.* Five percent *don't know.*

BONUS FINDINGS

- This option was most important to women in the thirty-five-to-fifty-five-year-old group, and least important to women in their middle twenties and early thirties. Among men there is little variation according to age.
- Gays and bisexual men find these qualities much more important than heterosexual men do (38 percent for gays versus 25 percent for heterosexuals). However, lesbians show an opposite reaction. Thirty-two percent of lesbians rank this choice unimportant, as opposed to 7 percent of heterosexual female respondents.
- Male college graduates are more prone to value common interests highly than are men who never attended college.

In the essays, common interests are usually mentioned in passing but are rarely the center of discussion.

Woman, Los Angeles, CA: There are a whole lot of things I could mention in terms of what attracts me. Brains, brawn, intelligence, mutual likes and dislikes, imagination, quality of feelings, and many more that would take me too long to list.

Woman, Oklahoma City, OK: The thing that turns me on the most in a man is when he treats me like a lady. He should attend to my feminine needs and make me feel very special. I like a man who talks my own language and who shares the same tastes, attitudes and background. I think it's hard for people to make it, for instance, who come from very different ethnic or social upbringings. I also like a man who knows how to behave properly in public, and who is well mannered. Clean mind and body alike are a must. I like men who dress with a flair but not men who over-dress.

"I think a de-emphasis on common interests and background is a healthy thing," maintains Dr. Faerstein. "What is becoming of increasing importance today is the person himself or herself. Background is not as important as it once was, and I think that singles are meeting each other on more equal terms. What they bring in terms of their own histories is not as important as what they bring in terms of individuality and intelligence."

g. Integrity, Sensitivity, Kindness, Understanding

Here, by a long shot, is the winner among the choices. A majority of 65 percent of single men say that the above qualities are *very important* attractions. Eighteen percent say they are *somewhat important.* Only 5 percent don't care one way or the other, and only 6 percent say they're *not important at all.* Six percent *don't know.*

With women, the response is even greater. Eighty-one percent marked this choice as *very important.* Ten percent say it is *somewhat important.* Only 2 percent say they *don't care one way or the other,* and only 4 percent state flatly that these are *not important at all.* Four percent *don't know.*

The results of this question give the lie to certain stereotypes concerning singles. There are in fact two roles into which American singles are often cast. The first portrays the single as a bark adrift between empty sexual affairs, a lost soul frantic to find a mate. The second imagines him or her as the abandoned "swinger," moving from one bacchanalia to the next, selfish, self-indulgent, an adversary of everything traditional: marriage, morals, perhaps even motherhood.

One purpose of this survey is to determine how closely these images apply. We learned that while such stereotypes do sometimes resemble reality, they remain stereotypes principally because they are exaggerations of their models. The survey demonstrates that the lonely life and the life of abandon, while both are aspects of the singles scene, are neither as independent of each other nor as extreme as popular opinion would have them be.

Of the two stereotyped roles, the swinging single has especially been the target of both scorn and envy. From the findings it appears that though singles are certainly concerned with sex and are unquestionably out to enjoy themselves, a majority are not as attracted by a partner's tangible assets—money, looks, sexual appeal, and so on—as by his or her positive personal characteristics: *integrity, kindness, understanding, and sensitivity.*

That a large majority voted for these qualities reveals singles to be more committed to traditional values than is often supposed. While placing some emphasis on the glamorous options, respondents still consider personal *emotional qualities* more important attractions than purely tangible ones.

The following essays are representative of this attitude. Note to what extent the "fundamental caring virtues" (as one essay writer termed them) are stressed:

Man, Winston-Salem, NC: I'm looking for a woman who can make me feel cared for and wanted. That's all. She should look like a happy person, content within herself. Attractiveness on the outside depends on the inner personality. She should be honest, direct, kind, knowing where she stands. Honesty is the foundation, because without it there's distrust, jealousy and sometimes hostility.

Woman, Seattle, WA: I'll tell you something I've told only a few men in my life. I feel it's a very important key for any man to understand about women. Remember that song from the movie *Camelot*? *Love Her.* The point of the song is that to win a woman a man has only to "love her, simply love her." I still think that is the great secret that all the books written on the subject of men and women forget. A woman wants to feel cared for, taken care of, treasured for her own personal qualities. If she is then she'll do anything for a man.

Man, Atlanta, GA: I am in my middle forties and have been through a number of scenes with women. I've married once briefly when I was young but otherwise have been single all my life. I've met one woman among hundreds who I would say was a total turn-on for me. I met her when I lived in a commune in the Blue Mountains about fifteen years ago. She was part Indian (American Indian) and part Negro. She had two children and she was what most men would call ugly. She came to the commune after I'd been there several months and she lived in the cabin next to mine. One day when we were pumping water at the spraying well I started talking with her. I soon found her to be a tremendously interesting woman. She had been on a reservation, had once walked across the Mohave Desert and had lost a young son by drowning. She had a lot to say but she never let that get in the way of what I wanted to say. We had a rapport because she seemed to have a fully honest mind. She really listened to everything I said. She was kind to her children and to all living things, even though her children were both from a different father and neither of these fathers had been decent to her. You sensed that she was a person who would help and care for you. She never got sick, never complained, would come to the aid of someone even if that person were her deepest enemy. There was something plain goodly about her which made me forget how ugly she was, and to fall in love with her. She even began to look beautiful to me after I had been with her for a while. I moved in and we lived together for about three years. Our lives were happy ones, and I came to think of her children as my own. Our happiness came to an end when some local neighbors who had always hated us set fire to our commune huts, then complained to the local police that we had set fire through carelessness, and were a menace. The commune was broken up after that and this woman and I set off together in our beat-up Chevy. We had some other adventures but gradually moved away from each other. Somehow being away from the commune made things different. One morning I woke up and she and the kids were gone. I had been expecting it and no note was necessary. Today I remember her as the most honest, forthright, loving, decent person I've ever known.

Finally, after such a long and detailed list of attractions we tried to find out what it is that turns a single man or woman *off* during the first meeting.

Responses to this question overlap with those found in the question about what turns people on and a capsulization of these answers shows how the two sets of responses complement each other.

**12. Which of these items (pick two)   Men
most turns you off in a woman?**

a. Excessive good looks	7%
b. Unattractive appearance	43%
c. Lack of money and position	3%
d. Unattractive personality	51%
e. Lack of intelligence	32%
f. Lack of sex appeal	18%
g. Extreme feminist attitudes	25%
h. Don't know	1%

**13. Which of these items (pick two)   Women
most turns you off in a man?**

a. Excessive good looks	5%
b. Unattractive appearance	27%
c. Macho attitudes	40%
d. Unattractive personality	39%
e. Lack of intelligence	35%
f. Lack of sex appeal	8%
g. Weakness and lack of self-confidence	34%
h. Don't know	0%

> **BONUS FINDINGS**
>
> - Only 7 percent of single men find excessive good looks a discouragement at first meeting (is it a myth that single men are frightened off by beautiful women?), while less than 5 percent of single women find excessive good looks in men a turn-off. However, the older a woman gets, the more she is likely to be repelled by excessive good looks.
> - Blue-collar men are more likely to find extreme feminist attitudes unattractive than either white-collar or professional men. Professional men, on the other hand, tend to be more put off by lack of intelligence in a woman than either blue-collar or white-collar men.
> - The more money a man makes, the more he finds unattractive appearance in a woman a turn-off. With women there is no variation of attitude among different wage-earning levels.

Perhaps the most interesting response to the question of what people find unattractive is the single woman's assessment of macho attitudes. In terms of percentage, women rank it very high on their list of turn-offs, on a par with unattractive personality.

Woman, Hollywood CA: I hate macho men who think they are so great and powerful. Just let me see a man swagger around with his shirt unbuttoned and his sneer for women of the world on his face and I flee.

Woman, Winston-Salem, NC: I have a lot of trouble with men who come on too strong with the male machismo act. Such men are always parading around trying to show off their masculinity. I believe that if they were really masculine there would be no need for such a show. Men like these are dangerous for women—they will go to any lengths to make women submit to them, as this is the only way they can feel like real men.

Woman, Pittsburgh, PA: Turn-offs: A man who throws his weight around; macho men who come on too strong and are so self important, and think they are irresistible; men who are never wrong and put women down. *Turn-ons:* A man who treats me as an equal both physically, mentally, and heartwise. A man who is man enough to admit when he's wrong. A man with enough confidence to allow me space to be myself.

Dr. Faerstein defines "macho" as follows: "A macho man is one who uses his gender to put a woman down; who is condescending toward a woman, calling her names like 'baby' and 'honey' and not respecting what she says or what she stands for; who treats her like an object, stressing his brute power at the expense of her lesser physical strength. A macho man acts very self-assured with a woman. Even if he gets rebuffed he never considers it his *own* fault. It's always something wrong with the woman. In general, macho means treating a woman as if she were a second-class citizen."

We are today seeing a new attitude among women toward this macho pose, claims Dr. Faerstein. "This is why so many women chose it as a turn-off. Women's consciousness is being raised among all generations today, even among older groups. When you look at somebody of the opposite sex, ideally you are looking at him or her in hope of a *real* relationship, not just as someone you can use or push around. Unless you are a sick person, you are not trying to look for someone to dominate you or for someone you can dominate. In the past a woman might have accepted this kind of dominance from a man because it was the accepted thing and a macho attitude among men was expected. Today, however, a woman searches for a man who is going to treat her as the intelligent, aware person that she is."

FURTHER TURN-ONS—AND TURN-OFFS

A number of the same themes appear over and over when singles discuss what most attracts and repels them. The wording is so similar that certain particular lines and phrases can be exhibited as typical of the entire group.

A most important prerequisite for women is that a man be "neat and clean." "Well-groomed" is a common description. "I hate men who are slobs," one woman writes, "even if they have a million dollars and look like Paul Newman."

The phrases "different looking" and "individual looking" turn up in women's essays more frequently than the word "handsome." All varieties of looks are extolled from "rugged" and "manly" to "debonaire." (One woman said she likes her man to appear "exquisite.") Almost all women require men to be satisfactorily washed. Cleanliness is the bottom line. Women also like a man who is well tailored. In fact, judging from the frequency with which clothes are mentioned, the power of good dressing to attract a woman should not be underplayed.

Woman, Chicago, IL: I'm a sucker for a man in three-piece suits. After that I like cardigan sweaters and tweeds. A pipe and tweed suit are an unbeatable combination.

Woman, Detroit, MI: I'm very turned on by men who wear tight-fitting pants (but not too tight) and body-form shirts. I dislike men in silk shirts but silk jackets are a turn-on if they're white. No running shoes, please.

Men care less about overall looks than women, and more about specific body and facial features. They often use phrases such as "I like large breasts," and "should have good legs." Women who are "stacked," "have delicate features," "large, full hips," "long hair down to shoulders" are all valued.

On the other hand, women should not be too "done up," "too made up," "too skinny," or of course the great bugaboo, "too fat."

Man, Sacramento, CA: I can tell you what a woman should *not* be. That's too bossy, brassy, shouldery, plump and fat. She should have a nicely taken care of body without blubber of any kind. I like women who exercise and like their bodies. It's a sign of sensuality. Women should take care of themselves and appear good to the world.

Man, Memphis, TN: I avoid women who overdo their make-up with the blue eyelids bit. I like simple looks but pretty ones. Women should dress well but avoid crazy styles like the kind you see in fashion magazines. Women who walk like clodhoppers turn me off. I like the classy type, new clothes, good figure, who stays in shape, keeps her stomach flat.

Men are also attracted by the way a woman *uses* her body:

Man, Little Rock, AR: When I was in the service in Japan I learned that there is a way a woman can move whereby just the sight of it turns on a man. It's not a hip-swinging walk. It's one of natural grace. The most sexy women I ever met was in a bathhouse in Tokyo. She helped bathe me. I guess she was a Geisha girl. She didn't put out or anything, just washed the service men who needed a bath. Just the way she smiled and her clothes swished (and smelled of perfume) when she moved. Everything about her was graceful and I've never forgotten her, especially when I see American women who are on the whole ungraceful in their movements. Orientals realize that sex-appeal is in the way you move as well as in the way you look.

An attractive woman exudes her own special "style." No one else is quite like her. She dresses in her special way, her tastes are her own, she makes up in an individual manner—or doesn't use makeup at all.

For women an important preference is that "a man pay attention when I speak to him," that he "listen to what I say." It appears, in fact, that one of women's greatest requirements is simply to be taken seriously by men. Highest on their list of the offensive is to be patronized or treated as a second-class intellect:

Woman, Independence, MO: Most important is for men to recognize me as an independent, thinking person who has something to contribute. I am not a stupid "broad," and any man who makes me feel this way will lose my interest quickly.

Woman, Grand Rapids, MI: Men I have gone out with fail to realize that all they have to do is act *fascinated* with me and I will be fascinated by them.

Woman, Portland, OR: Men don't understand women because they judge women by themselves. Since they are turned on by bodies, tits, and nice clothes they think women are turned on by similar physical attributes. Women are turned on by men who treat them as a person, not as a target for the night. Women are turned on in their minds, not in their bodies, in their hearts and not in their crotch. How could thinking that I'm some man's plaything turn me on for a moment?

Woman, Boston, MA: Turn-ons: a man who listens to what I say rather than one who waits for his chance to speak.

A man who cares about what I say, and who tells me so.

A man who likes me for my brains, integrity and willingness to share rather than for the size of my waistline.

A man who treasures me for what I am and not for what he thinks I should be.

Men ask for attention and recognition too, but in a somewhat different manner, more in terms of their "problems" than of their need to be recognized as equals. Men continually mention "a woman you can really talk to," one who will "understand my troubles" and "stand behind me." Many men complain that women are just "out for a good time"—which seems to be the female equivalent of "being out for what you can get." And they stress their need for emotional buttressing:

Man, Washington, DC: A woman should be sincerely caring about my real needs, wants and desires. I should be able to come to her with my problems, even the most intimate ones, and she would take an interest. She should stand behind me, be ready to help, to listen, to heal me when I'm ailing.

Man, Houston, TX: I like a woman who will stand up for me when I'm wrong, but who will tell me later that I *was* wrong. A woman who is sure of herself but knows she needs me. A woman who knows when to talk and when to be silent, who can communicate with me about my problems and give me real help in times of crisis. A woman who totally supports me no matter how tough the going. A woman who is my true friend.

Another preference among women is a man who is "open with his feelings" and "not afraid to show his emotions." This theme forms a leitmotif throughout the survey:

"I like a man who can expose himself emotionally. I like a man who is not afraid to cry."

"Men who can't tell you how they really feel when you say 'How are you?' are hung up."

"The rarest thing in a man is the ability to feel. Paradoxically speaking, it is also the best thing. A man who *feels* is worth his weight in gold."

"A turn-on is being made to feel by a man who can feel."

"Why are so many men so constipated inside? When a man opens himself up and takes a chance it is tremendously exhilarating for a woman to see."

"Feeling, feeling, feeling! Men are so dead inside! All they want is sex!"

Woman, Nashville, TN: Men should be open with their feelings but not crazy. I mean the type of guy who's real nice to you tonight, tells you he cares for you. Tomorrow he gets mad because his boots are dirty, and then you're a pig, you're no good, you stink! He swings back and forth. I've known a lot of them like that. That's not really being open with feelings but that's being sick. I think a lot of men mistake the two. They think it's just great to act crazy and believe that women like it. Well, they don't.

A woman from San Francisco phrased it in a strange, intuitive manner: "I want a man who's strong on the inside but soft on the outside, yet who's strong on the outside and gentle within."

"Honesty," "sincerity," "sympathy" rate high for both men and women. Some eight or ten of these fundamental caring virtues appear in almost 80 percent of all essay responses—"thoughtful," "warm," "affectionate," "patient," "friendly," and so forth—confirming findings in earlier questions.

A sense of confidence is also esteemed, especially among women. A man who exudes self-assurance and *savoir faire* is a perennial favorite. But men take heed. The plea for confidence is often tempered with a strong caveat: "Brute" is out! "His confidence," writes one woman, "must not be exclusive or destructive of mine. It must not come simply from the fact that he is bigger and stronger than I am."

Physical manliness is attractive in its place, many female respondents claim, but not when carried to the point of physical intimidation. As with self-confidence, strength in a man is pleasing only as long as it bolsters a woman's self-image rather than threatens it:

Woman, Washington, DC: Although I am not an avid feminist, I am attracted by a man who is self-confident and yet who I feel equal to. To be washed out in a relationship by a man's brute strength is not appealing. The type of man I like is one who makes me feel strong because he's strong.

Woman, Manhattan, NY: What I like in a man is self-assurance about where he's going in life, who he is, what he wants in a woman, what he likes and dislikes. What I hate in a man is the arrogance which macho-men types display: conceit, arrogance, egomania. Men who swagger around and think they're tough and irresistible seem more homosexual to me than straight. In my opinion, a real man is one who can be tough or tender as the situation demands. He is a man able to respond to a woman's needs, not a man who shouts a woman down whenever he's incapable of rising to the task. Macho is just bluff and a cop-out excuse for a real man."

SUMMING UP

Over the past years, as the number of singles has increased, as marriage has ceased to be mandatory, as urban life has expanded and small town life waned, as divorce has become more common and sex less closely monitored, the results have worked an important change in the ways men and women meet. Today single persons can still expect to meet a majority of their romantic partners through friends, introductions at social occasions, and at work—the more "legitimate" avenues of contact. But concurrently, the number of liaisons formed through singles functions, bars, dances, pickups, and so forth has dramatically increased. Though such methods were frowned on as recently as a decade ago, most of them have now attained at least quasi acceptance. The changes in the fabric of society have caused comparable changes both in people's tolerances and in their romantic needs.

The results of these changes have caused a movement away from private, personal, and mutually introduced meetings and toward meetings that take place in impersonal and public surroundings. Singles gravitate at an ever-increasing rate toward what might be termed "introductionless contacts." This trend will probably continue as long as the transient and impersonal nature of modern life continues to accelerate.

Singles offer a wide spectrum of opinions about the pros and cons of introductionless contact. Certainly, they tell us, such means make meeting easier than ever before; and in urban communities where the atmosphere is formal and impersonal this is no minor thing. At the same time, singles complain, these means can also be alienating, chancy, and occasionally dangerous. Though introductionless contacts are usually safe, the single takes his or her own *psychological* chances when opting for them. Any foray into what singles again and again refer to as the "meat market" carries the danger of exploitation and rejection. "The secret seems to be to pick carefully," advises Dr. Sollod. "If you're easily hurt, many of the singles functions can be psychologically damaging. Many people who frequent singles bars report negative reactions, even if the bar is camouflaged with a down-home decor. If you're oversensitive, these functions can be psychologically painful. If, on the other hand, you feel you have enough ego strength to face possible rejection, then go ahead, as the possibilities for meeting interesting, vital people are certainly there."

As to what it is that attracts singles, we learn from findings that while sexual appeal, money, and appearance are undoubtedly assets, they are usually assets only *initially*. When asked to list their priorities about what attracts them most, a majority of singles give first place to—we use the term again—the fundamental caring virtues. In the long run, it is emotional receptivity and openness that captures hearts and not the external allurements.

"What amazes me," remarks Dr. Sollod, "is that this revelation should come as a surprise. We are, after all, still human beings and still creatures of feeling. People should realize that the really attractive things you see in a person are the things that that person does *to make you feel good.* Certainly that person's looks never made you feel good. Certainly his or her money never did either. But that person's interest in you, her or his sense that you are a fine person—that's what makes the person attractive to you, and that's what a turn-on is all about."

Chapter 2

Dating ||||

Problems, Issues, and Pleasures

In this Chapter on "Dating" we ask:

1. Do you feel it's all right for a woman to ask a man out for a date?

2. How do you feel about asking a man out on a date?

3. From your experience, what are the most important things you would like to know about single men/women? What are the most important things members of the opposite sex should know about you as a man/woman? What would you like to tell men/women about yourself?

4. Should a woman ever pay for a date?

5. In your opinion, what effect has feminism and increased women's consciousness had on your attitude toward dating? Has it helped the relationship between the unmarried sexes or hindered it? How?

6. Can a single man and woman be friends without romantic involvement?

7. How do you feel about friendship with people of the opposite sex? If you have such relationships, what difficulties, if any, have come up? If you have no friendships with single people of the opposite sex, why not?

8. Describe your dream date: What single man/woman would you choose (he/she can be anyone you like, real or imagi-

nary, famous or just a friend)? Where would you go (any country you like, any restaurant, resort, palace, city, etc.)? What would you do? How would you end the night?

9. What is the most frequent reason you stop dating a particular woman?

10. What is the most frequent reason you stop dating a particular man?

11. It has been noted that if a man sleeps with a woman early in the relationship, this often causes him to lose interest in her—and conversely, if a woman refuses to have sex right away, this also turns a man off. In light of this "no-win" situation, how do you think a woman should behave herself sexually? What exactly is it that men want from women in this department?

12. Do you find that if you refuse to sleep with a man early in a relationship, he loses interest? Or, if you do sleep with him quickly, his interest also declines? Why do you think men force women into this "no-win" situation? How do you deal with it when it occurs?

13. How do you judge the majority of the women you date?

14. How do you judge the majority of the men you date?

15. How has single dating been for you on the whole?

With the many shifts in values that have occurred over the past decades, the traditional form of dating—man asks woman, man pays for woman, man pursues woman—has undergone conspicuous changes. Whether these changes constitute modifications on old themes or indicate a more basic transformation is a question we set out to answer.

WHO ASKS WHOM, TO WHERE, WHEN?

We started with one of the more ticklish issues by asking our respondents whether they think it acceptable for a woman to ask a man out on a date.

Major Finding: Almost two thirds of single men think it is all right for a woman to ask them out for a date.

---

1. *Do you feel it's all right for a woman to ask a*   **Men**
   man out for a date?
   a. Fine. But let her know most men take it as a sexual
      come-on.   15%
   b. Of course! It's time the old standards were
      changed.   54%
   c. Yes. But never the first time: that's the man's pre-
      rogative.   9%
   d. It's rarely, or never, happened to me.   10%
   e. No. It takes all the fun out of the chase.   2%
   f. No. Then a woman seems desperate and loses her
      appeal.   5%
   g. Don't know.   6%

If we total the percentages in options b and c—this includes men who are willing to be asked out on any date but the first, and those who find it acceptable under any circumstances—we have almost two thirds of the male vote. Women are even more emphatic in their positive response:

Major Finding: Almost three quarters of American single women think it is all right for a woman to ask a man out on a date.

---

2. **(Women's questionnaire)** *How do you feel*   **Women**
   about asking a man out on a date?
   a. I'd like to but I can't get up the nerve.   24%
   b. When I've done it it's usually turned out fine.   25%
   c. Whenever I've tried it's led to some kind of trou-
      ble.   3%
   d. I think it's wrong.   13%
   e. If the man is enlightened, he'll be pleased; if not,
      he's probably not worth it.   22%
   f. It makes a man feel pushed and/or emasculated.   7%

g. The way things are set up today, it's ask or lose
   your chance.   5%
h. Don't know.   3%

If we add up the positive responses to this question (options a, b, and e), we find that almost three quarters of single women are willing to ask men out on dates.

BONUS FINDINGS

• Women who have been single for more than ten years are the *least* likely to ask men out. Women *most* likely have been single from three to nine years.
• The more education a woman has, the more likely she is to say that her dates have turned out fine when she's asked men out. Thirty percent of the women who graduated from college and/or have a graduate degree indicated this, versus 2 percent who attended high school only.
• Divorced women are almost twice as likely to say it is wrong to ask a man out as are women who have never married.
• Between the ages of twenty and thirty-five, 23 percent of women claim they can't get up the nerve, while 26 percent of women in their middle thirties and early forties make the same claim. "Nerve" does not necessarily increase with age.
• Blue-collar women have considerably more trouble asking out men than do professional or white-collar women. Twenty percent of professional women say they can't get up the nerve; 30 percent of blue-collar women make the same claim.

Both men and women believe that female initiative in dating is acceptable and even laudatory. Yet behind this plurality lurks some nagging questions.

While both sexes are in favor of females' playing an increased role in date making, women are considerably more enthusiastic about it than men. One might suppose that men would support a vacation from the chase, that they would be delighted to allow women to sit on the other side of the fence for once, to undergo the turn-downs, the rejections, the anxiety of having always to break the ice. Male sexual mythology has long given first rank to beautiful women who pursue men. And yet, when offered this prerogative, men prove surprisingly careful and are a good deal more reserved in their clamor for role reversal than women.

"Some men like to be pursued by women," says Dr. Virginia Sadock, Director of the Program for Human Sexuality and Associate Professor of Psychiatry at New York University School of Medicine, "but if given the choice, many would prefer to remain the pursuer. This is the way men keep control. If a man is pursued by a woman, he may lose his superior position. Men imagine they want to be chased more than they really do."

The imagination-reality axis is a crucial point about which many important issues of singles life turn. As social critics have frequently pointed out, American men have been exposed since their childhood to conflicting messages concerning women. On a normal societal level, the courtship script reads: man the aggressor, woman the pursued. For centuries both parties have accepted this as the going convention. However, from the heart of pop culture comes the famous, if tongue-in-cheek, maxim "A man pursues a woman until *she* catches *him.*" And from pop culture too come the voices of ads, film, rock music, pornography, comic books, and other contemporary folk sources, where women are consistently featured in the role of dynamic sexual and even physical aggressors.

There is much confusion created by the head-on meeting of these two messages, and men often resolve the conflict by compartmentalizing rather than synthesizing. On the ordinary level they expect women to be passive and reserved. But in the world of their fantasies—which is given expression collectively through the media—Circe is allowed free rein, and it is here that Superwoman and the porno centerfold prevail.

Caught between new freedoms and old ethics, singles today find themselves divided in their attitudes. "I think one has to interpret the question of women asking men out by distinguishing between what people say and what they do," claims Dr. Peter Stein, sociologist and authority on singles behavior.* "Many college men still hold a pretty traditional value system in terms of dating and what they expect from women. This puts a woman in a dilemma—she gets two messages at once. One is to be more liberated, more assertive than she used to be.

* See *Single Life.* St. Martin's Press, 1981.

The other is that the men will tolerate *just so much* change and no more. So what is the woman to do? She tries to do both and ends up acting ambiguous. She then gives the guy a double message. She talks a liberated, assertive line, but her behavior may or may not correspond."

Another question is why, if both sexes are in favor of unisex roles in dating, there is so little evidence that a majority of single women actually *take* the initiative?

Some women do, of course, especially in the larger cities. But while the wish is often there the will remains reluctant:

Woman, Kansas City, MO: This survey is not the only place where I've recently been up against the question of whether or not to call a man up for a date. Many women's magazines give the greenlight on it. I know some friends who do it but more who don't. Why? Well, I think both because of fear of rejection and because of our training as kids that it's wrong to be the one to do such things.

Woman, Urbana, IL: I have occasionally tried to meet men by asking them out on dates. Once or twice this worked out and once it blew up in my face. It just left a bad taste in my mouth every time I tried. I don't try any more but prefer meeting men at work. Sometimes I meet them in friendship situations too.

"Why do people hesitate to ask out someone they like?" We asked prominent New York City psychiatrist and author Dr. Anthony Pietropinto. "Rejection, of course. It hurts too much when you hear 'no.' And I believe this particular kind of rejection is harder for a woman to take than a man.

"In our society men are conditioned from adolescence to being shot down by women. It's all part of the game, they're told. Women are generally not told the same thing. They are raised to see themselves as the shooters, not the shot."

"It's not exactly that men have overcome the fear of rejection," adds Dr. Sadock. "It's that they go ahead *in spite of it.* But women don't. They're not taught how. And this inexperience holds over into the world at large; it affects women when they are turned down for jobs, when they ask for raises, or higher positions.

"Women have been cast in the role of *pleasing* rather than demanding, and it is difficult for them to make the adjustment."

How *does* a woman overcome her fears? "Bite the bullet," replies Dr.

Sadock. "That's all you can do. The only way to get over this problem is to forge ahead, ask, demand, do despite your fears."

"There are several ways women can ask men out and avoid rejection at the same time," adds Dr. Pietropinto. "If a woman doesn't wish the man to take her invitation as a sexual come-on, it's important that she not be too direct. A woman should make sure she has some specific place to go, some plan, then make her invitation appear spontaneous: 'I have this ticket to a show, would you like to attend it with me?' Something like that. Make the invitation offhand and far enough in advance so it doesn't look like you're frantic. Say something like: 'In two weeks I have these tickets for a show. My girlfriend couldn't make it, would you like to come in her place?' This way you appear casual. If he says no, you save face. It's all in how you ask."

Though Dr. Pietropinto's advice may strike some women as the kind of game-playing they wish to avoid, for others it may prove a concession to necessity, the mandatory strategy required to protect one's own self-esteem. The other side of the question, of course, is the man's place in all this. Men, warns Dr. Sadock, don't always realize their rights of refusal. Just as women haven't learned to cope with having their approaches spurned, men haven't learned how to say no to an invitation from a woman. "Men *do* have this right," says Dr. Sadock. "They should not go out with a woman they don't care for *just* to spare her hurt feelings. Men must realize that if a woman is asking, she is also taking the chance of being turned down."

Ambiguity toward reform in dating protocol is especially evident from answers to the next essay, in which we queried singles on what they would like to know about members of the opposite sex.

3. *From your experience, what are the most important things you would like to know about single men/women? What are the most important things members of the opposite sex should know about you as a man/woman? What would you like to tell men/women about yourself?*

Woman, St. Louis, MO: Despite Lib's rhetoric, I can't see where that much has changed in our society. I'd like to know why, from men and women alike. Both of them. What's stopping women from taking responsibility for relationships? *Must* the man always run things? Is it the fact that we are all so conditioned as young women? I don't excuse myself on these grounds either. There have been many times when I've wanted to come up to a guy and say "Hello, how are you doing?" But like a good girl, I don't.

Man, Baltimore, MD: I would like it if women were more aggressive about going out together. When women have asked me out (it's only happened a couple of times) I have felt a lot of feelings at once—like I was being attacked, like I was flattered, like I was being propositioned. Something in me (I am part of the over-thirty generation and old fashioned maybe) didn't feel great about it when it happened. A carry-over from my past. I would like it though if women weren't quite as shy and quiet about telling you they're interested in going out, but I don't like feminists.

Woman, Los Angeles, CA: Men should know that women's time has come, and that men will no longer rule. This means that an army of bright, equipped, intelligent and aware women are being formed in society who will set the tone in all aspects of male and female affairs. The time will come when women will call men, just as much as men call women. When a woman wants to go to bed with a man she will seduce him *as she pleases.* Why don't women have the same sexual and personal rights as men? They should and *they will!*

There are, of course, variations in attitude among the different status groups answering the essays. The following profiles are formed from composites of the respondents who replied positively to this question concerning female aggressiveness.

PROFILE: What type of man is most likely to approve of a woman's asking him out on a date?

> PROFILE SUMMARY: He has never been married, or, if he has, he has been single now for several years. There is a good chance he is a widower. He is an older man, from forty-five to fifty-five, has gone to college, works at a professional occupation, and makes a good salary. Generally he comes from an upper-middle-class background. He lives alone or perhaps with a woman.

The older, more mature man blazes the trail for female rights in dating. This is somewhat unexpected since, throughout the survey, respondents over thirty-five tend to be more conservative concerning courting procedure. However, immediately behind the older single in percentage points comes the young male college student. He too champions women's dating rights, so much so that he demands a profile of his own.

PROFILE: What type of man is most likely to approve of a woman's asking him out on a date? (Runner-up)

> PROFILE SUMMARY: He's never been married. He lives with members of the same sex (that is, in a dorm or community-living situation), and is between twenty and twenty-four years old.

Between the younger man and the older lies a gray area. Those between the ages of thirty-five and forty-four are more guarded in their enthusiasms concerning female forwardness. Although the percentage spreads are not enormous, they are significant enough to indicate a trend. "Men in their thirties are in a peculiar position," says Dr. Pietropinto. "They were brought up in a time of conflicting values—the sixties and seventies, when morals and standards were changing violently in such things as sex, politics, the family. These men may feel torn over questions of female assertiveness. Part of them is influenced by traditional views of the subject, the kind they were brought up to believe. Part of them is influenced by contemporary views, which are much more liberal and loose. College men, on the other hand, have grown up with ideas of female assertiveness which are part of the Woman's Liberation platform. They have less problem accepting these ideas. As for older men: when people get older, they get more relaxed about relationships in general. What was once embarrassing and anxiety-producing becomes okay in middle age. If an older woman wants to suggest a date with an older man there's less fuss to be made over it, less to lose."

Disapproving Males

A wide difference in opinion looms between the college-educated professional and the blue-collar worker. This can best be seen in the following profile:

PROFILE: What type of man does *not* approve of a woman's asking for a date?

PROFILE SUMMARY: He is a conservative blue-collar worker. According to many past studies,* the blue-collar male is consistently found to be most conservative in his valuation of women's rights. Our findings in no way contradict this. The man most likely to disapprove of female aggressiveness holds a high school diploma or less. He has been divorced once, and has been single more than ten years. He feels most strongly of all the male respondents that female aggressiveness takes the fun out of the chase and makes the woman lose her appeal. He is least in favor of changing the old standards and is most vocal in his feelings that if a woman is going to ask a man out it must never be on the first date, since this is "a male prerogative." He is between the ages of twenty-five and forty-four.

Traditionally the "hard-hat" male element has been less tolerant of forward courtship behavior among its female population than any other class of men. Many blue-collar members are first- or second-generation Americans, still connected to the Old World ethic that sees women without chaperones as *ipso facto* prostitutes, and where virginity is next to godliness. Surely a cultural issue is at stake here, the age-old difference in values between the American upper- and lower-middle class.

Guilt and the Aggressive Woman

Major Finding: Most women would like to be more aggressive in their dating methods but are held back by a sense of guilt.

In responses to various essay questions, women reveal their wish to take the initiative with men. They feel intimidated by the prospect, however, and "repressed"—a word that pops up frequently.

Woman, Manhattan, NY: I see guys all over the place that I'd like to date. In my office, at parties, some of them even look good to me at singles bars. My girl friends feel the same way. We feel so repressed.

* Daniel Yankelovich, *The New Morality: A Profile of American Youth in the 70s.* McGraw-Hill, 1974.

My mother always told me that a man should come after you, he should want you, and to this day I just can't get the courage. If I even dialed the phone I'd probably get tongue-tied, and what would I say? Even worse, what if I was turned down? I couldn't handle the rejection.

Woman, Chicago, IL: I always felt somehow that it wasn't "right" to ask a man out. He would think I was desperate. In addition, I always had guilty feelings about it—like, why was I so desperate to even think of asking, what was wrong with me? Why did I have to be so aggressive about dating? This guilt trip kept me from asking, along with my own embarrassment about the situation. I'm in my thirties and I see younger girls doing it so I'm thinking more seriously about doing it myself.

The question of whether it is "right" to ask a man out troubles many women. For some it is a moral or religious question. Others simply feel an abstract kind of guilt. Whatever the root of the problem, the dilemma is a source of confusion, ambivalence, and even shame.

"In my practice," says Dr. Merle Sondra Kroop, Director of Education and Training, Human Sexuality Program at Cornell Medical Center, "I rarely hear women say the words 'I want to' about anything in their life. Usually they say 'I should.' Which means they are bound by guilt, images of what will make them seem like 'good girls' to the world. I've heard women say 'Of course I *know* I should take the initiative but I feel wrong about it somehow.' Usually women think they will insult men, offend the male ego by being too aggressive. Many women feel that asking a man for a date takes the romance out of it, and they feel the loss of being taken care of. Worst of all, they equate asking a man out with being desperate and asking for sex. All these things make women feel guilt."

Several of our respondents volunteer information on how they approach men without self-reproach.

Woman, Detroit, MI: I want to say something here to other women who may be reading this report someday: Don't be afraid to be the instigator in a love match. For years I sat around waiting for the damned phone to ring. When I met Bob at work I especially waited and waited. But Bob was shy and I never got the call. Finally I just called up and said, "Hi, this is Barbara from the cosmetics department. I feel really funny doing this and I hope you'll understand, but I enjoyed talking to you in the rec lounge a few times and I wanted to continue our talks over a cup of coffee." Well, in return he sounded so happy. Because it turns out he was dying to ask me out but for some reason thought I was engaged to my boss!

Woman, Fort Worth, TX: One of the ways in which I meet men is by coming right up to them if I like them. It usually works. This should be done cleverly or they'll get scared off. Men are sort of like gorillas. They look big and strong but they're scared off if you're too aggressive. That's the key thing, don't *seem* too aggressive but be aggressive in a lady-like way. A good case is when I met a fellow I liked at the wedding of a friend of mine. I really wanted to make contact with this guy, so I got his name from the friend who got married, and I called him up. I pretended I was calling (with my friend's permission) at the request of my friend to tell him about picking up some packages or something. To tell the truth, he didn't remember me from the wedding. But let not thy pride stand in the way, Woman! I forged ahead anyway. I kept talking to him and pretty soon we had a conversation going. It was he who finally suggested we meet. So I asked him out, but he thought he was asking me out.

For women who *have* asked men for dates, we wondered what the effects were of being rejected.

We spoke with a young woman named Elaine, who is today in her early forties and happily married. Five years ago she was working as a businesswoman in a mid-sized Eastern city and, like many successful businesspeople, had little time to date. At one point she decided that since her time was limited she wouldn't waste it. "In those days when I met a man I liked I would simply ask him out," she tells us. "I'd do it in the way a man might ask a lady out. I'd say 'Why don't we get together for dinner sometime?' or 'I think you're nice—I'd like to see you again; why not call me?'

"About nine men out of ten would call. Men are just as lonely as women. Women have this thing that men can get women at the drop of a hat because they're the aggressors. But in my experience it's not so. Lots of nice men are very shy. They just need a polite push. You can ask them out without being obnoxious about it. Just be natural and friendly.

"Things are a lot different today than when we all grew up, and a woman can get away with a lot of things she once would have paid dearly for. When I asked a man out and was turned down it stung. But it just stung, it didn't kill me. I mean, I'd been around long enough to be rejected by men in other ways. This was just a different form of it.

"I guess the hardest thing was when you really liked a guy and put yourself on the line for him. You'd call him up and ask him out, and he was very nice about it and all that, but he was busy that night, you understand. That's hard. You've gone out on a limb and had it cut away from under you. The thump can be heard a mile around. But I'd still say that the large number of successful times I've had with men I asked out outweigh the embarrassments and rejection."

Helen, a psychiatric social worker in Cleveland, is equally positive about forwardness in dating. "If it wasn't for my stubborn Irish pushiness," she says, "I'd never have known Rocky."

Rocky is a disc jockey, a minor celebrity in Cleveland. Helen met him with friends at a downtown bar. "The moment I set eyes on this guy I knew he was for me. I had no idea who he was, that he was a successful jock or anything, just that *he* was the one.

"I didn't have much glitter going for me, I'll tell you. I was a thirty-two-year-old divorcee with a kid and a job that was next to charity in pay. All I had was my personality, my looks, and my nerve. So I did the only thing I could do under the circumstances: I called Rocky and asked him if he would like to meet me and my daughter at the park next Sunday. I closed my eyes and waited for the bullet between the eyes. But instead he said it sounded like fun and that he'd be there—and I hadn't even been sure he'd remember me when I called!"

That Sunday they met, and Helen fell deeper into love. "Our talk flowed so smoothly and evenly. We liked the same music, the same people, the same movies, the same foods, everything checked out. When we said goodbye he promised he'd get in touch soon."

But soon wasn't soon. A week passed. No Rocky. Then another week. He was busy, she told herself, up half the night with his radio show, probably traveling, who knows? Silence. "Finally my impatience got the best of my pride. On a blue Monday night I called and asked him if he'd like to meet me again with my daughter at the park. He said he was busy—but would I have dinner with him next Thursday? We went out, and the same good-vibes kind of evening happened. Then, no Rocky again."

For eight months Helen took the lead. Rocky was always obliging, always they clicked. Rocky truly enjoyed visiting Helen's apartment; and for Helen's daughter, it was love at first sight. He liked Helen's cooking, he liked Helen's looks, he liked Helen's laughter and her way of thinking. He liked Helen. But after the date was over it was always the same, no return calls, no visible progress toward a commitment of any kind.

"I was getting discouraged and fed up. Rocky was too passive. I figured it was because he had so many women chasing him and I was just one of the bunch. We had had sex and it was beautiful. It made me feel closer to him than ever. But now I began to sense that I was just being taken for a ride. So I called him and said so. I told him I was tired of this one-sided affair, that I felt I was being used, and that I wouldn't see him again. He seemed taken aback but tried to sound casual. That was even more infuriating. I hung up in a huff.

"Several weeks went by. Many times I was tempted to get in touch but didn't. After a month, and I couldn't get the guy out of my system *one iota,* I gave in. What the hell! I just called him. Then, presto! He was overjoyed to hear from me. He said he couldn't stand not being together, that he wanted to call me but thought I really didn't want to see him. That was three years ago. We still live together today."

Our singles and experts agree, moreover, that if a woman is going to take the aggressor's part, she must be prepared for rejection as well as success. If she can handle the repudiations then she is freer in this area today than at any previous time.

"To get over the rejections and the guilt of aggressive dating behavior," says Dr. Pietropinto, "a woman must spell out to herself what she's really feeling guilty about. Chances are if she understands this she won't feel so guilty. First, she probably feels hesitant because her mother told her that nice girls don't do such things. But her mother spoke from another generation, another time. Things are different today.

"As for guilt, this implies we are doing something *wrong.* Ask yourself: Are you? Chances are your own reasons for contacting a man are quite reasonable and wholesome. Ask yourself why you are asking the man out. Go over your real reasons. If you know in your heart that your reasons are honest and well-meaning, then what cause could there be for feeling guilt? Get your own *self-approval* for what you do first. That's what really counts. Once you have that, neither guilt nor rejection can bog you down."

All in all, our survey shows that while the prejudice against a woman initiating a date is by no means defunct, it is presently reduced to the point of being just that, a prejudice (as opposed to a taboo), a prejudice that is as much rooted in female insecurity as in male resistance. What a woman must realize, singles say, is that if she is going to take the aggressor's part she must prepare for rejection as well as success. If she can handle the repudiations—and the advice offered by singles and experts addresses itself to how best to mollify these—then she is freer today than at any other time to try it.

For further light on the subject of attitudes among singles toward female aggressiveness, we asked a related question, one that pertains to the ever-sensitive issue of paying for a date.

Footing the Bill

Do single women feel that paying for a date is an important issue? Or is this the concern of a small circle of feminists? How do single men feel on the topic? Just how large an issue is it?

4. *Should a woman ever pay for a date?*   **Men**
   a. Yes.   28%
   b. No.   16%
   c. Occasionally.   26%
   d. If offered in a sharing spirit; when done as a statement of independence it turns a man off.   16%
   e. Yes, it's time women were more independent about such things.   8%
   f. No. Tampering with traditions upsets the balance between the sexes.   4%
   g. Don't know.   2%

At first glance, the men's response seems to support women who want to pay their own way.

Major Finding: *More than three quarters of men feel that women should pay or occasionally help pay for a date.*

There are, however, provisos:

- Although three quarters of men respond positively, only slightly more than a third volunteer an outright "yes" (options a and e).
- The rest of the men who say "yes" offer qualifications, maintaining that it's only all right *occasionally* or *if offered in a sharing spirit.*

Today's men are willing to share their one-time exclusive prerogative, but they are still not eager to surrender it completely. The questions of *how much* a woman pays, how *often, when* she should offer to pay, and perhaps most crucially, the *way* she offers, remain problematic.

"Before," says Dr. Pietropinto, "when the man paid for a date, the woman felt obliged to repay him, sometimes with sex. Now the man feels obliged to repay the woman. But how? He isn't quite sure. Should he ask her back? Should he reciprocate? Does *he* have to go to bed with *her* now that she's paid? The etiquette for paying simply hasn't been invented yet."

There are, of course, varying reasons why a woman might wish to pay. She may simply want to share the burden with the man, to help him. But problems remain, warns New York City psychiatrist Dr. Merle Kroop. "On an emotional level, unconsciously, many women are expressing a lot of disappointment. They just don't feel cared for, loved, or appreciated when they pay the bill. It's the old buddy-buddy thing, they say, like being out with the girls. Paying for men lacks romance, women tell me. There is something too matter-of-fact about the whole thing that makes them think the men don't care."

There are problems for men too: "If the man doesn't pay," says Dr. Pietropinto, "he may suddenly feel out of control, useless, like a gigolo. You can't take people's roles away from them and expect them not to respond. If the man insists on paying but the woman won't budge, the man may become withdrawn, and the chances are less likely he will respond to her romantically."

"Sometimes women don't want to get romantically involved," says Dr. Kroop. "It's a particular kind of protection, a way of making the point that this relationship is mine as well as yours, and I don't owe you a thing. It can also be a statement of feminism, of a woman's desire not to be dependent on the man or beholden to him."

When a woman pays on principle, Dr. Pietropinto explains, she should do so in the proper spirit. The object of a date is to develop a relationship, or simply to have a good time, not to engage in social debate. "If a woman on a date wants to win points for some 'ism' or for a belief, she has this right, but she should be aware that she may alienate the man while she's doing it. If she wants to let her principles be known, she should do it carefully, graciously, and not in a fighting manner."

The problem for women, therefore, seems to be how to navigate the extremes, how to turn what may appear as a threatening request into an acceptable and even pleasant gesture. For men it is a matter of how to accept this gesture without feeling loss of manhood.

"Men and women should take turns paying," says Dr. Kroop. "That way you have the pleasure of being both host and guest. As the host, a woman keeps her sense of control and dignity without losing the feeling of being cared for. She knows that next time around the man will handle things. I've never heard a woman say she feels guilty about paying. Only about *not* paying. I believe it is an important thing for her to do, for her self-esteem. But it must be done in the right way."

"There are a number of ways that women can help pay for dates," adds Dr. Leonard Reich, Assistant Professor of Clinical Psychology at C. W. Post College in Long Island, New York. "First, there's the Dutch treat—each pays for him- or herself. Another is simply cutting the bill in half. Or alternating. Or the woman can say 'Let me pay for the wine.' The idea to get across is that paying is a friendly gesture, not an attack. The woman is saying she doesn't agree with the old role models; they are unfair to *both* men and women. This way, she thinks, it's more equitable and honest on both sides. The real issue is not the exact method you use to pay, but getting the idea across that you're doing it in the right spirit."

When we asked women whether they felt they should ever pay for a date, 28 percent thought it would be a nice occasional gesture, similar to the 26 percent of the men who felt that women should pay occasionally.

Eight percent of the men and women alike think it is time that women were more liberated and independent about such things.

Almost a third of surveyed women feel that if the man asks her out, she assumes he will take care of such things. This is the old-line view and evidently it is still shared by a sizable proportion of single women. The findings also reveal that while four out of five women under 25 do *not* want a man to handle the paying, 30 percent of those over thirty-five years old, and 40 percent over forty-five, *do.*

Of the younger female respondents, college women are most in favor of change. While more than a third of non-college women claim they want a man to handle the check on a date, fewer than twenty percent of college women agree. Equally adamant are women with high-income earnings. Twice as many women in the high-income bracket as in the low feel it's time women were more liberated in such matters.

Conclusion: The woman most insistent on paying her own way is young, educated, and a good wage earner. The woman who makes a lower wage, has not attended college, works in a less prestigious job, and is over thirty-five is not so certain.

"The more control a woman has over money," Dr. Pietropinto says, "the less likely she is to rely on men. If a woman is poor she usually has low hopes for the future. So she turns to men for her future and must be more agreeable to their demands. Let's face it, money and education go hand in hand. If a woman doesn't have an education, she's probably—probably, I say—not going to have a big salary either. It all fits into a kind of general sociological picture: educated women are ordinarily higher wage earners and usually more forward looking. The more a woman is exposed to new ideas, the more she'll lean toward the radical, the modern. That's generally the trend."

Among men the differences in age, occupation, and education are equally apparent. Almost a third of the men under twenty-five believe a woman should pay for a date. Less than a fifth over forty-five are in accord. College graduates are almost twice as likely to believe that women should pay as are those without high-school degrees. Professionals are a third again more positive than blue-collar workers.

Conclusion: American singles view the issue of women's financial independence through the eyes of their own sexual, cultural and educational bias. Though there is agreement among both sexes that women should become more prominent in courtship affairs, there is a lack of unanimity on the subject among particular age groups, different class levels, and different professions. In fact, the question whether women should pay now looms as a symbolic issue on which many other loaded social and sexual questions hang—issues such as moral conflicts between class groups, generation gaps among singles, the effect of feminism on American values, the effect of education on one's general worldview; it is a debate in which many of the basic conflicts of our time become apparent.

"Money is power, caring, giving and at times hating," says Dr. Reich. "That's why it's such a pregnant and emotional thing that affects all of us. With the question of payment and women's rights, we're mining new territory and we haven't begun to see the repercussions: what it means, how all our feelings will be touched. Now that women are in the labor market, they'll have as much access to money as men, and that means a new world. If we extrapolate the trends we have here, we'll find that in the future it may *be* the norm for women to be the breadwinners, the heads of the family, the decision makers, the bosses and chiefs. It's possible. And are men really built to take this? Are women? Will it be productive of a healthy and happy society? Does equality of the sexes automatically ensure their well-being? Having money, having financial domination in a situation, can represent power for us—but hopefully it won't represent 'power over.' Hopefully it will be the vehicle of equality among us, the power for both to say, 'I am competent, I am equal, I am okay.' "

For many singles the question of who pays the bill has not only a social significance but a psychological and an emotional one too. The case of Reggie R. illustrates this clearly. Reggie is a talented film editor living in San Francisco.

"When I first came to San Francisco, fresh out of film school," he tells us, "I met a hotshot blonde film editor who was so good she was already cutting a feature. I asked her out, and after futzing around with me she finally agreed to meet at a restaurant in Chinatown.

"The dinner was okay. We made the kind of typical semi-sincere, semi-game-playing chitchat men and women make over a plate of food. When it came the time to pay I reached for my wallet. She almost jumped out of her chair.

" 'What's wrong?'

" 'I'm going to pay the bill,' she said, like she was issuing a command.

"Now I come from a smallish town in Pennsylvania, and though Woman's Lib has not gone unnoticed there, I'd never come up against *this* one. I said, 'No, I'll pay,' trying to dismiss it, but she insisted. The more I insisted the more *she* insisted. So I finally asked her what was such a big deal. Then she stopped me in my tracks by asking me why *I* was making a big deal out of it. What was *my* hangup? To myself I admitted that something inside me was really riled up. I was furious out of proportion at the simple fact that this woman wanted to save me a little bread.

"Our tilting went on for a while till both of us were getting really pissed off. She started raising her voice and saying that I had no right to think she was going to be beholden to me. I found myself shouting back at her that she was a 'castrator.' In the end we split the check. She walked home and I never spoke to her again.

"About six months later I was in therapy and I talked about this incident with my therapist. And he focused my attention on the fact that

I was calling her a 'castrator.' I realized that it really *was* a sex and power trip at heart, that she was somehow deballing me by taking away my—what seemed—native right to pay the check. Money was power, all right. And the fact that I controlled the money was even helping support what I thought was my identity as a man.

"The therapist pointed out that the girl's violent insistence on paying the check was also neurotic. She needed to get the upper hand no matter what. She needed to control the situation just as much as I did, and the two of us both ran into each other's neuroses like raging bulls. Where that kind of intensity occurs over apparently small things, the therapist said, look behind the scene for big matters."

We asked Reggie what happens today when he goes out with women who want to help with the check.

"The therapist suggested that when I date a woman who feels strongly about paying the bill I let her pay, but that I tell her I don't feel comfortable about it. I tried this, and the women I did it to didn't like it very much. But it sort of cleared the air and made *me* feel better anyway. One woman, a real feminist, thanked me for my honesty— though she still insisted on helping pay the bill."

SINGLES AND THE WOMEN'S MOVEMENT

The Women's Movement stands behind many of the changes of the last decades. Feminism is mentioned in the essays time and again, and feminist themes run through the survey like a thread. There is no doubt that feminism has deeply penetrated the American mentality.

How do singles feel about feminism's influence now that the Movement is several decades old? We asked:

5. In your opinion, what effect has feminism and increased women's consciousness had on your attitude toward dating? Has it helped or hindered the relationship between the unmarried? How?

Major Finding: Approximately two thirds of men and approximately three quarters of women have positive things to say about Women's Lib.

Though many answers are qualified, most singles are positive in their overall appraisal of feminism. At the same time, a divergence, sometimes amusing, sometimes troubling, can be observed in the reasons *why* the sexes agree. One example is the relationship between feminism and sex. Many male respondents delight in feminism because they believe its liberal attitudes have made casual sex more available.

Man, San Antonio, TX: I find it much easier to ask women out because I know I'll get laid. Helped it, helped it, helped it. Lots of screwing.

Man, Washington, DC: Whenever I want to be sure of scoring I go out with a feminist. They are so anxious to prove themselves equal to men they'll have my pants off before I have their's.

While many men were pleased at the sexual openness of liberated women, many women praised feminism for a very different reason. "Feminism frees me," the oft-repeated phrase reads, "from being a sex object":

Woman, Pittsburgh, PA: The feminist movement has definitely helped. At least the potential for improvement is there, if people will let feminism free them of the old sexist, stereotype attitudes. For myself, I now know that men value my company because of my intelligence, not because I'm an available body.

Woman, Manhattan, NY: For some time I used sex as a way of getting men to tell me I was okay. If they had sex with me I felt they liked me. What it really meant was that they used me. After becoming involved with the feminist movement I learned that the way to have a relationship is for a man to respect you as a person, not a sexual "thing." Today I am much choosier about the man I sleep with. First he must like me for what I am. Only then can we have sex.

Marriage is another issue where agreement converges but reasons for this agreement contrast. Many women claim that feminism, by delivering them from the tyranny of a man-centered world, releases them from the belief that marriage must be the center of their lives.

Woman, Dallas, TX: I find myself dating a lot *less* because I feel men are now not "the only thing in the world," as I used to, and that there are more important things for a woman to do than get married and have kids. When I go out with a guy who's on the make I have no reservations about doing exactly what I feel—cutting the date short and going home.

Men feel liberated from the burden of marriage too, but for different reasons:

Man, Phoenix, AZ: Feminism has improved the situation. Women are much freer—willing to try things. It has actually liberated men too, made it easier to have sex and enjoy it without worrying about marriage.

Single women often praise feminism for its insistence on women's right to be more independent, to have a say in their own lives, to stake out territory once claimed by men. Many women respondents consider greater mobility and freedom the finest jewel in the feminist crown. Some men were pleased too, though they are often a bit smirky about it.

Man, Lansing, MI: Women have become more independent and aggressive. That works out fine for me. They do all the work I used to have to do. They seduce me. They want to pay their own way, so I save money. They invite me to their summer places. They even want to get on top during sex. And they want to be independent about it too, so I don't have to worry about getting hooked. Now is the best of all times to be born a man. A man can have his own harem of eager women, and these women will end up paying for the privilege. Fantastic! Hurray for Woman's Lib!

Man, Little Rock, AR: With women trying to rule the roost it takes a lot of the pressures off. I was brought up, you know, to ferry women around and get charged for the pleasure. Be a pleasant gentleman, Bob, my mother told me. Treat the ladies like ladies, God bless them. Now the ladies want to run things. Now the ladies don't want to be treated like ladies anymore, God bless them. So I don't.

Man, Providence, RI: In 1968 I was very much in love with a girl I went to college with. We went everywhere and did everything together. I was basically fair and sharing with her. Though I'm old-fashioned enough to demand traditional roles in a relationship—like, unreasonable as it may sound, that a woman know how to cook, that she like being a wife and mother, that she enjoy having me take care of her, outrageous things like that. Anyway, when Lib became really popular in the early 1970s my girlfriend began to become very influenced by it. She decided she didn't want to get married after all. She wanted to get a job, to have a career, not to get married, not have children. She informed me that her personal "growth" was more important than her love for me. That was the straw that broke the back. I suggested that her personal growth might be in sharing a life with me, but no, she insisted it was in her succeeding in costume design and that was what would make her life complete. We finally split up and I often think about her and wonder if she regrets her decision.

The most common complaint single women make against the Movement is that it takes away their "right to be a lady." This comment crops up many times:

Woman, Toledo, OH: I feel some women have become blithering idiots about this feminist thing. It is up to *you* and only you, not a group. You do what you want and anything less is a weakness. I've never had a problem being a woman. It's my right. I love it, and I like men the way they are. I have no intention of taking away their identity by terming it with some unpleasant sounding title like "stereotyped role."

Woman, Danbury, CT: Most men expect you to be much too liberal and unlady-like in the following categories:

1. Sex
2. Dirty talk
3. Go with the flow (no matter where it's flowing)
4. Have a relaxed attitude towards commitment (that is, have no marriage or family plans for the future)
5. Be a big spender (that is, take men out and not vice versa)

None of these appeal to me. Let the feminists rant and rave about their freedoms. I prefer to remain a lady.

The complaints, however, are outweighed by favorable comments. We frequently read that the Women's Movement has given women the right to be themselves:

Man, Dallas, TX: It's helped women be more frank with men, more direct, more honest. And men can now be the same back, too. The old games of our parents' generations are on the way out.

Women's Lib has allowed women to give free rein to their intelligence and talents. Many men, remarking on how they dislike the "dumb blonde" syndrome, comment that the Movement has made women less fearful of showing their intelligence:

Man, Hollywood, CA: I have dated only one woman that I consider a feminist. The relationship was very exciting and refreshing, compared to most others I've had. It brought out many new ideas and feelings in me that I had never experienced before. She was so free with her thoughts, ideas, creativity and such. It just flowed out of her and I learned lots of things. I'm used to the dumb blondes in Hollywood and she blew my mind.

Thanks to the feminist influence, relationships are now more open and honest, respondents report.

Man, Cleveland, OH: The Woman's Movement thing has taken what used to be a ritual (dating) and turned it into a freer and more serious game—with more options for both players. But it's a trial too. Underneath it all I think women are having to put more on the line now. They've got what they wanted and now they have to prove themselves in their equal world.

Some men claim to be unaffected by Women's Lib, treating feminist issues and demands as if they were settled affairs.

Man, Oklahoma City, OK: I've not been affected much by Women's Lib. Mainly because I think women are equal, and have a right to be politically and sexually equal to men. I don't have much need for Women's Lib to tell me this.

Man, Manhattan, NY: Hell, I've been pro women ever since I was in high school. My mother and father raised me that way. It's not even an issue with me. I wouldn't call myself a feminist or anything like that because belief in feminism and women's equality is just part of my natural makeup.

These and similar pronouncements, by their unquestioning acceptance of ideas that were almost unheard of several decades ago, show to what extent feminist philosophy has become a part of singles' awareness. Certainly those over thirty-five know well enough how things have changed. Even in the 1950s a woman's place was very much in the home; sex before marriage was taboo; and pregnancy out of wedlock was spoken of in hushed tones. Only the bravest woman could enter the professional working world, and then usually in a menial position—only the most far-sighted man was willing to employ a woman in a responsible position. As for women's assertiveness— women calling men, women making dates—these ideas had, to put it simply, not even reached the drawing board.

American attitudes have changed enormously over the past decades, far more quickly and thoroughly than historians or sociologists could have predicted; but the changes have often happened largely without the participants' own recognition. Many men and women, especially younger ones who have grown up with feminist ideals, now take for granted social changes which were not so long ago forged in fire and blood and which represented a radical departure from the past.

Man, Portland, OR: I don't know what all the fuss is about feminism. It doesn't seem that important to me, to tell the truth. The battle is largely imaginary if you ask me. In my college men and girls are equal. My girlfriend and I consider each other as equals, both as sexual partners and as people. Women can get jobs just like men. Most of the faculty and administration here has more women on it than men. I don't see why people make so much noise over it all.

Finally, women tell us, "Now I can be myself!" The following essay stands as a kind of manifesto for the assertive, self-proclaiming, free-willed, modern single woman:

Woman, Tampa, FL: Feminism suits my nature. It gives me the courage to say "I am myself," not some cutout I read about in a magazine, not some stereotype my parents tried to convince me to be. I am what I am. And I say this to men: You can take me as I am, and you can get out of my life if you don't like it. You can hang around wishing I were more the way you want me to be. But it won't do you any good. You can try to change me but you can't succeed. You can try to dominate me but I'll not have it. If you choose to accept me as I am then I'm happy to call you friend. If not, it's your loss. I will not wait on you or live by your pronouncements. Probably I won't agree with you very often. But if you love me as I am, then I will love you as you are. And that's a big thing.

The Platonic Friend

Two claims are commonly heard in female essays concerning feminism. First, that feminism frees women from dependence on men. Second, that women now feel more comfortable in nonsexual relationships with men. For the first time, they say, it has become acceptable for a man and a woman simply to be friends.

6. *Can a single man and woman be friends without romantic involvement?*

Of all the questions in the survey, none received a greater majority of positive responses.

Major Finding: ***Ninety-one percent of men and 93 percent of women feel singles of the opposite sex can, and should, be platonic friends.***

Singles often tell us that they have *many* friends of the opposite sex. Among the social groups, all rank friendship between men and women as a preeminent ideal. This finding is reinforced by responses to the next essay question:

7. *How do you feel about friendship with people of the opposite sex? If you have such relationships, what difficulties, if any, have come up? If you have no friendships with single people of the opposite sex, why not?*

Woman, Syracuse, NY: Having platonic friendships with men allows for the more noble side of both parties to come out. Love sometimes brings out the worst in people as well as the best. Friendships produce feelings that are a little more dependable and lasting. Most of the people I know today are beginning to branch out in their friendships, and to have opposite sex as well as same sex friends.

Man, New York, NY: Here, here! We are certainly ready for this big step—it's about time. I don't know many people who don't want to be friends with both sexes. We are more enlightened on the subject now.

Some of the best parts of friendship are having women friends who can tell me what makes the female tick.

As there are rules of love between men and women, so there must be laws of platonic friendships too. But what are they? There are few models to imitate since the phenomenon itself is still in the process of development.

One thing we learn from essays is that attitudes toward platonic friendships differ at different stages of life. Young people commonly depend on a platonic friend for information about how to steer the complicated waters of sex and love:

Woman, New Orleans LA: There are times a girl needs a boy's viewpoint on sex. At college I go out with lots of guys and plenty proposition me. So I will call up one of my male friends and talk it over with him. Often he can give me viewpoints I couldn't think of myself. He'll explain the male mind to me (an eternal mystery) and help me understand myself better. It's helped me avoid several *big* mistakes!

Singles with children come to depend on members of the opposite sex for the support they might otherwise have received from their mates. Since the divorce boom, the custom of mothers' befriending each other over the sandbox has been broadened to include single fathers, both sexes helping each other grope their way through the difficulties of single parenthood:

Woman, Chicago, IL: Being a divorced mother with two children, I find that several of my friends are men with children. These relationships are precious. We get together a lot and it sometimes seems like a family again. Men give me pointers on being a father, and I teach them the fine points of mothering.

Older singles often find members of the opposite sex simply nice to be with. Though they are of the generation that generally looked more askance at platonic friendships than people do today, many singles over forty-five write in the following vein:

Man, Cleveland, OH: As I get older I realize that the barriers between the sexes are unnecessary, and that it is perfectly right for man and woman to be friends. Not lovers necessarily. I enjoy friendships with women now at my bridge club and at night over the phone.

Respondents often remark that they can trust members of the opposite sex more than members of their own. Women claim other women are too "competitive," too "catty" or "devious." Men say women know how to sympathize more than a man, that they interpret situations with greater clarity and cleverness:

Woman, Manhattan, NY: The majority of my friends are members of the opposite sex. I chose these friends not because it looks good to have many male friends but because I enjoy the openness, outgoingness and love of life that men have over women. I feel that women tend to be false or fake. It takes a lot longer to know how a woman really thinks. Whereas I feel at home with men from the beginning, and not necessarily for sex reasons.

Men turn to women for the kind of warmth and empathy they don't often find in fellowship with other men. "Research on male friendships suggests that most males are not very emotionally intimate with other males," writes Professor Robert A. Lewis in the *Journal of Social Issues* (No. 1, 1978). "Two studies suggest that, although men may report more same-sex friendships than women do, these friendships are not close or intimate." For most men, says Lewis, intimacy is problematic even with a best friend. In a recent nationwide survey, he reports, a majority of males admit they have never told their best male friends that they *like* them. "Males tend to place greater confidence in, consult more about important decisions, and spend more time together with their best female friends than their best male friends."

"I have helped many men patients to see how important female friendships can be," Dr. Kroop relates. "They offer a lot of benefits that men won't get from their male friends. I think men's friendships tend to be a little superficial. Men are raised to achieve, to succeed, to win. Women are taught to perform the sort of social rituals that gain one friends. Men have to put on an act for their male friends, to be macho and prove something. Women don't have to do this. It's all right for them to be emotional with one another."

There are also benefits for women in a platonic relationship. "If a man is not sexually involved with you, he won't be competitive, as women often tend to be with women," claims Dr. Kroop. "He can give you courage and advice in areas in which you may not be experienced, such as handling your finances or getting a raise."

How can one have a friendship with a member of the opposite sex without letting sexual involvement get in the way? "If you say to a man who likes you 'Let's just be friends,' he'll probably take this as a condescending brushoff," says Dr. Kroop. "But if you genuinely believe that a friendship is important and possible, you can create it in many subtle ways. Be kind to him but not seductive. Remain emotional and giving without being sexual. If he does make an advance tell him he's attractive but that you think you'd be better off together as helpers, allies. The important thing is that the woman be sincere. The man will usually go along with you.

"Gay men make good friends also. I know a lot of women who have boyfriends and homosexual platonic friends at the same time. The homosexual has no axe to grind. If he's your friend you know he values you as a person, not a sex object. This is very reassuring. Gay men are often more sensitive than straight men. In many ways they're more emotional and understanding. Whatever choice you make, it certainly pays not to limit your friendships, but to be friends with any man or woman who can fill your needs."

Woman, Los Angeles, CA: There's a guy named Charley at the office who I like very much. But he doesn't turn me on and never did. When we were first seated near each other and started talking it was clear that he had a sexual relationship on his mind. We went out a couple of times and this was verified. I liked Charley a lot and I wanted to be his friend. I decided to have a talk with him. The danger I felt was that I would hurt his feelings, so I had to be careful. I told him that I had just come out of a bad affair (which was true) and didn't want to jump into anything. That I really liked him, thought he was attractive but that I felt the two of us together would be better as friends. I told him a little about my feelings that it's best men and women don't always look at each other as potential sex objects. Then I asked him pointblank: please be my friend. I like you. He did. And we've been just that now for three years.

"The enormously affirmative response to this query," says Dr. Kroop, "raises the question whether our society places too much emphasis on romance and not enough on healthy nonsexual companionship. Men often feel they must make a pass to preserve their manhood; women feel there is something 'weird' about going out with a man without being sexually interested in him. People should listen more to their feelings in these matters. They should ask themselves if they really want to be a lover with this person, or just a friend."

DATING: PLEASURES AND DISPLEASURES

What do respondents feel about dating itself? Have they enjoyed it? Has their social life been a letdown? A pleasure? A pain? Or a little of both?

In order to judge outcome against expectation it is sometimes helpful to begin with the ideal and measure down from there. Just what ideal is it that singles hold?

Dream Dates

8. *Describe your dream date: What single man/woman would you choose (he/she can be anyone you like, real or imaginary, famous or just a friend)? Where would you go (any country you like, any restaurant, resort, palace, city, etc.)? What would you do? How would you end the night?*

Woman, Des Moines, IA: The man that I would consider a "dream date" would not exist on this planet. I imagine that I would be out in the country alone some quiet evening and a small space craft would land in a nearby field. I would walk over to examine it and out would step a being from somewhere other than earth. He would look almost human but he would have deep, clear blue eyes. He would be of a level of intelligence that would far surpass any earthling. He would have a complete understanding of the society here on earth and be able to communicate with me in any language. I would go with him on a spaceflight around the Milky Way on our first "date." It would be purely platonic.

More often, dream dates are closer to earth and a bit more earthy:

Woman, Los Angeles, CA: We would fly on his private plane to a remote island in Greece with our own villa. We would go to a lovely restaurant and have delicious seafood, salad and Dom Perignon champagne. We would dance slow and romantically till late at night, then back to the villa. There we would go for a midnight swim, then into the house and a bath in pure champagne. Soft music, low lights. Two slaves, one man and one woman, would appear from nowhere, and give us both body rubs, stimulating us sexually for one another the whole time. The slaves would smear our bodies with fragrant oils, then they would give a sexual performance for us while we watched. They would run the gamut of sexual display from ordinary intercourse to intricate kinds of kink, all sorts of delights while the two of us caressed each other and watched. Afterwards, as we watched, we would sip a brandy or perhaps take a bath now in pure jello. Finally we would make love ourselves as the slaves watched this time. Wow!

Man, Atlanta, GA: I am walking down a beach that's broad and empty, and it's not too hot, and I am naked. Coming from far down the surf is another single figure. As we approach each other I see it's Helen, a girl I knew in Junior High School. She's naked—and grown up now to be a full woman. It's all beautiful and I have an erection that's as natural and free as a tree in the breeze. She looks at me and I look at her and we smile and sit on the sand and don't talk. But my body is saying "Oh, the pains I've been through. I'm so worn out and used since I knew you before—when we were both untested." And her body says to me: "I've been used like a road. There would be deep ruts and tire tracks all over my breast and belly if nature didn't always repave the surfaces. When I knew you I was new." She touches the tip of my erection fondly and looks in my eyes. I cup my hands under her breast and look into her eyes. We go to a waterfront dock where there are people eating and dancing. Our nakedness makes them all feel guilty. We drink, we dance. We softly, very softly, touch each other very often—and we feel a part of the sand, the sea, the sky. Everybody stops doing what they are doing to watch us become closer and closer to each other. Then they too soon merge into the dream of it all. Our bodies are near each other. The smile on our faces floods our bodies and the heavens. Now everyone knows that God is innocence.

Respondents vividly depict their dream dates. The pictures include minute details of such things as the shape of a belt buckle or the make of a pair of jeans:

Woman, Independence, MO: My dream date would be fairly tall, tanned, sunbleached hair, and a nice but not overly muscular build. He would weigh about 180 pounds. He would wear an ID bracelet with beautifully inscribed letters on it, and wear his blue shirt open at the chest with a simple silver chain around his neck. At the bottom of it would be a small silver tag with *my* name inscribed across it. He would be a classy, not a loud dresser—perhaps a nice blazer, dress pants, a little gold jewelry, perhaps a gold chain, ring and watch. He must not wear dungarees or a hat. His shoes should always be brown, not black.

Only 10 percent of the respondents chose well-known personalities as their dream dates and these presented few surprises. Most popular for women are Burt Reynolds and Robert Redford, with several references to Muhammad Ali and Paul Newman—and one for Henry Kissinger ("He's so roly-poly and intelligent"). Female nominees include Ann-Margret, Cheryl Tiegs, Cheryl Ladd, and Olivia Newton-John. Whenever particular stars are chosen, the scripts are heavily erotic.

Woman, Los Angeles, CA: My dream date would begin with Jack Youngblood (L.A. Rams) picking me up at my house, him in a tux and me dressed in a light blue dress. We would fly to San Francisco and be picked up there in his baby-blue Cadillac, go to Fisherman's Wharf, Grotto #9. Overlooking the water, we sit and drink, and he fondles my body over white wine and a lobster dinner. We walk along the wharf holding hands, talking about what kind of life we could have together, football and politics. We fly home at midnight, he drives me home, and I invite him in. I thank him for a lovely evening. He softly kisses me, he continues to kiss me, and takes my hand and leads me to the bedroom.

Write-ins from homosexuals usually read more or less the same as write-ins from heterosexuals, allowances being made for gender switch.

Woman, Newark, NJ: This question is one that I can not answer adequately because it implies contact with a man. I am strictly a lesbian. However, I *can* describe my dream date in terms of femaleness. In appearance my dream date has dark brown eyes and a dark complexion. She has long hair that is lightly curled and a sweet glance. She's definitely not a heavy girl, but has full hips because I like the softness there. The ideal place to go would merely be out of town. No special country or destination. This is important because I can feel comfortable and open with affection when I know people around me are unfamiliar. I would take my dream date to an expensive restaurant—the *most* expensive, of course. We would stay overnight in a hotel, terribly ritzy, and would probably have sex. But this is *not* a requirement. I find that cuddling is equally satisfying.

Many respondents stress the moral and Christian qualifications of their dream date:

Man, Omaha, NB: My dream date is a good Christian girl who would enjoy my company in a fine restaurant, and then we would go to church, and after church meet with the young singles and have a good time. We would take a ride in the moonlight, give her a bit of loving but without going "all the way"—then get her back on time, I mean at a respectable hour, and go home and dream of the time when she will be mine. There is something wonderful about waiting for the girl you love. People have forgotten this today, marrying a virgin, and wonder why their lovelife ends up wrecked so much of the time.

Interestingly, more than half the men and women end their dream dates with "a big kiss" and nothing more. Time after time respondents say the evening will *not* terminate with sex (the "not" usually underlined) but with a platonic hug or a parting promise. Though for many people sex is the ideal way to consummate a perfect romantic rendezvous, for many others it lessens the experience, hinting at an ulterior motive, a suggestion that the dream date is out for something more than the respondent's plain lovability. Many subjects, however, report that they and their dream date *will* fall in love—but that there is world enough and time for sexual consummation at some future meeting.

Again, the respondents are detailed in their specifications concerning their dream date's looks, character, and personality.

Woman, Kansas City, KN: He is 6'2", dark and handsome. He is moderately wealthy. Witty. Sharp dresser. Neat and clean. Very intelligent. Affectionate. Understanding, lovable. Rarely bothered by small things in life. He would be a physical person, holding hands, eye contact. He's in good shape and athletic. A *great* lover, of course; totally understanding. Personality—genuine, funny, can take a joke, kind, considerate, gets along well with others, puts up with my nonsense.

Man, San Diego, CA: My woman is extraordinarily beautiful with blonde hair, straight nose, hair in a ponytail that reaches down to her waist, body like Cheryl Tiegs, legs like a model. Her father owns a big shipping line but he has never spoiled his daughter, so she is sweet and pure. She is cheerful, always happy, knows how to take it when I'm angry, knows how to laugh and make me laugh. She is compassionate with others and understanding of me. No matter what I do she forgives me and lets me have my way. And as a lover she is—well, out of this world!

As one respondent remarked after enumerating his list of perfect qualities: "There's probably no woman like this anyway." And there probably isn't. "The idea behind this question of the dream date," says Dr. Robert Sollod, Associate Professor of Psychology at Cleveland State University, "is to create an ideal mate. However, an ideal does not presuppose an irrationality or an impossibility but simply a person who realistically suits our needs. What we see in the answers here is the impossible dream, the impossible romantic hope. It's worth considering that these overblown expectations may hint at the reasons why so many singles relationships fail. Often neither person begins dating with reasonable expectations; both may have impossible standards. When these standards aren't met, instead of realizing that no one will *ever* measure up to our ultimate ideal, both parties break off and go in search of the unattainable."

On the other hand, Dr. Sollod adds, fantasy-mates do have a helpful place in our lives. "If a person didn't have ideals he wouldn't know what he was searching for. One has to look beyond the unrealistic sides of the fantasy," maintains Dr. Sollod, "into the areas that can be of help. A good way to do this is with the following exercise: As completely as you can, make a mental picture of your dream mate. Try to see him or her in your mind's eye. What are this person's particular physical features? How does the person speak? What qualities of the dream mate are absolutely required and what could you do without?

"Ask this fantasy person all the things I mentioned. Ask what *he or she* wants from you. Tell the person what you have to give to her or him. Get to know the person. Study him or her. In this way, by keeping your ideal realistic and by approaching it as if he or she were a flesh-and-blood individual, you become aware of your own deeper feelings. And this can reveal to you what you really want in a mate. It can help you know yourself better and learn what you're looking for."

Saying No

It's a long way from the perfect date to the drudgery of saying no, but the latter is a far more common concern of singles life. We quizzed respondents concerning their most common reasons for breaking off a dating relationship.

9. **What is the most frequent reason you stop**   **Men**
dating a particular woman?
    a. I find her dull and superficial.   30%
    b. She refuses to have sex.   6%
    c. She is immature or neurotic.   20%
    d. She is a poor lover.   3%
    e. It's usually my way to go out with a woman a few
       times and then move on.   15%
    f. She presses me too quickly for intimacy and in-
       volvement.   10%
    g. She loses interest.   12%
    h. Don't know.   5%

10. **What is the most frequent reason you stop**   **Women**
dating a particular man?
    a. I find him dull and superficial.   34%
    b. All he wants is sex.   13%
    c. He is immature or neurotic.   18%
    d. He is a poor lover.   3%
    e. It's usually my way to go out with a man a few
       times and then move on.   8%
    f. He shows no sign of serious interest or involve-
       ment.   13%
    g. He stops calling.   7%
    h. Don't know.   6%

Major Finding: Half of single men and women stop dating each other because they find their partners to be either dull, superficial, immature, or neurotic.

Both men and women cited "dull and superficial" as the biggest source of aversion. Women feel more strongly about it than men, but there is close agreement among the various groups in both sexes that a vapid personality is the greatest cause for terminating a relationship.

The second most common reason for ending an involvement with another is that the partner is "immature or neurotic." In both cases the cause of rejection is found not in appearance, not in sexual assets or liabilities, not in monetary worth or public profile, but in the personality.

Only a handful of men (6 percent) claimed they stopped dating a woman because she refuses to have sex or because she is a poor lover.

BONUS FINDINGS

- Widowed men are most bothered by women who press them too quickly for intimacy. Men divorced twice or more tend to care least when this happens.
- The more education a man or woman has, the more likely she or he is to stop dating someone because he or she is too dull and superficial.
- Women over forty-five are more prone to stop dating a man if all he wants is sex than are women in their middle thirties. As compared to women who have college degrees, twice as many women with only high-school educations will stop dating men if all they want is sex. The man most likely to stop dating a woman because she refuses to have sex tends to be in the forty-five or over range. The man least likely is between the ages of thirty-five and forty-four.
- The older a woman gets, the less tolerance she has for men who only want sex. Blue-collar women are almost twice as likely to be put off by this trait as professional women.
- A woman single two years or less will usually *not* stop dating a man who fails to show signs of serious interest. Women single three years or more are far more likely to terminate an affair on these grounds.

And only 3 percent of women report they stopped going out with a man because he is sexually inadequate.

Three percent and 6 percent are pretty small figures. Again, sex trails personality as a source of attraction. In light of the common belief that a man must be a sexual prodigy to keep a woman's affections, this is an interesting revelation. In our culture, a good deal of masculine energy is spent in cultivating the appearance of confident sexuality. Yet the survey demonstrates that though sex-appeal may often be a powerful first appeal from across the room, it is neither the ultimate attraction that brings singles together nor the force that keeps them united.

What is equally noteworthy—besides the fact that sexual appeal is subordinate to personality—is the fact that *half* of single men and women apparently find each other to be dull, superficial, immature, or neurotic. Dr. Mary Ann Bartusis, former member of the Board of

Trustees of the American Psychiatric Association and Clinical Associate Professor of Psychiatry at the Medical College of Pennsylvania, believes that this represents a case of unreasonable expectation and subjective judgment. "Singles often expect they'll fall head-over-heels for someone on the first date," says Dr. Bartusis. "They are viewing every date as a step to the altar. On a first date a person learns how compatible she or he is with the other person. If they don't share their interests and tastes, they immediately dub each other boring or superficial. What this really means is that the date doesn't like what we like or think the way we think. It does not mean the person is inherently lacking in positive qualities, nor does it mean that the person will not become more attractive in our eyes if we give him or her more of a chance."

Dr. Bartusis believes that singles should approach each other in the spirit of exploration as well as hope. "It takes a number of dates to help us decide what we're really looking for," she says. "Instead of putting dates down for being incompatible or boring or whatnot, we might thank the other person for helping us decide what we want and what we don't want in another partner. I call this 'creative dating.' Each date we have, though he or she doesn't turn out to be *the* one, helps us to find that 'someone' we *are* looking for. It should be viewed as a process, one of weighing, building, sifting, refining. This is what I mean by 'creative.' "

The "No-Win" Date

The query on why people stop dating leads to a question that has probably troubled women for centuries. We asked men the following:

11. It has been noted that if a man sleeps with a woman early in the relationship, this often causes him to lose interest in her—and conversely, if a woman refuses to have sex right away, this also turns a man off. In light of this "no-win" situation, how do you think a woman should behave herself sexually? What exactly is it that men want from women in this department?

To women we posed the same problem in somewhat different terms:

12. Do you find that if you refuse to sleep with a man early in a relationship, he loses interest? Or, if you do sleep with him

quickly, his interest also declines? Why do you think men force women into this "no-win" situation? How do you deal with it when it occurs?

Approximately a quarter of the men and women stated that they had rarely run into this problem, or that it was usually of no great consequence. The rest were concerned to varying degrees, and many offered explanations and remedies:

Woman, Memphis, TN: The whole situation doesn't really bother me. I enjoy sex and I'm aware of my sexual appeal. If a man can't handle the fact that I would give in to it so soon then he isn't my type of man. If all he can see is my lack of "morals" then he's not going to really look at me as a person.

Woman, Boston, MA: The "free" lifestyle really means that women are not free to make options. There's no real way to deal with it. It's no-win for women—and win all the time for men. It's turned all pretty women into cunts. I hate it, basically.

Man, Grand Rapids, MI: If a woman sleeps with me early, I feel she is not sincere. If she refuses to let me touch her right away I'm not offended. What's important over everything is that she be honest and let me know how she feels morally on the question. I'll honor her opinions.

Man, Omaha, NB: If a woman is charming and/or interesting to the man, and there is an attraction, then early sex will not hinder the relationship. If sex occurs for lust only, on the other hand, it will not sustain a long relationship. In other words, the length of dating time before sex is less significant than the psychic/emotional/intellectual underpinnings.

Man, San Francisco, CA: I feel that a woman should keep a man guessing at all times. Never give 100% to a man or he'll get bored. Women should have sex *only* when they feel like it.

Man, Los Angeles, CA: I think men want *honesty* above all in the beginning of a relationship. Whether or not a woman wants sex immediately is relatively unimportant as long as he understands *why* the woman feels and thinks the way she does. Game playing and dishonesty have been the curse of all relationships.

Man, Chicago, IL: As to how a woman should behave, I think she should protect herself against sexual exploitation and otherwise do as she wants and to hell with what the man wants!

One female respondent speaks for many when she says: "Sex is appropriate only when there is emotional involvement. Otherwise it acts in a negative way, driving people away from each other rather than bringing them together." Lack of feeling between partners is the reason most often quoted for the sexual double-bind. "People should care before they get involved," writes a man from Seattle. "Otherwise sex can actually turn people off to each other. Immediate sex by its definition can't have any depth to it. The people have hardly met, so how could it? Why be surprised when the man backs out? Women think if they give themselves to a man the man will feel a responsibility toward them, and a special bond; but many men feel just the opposite. Since they don't care emotionally about a woman—and while they realize that having sex with her does demand an attachment—they get scared and run away."

Many singles feel that women are apt to mix up sex and love:

Woman, Portland, OR: I finally learned that emotions and sex are different. A man can dig a woman sexually, yet have absolutely no feelings for her. Sometimes his sexual feelings cause him to dislike her once he's had her, and he takes pleasure in dumping her.

Man, Providence, RI: Women mix up feelings and sex with each other. They think that if they allow a man to sleep with them love will automatically result. This is an absurd bit of thinking. Women should realize that a man has a *sex drive* and a man has a *heart,* and that the two are *different.* Each can get along quite well without the other. Women should also realize that a man has to care for her *first.* Sex won't make him care. After he cares *then* they can have sex to their genitals' content, and it will improve things. But not before, that's the mistake. We do things too quickly in this world, and I mean everything *including* sex.

It is frequently stated that men who demand rapid sexual relations are often hostile to women; giving in to such men simply provides food for their neurosis. "Sleeping with a man quickly," says a single man from Oklahoma City, "because he threatens to leave, is doing what the man secretly wants you to do—it proves to him that women are whores, just like he thought, no good, and he has a perfect reason now for using them and then getting rid of them."

In reading the essays in this section one senses that both single men and women often feel victimized by a setup that neither really enjoys but that both obey out of fear of alienating the other. The system is self-perpetuating: The man thinks the woman will judge him unvirile unless he quickly proves himself sexually; the woman thinks the man will lose interest unless she is quickly available for sex.

"If a woman desires an enduring relationship," says Dr. Carol Nadelson, Professor of Psychiatry at Tufts New England Medical Center in Boston, "but she constantly finds herself sleeping with many men and then being rejected, she should stop blaming the men and forces outside her, and look into herself. Why *does* she keep getting into no-win situations? There's a lot here that is operating on an unconscious level—self-destructiveness, fear of involvement, etc.

"Of course some men take advantage and use women, but both men's and women's judgment can be colored by their unconscious motivations. You frequently find people of both sexes who actually pick people who *can't* give, who *don't* want closeness, who *don't* want sharing and love. If women or men find they are continually in superficial, fast-sex situations, they should ask themselves if there isn't a deep-seated reason behind it."

DATING: SOME FINAL EVALUATIONS

Finally we asked our respondents how much they enjoyed the majority of their dates and how in general they evaluated their dating experience.

13. (Men's questionnaire) *On the average, do you find that a majority of the women you date are:*
   a. Sincere, decent and open
   b. Interested in a nice evening but nothing serious
   c. Anxious only to find marriage
   d. Looking for men with money, fame, and power
   e. Superficial, missing that certain "something"
   f. Generally undesirable
   g. Generally desirable
   h. Don't know

14. (Women's questionnaire) *On the average do you find that a majority of men you date are:*

   a. Sincere, decent, and open
   b. Simply on the make
   c. Superficial, missing that certain "something"
   d. Well-meaning, but afraid of intimacy and commitment
   e. Just interested in their jobs, sports, comforts, and someone to wait on them
   f. Generally undesirable
   g. Generally desirable
   h. Don't know

BONUS FINDINGS

- Almost 40 percent of divorced men say the women they date are sincere, open and honest. Only 29 percent of twice-divorced men make this same claim.
- Far more commonly than low-income bachelors, those with a high income perceive the women they date as anxious only to find marriage.
- As compared with men who have college or graduate degrees, men who hold only high-school degrees are twice as likely to see the women they date as interested in a nice evening but nothing serious.
- Highly educated, high-wage-earning women more commonly view their dates as sincere and decent than women with high school only and middle-income earnings. Almost three times as many women with high-school-only backgrounds see men as being on the make as compared to women with college degrees. Twice as many blue-collar women as professional women see men in this light.
- Practically a quarter of women in their thirties view men as well-meaning but afraid of intimacy.
- One blue-collar man in five says the women he dates are interested in a nice evening but nothing else. Only one professional man out of ten says the same thing.

Men are almost evenly split between satisfaction and dissatisfaction. Fifty percent think the women they date *sincere, decent* and *open* or *generally desirable.* Eleven percent find women *superficial,* 6 percent *anxious only to find marriage,* 9 percent *attracted to money, fame and power,* and 2 percent *generally undesirable.* Another 2% answered *don't know.* The most common reason for male dissatisfaction is that women are interested in a nice evening, but nothing serious (20 percent). This is ironic, since women think the same of men. Their most common grievance is that men are well-meaning but afraid of intimacy and commitment.

Man, Cleveland, OH: Dating has been chasing a phantom. Trying to find a girl who's not just fluff, one who is not just interested in disco and a good time. That's okay in its place, but a man wants something more—someone to talk to about life, work, friends, politics. So far I've been divorced for eleven years and haven't met a woman who fills the bill.

Woman, Washington, DC: The problem in this city is there are so many more women than men. I don't know. Maybe that's why I can't find a guy who is serious about life and not afraid to give himself wholeheartedly to a relationship. Men are so afraid of being serious and committed. It reminds me of legends of fairy tales of knights who are walled up in castles for a hundred years. Men are so walled up in their feelings and fears.

Women are less satisfied with their dates than men. Thirty percent find their dates *sincere, decent* and *open,* and another 10 percent find them *generally desirable.* This makes 40 percent. The rest express dissatisfaction that ranges from mild annoyance to outright anger.

"Men are more satisfied with their dates than women because men have lower—or I should say *different*—expectations," claims Dr. Bartusis. "A woman usually seeks emotional fulfillment on a date. For a man, sleeping with a woman is often enough. With men, sleeping with a woman can be a sign of success. For a woman it can be a sign of failure."

Women, Dr. Bartusis claims, are primarily concerned with the emotional quality of the relationship. "Since the emotional aspect is the hardest part of the relationship, women are more consistently going to be disappointed in dates because, let's face it, it is usually easier to have sex than to be emotionally involved. Despite the fact that many women today are liberated in their attitudes, I think women are still more interested in marriage and a happy home life than men. That's what makes the difference, and the disappointment."

THE FINAL QUESTION

15. *On the whole, has single dating been for you:*
    a. Highly enjoyable
    b. Frustrating but worthwhile
    c. Something to be endured until the right man/woman comes along
    d. Fun but nothing too significant
    e. A tedious grind
    f. Less exciting than I'd hoped it would be
    g. Don't know

Major Finding: Approximately two thirds of men agree that their dating experiences while single have been profitable and enjoyable.

- Approximately a third of men who have positive feelings are unqualified in their praise. *Highly enjoyable* is how they describe their dating encounters.
- Another third are mildly pleased or pleased in qualified ways. One group calls dating *frustrating but basically worthwhile* (17 percent). The other says it is *fun but nothing too significant* (15 percent).

When men complain about dating it is almost entirely because dating is *something to be endured until the right woman comes along.* Twenty-five percent of single men checked this answer. Eight percent say it is *less exciting than I'd hoped.* Two percent answered *don't know.*

A majority of women consider their dates satisfying, though women are more restrained in their approval than men:

Major Finding: Slightly fewer than two thirds of women agree that dating has been a positive experience.

A majority of women who enjoy dating do *not* claim it is *highly enjoyable* (only one out of five). The majority deem it *fun but nothing too significant.* The most enthusiastic are those who belong to the highest income bracket. Lower-salaried women enjoy it least.

BONUS FINDINGS

- The man who finds singles dating highly enjoyable tends to be a high-wage-earner, a professional, and probably lives with a woman at present. Age is not a factor in his enjoyment. Men who find singles dating least enjoyable live at home with their families and are in the lowest income bracket.
- Men who live at home with their families are the most likely to say dating is something to be endured until the right mate comes along. Men least likely to echo this sentiment are those living with a roommate of the same sex.
- Almost 25 percent of men in the thirty-five-to-forty-four age bracket find singles dating frustrating but worthwhile. Half that figure (13 percent) in the forty-five-to-fifty-five age group agrees.
- Women who find singles dating most enjoyable are in their early twenties, have never been married, and are high wage-earners. Women who enjoy it least are twice divorced, and are low-to-middle-income earners.
- Almost one out of three women divorced twice says that singles dating is fun but nothing too significant.

Many factors thus determine whether dating will be a happy or unhappy experience. Paramount among them are age, class, education, and especially earning capacity. Income *does* make a difference: The wealthier a person is, the better that person's job, the greater worldly success he or she has achieved, the *more* enjoyable his or her dating will be. Money in the singles world equals accessibility to pleasurable options, to travel, to interesting places and a wide variety of people. Despite myths to the contrary, money can buy, if not happiness, then at least an ample slice of the good life.

On a deeper level, we learn that in many instances the real issues of dating are not such details as who pays for the meal or who holds the door. The real issue is *who holds the power.* This is the basis of many dating dilemmas, the issue that reveals itself behind a hundred different façades. Whereas well-adjusted married couples may settle the hard-nosed problems of power by negotiated agreements, discussions, contracts, or traditional sex-role divisions, for singles, questions of power must be negotiated *with each new partner,* and at times this pressure can overload the circuits. Since among the underlying questions of the power struggle are whether or not to indulge in sex, when, with whom, and why, the dynamics of the situation can become extremely complex, demonstrating why the power-money-sex triumvirate looms as large as it does in the lives of the unmarried.

Finally, despite whatever drawbacks it may have as a means of courtship, dating is quite simply the only system we have. With the disappearance of the old-fashioned matchmaker, and with the independence of the unmarried person from family direction and traditional social roles, men and women have increasingly become the captains of their own fate.

Dating, as we know it now, is actually something of a new social institution, and in a certain way we are witnessing its rise and growth. "Let's face it," one respondent says. "If you're single you're not likely to meet your dates in a church anymore, or through your darling old mother, or in someone's parlor over an arranged cup of tea." Dating is now the only game in town, and all singles are its players. "Dating is a process, a means to an end," writes a single man from Chicago. "Might as well try to get everything out of it we can because the end may or may not turn out the way we want it but, you know, there's always something valuable and growth-productive in the process. I say: *Vive le Process!*"

Chapter 3

Mating||||

Sex and the
Single Person

In this chapter on "Mating" we ask:

1. How do you feel about sleeping with a woman on the first date?

2. On the average, how many dates do you have with a woman before you sleep with her?

3. On the average, what is the number of dates you require before you sleep with a man?

4. Do you—or would you—ever initiate sex on a date?

5. How do you feel about women who initiate sex?

6. What is the main reason you invite a man to your apartment for dinner?

7. Why do you think a woman would invite you to her apartment for dinner?

8. How many sexual partners do you estimate you have had while single?

9. How would you characterize the experience of casual sex or a one-night stand?

10. If you ever slept with a stranger or casual acquaintance purely out of sexual attraction, how would you describe the experience?

11. Do you believe it's possible to be meaningfully and sexually involved with more than one man/woman at a time?

12. Do you ever have sex with a man or woman because you think he or she expects it? Do you ever have sex when you don't want to? When, how often, and under what circumstances?

13. Do you think love is a prerequisite for good sex?

14. What makes a man/woman a good lover?

15. Describe how an ideal lover would treat you in and out of bed.

16. Once you have decided to have sex with a man/woman, what would you generally refuse to do?

17. What are your favorite sexual fantasies in masturbation and sexual intercourse? Please describe them in detail. What sexual acts and/or fantasies do you consider perverse?

18. What sexual variations, if any, do you indulge in?

19. If you indulge in any sexual variation such as group sex, voyeurism (watching others have sex), bondage (tying or being tied up), S&M (giving or receiving pain), or any other, please tell about your involvements. Where do you contact partners? What takes place, and where? Please describe your feelings about the experience.

20. On the whole, how skilled have you found single men/women to be at making love?

21. How do you view yourself as a lover?

22. How has your sex life been as a single?

23. Have your feelings about sex changed over the past several years? Do you find it as interesting and important as ever? Are you more adventurous about sex or have you become more conservative? Why?

There is no question that sex plays a dominant role in the life of the single person today. The sexual revolution is decidedly with us, and in many minds singleness and sexuality are synonymous. Indeed, many people are unmarried not simply because their mate was tiresome or times were hard, but because monogamy itself proved too inhibiting.

This situation is due to many factors. The awesome number of sexual alternatives available to single men and women places an immense strain on the institution of matrimony, and a number of ex-husbands and -wives have chosen to desert marriage *specifically* for the pursuit of sexual adventure. Sexual opportunity and single life often go hand-in-hand. Many questions, however, remain unanswered. How liberating are the new sexual attitudes? How frequently are they translated into fundamentally new patterns of sexual behavior? What do singles tell us about sexual freedom and sexual hangups? About the part played by sex in their lives—the importance of sex, the difficulties of it, the value of it?

This is so significant a topic, one that has received so much attention on so many fronts, that we have devoted a number of questions to it, hoping to determine just how "swinging" singles really are, to learn what it really means to be free, sexual, and unattached in the 1980s.

1. (Men's questionnaire) *How do you feel about sleeping with a woman on the first date?*

Major Finding: Almost 75 percent of men are indifferent or actively opposed to sleeping with a single woman on the first date.

This large majority, close to three quarters of the respondents, breaks down in the following way:

- Approximately a third of men say *it doesn't make much difference.*
- Twelve percent say *it takes the challenge and mystery out of the relationship.*
- Seven percent prefer a long courtship before actually having sex. And one out of five single men feels that *if she does it for me she probably does it for others as well.*

Apparently men take a kind of patient, wait-and-see attitude not usually credited to them. But it is early to jump to conclusions. We also asked men:

2. On the average, how many dates do you have with a woman before you sleep with her?

Major Finding: Almost two-thirds of men sleep with a woman on the first to third date; 80 percent sleep with a woman on the first to fifth date.

We asked women a similar question:

3. On the average, what is the number of dates you require before you sleep with a man?

Major Finding: Fifty percent of women sleep with a man on the first to third date.

BONUS FINDINGS

- Compared with the man who has been single for two years or less, twice as many men who've been single at least ten years expect a woman to sleep with them on the first date.
- Almost half of women divorced *twice* will sleep with a man on the first date. Only one third of women divorced once will do the same.
- Men in their early twenties and men in their forties say it doesn't make much difference if a woman sleeps with them on the first date. It's the man between twenty-four and thirty-four who expects more.
- Twice as many men in their early twenties (as compared with any other group) prefer a long courtship before actually having sex. Ten percent of men under twenty-four years of age expect the same. Only 5 percent of all men over twenty-five prefer a long courtship before sex.
- One third of women who have never married say it usually *takes them several months and many meetings* before they are ready for sex. Only 10 percent of women divorced twice or more feel the same way.

If men are relaxed in their expectations and women slow to respond, there is small evidence of this from what appears here. As many questions emerge from this set of findings as answers. The first and most obvious discrepancy is between men's avowed indifference to rapid sexual contact, and their actual behavior. Almost three quarters say they're in no hurry. Yet two thirds bed their dates in three evenings or less. Are men impelled toward sexual performance to prove themselves even while they secretly prefer to wait, or is the short waiting period that does exist honored only out of custom and propriety?

Dr. Richard Samuels is a clinical psychologist, sex therapist, and Director of the Center for Sexual Relationships and Enrichment in Teaneck, New Jersey. He feels that while men may be hesitant to sleep with a woman quickly, this hesitation is based on moral do's and don'ts rather than on essential wishes. "In one case you ask men to report what they *think* they should do with a woman in the early dating stages. The second question asks what they really do when the moment arrives. That's quite different."

As to the woman's part in all this: "I have found in working with single women, and in speaking to numerous single groups, that a large number of women are pressured into having sex early on, and that they are driven to it by the myth that if you don't have sex by the third date you will lose the man. Many single women are just coming out of marriages and are terrified by what they view as a kind of sexual 'pressure cooker.' They feel pushed and even compelled to perform sexually."

Many responses to essay questions dealing with sexuality support Dr. Samuels' image of a "pressure cooker."

Woman, Chicago, IL: When I got out of a bum marriage and started dating again the first months were difficult. The feeling I got from many men was that they expected me to give myself to them right away. If I didn't then they would lose interest. I slept with some men because of this pressure.

Woman, Burbank, CA: One of the hardest things of sexual life in being single is that men expect you to have sex quickly and at the time it's happening you're scared to say no, so that you feel squeezed in the middle between your real wishes and your real fears.

How, we asked Dr. Samuels, can a woman handle this pressure-cooker syndrome?

"What I tell the woman I see in individual therapy is this: that if you do something you don't want to do sexually, you are *not* going to feel good about yourself—whether you like the man or not. It's most important to clarify in your own mind the meaning of sex in a relationship. If sex becomes an element through which you can manipulate a man, or through which he can manipulate you, you are not going to feel good about yourself."

Further analysis of the findings shows us that almost four times as many women as men report that before they can sleep with a man "it usually takes several months and many meetings before I'm emotionally ready." However, a third of single women say they will sleep with a man on the first date if they like him enough, while only 15 percent of men say "I generally expect sex on the first date and enjoy it." Women's increased willingness in this department seems to be a correlate of time, place, and attraction.

Woman, Burbank, CA: It doesn't make much difference to me whether or not I sleep with a man right away. I will if he's very nice and we have a comfortable, non-threatening place to go to do it. The rush-rush is absolutely no good, but if it's all right with both of us, then okay.

Woman, Urbana, IL: I do not believe that fast sex with a date is a good thing, especially on the first date. However, I have at times indulged in sex with a date on the first night if he seems especially nice and considerate. One man brought me to his $200 a night hotel room after the date and how could I say no?

While men report sleeping with approximately two thirds of the women on the first few dates, only one half of women report a similar experience. The second half feels that more time, sometimes a great deal more time, is necessary before they are ready for sex. And this is not to mention the almost one out of ten who tells us that sex of any kind before marriage is wrong.

Greater conservatism on the part of women is manifest in most concerns of single life throughout the survey. Though women in the survey seem a good deal less custom-minded than women of twenty-five years ago, they still lag behind men, perhaps in the same ratio as always, in their willingness to experiment, their desire to overturn moral convention, and their haste to alter time-honored norms. Whether this "lagging behind" is healthy or unhealthy depends, of course, on whether one views the increased loosening of sexual strictures as social progress or decline. In a later chapter we will learn how singles themselves feel about this question.

WHAT SINGLE MEN AND WOMEN EXPECT IN THE WAY OF SEX ON THE FIRST DATE

Sub-group findings provide further facts about speed of sexual contact. What kind of man and woman are most likely to sleep with a partner on the first date? What man and woman tend to refuse with the greatest frequency?

PROFILE: What kind of man expects to sleep with a woman on the first date?

> PROFILE SUMMARY: Basically, two varieties of men expect to sleep with a woman on the first date. The *first type* is from the low to lower-middle class. He has attended high school or less, works at a blue-collar trade, and earns under thirteen thousand dollars a year. He is usually a young man (though not a student) between the ages of twenty-four and thirty-four. He's been divorced once or twice, or more.
>
> The *second type* is the higher-wage-earning professional. A college graduate, he has been single less than ten years and is over forty-four years old. What unites these two men is their gentleman's agreement that sex on the first date is a prerequisite for satisfaction. What separates them is the reason why they think so. The first, the young blue-collar worker, checked that he *expects* sex on the first date. That is, it is a man's right to claim immediate sexual gratification and a woman's duty to provide it. The second, older, professional man believes in sex right away, but in this case because, as he checked in the multiple choice entries, *Women are becoming more free in this department and it's better for all of us.*

While the first response speaks from a cultural judgment, the second is based on a social ideology; and in this way two dissimilar attitudes offer the same conclusion, though via entirely different routes.

PROFILE: What kind of man least expects to sleep with a woman on the first date?

PROFILE SUMMARY: Two types again. Most conservative is the man who prefers a long courtship before sex. He's never been married, lives with his family, is twenty to twenty-four years old, and is a student. He is, in other words a bright, idealistic young man, probably highly ethical or religious. Also, he is most emphatic on the issue that *if a woman does it for me, she probably does it for others as well.*

The second type has no set opinion on the matter, saying *it doesn't make much difference.* He's between twenty-five and forty-four, is a college graduate, earns in the high-income range, and works in a professional capacity or at a white-collar job. He's been divorced twice or has been single most of his life—the portrait, most likely, of an experienced man.

PROFILE: What kind of woman expects to sleep with a man on the first date?

PROFILE SUMMARY: This woman has been divorced twice or more. In fact, a multiple divorcee is *a third* more likely to sleep with a man on the first date than a woman divorced only once. She is twenty-five to thirty-four years old, has had some college but doesn't hold a degree. She earns an average income, not too high or too low. Chances are she's just become single or has been single for only a few years. She is, in other words, a middle-of-the-roader, not a highly educated professional, not a semi-skilled laborer—an average white-collar worker, an office person, a saleswoman, a woman in a low-level management position.

PROFILE: What kind of woman least expects to sleep with a man on the first date?

PROFILE SUMMARY: This type of woman is twenty to twenty-four years old, or forty-five to fifty-five—quite a split, but one that demonstrates how the most conservative respondents are often either the very young singles (college students as a rule) or the older singles, those raised in the 1940s and early 1950s. (Singles between the ages of twenty-five and thirty-five, on the other hand, tend to be the most liberal of our group.) The woman who least expects to sleep with a man on the first date is a student or, if she's older, a professional. She has never been married, or she is perhaps widowed. A good number of women in this category are celibate or receive their sexual pleasure by means of self-stimulation.

In summary, while singles are generally no strangers to sex on the first date, they exhibit conflicting emotions concerning its desirability. Women are more reticent than men, though they are potentially as willing, *provided* the emotional setting is correct. In both sexes we find a reserved, traditional attitude existing side-by-side with a more modern, aggressive one. This conflict is especially common among women. Just how reserved, aggressive, and ambivalent they are about the issue we learn from the next set of questions:

4. (Women's questionnaire) *Do you—or would*   **Women**
you—ever initiate sex on a date?

a. All the time. It's my right as well as his.	10%
b. Only if I'm really turned on and he hasn't made any advances.	18%
c. Only through verbal hints, body language. Never by a physical act.	31%
d. It's a man's place, not a woman's.	14%
e. Only if an excessive amount of time has passed and the man has still made no approach.	4%
f. I've initiated sex but usually feel badly afterward.	3%
g. I'd like to but think it would reduce my appeal in a man's eyes.	13%
h. Don't know.	7%

Major Finding: *Two thirds of single women have or would have initiated sex with a date in one form or another.*

Two thirds of women (answers a, b, c, e, and f above) say they would take or have taken the sexual lead in one form or another. But this is deceptive math and requires some clarification. Note that a large portion of females who would initiate sex say they would do so only through body language and not, as it were, by direct attack. Another substantial percentage prefer to wait and will take the initiative *only* if they must.

What this finding really says, then, is that, while many single women have made overt sexual approaches to a man, most assertive women still confine their overtures to the more traditional strategy—seduction, arousing the male by means of intoxicating body language, verbal suggestions and subtle wiles.

Obviously there is a marked difference in these two approaches, the direct and the oblique (as we could call them), and practitioners of each clearly demonstrate by their choice how they feel about the issues of sex, themselves and the times. Among women in favor of sexual assertiveness, as we have seen, only 10 percent say they *initiate sex all the time*. Though we hear much about the sexual equality of men and women today, and though this idea may be theoretically espoused by many, evidently the theory has not been widely translated into practice, at least not yet. A profile of the bold woman, the one most militant on the subject of women's sex rights, shows her as follows:

PROFILE: The sexually militant woman.

> PROFILE SUMMARY: The woman who favors direct initiation of sex has never been married. She belongs to the upper-income bracket, is between twenty-five and thirty-four (only a small number of women over forty-five say they have *ever* made direct sexual advances), is a college-educated white-collar or professional worker.

WHEN WOMEN INITIATE SEX

Through the years women in our society have often been belittled for taking the sexual lead. Traditionally the woman waits for the phone call, the follow-up date, the sexual request. It is her duty to remain passive and at the same time alluring. To push sexual matters is to take the chance of frightening off the man. It is stealing away his traditional prerogative.

Our survey shows that this value has changed—to an extent.

While only one out of ten single women in Question 4 is militant enough to claim sexual aggressiveness as her privilege, one out of five says she will take the sexual lead if highly attracted to a man who has not yet made the approach. Another 13 percent say they would like to be more aggressive but are too shy. Add these points of view to the rest mentioned and we have a picture of the American single woman as a person far more aggressive than women of the past, yet one still careful concerning her sexual behavior, still largely reluctant to make forceful solicitations, still uneasy about how active or passive her sexual role should actually be. Today's single woman is in the process of balancing her new-found assertiveness with more traditional culture-sponsored views of what it means to be a woman. As with many balancing acts, it is not always easy.

Woman, St. Louis, MO: Sometimes I am very turned on sexually to a man and would start something but am afraid of saying so and my guilty feelings at trying to be too forward. Women have sexual feelings too, you know. I want you to let men know that this is the case. They seem to think we can turn them on and off just at their pleasure. The trouble is we've been so brainwashed since birth that it's too embarrassing to try and make our feelings known. Men just think you're "loose" or a "Jezebel" when you do. Then they either treat you like a slut and "expect" you know what, or they find someone else.

Woman, Pasadena, CA: Listen, I've been sexually aggressive with a lot of men and where did it get me—nowhere! It was just a big guilt trip. In addition, many of the guys just dropped me. Men out here come on so strong that sex has become like a good-night kiss. I'm only living here six months and things were slower in the midwest city I was born in. I thought that's what the scene was here, you could be yourself, or even be what the guys wanted you to be, and you were accepted. A farce! They say one thing, and play it another way.

Woman, Boston, MA: I suppose if I were a little less inhibited I could make some advances toward a man I cared about, but it would have to be indirect—and very subtle. What I probably would like to do is just show that I care and would be open to the thought of a physical relationship. But my religion gets in the way. I grew up in parochial schools and I sometimes get overwhelmed with guilt if I even think about showing some physical overtures.

From the essays on dating and sexuality it is obvious that the greatest problem women face from sexual forcefulness is guilt. The essay excerpts above are three from a heaping pile. But before exploring this prickly situation further, let's see what men feel about women who initiate sex.

5. (Men's questionnaire) *How do you feel about*   **Men**
women who initiate sex?

   a. It really turns me on.   31%
   b. I wonder if there isn't an ulterior motive behind
      it.   8%
   c. It means a woman is promiscuous.   5%
   d. I resent being "helped along."   4%
   e. If it's done subtly, in a feminine way, it's nice; if in
      a pushy way, it's a turn-off.   47%
   f. I find it a turn-off in every way.   5%
   g. Don't know.   2%

Major Finding: *Over three quarters of men feel it's acceptable for a woman to initiate sex.*

By adding the percentages in answers a and e, we get a strong yes—but with stipulations. There are two schools of thought among men on this subject—some relish the hard sell while others appreciate the soft sell. Those who favor the hard sell, accounting for about a third of men in Question 5, say quite directly that women's sexual aggressiveness *really turns them on.* There are no qualifications, simply a complete affirmation.

More careful in their assessment are a larger group, who claim aggressiveness is okay *if done subtly, in a feminine way.* This attitude comprises the majority of male respondents, just as the majority of women opt for the seductive rather than the confrontative approach. We might, of course, ask what exactly is a "subtle, feminine way"? And when does it cease being subtle? Several male essays start us off.

Man, Washington, DC: It's exciting when a woman comes on sexually. It's best when she does it with the French finesse. She can signal her sexual spark with her body. If she wants to have sex she can talk about it. She can mention some of her own sexual experiences with a certain tangy look in her eye. She can flirt. I love flirts. She can kiss me suddenly without my asking for it. She can even say she's interested in me sexually, but not delivering a feminist monologue. A gentle touch on my knee; an invitation back to her apartment, soft music, sitting close to me; good perfume and not too much make-up; looking into my eyes with "that look"; breathing hard; taking my hand; making little sexy sounds; moving her mouth into sexy little shapes (but not too self-consciously); "accidentally" touching me with her breasts; jutting out her breasts; talking low and sexy. Every man has his own list. If a woman wants to find out about it, ask him.

Man, Seattle, WA: The women I go out with often let me know in no uncertain terms that they are "hot" ones. A bit of fun is taken away but on the other hand a man doesn't have to work so hard anymore. It's changed a lot even in the past five or seven years. When a woman tries *too* hard it's sort of pathetic. She seems desperate. They blame *us* for losing interest. "I've given you my self, haven't I?" "Yes, sweetheart, but not in the right way. Nobody wants what they think everybody can have for a fingersnap."

Man, Baltimore, MD: I fear female assertion because it makes me feel I'm on the spot to perform. But then if I perform well I'm happy she "done" it. The new aggressive thing is okay as long as the man can meet the woman's needs. When he can't meet her needs he feels like an inadequate fool.

In numerous essays the word "subtle" is used to describe the proper feminine approach. We also find phrases such as "she should be gentle in her approach"; "should not use meat-cleaver tactics"; "a woman who knows how to seduce without seeming like she is seducing"; "must be ladylike even when she is coming on strong"; and so forth. Occasionally, however, an essay favors the hard-sell feminine approach:

Man, Jersey City, NJ: Am most turned on by women who grab me. Like being stroked right away. Let them do the work to start things off—turns me on that way—like it when woman kisses me first, good deep French-style kisses—she comes on and lets me know where it's at—like it when woman takes off her clothes without being asked. Like it and am turned on when woman initiates sex.

This is rare, however. When men discuss female aggressiveness, they ordinarily ask that it be tempered with what one respondent called "good old female 'chase me till I catch you' kind of style."

Man, Oklahoma City, OK: I am not at all discouraged by women who initiate sex, but am uninclined to go after the kind that tries to undress me, or to carry me into the bedroom. *Vive* the woman who knows how to undress you with her eyes.

Preferences among men for either hard sell or soft sell assertiveness follow their own special dynamic within each social class. Blue-collar, white-collar, and professional men are all quite certain that they support female aggressiveness. Educated professionals and white-collar workers, however, prefer their aggressiveness subtle—for some, in fact, subtlety appears to be the *sine qua non* of acceptability—while the niceties of approach are generally of less importance to many blue-collar men.

Simultaneously, men who disapprove of sexual forwardness are mostly from the blue-collar world, too, and here we find a significant polarization within a single class. Blue-collar men are almost twice as adamant over the fact that sexual assertion *means a woman is promiscuous* or that aggressiveness is *a turn-off in every way.*

A gap is here, not only between blue-collar and white-collar/professional sexual morals, but within the blue-collar world itself, where a particular ambivalence toward women looms clearly. Women may be viewed either as willing sex objects or as lofty, virginal, and sometimes holy mothers.

This split image of women, though present to some degree in all stations of society, has traditionally been most noticeable among singles in the lower middle classes, and is commonly known by therapists as the "prostitute-madonna" complex. "For many men it's a relief to have sex with a woman on the first or second date," reports Dr. Samuels, "because this immediately eliminates the woman from consideration as somebody he might want to be involved with. She becomes the symbolic 'prostitute.' If he did become involved with her, she would symbolically become his 'madonna.' "

Even though there is disagreement within American manhood, the fact remains that most men are in favor of women's inciting sex. This is a meaningful finding, especially since the problem of guilt still has high priority among women.

Woman, Tombstone, AZ: Though supposedly women are liberated today I find myself that I am incredibly guilty about asking a man out on a date. I certainly would *never* try to talk him into bed with me, it would make me feel horrible and dirty.

Woman, Philadelphia, PA: The experiences I've had at suggesting sex have been taken up quickly by the men I've been with. They seem to enjoy the sex but honestly, it makes me feel badly. I just don't sit comfortably in the role of sexual aggressor. There is no way I can sort of shoulder my way up to a man and proposition him. It is hard also to even talk about sex, as I was brought up in a generation which considered sex a private thing.

"When women who are uncertain about sexuality decide to initiate it," says Dr. Avodah Offit, author of *The Sexual Self* and *Night Thoughts: Reflections of a Sex Therapist,** former Director, Sex Therapy Unit, Lenox Hill Hospital, New York, and psychiatrist in private practice, "they often act far more aggressively than necessary. It's like using a bulldozer to dig up violets. They haul out this vast machinery to insist on something that would have come very easily otherwise." Sexual aggressiveness, says Dr. Offit, is a function of the way a woman approaches a man. "Being sexually assertive includes being sexually reassuring. Accepting, knowing how to bring a man out sexually, letting a man know that she is interested, cooperative—these are all a part of it. This is different from a woman who *demands* sex. What I teach in sex therapy is a path to simple affection. 'Do you really feel affection for this person?' I have people ask themselves. 'Do you like one another?' When we really want the best for another person, the proper uses of sexual self-assertiveness will fall into place."

There are, of course, Dr. Offit adds, men who find any sort of a request a "demand," just as there are men who feel ignored if a woman doesn't initiate sex. "Some men are flattered when women initiate sex. Some are surprised. A few are shocked. A woman should ask herself certain questions to learn her own deeper feelings on the subject. 'Am I comfortable asking for what I want in sex?' 'Do I usually take the lead?' 'Why?' 'Am I comfortable at it when I do?' 'Do I regard sex as a reward or a prize?' 'What is my attitude toward sex, and men?' 'Do I like to take the lead, or do I prefer things to go more slowly?' She

---

* Both, Congden and Lattè's.

should ask herself these questions to get an idea of her sexual personality, and to learn how assertive she really wants to be."

How, we asked Dr. Offit, can women learn to shape their own approach to sexual aggressiveness and not just follow the fashion or fad? "It all depends on the individual. There are many ways. Some women can use an approach the way some men use a 'line.' Others wait for a man to approach them, although they also make suggestive overtures. Still others try to evaluate what will tempt a man—the active invitation, or the passive one, or none at all—and act accordingly. I myself believe the indirect approach is the most frequently successful because it is the least threatening. If men do not feel commanded to perform, they may be *seduced* into doing so. However, a woman is probably well advised to become more sexually assertive on the grounds that she is more likely to meet a sexually confident man that way. The man who can respond wholeheartedly to a female invitation is likely a stronger person than the man who must always be in charge. In sex, like business, it often takes more strength to receive than to give."

Does this mean that women will eventually be as assertive as men? "Hopefully a balance will be reached. I believe this question of assertiveness should be a two-way street. Most men want women more assertive, just as women want to become that way."

YOUR PLACE OR MINE: INVITATIONS TO THE HOME AS A SEXUAL COMMITMENT

In many essay questions respondents discuss sexual issues in reference to their home or the home of their dates. The private dwelling has a symbolic as well as a literal significance, for it is here that relationships often start and finish. We were curious to know to what extent invitations to the home are viewed as sexual invitations. In the past few years it has become increasingly common for a woman not only to ask a man out for a date, but also to ask him back to her place when the date is over.

Several women respondents write that their homes are designed with romance in mind.

Woman, Evanston, IL: When I've known a man a while I'll invite him to my place which I have set up, to be candid with you, with love making top o' the list. I have a waterbed and mirrors on my ceilings which I can reveal by pulling a drawstring. I have leather curtains and a leopardskin bedspread. There's a lot of soft velvety pillows, and a lining inside my bedspread. It's as good as something you'd see in *Playboy* but it's out of *Playgirl.* Do the guys like it? It takes their heads off, that's what! I plan to put a motor under the bed so that it turns— slowly—as we make soft, oily love!

Is the above essay representative? Do single women view their homes as outposts of seduction? Is an invitation home an invitation to make love?

6. (Women's questionnaire) *What is the main reason you invite a man to your apartment for dinner?*	**Women**
a. Usually just as a friendly gesture.	22%
b. As a prelude to romance and perhaps sex.	4%
c. As a way of personalizing the relationship but not usually for sex.	28%
d. I don't have a plan—I just let things happen as they will.	23%
e. I almost never invite a man to my apartment.	12%
f. If it's a first or second date it's just friendly; if we've been dating for a while it's usually for romance and perhaps sex.	10%
g. Don't know	1%

Major Finding: An invitation to a woman's home is not an invitation to her bed.

Only 4 percent of women invite a man to dinner *specifically* as a prelude to sex. Allowance must be made for the almost one quarter of female respondents who claim they just let things happen as they will, plus the number who claim the evening may be for sex "if we've been dating a while." But though this modifies, it does not alter the conclusion, for the majority of single women state that an invitation to their lodgings is by no means a specific sexual bid. Interestingly enough, men are aware of this.

7. (Men's questionnaire) *If a woman invites you*   **Men**
to her apartment for dinner do you feel this is:
   a. An invitation to sex   8%
   b. A friendly gesture   14%
   c. Could mean either, depending on the man's se-
       duction technique   17%
   d. If it is the first or second date it is just friendly; if
       the fourth or fifth it is something more serious   9%
   e. It is a way of personalizing the relationship but is
       not necessarily for sex   52%
   f. Don't know   —

Nonetheless, though there is an apparent agreement on the part of both sexes over this question, such invitations are often, in fact, the cause of mixed signals between dates. We learn this from essay answers. The usual scene is as follows: Woman invites man for friendly get-to-know-you evening, man misreads invitation as sexual invitation. Woman feels betrayed, man feels betrayed.

This is a delicate issue, one that will often cause women to give up entirely on hospitality for fear of being misinterpreted. What we must assume is that while most men do not necessarily take dinner invitations as a direct proposition, many (for instance, those who checked answers a, c and d above) may believe that with some coaxing an already promising situation can be turned into a sure thing. Perhaps this is the source of the misunderstandings we encounter in the representative essay answers given here:

Man, San Francisco, CA: I have been invited by women, one in particular, to come to their house all alone for brunch on Sunday morning. Now that would seem like an ideal time to get it on. Why else would I get the invitation if not to get intimately acquainted with this girl? In fact, the whole thing fizzled. She treated me like a king, cooked up a batch of eggs, bacon, potatoes, crisped corn and hot coffee. The meal was delicious. I was feeling like a mellow fellow and tried to put my arm around her and she got up and went over to the other side of the room. That was about the gist of it. I left with my stomach full and my sexual desires unfulfilled.

Woman, San Diego, CA: I believe that men do not understand that women are *not always on the make.* Why can't we just go out, have dinner together, or even go to one another's place of residence without the all-present sex thing hanging around? Men and women *can* be friends. They don't have to hop into bed.

What does all this tell us so far about the level of sexual aggression of the new American single woman? Simply this, that today's single woman is more assertive, more aware of her sexual needs, more active in her claims. And also, that men are more tolerant of this new feminine attitude and less chauvinistic than in a previous age.

Yet, while customary roles have altered they have not changed at their roots. They are modified perhaps but not yet transformed. They may *be* transformed, of course. As younger generations move up, as values continue to metamorphose, as taboos fade and sacred cows disappear, what today shows up as a trend may tomorrow become a norm. As matters stand now, however, a sizeable portion of singles still abide by the customary male–female courtship roles. This means that as of the early 1980s it is not yet the norm for women to play sexual host and sexual instigator to the man. And while men are more willing than before to relinquish *some* control of their courting privileges, it is usually still men who make the first overtures and who take the sexual lead. Finally, while a portion of single men and women believe this social dynamic should be utterly changed, a majority believe it should not.

HOW SWINGING ARE SINGLES?

8. *How many sexual partners do you estimate you have had while single?*

Answers to this question indicate how sexually active American singles are and which segments of the singles world are most active.

NUMBER OF SEXUAL PARTNERS WHILE SINGLE

Men

Length of time you have been single

Number of Sexual Partners	Percentage of Respondents	2 years or less	3–9 years	10–30 years	ALL MY LIFE
None	4%	5%	2%	4%	5%
One	6%	13%	3%	3%	4%
2–4	15%	26%	10%	14%	13%
5–9	14%	17%	13%	17%	14%
10–19	20%	18%	27%	17%	20%
20–49	19%	14%	19%	20%	21%
50–100	10%	4%	12%	8%	11%
MORE	10%	2%	12%	15%	11%
Don't know	2%	1%	2%	2%	1%

NUMBER OF SEXUAL PARTNERS WHILE SINGLE

Women

Length of time you have been single

Number of Sexual Partners	Percentage of Respondents	2 years or less	3–9 years	10–30 years	ALL MY LIFE
None	9%	14%	7%	7%	9%
One	14%	18%	13%	11%	13%
2–4	28%	30%	28%	32%	24%
5–9	17%	14%	17%	15%	22%
10–19	13%	9%	15%	13%	15%
20–49	11%	8%	13%	10%	12%
50–100	3%	2%	3%	5%	3%
MORE	2%	1%	3%	3%	1%
Don't know	3%	4%	1%	4%	1%

HOW MANY SEXUAL PARTNERS DO YOU ESTIMATE YOU HAVE HAD WHILE SINGLE?

Men

Number of Sexual Partners	Never Married	Divorced Once	Divorced Twice or More
NONE	5%	3%	2%
One	4%	10%	1%
2–4	14%	18%	9%
5–9	14%	14%	12%
10–19	19%	23%	26%
20–49	21%	17%	21%
50–100	12%	7%	8%
MORE	10%	7%	19%
Don't Know	1%	1%	2%

Women

	Never Married	Divorced Once	Divorced Twice or More
NONE	10%	9%	3%
One	13%	16%	12%
2–4	23%	28%	21%
5–9	20%	15%	22%
10–19	15%	15%	9%
20–49	12%	10%	19%
50–100	4%	3%	4%
MORE	1%	1%	6%
Don't Know	2%	3%	4%

BONUS FINDINGS

- Almost two times as many twice-divorced men as men who had never been married claim they have had a hundred or more partners while single.
- Education and income are *not* meaningful factors in how many sexual partners a man or woman has while single.
- Approximately one fifth of all single men between the ages of twenty and fifty-five have had at least ten to nineteen sexual partners.
- Gays in general show different sexual patterns from heterosexuals. Rather than load the column with lengthy descriptions, we will give the numerical statistics:

Men

Number of Sexual Partners	Heterosexual	Homo/bisexual
None	2%	10%
One	5%	10%
2–4	16%	5%
5–9	15%	11%
10–19	22%	16%
20–49	19%	17%
50–100	10%	18%
MORE	10%	11%
Don't know	1%	2%

Women

Number of Sexual Partners	Heterosexual	Homo/bisexual
None	4%	4%
One	14%	5%
2–4	30%	15%
5–9	18%	27%
10–19	14%	25%
20–49	12%	8%
50–100	3%	8%
MORE	2%	6%
Don't know	3%	2%

Single Men Are More Sexually Active than Single Women

Single men tend to have more sexual partners than single women. The percentages remain more or less equal up to the five-to nine-partners point. After that men far outdistance women in number of sex partners and, we thus assume, in frequency of transient and casual sex.

In this context, Dr. Stephen Levine, Associate Professor of Psychiatry at Case Western Reserve University in Cleveland and Director of Case's Sexual Dysfunction Clinic has a pertinent if not entirely popular observation. "Men seem on the average to have higher sexual drives than women," he claims. "Young boys already have male hormones in their bodies, and biologically I think it finds expression in higher frequency of sex life. On the average men masturbate more often, tend to have more extramarital affairs, and want to perform sex more often. Women, on the other hand, I believe tend to be healthier about sexuality than men."

According to Dr. Levine, men want to dissociate sex from emotional closeness. Over a long haul, explains Dr. Levine, "Women's expectations are more in keeping with mental integration." Dr. Levine presents as an example men who are frightened of emotional closeness. "These men tend to have a number of brief encounters, a lot of sexual activity without much substance. Emotion and closeness scares them away."

According to our statistics, *almost 20 percent* of men claim anywhere from twenty to forty-nine sexual partners while single, and one out of ten claims having had more than a hundred. Let's look at the profile of this sexually active individual.

PROFILE: The man who has had a hundred sexual partners or more.

PROFILE SUMMARY: This man has been divorced at least twice, which means he's a casualty of at least two different intimate situations and probably many more. (This is reinforced by the fact that if he does not live alone, he lives with a female partner.) He is from thirty-five to forty-four years old, is a white-collar worker, and may or may not have attended college. He is, in other words, an older, upper-middle-class playboy type who has probably been through a wide range of unsuccessful situations with women and who finds his pleasure mostly in relationships that are by their nature brief and that perhaps risk very little of an emotional or personal nature.

This brings us to the subject of hypersexuality among singles. "Concepts of what is normal, borderline, and abnormal," Dr. Stephen Levine tells us, "are something most social scientists avoid discussing. Hypersexuality in particular is not only manifested by the number of partners one has but also by actual frequency of intercourse plus the 'drivenness' toward doing it. A real Don Juan gets his thrill from *the seduction itself*—the hunt. The actual sexual experience is not that important to him, and such a man rapidly loses interest in his partner after he has been victorious."

According to Dr. Levine, hypersexuality first of all represents the expression of anger toward women and, second, an enactment of a man's fears of psychological intimacy. "Men sometimes brag to me, describing themselves, if you will excuse the expression, as 'cocksmen.' They may be powerful, seductive, manipulative people who use women and generally have chaotic relationships with them. When the woman tries to get more from this man besides genital exercise, he views her as a 'dumb broad,' a 'screwed-up chick.' "

Dr. Levine reports having treated the hypersexuality syndrome several times. "The first case of this was a man who at age thirty-four told me he had had between two hundred and three hundred sexual partners. He traveled quite a bit and had a series of very brief relationships with women. At age twenty-seven he became engaged. He met the 'perfect' girl and they planned marriage. The trouble was he couldn't get an erection with her, and she wisely ended the engagement. He returned to his ways for another seven years, at which time he met another 'perfect' woman and this time married her. But again he couldn't consummate his relationship. So, you see, what appears to be super-studhood often reveals itself as an inability to become intimate and to integrate tender with sexual feelings."

What can we conclude about the average number of sexual partners claimed by American singles? For men this is difficult to pinpoint. The percentages are rather evenly distributed, ranging from two sexual partners up to fifty. There is no stereotyping, no average number of sexual partners. The typical single man is as likely to have a seraglio of different women as he is to be a one-woman man.

For women it is easier to be precise. The majority of American single women have had from one to nine partners while single. This is a median figure and an approximate one at that, but it falls in the right ballpark. Despite sexual liberation, women are still far more reluctant than men to take on many sexual partners. Single women are still selective in their sexual partners (note that only the smallest number of women report more than fifty). A majority are still careful over the question of sexual contact and involvement.

Only a Tiny Percentage of Single People Are Virgins or Are Now Celibate

Four percent of men and 9 percent of women have had absolutely *no* sexual partners since becoming single. Most numerous in this category are widows and widowers, many of whom are still traumatized by the death of their mates and are not ready for another sexual relationship. Next comes the young never-marrieds who have not had the exposure, opportunity, or inclination, or who choose to remain chaste on religious or ethical grounds. Then come those who simply have no sexual drive whatsoever, though these are rare. Finally, there are the older singles of both sexes, mostly over forty, our lifers.

Roundly speaking, the percentage of celibates—4 percent men, 9 percent women—indicates how many abstainers and virgins there are among the singles population. It's a rather small number, one that shows to what extent the norm of virginity among unmarrieds has fallen out of fashion.

9. *How would you characterize the experience of casual sex or a one-night stand?*

Major Finding: Only 20 percent of single men and 6 percent of single women recommend casual sex or one-night stands.

Those who praise casual sex come predominantly from the young and the never-married groups. As age increases, so does disillusionment with casual sex. By the time a single man or woman is near middle age, he or she is *half* as likely to praise casual sex as the young.

PROFILE: The single man who enjoys and recommends casual sex and one-night stands.

PROFILE SUMMARY: He is between the ages of twenty and thirty-four and has never been married. If he is homosexual he's more in favor of one-night stands than if he is straight. Oddly enough, if he is living with a woman he is more apt to champion fast sex than if he is living alone— twice as likely, in fact. He has gone to high school and may have some college, works as a blue-collar worker, and is in the low-to-middle earning strata.

BONUS FINDINGS

- Never-married men are *twice* as apt to recommend one-night stands as are men who have been divorced twice.
- A quarter of all widowers feel casual sex makes one *bored and cynical.* Only 5 percent of never-married and divorced men agree.
- Absolutely *no* widows recommend casual sex.
- The blue-collar man is *least* likely to feel empty after a bout of casual sex, the student *most* likely.
- The more education and money a man has, the *less* likely he is to recommend casual sex.
- Far more lesbian/bisexual women recommend one-night stands than do heterosexual women. Six percent of heterosexual women call it *a great high*—32 percent of lesbians do the same. Among men, homosexuals/bisexuals are also more enthusiastic about one-night stands, but to a lesser extent than lesbians (20 percent of heterosexual men recommend it, as do 25 percent of homosexual men).

PROFILE: The single woman who prefers and recommends casual sex and one-night stands.

PROFILE SUMMARY: First, remember that we are dealing with a small number of women here, 6 percent, so this profile will give only a rough estimation of fact. The woman in question has never been married, is aged twenty to thirty-four, is a low-wage-earner who works at a blue- or white-collar profession and has been single all her life. Her chances of being homosexual, however, are decidedly less than a man's and she probably lives with a group. For both men and women, the more permissive single is young, has never been married, and is from the lower to middle socio-economic strata of society.

Next, why do those who oppose casual sex and one-night stands do so?

- *It's pleasant but later one feels empty* (29 percent men, 25 percent women).
- *There's something wrong with it which I can't explain* (12 percent men, 28 percent women).
- *It's mechanical, without real emotions* (15 percent men, 18 percent women).
- *It makes one bored and cynical about sex* (5 percent men, 5 percent women).

Some stay neutral on the subject.

- *It's simply part of a lifestyle, no better or worse than being married, living together, etc.* (15 percent men, 9 percent women).
- *Others indicate they "don't know"* (4 percent men, 9 percent women).

In essay questions, reports of casual or, as it is sometimes called, "recreational" sex are peppered with such phrases as "makes me feel bad afterward" and "a meaningless experience." Many speak of "emptiness" or "letdown," especially after the act has been consummated. We asked singles:

10. *If you ever slept with a stranger or casual acquaintance purely out of sexual attraction, how would you describe the experience?*

A majority of the essay responses were negative. Typical lines and phrases included:

Woman, Dallas, TX: The man couldn't perform very well. I was left with a very cold feeling.

Man, Nashville, TN: Many one-night stands and a few one-hour stands . . . empty, desolate, dead, hopeless.

Woman, Nashville, TN: Sometimes nice but in the morning I want to get rid of the man quickly. I feel like running. I give him the bum's-rush right out.

Man, Houston, TX: A few minutes after I come, I feel very sad or I get a loathing for the woman I'm with no matter what *she's* done or what she's like.

Man, Palo Alto, CA: Have had so many of them I can't even remember the faces, let alone the names. I usually feel reviled when it's over, yet I'm driven towards a casual sex time again the next night. I feel driven by my sexual urges, as if something is riding me like a horse and I can't get it off my back! Obviously one-night stands are not the way to relieve the feeling because I keep coming back for more of same and enjoying it less.

Women often describe casual sex as "lonely" or "dirty." Men are more inclined to characterize it as "meaningless" or "empty."

Among those who praise transient sex, men are more enthusiastic in their appraisal and often describe it as a "fulfillment of a fantasy."

Man, Montpelier, VT: It's only happened twice, and both times it was beyond reality for me. First time I was picked up by the most beautiful woman I ever saw and brought to her place, sucked and fucked royally, and brought back to where we had met. I never saw her again and I never knew who she was. The second was an older, also beautiful woman. She went through my fantasy numbers from A to Z as if she had ESP. She was less mysterious than the first woman. I never saw either of them ever again, but the memories represent the finest sex I ever had.

Man, San Diego, CA: It happened when I was a crew member on a sailing ship. In port the night before a race when I was the only one on board, I noticed an exceptionally attractive young woman on the pier, wearing an Indian sari that waved in the breeze. We began talking and I invited her to share my evening meal. After dinner, carried away by the sea, the moon, and each other, we had sex. She left in the morning and we never saw each other again. But I've never forgotten the experience. I think it was the best single sexual experience I had. She had a beautiful body and loved to make love. She touched me all over as if she really cared about me, though she knew I was only passing through. And we tried all kinds of things I had never tried before. We had oral sex, something most women I knew wouldn't even consider trying. There are therefore many advantages to having sexual experiences like this. First, the sex can be particularly good when you don't have to think of the future, about impressing your partner so that she'll want another date. You can throw yourself with wild abandon into thoroughly enjoying the sensual and sexual experience. When you have nothing to lose, you can act out some of your sexual fantasies. You can open up and talk about things you don't usually talk about. You can reveal yourself. You can also find a different pleasure in pleasing your partner, giving to her because you like her the way she is *right then*. When your motives are pure like this, your partner can feel it. And you won't be paying her back for what she did for you in the past because you've got no past. You aren't building up credit for the future, because there won't be any future.

Occasionally men speak of a kind of "peak" sexual experience. The very transience and anonymity of the encounter seem to heighten the enjoyment, as in the essay above. Women will also mention anonymity as being a kind of sexual "uninhibitor."

Woman, Weed, CA: The one time I had "instant sex" was in my first year of being single. I was terribly depressed and so went to visit my aunt in San Francisco. Went out to a bar and met a tall brunette man who seemed understanding and intelligent. To get to the point: We drove out of town a short distance to some hills there. He took out a blanket and spread it under the stars. We had some wine and his portable radio. We made delicious, loving love there. Yet I didn't feel guilty and it was very enjoyable. During the sex I realized that this was a kind of fantasy for me, having sex with a complete stranger. I was aroused by this fact and I believe it was what helped me that night to have several wonderful orgasms. I do not always, not usually even, have orgasms, or the ones I had with my husband were small. I'm not certain they were orgasms or what, but were nothing to compare to what happened that night.

"Often in marriage people are locked into a destructive relationship," says Dr. Levine. "When they finally are divorced, they are interested in a dimension of life they've never known. They don't want to get involved. And so a man or a woman goes out and finds he or she can bed down with somebody nice in a casual situation. It's satisfying because they are reassured of their attractiveness and desirability. A woman who, for example, couldn't have an orgasm with her husband may find in her first post-separation experience that she *has* an orgasm.

She discovers that she wasn't crazy, or inhibited, that there wasn't anything wrong with her. Many men who have had no desire for their wives, and have been impotent, function very well post-maritally. It's satisfying for them not necessarily because they like the person but because they are getting an affirmative answer to a very personal question: Am I sexually adequate?"

On the darker side, respondents' descriptions of casual sex sometimes hint at psychological problems of varying complexity.

Woman, Louisville, KY: Do I have casual sex? Yes, yes, yes, all the time, whenever I can. Only that. It's the only way to fly. With whomever I want, whenever, all the time. Whew! No getting tied down or tired for me. I just want dicks, dicks, dicks, all the time, and make sure they're new ones. Make sure I never have the same goddamn one twice. If a guy who screws me tries to hang around afterwards I slam the door in his face.

Man, Jersey City, NJ: Most of my relationships with women are quite brief. I find that after I have sex I quickly lose interest in a woman. To date, I have not been able to fall in love or have an affair for very long, as I lose interest in that too. I find that I just prefer having fast, neat sex with women and then moving on. No one gets hurt and we both enjoy ourselves. I would hate to have to hang around with a woman after we have finished the business of making love.

"Habitually engaging in sex with strangers may represent an acting out of severe neurotic conflicts," Dr. Barbara Bess, Associate Professor of Psychiatry and Assistant Director of Residency Training in Psychiatry, New York Medical College, New York City, writes in a professional journal.* By sticking to impersonal situations, people who feel threatened by rejection risk neither rejection nor acceptance, pleasure or pain. "One-night stands with strangers," she writes, "preclude rejection since the potential sex partner means nothing to such a person."

Woman, Santa Fe, NM: Yes, I have had many sexual relationships which you could call casual, almost all of them with strangers or men I scarcely know. I suppose I have taken a kind of protection in the fact that these men were strangers to me and meant nothing. It doesn't matter if a stranger hurts you because you are not emotionally invested

* *Medical Aspects of Human Sexuality,* September 1979.

in him. Of course, you pay the price for this by rarely having sex that is meaningful.

Dr. Augustus F. Kinzel, a psychoanalyst in New York City, claims that if impersonal sexuality becomes the primary mode of behavior, then something is wrong.* This impersonality may result from a number of underlying problems:

1. sex to compensate for an ungratifying family life
2. sex to maintain a hold on reality
3. sex to offset homosexual fears
4. sex as an assurance of personal masculinity or femininity
5. sex to rejuvenate or to stem the aging process
6. sex to foster the illusion of youth
7. sex to place oneself in a mothered position
8. sex to prevent the sense of abandonment

When any of these needs becomes the predominant part of the sexual drive, Dr. Kinzel maintains, it is an indication that the sexual act has become an expression of neurosis.

"If you look at the frequency of casual sexual intercourse," says Dr. Samuels, "and the number of partners, you really can't always tell if it's healthy or unhealthy. You have to do further examination and find out how the person *feels* during casual sex and what his or her motives are." If the motives are based on anger, or feelings of inferiority, or questionable sex-gender identification, or fear of rejection, then clinical help may be in order.

Some respondents describe casual sex as lessening sexual excitement:

Man, Boston, MA: After the thousandth one-night stand you just lose interest. It becomes hard to get it up. Even for pretty girls. Sometimes you find yourself chasing after women, but when they fall into bed with you easily you can't stay interested while you're making love. I've caught myself thinking of sports, or certain investments I've been considering in the middle of a so-called love-making session. So far I have not been impotent or anything like that, but sometimes the woman has to work hard to make me hard. This is not a very "macho" admission,

* *Medical Aspects of Human Sexuality,* March 1979.

but in the interests of social science, I offer it to those young men in the reading audience who think that heaven itself is a harem full of willing women. It is, boys—but only for a time. Later on it can take a turn and become more like hell. Well, not hell exactly . . . more like limbo.

Man, Framingham, MA: After the initial setup is made in casual sex the actual happening of the sex act is very disappointing for me. There is no real communication or emotion between us. When one of us tries to force it it gets phonier than before. Once in a while you find a woman who is just naturally caring. In California I had a fast sex thing with a motor secretary who was naturally loving and caring. It was this fling with her that made me realize how empty and dull sex is on a one-night stand basis.

Woman, St. Louis, MO: I slept around a little after my separation. This quickly ended when I realized I wasn't enjoying the sex itself. It was fun to flirt with a stranger and have fantasies about him. In bed the whole thing was dull and once even painful.

Postcoital depression is mentioned by many respondents:

Man, Oklahoma City, OK: I've had casual sex with many women. It's great up to the orgasm. Boom! After that I feel like killing myself and sometimes the girl I'm with (not literally, don't worry, I'm not a murderer). It's amazing the letdown between before and after; it's like night and day.

Woman, Seattle, WA: I often find myself seized with a sense of despair after having made love with someone I don't care about. I fantasize about whether I will ever find a man who I can really love and who will love me back. The funny thing is that I often go to the bar I like out of loneliness. I want some warm, loving company. When I pick up a man though and make love with him the opposite happens. I feel more lonely than before.

Casual sex may answer many needs, some neurotic, some not. Loneliness, ennui, the search for companionship, the urge to conquer, the need for sexual reassurance, the need to view oneself as an attractive person, the love of variety and adventure—all may be urges that drive one on, and it is the wise man or woman who know his or her own motivation. As Dr. Bess points out: "Both men and women use casual sex to boost their egos, especially after marital discord. Sex with strangers is not an uncommon phenomenon. Those who participate range from people with serious psychopathy to those who are relatively healthy individuals."

Multiple Sexual Involvements

11. *Do you believe it's possible to be meaningfully and sexually involved with more than one man/woman at a time?*

The relatively severe judgment brought to bear by singles concerning casual sex is repeated concerning involvement with more than one partner during the same period of time. (This is not to be confused with threesomes, group sex, and so on.) Singles lumped casual sex and multiple involvements under the same heading, and delivered an equally stern judgment on both:

Major Finding: Approximately three quarters of single men and almost 90 percent of single women feel it is difficult or impossible to be meaningfully and sexually involved with more than one person during the same period of time.

- Some 18 percent of single men and 31 percent of single women totally dismiss the notion that multiple sexual involvement can be meaningful. Twenty-seven percent of men and women claim it can be meaningful *only under rare circumstances.* Thirteen percent of men and 15 percent of women say *it happened to me but it was extremely difficult.* Fifteen percent of men and 16 percent of women say *it can be done but ultimately it hurts one's ability to love.*
- Nineteen percent of men and 10 percent of women claim *I am frequently involved with more than one man/woman and get fulfillment from each.* Seven percent of men and 1 percent of women prefer such an arrangement, claiming *it is the wave of the future.* Finally, 2 percent of men and women checked *don't know.*

Most singles who have had experience with random sex declare that the rewards are less than the promises. There are, of course, those who extol the pleasures of casual sex and multiple involvements. In this case a quarter of our men and 10 percent of our women are in such a category. But the majority disagrees.

What does this tell us about sexual exploitations and reality? To what degree are singles conditioned to expect happiness from activities that in fact often prove disappointing? "The attitude among many people today," claims Dr. Samuels, "is that sex is a recreational activity, like a sport of some kind. This attitude is largely promoted by the media. But for many people sex is still connected with ideas of love and affection. So when they indulge in sex without love they feel bad about it. You can take the view that sex is recreational, that it is simply procreational, or that it is an expression of love. We can only hope that people will clarify their own viewpoints and act accordingly."

On this question of non-singular involvements, New York psychiatrist Dr. Anthony Pietropinto has a somewhat different slant. "Multiple involvements can be helpful at times," he claims, "especially for people who cannot make a commitment at a given time in their life. For example, someone who is building a career and traveling a lot, who has demands on his or her time that would make him or her, frankly, a bad spouse. It might be right for such people not to make strong emotional commitments for a while but rather to have casual pickups here and there. Multiple friendship-love affairs would be even better.

"The question concerning 'meaningful sexual involvement' revolves around the use of the word 'meaningful.' For most people, meaningful has to mean love, but the all-or-nothing attitude is not necessarily the best. Certainly if you are single you can have an affair that is wholesome, interesting, and full of mutual respect, without being in love. And if you can have one, why not several? Love, of course, is something else. It may not be so easy to carry on several real love affairs. But meaningful ones in the sense I have just outlined? Why not?

"There is," continues Dr. Pietropinto, "a gray area in human relationships. There are a lot of people whom you can get along with, whom you can admire, laugh with, whose company you enjoy—yet who are not compatible enough to spend the rest of your life with. You don't necessarily have to love them. It doesn't have to be just sex or just love. I think one of the problems with the singles scene is that people get into physical relationships with a degree of emotional detachment. It's a schizophrenic situation. From the beginning they bring an attitude of 'I don't want to be involved,' and this naturally carries over into 'I don't want to be your friend, I just want to use you for sex.' It doesn't have to be this way. Friendship doesn't necessarily make sex impossible—and vice versa."

12. *Does casual sex damage one's ability to love?*

Approximately 15 percent of respondents checked that multiple sexual involvements *can be done but ultimately it hurts one's ability to love.*

Woman, Winston-Salem, NC: My greatest complaint about sleeping around is that it makes it harder for me to zero my affections in on one man. I feel that if I spread my affections, and hence my body, around too much there will be nothing left for the man I choose as a husband. A woman *must* discriminate in sex or she loses something precious of her womanhood.

Man, Dallas, TX: At one time I had many, many, many women. Too many! I began to feel lonely and cut off from others. The more women I had the less I could feel about them. I became an "emotional eunuch." I was lying a lot and pretending. It took years for me to pay the price of all those flings. I feel that it is just now that I am able once again to think about really caring for a single person. I got my head together by being celibate for a while, going on several spiritual retreats. My soul needed care. I feel that I had wrecked it somehow by fooling around too much.

Man, Manhattan, NY: People tend to become what they practice a lot. I firmly believe this. I am a moral person. Not religious but ethical. I believe people must choose the highest good in every situation. With women I came to the conclusion that as a once-divorced man I could go two ways. I could swim along with the other fish and do exactly what they do, make it with the ladies in singles bars, pick up women, have intercourse with every woman and at every opportunity. Or I could be like the salmon and try to swim upstream, I could try and go against the grain and not do what everyone else is doing. I would pick and choose, and get sexually involved only after a period of acquaintance and acquired closeness. I decided this on the grounds of watching and observing several of my friends, young "men-about-town." Speaking as objectively as I can, I would say these men have done a first-class job of deadening their feelings toward the opposite sex. They have accomplished this by so much random sexual activity added on to much prevarication, line-handing-out, bullshit and outright dishonesty with women—they have become walking lies, and they pay the price—they lose their readiness for close feelings. Certain of them even complain about "not being able to get it up." Big surprise!

"People can wall off their feelings," says Dr. Pietropinto. "When a person hardens himself this way he is saying 'I am not going to let my emotions slip when we make love. I am going to remain uninvolved.' When a person does this too often he finds in the end that he really can't *get* involved anymore." At the heart of non-singular sexual involvement, Dr. Pietropinto claims, is a person's desire to satisfy the many conflicting sides of the libido. "Some women say 'I want a kind, gentle, sympathetic man,' and yet they are still attracted to the big, husky, macho type. They like a man who is young and vibrant and at the same time one who is older, who has a steady influence. This woman may have several different types of boyfriend, each filling one of these different needs. Neither men nor women want to give up any of these mates. To find a man or woman who combines *all* these qualities is almost impossible."

At the same time, says Dr. Pietropinto, "People want the feeling that they are not really alone, that there is somebody there to care for them. This is one reason singles are often so negative about casual sex. Deep down we know there are times when we are not that admirable, not that healthy, not that happy, not that sexy. And it's a nice feeling to know that somebody is always going to be there, so nice in fact that it is perhaps stronger than the need to have many different lovers to satisfy all your sexual sides. Permanent stability can only come out of a one-on-one relationship. Multiple involvements just don't fill the bill here."

Almost 20 percent of men and 10 percent of women claim they are *often involved with more than one man/woman and get fulfillment from each.* In addition, 7 percent of men and 1 percent of women say *I prefer such multiple involvements—it's the wave of the future.* Thus approximately one out of four men and 11 percent of women prefer nonmonogamous sex. Who are these people?

PROFILE: The man most likely to have many simultaneous involvements.

    PROFILE SUMMARY: The man likely to have many simultaneous involvements is older, between thirty-five and fifty-five. He is in a very high income bracket, has a good job, good education, good worldly prospects. He lives alone and has been single no more than two or three years. Most likely he's been divorced twice.

PROFILE: The woman most likely to have many simultaneous involvements.

PROFILE SUMMARY: The woman most likely to have many simultaneous involvements is a high-wage-earner, is college educated, and holds a good job. She is between thirty-five and forty-four years old with two divorces behind her. And while there is little to indicate that homosexual men prefer multiple sexual involvements more than heterosexual men, a woman is three times as likely to opt for nonexclusive involvement if she is a lesbian or bisexual than if she is straight.

Woman, Troy, NY: I feel that I'm not built to be a one-man woman. I've been married and lived with men. Both times I've gotten the urge to get it going with other men at the same time. And have carried on affairs while with these men. It is my "itch," as I call it. Unlike your run-of-the-mill woman, I do not feel guilty, wrong, insecure, stupid, inferior or a failure for sleeping with several men. A man looks good to me and I say to myself, "why not?" So far it's been a source of happiness rather than trouble for me.

Man, Indianapolis, IN: For six years I have been living with four women. I serve as their husband and when we do sex we do worship. I can honestly say that I love all four of them but of course in a different way. Each one brings something different to me sexually and personally, as well as materially. We seldom fight and when we do the entire group comes together and conferences over it until all troubles are satisfactorily worked out.

The lesbian preference for multiple sexual involvements mentioned in the profile above crops up with relative frequency in essay questions dealing with dating and sex:

Woman, Providence, RI: Being homosexual I never look forward to marriage. Neither do I wish to "marry" another woman as some of my female acquaintances do. I enjoy meeting and loving with a variety of women. Each woman brings a new technique of love making as well as something of her personality and heart. I do not wish to be tied down but prefer having several lovers who I can relate with.

Woman, Kansas City, MO: My scene is lesbian.
My preference is for lots of women.
I get off on orgies—so there!
I prefer young women to old, and I don't do butch!
I am not a man. I am a woman. I like other women.
Many of them.

The notions that one will end up "trapped" with a single partner, that it is possible to have more than one person at a time, and that people are not built for monogamous sex are all mentioned in defense of multiple sexual involvements.

Woman, Denver, CO: If I was tied down again to one man I think I'd kill myself. Being married was like being put into a box and rolled down the hill. Needless to mention, the key has been thrown away. The right to choose my own variety of men and have as many dates as I like is the best part of being single. I don't think people were made to be married.

Man, Grand Rapids, MI: There are many women on the market. Most of them are sexually available and on the loose. There have been times when I've found myself under a pile of women, and I have to come up for air. Going out (and down) with a lot of women is in my estimation preferable to getting trapped with a single woman. I am free to love and live as I please.

"Once you have tied yourself to one sex partner," says Dr. Pietropinto, "that gives the person a pretty strong hold over you. There could be the feeling that one is getting into a deeper commitment than he or she wants. A lot of people are afraid of this kind of intimacy. Somehow there is safety if you have more than one partner."

As to whether people are inherently monogamous, Dr. Pietropinto refers to his best-selling book, *Husbands and Wives.** "There are two conflicting instincts in human beings. In the animal kingdom there is a

* Anthony Pietropinto and Jacqueline Simenauer, New York Times Books, 1979.

segment that isn't monogamous. On the other hand, there is another segment, mostly among the birds, where the nesting phenomenon takes place, and where animals bond together in pairs to raise their offspring. If anything, man is emotionally closer to the animals that bond. However, both impulses are with us. It takes a lot of effort and cooperation for two people to raise a family, and this kind of emotional cooperation must predominate if man is to continue as a species. This emotional support can even make up for the fun of chasing around trying to get as many sexual partners as possible. But two things are always going on at the same time. Biologically we are attracted to more than one person. Emotionally we are drawn into the private nest."

Much of the enthusiasm for casual sex and multiple involvement comes from young people who are just discovering the power of sex.

Man, Denver, CO: The greatest thing of all about sex is that you can get it on with as many girls as you can handle. It's amazing! Cause it's so easy! I swear, sometimes I have an overload of girls calling me up while I'm fucking another. The other guys in my dorm have the same problems (some problems!).

Casual sex and multiple involvements are also commonly endorsed by singles who have recently passed through painful divorces and who wish to play as wide a field as they can:

Woman, Buffalo, NY: Since my divorce I have become "promiscuous" and am loving it. I have several men with whom I make love and they are all freeing for me, unlike the married drag who I have, thank the Lord, escaped from now entirely.

Swingers

Finally there are the reports from the "swingers." Swingers are a small but growing collection of men and women who make a lifestyle out of casual sex and mutiple involvements. Almost any form of "social" sex is practiced by swingers: group, mate-swapping, couple-hopping, various varieties of "kink." Unlike the "free love" societies of the 1940s and 1950s, however, which kept a low profile, swingers today are vocal in defense of their philosophy:

Man, Manhattan, NY: In the past year I have had almost 300 women and I'm still going strong. I have a new one practically each night. This is all part of my lifestyle as a swinger. I meet regularly with other guys and gals who feel the way I do, that sex is a natural and joyous part of life and should be brought out of the closet and entered into whole-heartedly—without *anyone* telling us it's right or wrong! This way of life gives me what I need. It gives both myself and my partner pleasure. It gives us both sexual equality, the kind women are fighting for. It helps us to "get it all out" and not pretend. We're not prudes here but we're not wild and crazy either as people think. There are guidelines which are set up to insure that no one gets hurt and that everyone gets the pleasure they deserve. Why hide in the closet when you really want to swing? I indulge in various sex practices besides sucking and fuck-ing, and get a thrill out of all of them. I highly recommend it. Our motto is: "If it feels good, do it."

Woman, Manhattan, NY: Last year a boyfriend of mine, who works for a small magazine in New York City, did a story on a swing club. He asked me if I wanted to go along and I said sure, being an adventurous kind. The place is pretty shabby in the lobby and I got uneasy. Some decent looking people came in the door and after a while I calmed down. My boyfriend talked to a couple of people upstairs while I sat in the lobby and waited. Then we were taken downstairs into a big area that was once a gynmasium, I believe, and where there is a pool, steam baths, hot tubs and that sort of thing. There's a place for disco dancing. I went prepared to either laugh or cry. I ended up liking what I saw, which was a lot of people having a good time. They actually were making love in a large room but it was fairly okay, and if you wanted to be more discreet you could go into one of the back rooms they pro-vided there. My boyfriend told me that some of the women were hookers which was why so many good looking women were in atten-dance. I did not indulge in the festivities but was amazed to see how openly so many people did. People walked around naked, both men and women, and old and young alike. There were people making love in the swimming pool and in the hot tubs. The lights were low and col-ored red, and you could see what was going on. My boyfriend learned from the manager that the same people tended to come back very often and there is an inner circle of swingers who are the best customers. I was surprised by the whole experience and wouldn't put it down if someone asked.

For a more detailed description on what swinging is about we talked with Larry Levinson, self-styled "King of Swing," and founder of the country's most famous swing establishment, Plato's Retreat in New York City, a made-over health club on Manhattan's Upper West Side. Here couples nightly meet and greet for swing.

"In swinging everything is done together," Levinson tells us, "the same as if you're living together. Say a man is a swinger. A girl at the office makes a play for him. What does he do? Does he screw her on the side? No sir, he takes her home. He introduces her to his wife or his girlfriend. She's probably got a boyfriend there already, you see. And they all swing. That way nobody's cheating on anyone, it's all in the open, no jealousies. The idea is togetherness, and being up-front."

Swingers often refer to "rules of the game" and the "swinger's code," a special form of morality often espoused by organized sex groups. "Swingers," remarks Dr. Pietropinto, "follow a strict code, and there is a strange incestuous closeness among the committed ones. They get to know each other, they are friends, and there is a tight little unit in which they tend to get possessive about their mates. They will often marry one of the people in the group. Swingers are a little different from the 'anything goes, what the hell' kind of attitude toward sex because they do have their own rules. It's okay to swing with someone else as long as your partner knows about it and is present as well. But God help you if you go out for a cup of coffee on the sly with someone that your partner doesn't know about!"

"At Plato's," says Levinson, "everything is out in the open. It's the solution to cheating. Lots of people who come here tell me that swinging helped their marriage. They say it helped couples get closer together."

Indeed, people who patronize Plato's are invariably coupled. It's the house rule—no man allowed in without a woman. Women, however, are welcomed free of charge. "I get a lot of single girls come in here alone. Beautiful women. The majority are between the ages of twenty and forty years old. The single women come in here because if they go to a singles bar, any one in the city, they're hassled. Here no one bothers them. There's so much sexuality around anyway nobody cares."

Though not exclusively a singles spot, Plato's does cater to the single men and women who find multiple involvements to their taste. "We got all kinds come in here, especially single men and gals who just plain like to get it on. Pleasure seekers, you know? You see, there's no pressure here, no pressure to take your clothes off when you first arrive.

It's up to you whether or not you want to swing. You can swing or you can watch. Or you can do both. I keep it very warm downstairs on the premises so if you want it's easy to strip. I own a Jacuzzi, there are lots of soft seats, the pool's inviting. The first hour you get here as a newcomer you look around and see that everyone is having a wonderful time. And you're sitting here dressed in a hot suit, while the others are jumping around. Why not? you say to yourself. Who would know? I'll just go in for a swim. Before you know it a beautiful girl walks up to you, she's twenty-one or twenty-two, a beautiful girl. Like something out of a book. Before you know it something wonderful happens and you're getting it on. Then you're a swinger."

Reports from respondents concerning swinging are infrequent. Group sex, as we shall see below, is practiced by only a small part of the singles population. By and large, men tend to be more enthusiastic about it than women. Here is what several women say on the subject:

Woman, Syracuse, NY: I have indulged in swinging parties and always wished I hadn't. I had a boyfriend who made me go. They were at a friend's house where a bunch of swingers came over for a brunch and then sex. I only stuck around for a few minutes because the thing was too hairy for me. Then my boyfriend made me go to several more, but I had the same reaction to them all. At one party my boyfriend practically forced me to indulge in the sexual activities, and that nearly broke us up for good.

Woman, Pawtucket, RI: For a short time in my life I was involved with swinging and a group of sex freaks. It made me feel dirty and disgusted with myself. It didn't even feel good when I did it.

"Swinging," says Dr. Pietropinto, "is a kind of compromise between monogamy and unbridled 'what the hell!' sex. It is an attempt to get the best of both worlds, where you have a commitment with one partner and at the same time see others. You can be more open about sex this way; you can do forbidden things.

"The potential harm in swinging is this: There is always a desire to have one person who will be exclusively your own. If you start sharing this person it means you will not find this kind of intimacy any longer. This kind of intimacy can't be shared. You can't have both in life—you can't have a lot of sexual partners and at the same time have the kind of intimacy that comes from commitment to a single partner."

UNDESIRED SEX

13. *Do you ever have sex with a man or woman because you think he or she expects it? Do you ever have sex when you don't want to? When, how often, and under what circumstances?*

Many respondents are adamant about the fact that they *never* have sex simply because it is expected. A kind of fierce insistence on this point runs through at least half the replies, demonstrating the degree to which independence and self-determination are precious to the single.

On the other hand, within the denials themselves there sometimes lies an ambiguity, which we can only assume the respondents themselves are unaware of.

Woman, St. Louis, MO: I have never considered such a thing. I am not in the habit of allowing myself to be talked or forced into things I do not wish to do. The only time I change my mind about sex is if a man shows me a very good time. That's the only time I might consider giving myself even if I didn't really feel like it. But other than this, never.

Man, Greensboro, NC: Of course not. What fun would it be? I have had sex though when the *woman* I was with didn't want to. Somehow both of us felt that night that we should make it even though we weren't really in the mood. Nobody forced us into it but we ended up on the floor of her apartment. It wasn't a very satisfactory night and neither of us got together again.

Woman, Burlington, VT: I don't think I have. Sometimes this issue gets hazy, you know, but I don't think so. Occasionally I do end up having fornication with a man I'm not that crazy about, who I have no intentions of having anything to do with. Men are very clever that way, they talk and talk to you and before you know it you're in bed with them. And you say: "How did I end up here?" You can't say it was against your will but neither can you say it was "with" your will. I think primarily such men play on a woman's vanity, her insecurities and her need to be liked and admired. At least that is my observation. Men seem to need to have sex with a woman very badly. I'm not so sure they *really* want to a lot of the time, but they feel that we'll judge them if they don't. The macho games are all twisted around but they're still with us.

At least half of the respondents recount experiences, often during transient meetings, when they were forced in some way into having sex.

Man, Pittsburgh, PA: Once I had sex with an overly aggressive woman who pushed me into it to prove she was "liberated." She was a true libber and out to make her point, that she was as sexually equal as I. The whole experience sucked. No feeling of intimacy or rapport.

Man, Los Angeles, CA: Women, of course, do not usually "push" you into sex, not in the way a man might do it. In the past few years, however, I have noted that women seem to expect sex more. They talk about it more and at the end of the evening they sometimes seem to be waiting. In this sense I have found myself sleeping with a woman when I didn't wish it. I did it, of course, to prove myself a man. When a woman challenges you in this way it is difficult not to respond.

Some respondents report unwanted sex due to peer pressures, or from fear of appearing "weird," "old-fashioned," "out of touch":

Woman, Birmingham, AL: I used to have sex when I just wanted to experience what I heard was the going thing. Or so as not to appear old fashioned, prim and proper. I do not anymore because that kind of thinking only leads to subservience and being used as a "sex thing." I enjoy saying "no" now when I don't want to have sex. It makes me stronger.

Other singles claim they acquiesce out of a wish not to hurt their partner's feelings. Reports of this kind frequently end on an unfortunate note.

Man, Greensboro, NC: I've only had sex with someone I didn't want one time. One night of all places, at a prayer meeting. I kissed and held the hand of one of the members (in brotherly fashion) and she didn't let go. Later she confessed to me that she hadn't had sex in five years and wanted me to do something about it. Because of the nature of her personality and her plight I agreed to bring her home. I liked her as a person but found her to be physically repulsive. But I went through with it and even walked her home in the morning before my roommate woke up. Needless to say, it's something I don't wish to repeat.

Finally we have occasional reports of forced sexuality.

Woman, Danbury, CT: Oh yes. Several times men have physically pressured me into sleeping with them. Whether I wanted to or not really made no difference. Whether I was raped or not is hard to say, but I definitely did not want sex at that time.

LOVE AND SEX

The subject of undesired sex leads to a related yet larger issue, one that troubles many single people and that has been hotly debated over the past few years. It is the question of whether love is necessary for good sex.

14. *Do you think love is a prerequisite for good sex?*	Men	Women
a. Absolutely.	15%	21%
b. One should at least like his/her partner.	22%	15%
c. Sex is better without love to complicate it.	4%	2%
d. Love makes sex better. But it's possible to have good sex without it.	40%	40%
e. Sex without love is empty and incomplete.	9%	18%
f. Sex is great any way you experience it.	9%	3%
g. I don't know.	1%	1%

---

*Major Finding: **Most singles do not think love is necessary for good sex.***

The consensus, reached by combining answers b, d, and f, is that though love augments sex, it is not an absolute requirement. Two people who enjoy mutual fondness and respect and are physically attracted will most likely enjoy going to bed together even though love is absent.

The largest vote was cast for answer d: *Love makes sex better. But it's possible to have good sex without it.* Next comes *One should at least like his/her partner*—a positive way of saying that love is not necessary so long as some kind of affection is present.

BONUS FINDINGS

- Men in the lower-income brackets tend to believe *more* in love than their counterparts in the higher brackets.
- Twice as many men in their early twenties (as compared with men forty-five and over) feel that sex without love is empty.
- Women who live with their families are more insistent that love accompany sex than are those who live alone. Least insistent are women who are living with a man.
- The twice-divorced woman is the most insistent that sex is better when not complicated by love. She is also the least likely to feel that sex without love is empty and incomplete.

"The problem," states Dr. Arnold A. Lazarus, Professor of Psychology at the Graduate School of Applied and Professional Psychology at Rutgers University in New Brunswick, New Jersey, "is that the word 'love' does not adequately convey the wide range of possible affection. After all, one can be infatuated with another person, be biologically attracted, or care for him or her as a friend—not to mention caring for one's parent or one's pet—all under the single name of 'love.' When singles claim 'love' is not necessary for sexual satisfaction, they do not suggest complete indifference as its opposite. For many singles, warmth and sharing as characterized by what has come to be known as 'like' are enough to make sex worthwhile, and even form a kind of love."

This is the central issue implied by respondents' answers to the question of love and sex—that affection has many degrees, and that maximum romantic intensity is not necessarily a requirement for a meaningful sexual affair. This point is expressed in several answers to the following essay question:

15. *What makes a man/woman a good lover?*

Man, Cincinnati, OH: A good lover would have to be in tune with what goes on in their partner's life. Awareness and consideration are vital. A good partner would try to please before thinking of themselves. They are considerate with one another and there when a listening ear is needed.

Man, Albany, NY: My ideal lover would have these attributes:

1. Honesty—I know the person is straight about her feelings.
2. Sensitive—About my and her own inner needs.
3. Integrity and Daring—Makes for an interesting life.
4. Relatively aggressive—I don't want to have to do everything.
5. Understanding—Of shortcomings and faults (sensually and other).

Woman, San Diego, CA: The perfect lover would be a perfect specimen of manhood. He wouldn't have to love me—just treat me fine, attend to my satisfaction. He should be gentle with me but firm. He should be a man.

Woman, Oxnard, CA: The most important thing that makes a man a good lover is his desire to please. A woman senses this in a man, and she knows when he is a hopeless egotist or someone who has your good at heart. Selfish, self-centered men, in my experience, may make technically good lovers because they've had a lot of practice at it but they don't know how to give of themselves, and that turns me off.

Almost all respondents speak of "attentiveness," "honesty," "openness," "consideration." Many say that a lover must be "sensitive to my needs" or "emotionally available." Only a few mention love directly. But though most singles claim not to require love *per se,* many ask for related emotional qualities such as "caring," "concern," "awareness of my feelings," "alertness to my needs." Sex without these qualities, respondents claim—blind, mechanical sex devoid of thoughtful feelings—is "egotistic," "self-centered," "self-serving," and often leads to a lowered sense of self-esteem.

Woman, Toledo, OH: I have been attracted to men purely on the basis of their looks, size, handsome qualities, etc. But I say no because those times I have had sex without love/caring I have known in my heart it was a selfish thing and a wrong thing to do. Women's lib can tell me all they want but I know men and women are not the same. I know these things deep in my woman's heart.

Man, Oklahoma City, OK: When I have sex with girls I don't care about and sometimes when I have sex with nice girls too, I feel like pure shit the next day. I wake up and see them lying next to me and I have to turn away. Their breath smells and so does mine. It's like a sample of how we feel about each other that next "ugly gray dawn." It makes me feel real bad I did it without giving a damn for myself or them.

Woman, Nassau, NY: After making love to a gentleman who I met casually at an antique fair, the next day after we had bedded down mutually, I started having a feeling that there was something in my throat. This feeling lasted about a week and near to drove me out of my mind. I checked it out with a doctor—I thought I had cancer but he said my throat was clear. The next time I had a fling with a man in the same brief way this same throat problem returned. It was accompanied by feelings of worthlessness and depression. I felt very guilty. Now each time I get involved with someone I care about strictly for the purpose of sexual release, I have this same itching feeling in my throat. Plus depression. I have no doubt that they are related to one another.

"Wherever there is guilt or a poor sense of self-esteem," Professor Lazarus claims, "there are few things you can generalize about. But here is one: when guilt is present there are two words I hear—'should' and 'shouldn't.' When it's 'should' it may be: 'I *should* have feelings during sex, I *should* love and care for this woman, I *should* be unselfish.' When it is 'shouldn't' you may hear: 'I *shouldn't* be having this sex with this person because I don't really care for her,' and so forth. Many people feel that as long as you are in love, and *only* if you are in love, do you have permission to enjoy yourself and not feel guilty."

Dr. Lazarus believes that love is unnecessary for the attainment of full erotic satisfaction and that it can at times actually have an inhibiting effect. "Casual encounters can prove more sexual than the kind experienced during marriage. This is because people deeply in love find themselves concentrating so intently on the affectionate components that their sexual impulses become diffused, and decreased erotic stimulation results. When people are in love they are privy to a wide range of conflicted feelings like warmth, concern, obligation, vulnerability, jealousy, fear of betrayal. These can complicate matters so much that the sexual part of the act becomes secondary. On the other hand, when raw, physical infatuation is in operation no such complications occur, and a couple can concentrate fully on sex. The idea is that love messages and sex messages are not synonymous."

Finally, Dr. Lazarus claims, casual sex—sex without love—may in fact turn into love. "There is often a special sequence of events that takes place when people first meet and make love. The sex comes first. There is touching, intimacy, contact—and it sparks something deep in people that otherwise might not be set off. Once contact is made, good feelings come, then more positive reinforcement, then more good feelings. Ultimately these good feelings shift gears, as it were, and enter another plane. What started out as pure physical attraction has been sublimated into deeper, more meaningful emotions. The very act of sex has helped create love."

Single women are more prone to require love during intercourse than men. This has, of course, long been the norm in Western society, so much so that for many women love and sex are part of the same fabric, and "making love" is another way of saying "having sex."

In our time, we see from findings, attitudes are shifting due to the influence of modern ideas. From responses we learn that almost half of all women now feel "like" is as acceptable a premise for sex as "love." This represents a dramatic change from the past. Further, more women demand the right to separate the two functions, sex and love, and to enjoy the first without taking on the responsibilities of the second.

Woman, San Diego, CA: I think what you will be seeing in the future is that women will no longer let men call the sexual shots. Women feel they have been repressed over this too long as it is. We have the *right* to make our sexual desires known! Perhaps we don't all want to marry the men we go out with. We just want sex once or twice, just like men. But men never think of this. They think we are all out to tie them down. Most of the men I make love with are just friends, and I do not get that serious with them.

Man, Lansing, MI: Women today want to use *me*—it used to be the other way around. I may want to get involved with a certain woman but she tells me she just wants to have sex without involvement. Sometimes it's they who want sex only one time. It's very hard to make this adjustment for men.

Man, Fort Worth, TX: Fast sex is all they want. What ever happened to old-fashioned love? Is it the modern world that is doing this to us? I don't know, but women today are so busy proving they are as good as men, and in the meantime they are getting hard, cross and dirty as men. It once was that the man chased the woman. Now the woman chases the man. It once was that the man propositioned the woman. Now it's the woman who propositions the man.

"In my hypothesis," says Dr. Lazarus, "we live in an age of fierce competition between male and female, with feminists attempting to gain equality on just about every front. Equality to them means similarity, sameness. When these women learn that men compartmentalize sex and can have sex without love, they believe it is their duty to do the same. They may *think* this without really feeling it. That is, they may set about to do it not because it comes naturally to their temperament but because it gives them the sense of being socially equal to men. That may be why in your survey so many women say they would sleep with a man without loving him—they want to be equal to men in that area."

Even in this age of the Women's Movement, says Dr. Lazarus, there seem to be fewer women who have the same trigger system as men. "I mean by that, if a man is very turned on by a redheaded woman with dark brown eyes, and if he spies such a woman on the street, he experiences an immediate erotic reaction. He doesn't know anything about her personality or character. And yet secretions and chemical changes automatically take place in him due to this visual stimulus alone. When women look at a man who is very good looking this doesn't as a rule produce the same instant arousal. It might produce a desire in them to hug, cuddle, or caress, or to have sensual rather than sexual experiences. But with a male, the sight of a sexy woman goes right to his sexual organs and instantly turns him on. A lot of people would say that sex differences are due to cultural training, that women are still taught to inhibit their sexuality. But I wonder about this."

The difference between having sex and making love brings up the fact that some respondents judge it possible, and even *necessary,* to separate the genitals from the heart entirely, and to enjoy sex purely as a biological pleasure. For this, liking one's partner is secondary to finding him or her skilled and appealing.

Man, Providence, RI: Let's face it—we're animals. I learned this in biology class but I think other people forget the fact. If you observe the animal world you see every creature fornicating at will, and doing so without guilt, moral restrictions, hangups, and so forth. If nature wanted us to hold back with each other why did she give us the full go-ahead on mating seasons? We're not restricted this way like other animals—we can make love any time of year and enjoy it as much. Celibacy is against the laws of nature. I always feel better when I have had sexual release than when I haven't. By taking full advantage of the sexual freedom of today's world we are just cooperating with nature's plan. And you know: "You can't fool Mother Nature!"

Nonetheless, as we have seen, only a small percentage of respondents (9 percent men, 3 percent women) agree that *sex is great any way you experience it.* The rest insist that positive, caring feelings must be present in order to enjoy the real pleasures of sex, even if these feelings are not undying.

The singles majority, therefore, is temperate but not prudish in its estimation of casual sex versus love. Most say no to one-night stands and to simultaneous sexual arrangements. Most do, however, say yes to sex without love—qualified by the understanding that *some* fond feelings be present, that "like" be there if not "love," and that "like," if not as productive of ecstatic sex as love, is still a good substitute until the real thing comes along.

Thus, while there are a number of singles who support casual sex, the majority do not. And though there are many reasons for this attitude, behind most rationales is a fundamental insistence that men and women by their nature require a single deep relationship rather than a number of sequential and even simultaneous ones. We could call this attitude a kind of covert monogamy.

The monogamous argument is of course deeply ingrained in the mind of Western man, and it should come as no shock that it shows up, if in somewhat camouflaged and modified form, among the unmarried community. For despite the intentions of reformers and those who wish to instantly rewrite all courtship scripts, to cause such a deeply underlying motif to vanish by simply declaring the revolution is far from realistic.

At the same time, we see once more that sexual values and mores have changed significantly, even over the past thirty years, making what was once a relative rarity, sex out of wedlock, into a routine and *expected* event. Does this tell us that the norm is slowly but inexorably shifting from monogamy toward transient sex, that the significant number who already support casual sex in the 1980s may be the majority by the year 2000, that Western man will soon view sex with as relaxed an attitude as he now looks upon other biological necessities like eating and sleeping, and that we shall sooner or later enter a Brave New World where anyone not promiscuous is considered a risk to the state? The question of where the sexual revolution is ultimately taking the singles community, and whether it is guiding it there or dragging it, is an intriguing and controversial one. In the last chapter we will learn how singles themselves feel on the subject. At this point, however, we shift emphasis away from the issue of how singles approach the sexual experience and toward the question of what they actually do while it is taking place.

SINGLES' SEXUAL TASTES: NORMS, VARIATIONS, AND DEVIATIONS

16. *Describe how an ideal lover would treat you in and out of bed.*

Just about everyone knew what they liked on this score:

Man, Pompton Lakes, NJ: An ideal lover would be shy and quiet. But when we have our clothes off she is a passionate, caring woman, and gentle. She would communicate with me about personal wants and her body parts and her fantasies. She would be willing to let her fantasies come out and seek new adventure. She would know how to handle my penis, how to use her tongue, how to move her thighs. She would have tricks experience taught her. She would never be dry. She would never grow stale.

Woman, Albuquerque, NM: To me what makes a man a good lover is his ability to be truthful and truly loving. You can have a great sexual partner but that means nothing if he is lacking love, understanding, truthfulness and respect for himself and for me. What I'm trying to say is that a man's regard for me determines whether he's a good lover in and out of bed.

These two answers are typical of men's and women's ideal romantic relations. Men often value sexual skills first, then personal virtues. Single men often see the question in physical terms. Women generally base their opinions on character judgments and emotional characteristics. This difference, long recognized by professionals and encountered throughout the survey, occurs frequently in a variety of responses.

Woman, Buffalo, NY: He has to be passionate, gentle yet aggressive too. No milktoasts need apply. An ideal lover would be very attentive to my desires and let me know of his own too. He would treat me as an equal in all things (besides sex) and respect me as a person. He must be thoughtful and courteous in and out of bed.

Woman, Manhattan, NY: I find that the way a man is *out of bed* has much to do with the way I will feel toward him *in* bed. Men do not always understand women. They get instantly turned on themselves by the mere sight of a bulging bosom, and they think women have the same hair-trigger reaction. Women want their lover to be close to them during the day in both thought and behavior. They want to feel loved, like sleek pussy cats, adored if you want a better word. Their lover should be just that—a love-er. A man who knows how to feel and to give (and take) affection well. A man puts money in his sexual bank with a woman if he treats her well in "off-hours" when they're not indulging.

Women continually talk of a lover who "listens to my needs," who "shows his enjoyment," who "has sensitivity both to his needs and mine." The phrase "during sex and after" crops up all the time. "Slam-bam, thank you, Mam, sex is the worst," says a woman from Oklahoma City. "In my opinion sex continues after the orgasm—it includes the cuddle-time afterward, the cigarette after, the warm night's sleep together."

Many female respondents stress that a good lover never forces sex when the woman is not in the mood. Women especially stress sexual honesty:

Woman, Albany, NY: The ideal lover never hints at wanting sex. If he wants it, he says so. I despise pats on the buttocks to the extent that I won't date anyone who does it. In bed I want him to touch me. I want him to make it clear that he enjoys my whole body and is not just hung up on some part; I want him to state without undue shyness what pleasures him; I want him to respect what pleasures me and not insist on what he read about women in some manual; and most of all, I want him to please himself, because if he doesn't then I have to worry about whether he's enjoying it instead of concentrating on pleasing myself. How can a person be natural when she's thinking, "I wonder whether he likes this?" or "Should I try that?" And that's the whole key: NATURAL.

Woman, Omaha, NB: My ideal lover would not lie about sex. He would not lie about what he wanted from me. Lies and sex do not mix.

My first husband had several hangups about sex but kept them from me to the last days of our breakup. When they came out they came out like a flood. He was plenty angry at *me* for not doing what he wanted, when in fact it was his fault for never telling me.

Some women require forcefulness, others prefer love to be gentle. All, however, make it clear that they like the man to give them a sense of confidence and expertise. "Fumblers are bumblers," a woman remarked.

Woman, Gary, IN: Many men do not understand that a feather-like touch is *very* tantalizing. They think the more pressure and contact the better. I have tried to explain or guide them but very few are able to get it. A good lover plays upon the body of a female partner as if it were a very delicate musical instrument, and his response to her verbal and emotional cues is all significant. He must have technique and *savoir faire,* and communicate his competency to me. If I feel I'm in the hands of a dolt I get alarmed.

Though the notion that women are excited by a man's emotional qualities rather than by his physical attributes is supported by the survey findings, this is not invariably the case, and in fact some observers feel that things may be changing.

Woman, Boston, MA: I'm turned on to a lover who is built well and who knows how to make love. His technique is what is important to me, and how he smells, how his skin feels, strange things that are important to me. If a lover has a funny smell I may be turned off.

Woman, Burlington, VT: A man should be a good balance between considerate and masculine. Just "nice guys" are of no interest to me. I like a man who is a man, who is built like a man, who acts like one, who takes charge and who you feel safe with when his big arms are wrapped around you. I don't mean to tell you I like heels or macho men, but men who are attractive, not flabby, who understand a woman's sexual wants.

Two common words in single women's vocabulary are "relaxed" and "foreplay." "Heaven knows I can't stand a stiff, awkward lover," writes a woman from Seattle, speaking for a majority of the respondents. "I can't stand to be with a man who is tight or up-tight," says

another. "Relaxation on his part relaxes me and I can enjoy myself."
Men are accused of pressing for insertion too quickly, of seeking orgasm before the woman is ready. Such phrases as "cuddling" or "creative exploring" appear in conjunction with descriptions of good technique, and men who understand that arousal rhythms are slower for
women than for men are given extra high marks:

Woman, Jamaica, NY: One sign of a good lover is his sexual bedside
manner. This must be slow and unrushed. He must play me like a
piano. Know when and how to excite me before we start intercourse. If
I'm not adequately stimulated by foreplay I will not be wet and ready,
and if I'm not wet and ready woe to the man and myself!

Woman, Baltimore, MD: In terms of sexual technique, I'd say that for a
man to really be an ideal lover and for us to have ideal love making, he
would have to have *patience.* This is something men are short on. Long
and gentle foreplay are what make a good lover. He spreads his attentions around in an unhurried and relaxed manner. He settles on all
parts of my body, not just my breasts or lips or whatever. Men who
know that arousal is a slow process in women are ahead of the game.
Why isn't sex education a mandatory part of our educational system?

Woman, Chicago, IL: The way a guy turns me on the most is with
foreplay and *without* jumping to the next step. If the guy doesn't attempt to force himself on me, I get turned on. But I don't like a guy
who wants to have instant sex without the necessary preliminaries. Pre-
and post-coital activity has as much to do with sex for me as the very
act itself does.

Other qualities women believe should be part of the good lover's
repertoire include the following:

"For me an ideal lover would be warmly seductive and romantic. He
would be sexually skillful and creative—not mechanical."

"I like a man in bed who compliments me on my body and makes me
feel like a full, desirable woman. I *dislike* it when a man totally disre-
gards my body, especially if it's the first time, because it makes me feel
put-down and neglected."

"I want a man who will pay attention to my needs but not so much that
he feels like he must stifle his orgasm until I climax. This only serves to

make me feel like I'm not pleasing him, thus making my orgasm more difficult to achieve."

"I like a lover who afterwards stays close to me and we talk, not about sex but about things we both like and know. I also prefer to spend the night together whenever possible, a good shower together and breakfast next morning. I don't like sentimental goodbyes, but a good kiss and 'I loved it.' "

"He speaks freely of what he likes and how I can help him become one with his own pleasure zone. He moves slow and easy, as if we have all the time in the world. If he sees something is tensing me up, he asks and doesn't ignore it."

"I like to feel like a partner when lovemaking, not just a necessary part of equipment for the 'procedure.' "

As we mentioned, men are more explicit in their sexual demands.

Man, Indianapolis, IN: To be a good lover a woman must be able to satisfy a man. Within this framework, my ideal lover would: 1) know how to move her hips; 2) be accomplished at fellatio and enjoy cunnilingus; 3) know how to make her breasts wiggle when we are making love; 4) know how to assume sensual and sexual expressions *naturally* on her face; 5) be creative with her hands, exploring all parts of my body, especially forbidden parts like the anus, inside my mouth, etc.; 6) to develop the muscles in her vagina so she can tighten and loosen them at will, 'milking' my penis, a big turn-on; 7) would know and like many sexual positions, and be as good on top as on the bottom; 8) would not be afraid to experiment with wild (not kinky) things—and even suggest them; 9) to live out my fantasies and have a few of her own; 10) to always remember to have *fun* during sex.

Man, Louisville, KY: I like a woman who is slightly aggressive in bed. I like to undress her and play with her breasts first. I especially like a woman with little cute, tight undies. It really turns me on! I like her to begin undressing me and to begin blowing in my ears and rubbing my upper and lower back with her soft, sensuous hands! Next, I like her to take off my underwear and begin massaging my penis with long flowing strokes. I especially like to have the underneath part rubbed. Then we would have long intercourse followed by a warm bubble bath.

Man, Hollywood, CA: Women who are older and have more experience make the best lovers. Young women are dumb about sex and expect you to do all the work. Women with a lot of experience and not many inhibitions make the best lovers and turn me on the most. You can talk to them.

Man, Tampa, FL: Slow love making is an art that few women understand. Women should know how to move their hands slowly over a man's body, massaging him as you make love. No one should be in a hurry. Nervous ladies are the worst lovers. Ones that take their time and give good head are the best.

Man, San Diego, CA: Communication. Beyond any doubt this is the most important element in sex. I'm not sure about the other things because they vary from woman to woman and man to man. Be sure you and the woman are on the same wave length, that's most important. Her signals to you are read by you—that's communication, and vice versa. You are both feeling the same thing *and know it!* That's communication. Communication is largely non-verbal. But not entirely, because it's important to talk out things too, and not assume the other person can read your thoughts. A couple should explore possibilities between meeting with their eyes and thoughts.

Man, Manhattan, NY: I like women who I can do crazy things with. I had a girlfriend who knew how to give massages by walking up and down my back. I had another who liked to read porno magazines with men. If you don't think that's a turn-on with women, try it someday. Women should be candid about telling you what arouses them. Don't let them get tongue-tied on the subject, or don't let them get silent because a lot of the fun goes out of it for both of you. You know, I like to put my hand under a woman's dress when we're in the preliminaries to sex and feel that she's gotten wet in the process. That means she's ready for me and not just faking it. Have you ever gone out with a woman who suggests making love in the back of a car? Crazy things. Women shouldn't be afraid to get a little rough just like men. I like sex hot and full of struggle.

Man, Dayton, OH: What makes a woman a good lover? This should be a woman who is unafraid to show what's inside her, and by this I mean she is ready and willing to howl! Frenzy is just part of it, however, as a good lover should have plenty of tricks up her sleeve. (I once had a girl stick her finger in my bellybutton and push down while she handled my penis—wow! I am eternally grateful.) Being long on technique, she should also show signs that she is enjoying the act and that I really turn her on (that is, assuming that I do, which I try to do as my end of the relationship). A good lover enjoys her sex as much as you do. Being attractive doesn't hurt but being useful with her body is even better. I have had plenty of unattractive women in bed who have proved to be dynamite lovers. The best of them don't let me do all the work but contribute with their own hip movements and they keep their hands busy all the time.

Man, Albuquerque, NM: A lot of sexuality is in the head. But since a majority of sexuality is also on a physical level, there would have to be chemical balance. A good lover wouldn't think that sex made a good relationship but she would like to have it as often as she could and be just as horny as I was (all the time). When making love we would not be shy about our bodies. It's all we have and shouldn't be afraid of them. She should be willing to experiment. If she knows little turn-ons like wanting to strip for you with sexy music, or dancing for you while you watch, that would be good too. A good lover should be full of surprises and the unexpected turn-on. You are never quite sure what she'll do next, and there is always a tension between you about maybe she'll just go crazy one of these times with passion. Another thing is that she whispers in my ear things like: "Give it to me!" or "Fuck me, baby!" Sexual dirty words are a rip when you're making love.

Variety and experiment seem a good deal more important to male respondents than to female. Many men express distaste over the standard "missionary" position, and praise lovers who enjoy different postures and unusual techniques. Some men are not shy about stating their wish to be catered to in bed. Although this attitude runs counter to the present taboo against macho, it appears in a number of essays and is evidently an urge that will not easily be defied:

Man, Akron, OH: One of the biggest turn-ons ever is a woman who is *totally* devoted to my pleasure. She would treat me as a Greek god. She would be entirely aware of every little part of me, how it gives me pleasure or pain. She would be willing to do anything I wanted. If she were like this I in turn would be very excited and would wish to completely fulfill her every want and desire.

Man, Framingham, MA: Women today think too much of themselves. I think that in bed women should not worry so much about their precious orgasms. If the man is good he'll take care of that. Most women I sleep with today seem to be so defensive on the subject that they forget the purpose of sex is to please the man too. In fact, I think if a woman really sets her sights to give the man total pleasure she will get the same in return, because he'll be so excited by it. Whatever happened to putting the man first?

Man, Louisville, KY: I can't exactly say all the things that make a woman a good lover, but the one for me that turns me on most is the idea that a woman is open and surrendering herself to me. The biggest excitement that was ever aroused in me was when this woman I had just met took me home and, after we were undressed, said to me: "I'll do anything in the world for you." I think most men would agree this is about one of the most exciting things a woman can say to a man.

A small but significant number of men claim intellectual compatibility as the preeminent characteristic for good love—once minds are in harmony, they claim, physical pleasures will follow:

Man, Armonk, NY: Since the majority of sexuality is mental, one would have to feel comfortable with their respective partner on an intellectual level. I have a saying that if you can mentally "fuck," everything else can blend together. In society today too much emphasis is placed on the physical rather than mental aspects of life. Don't people realize that it *is* one's mental attitude that decides how they will relate to a woman physically? Everything starts in the mind. If you are in love with a fat, ugly woman in your eyes she will be beautiful.

Women should be "inventive," "imaginative," and "uninhibited." This trio appears many times, often in the same sentence. "Routine" and "automatic" are dirty words. So are "passive" and "non-involved." Respondents commonly describe an ideal lover as one who "does not let me do all the work," or who "knows how to suggest new things." Most abhorred is the woman who is inactive during sex, who, as one man expresses it, is a "dead lay." "A real woman *participates* in the sex act," a respondent claims; "she doesn't lie back like a corpse and let me do everything. She realizes her participation is a source of great excitation for both of us, and that sex is a fifty-fifty deal."

Aside from the emphasis on physical needs, the requirements mentioned by men are not vastly different from those of women. Men ask their mates to be considerate, enjoy variation, be "willing to expose themselves emotionally," not be "in a hurry," to have "awareness of their partner's needs and feelings." The picture calls for a lover of technical skill, psychological sensitivity, passionate receptivity, and emotional depth. A few other excerpts from men's version of ideal lovers include the following:

"Uninhibited. Allows herself to follow her instincts. A good person without too many axes to grind, and without too much desire to castrate. Feminine without being silly about it, or too weak, childish, immature, etc."

"Tenderness is all important to me. She does not give me the impression that she is going to eat me alive or judge every little twist and thrust of my sexual performance."

"Is totally uninhibited. Gives great head! Lots of touching and constant attention to everything I say and do."

"Kind and respondent to your needs in bed. Yes, but would demand she be satisfied also. Empathetic, kind, respectful, womanly. Must be interesting, sense of humor. Beauty with stupidity is no good in bed or out of bed. She must be really *interested* in sex and not just do it out of a neurosis, to get something, etc."

"An ideal lover in bed is seductive and sexy—kissing, touching, caressing; not just passive. Out of bed she is trusting and communicating. The key to being a lover is love."

"Open-minded and willing to share fantasies. She is not afraid to talk about sex, nor does she become uptight when it is mentioned. She should not be worn out or laid a thousand times. I like a wholesome, unafraid outlook on sex by women."

Sexual Variations: What Singles Will and Will Not Do

17. *Once you have decided to have sex with a man/woman, which of the following would you generally refuse to do?*

Sex acts you would not indulge in: *(Circle as many answers as apply)*	*Men*	*Women*
a. Have oral sex	12%	20%
b. Show your body naked	3%	6%
c. Have sex with the lights on	7%	10%
d. Give vent to your full sexual feelings and instincts	10%	10%
e. Have anal sex	27%	56%
f. Tie up a partner or be tied up	48%	60%
g. I would do all of these	22%	8%
h. I would do none of these	6%	9%

These questions include a broad group of activities. Among neither sex are there many erotic practices that singles would *not* indulge in. Though still conservative, singles are at least theoretically open to sexual experimentation.

There are still, however, a sizable number of singles who would refuse to perform relatively conventional sexual acts. An aggregate 16 percent of women would object to having the lights on during intercourse or showing their body to a lover. "This reflects many women's attitude that 'sex is bad,' and that 'if I don't see what's going on then it's not going on,'" explains Dr. Sheila Jackman, Co-Director of the Division of Human Sexuality at Albert Einstein College of Medicine, Bronx, New York. "It's an unconscious but a very real problem. This attitude stems from an 'I don't like my body' problem. The most common reason for this is that many women believe they're too fat, too skinny, too lumpy, or have bad skin. They think that men are going to spend time studying their bodies. The reality is when men are enjoying sex no one stops to count pimples or notice how big breasts are. The partner is totally involved and couldn't care less."

Dr. Jackman offers several solutions for women bothered by poor body image.

"What I tell women to do is to place a red light bulb or perhaps several candles by their bed. Most women know their bodies look much softer and more appealing in candlelight, or under red light. The red light gives the body a whole different glow, and sets a mood. Women came back after doing this and say 'I can relax a little now. I don't feel like my body is under a microscope. This kind of light disguises the right things and enhances the right things.' It's also been a help for mastectomy patients.

"I have another technique I also recommend for the same problem. Many women are shy about revealing their genitals. It's one of the reasons a lot of them can't indulge in oral sex. What I tell them is to think about all the men's magazines that are published, and of the fact that men are spending *millions* to look at genitals. Rather than turn them off as most women think, genitals are usually a male turn-on."

The difficulties women experience about revealing their genitals brings to attention another alternative mentioned in question 16, that of oral sex. Considering the familiarity with which this is treated in sexual literature, it is perhaps unexpected to find that so many singles still refuse to indulge in it. Women who are most adamant are either very young, twenty to twenty-four, or older, forty-five to fifty-five. "In the first age bracket we are seeing youthful inexperience," says Dr.

Jackman. "In the second we probably have the carryover effect of the oral-genital sex taboo that was part of the sexual morality up to a few years ago."

Another response informs us that 10 percent of singles, men and women, would not *give vent to their full sexual feelings and instincts.* Once more we encounter a cardinal problem—fear of intimacy. "This fear stems from the feeling that 'I'm not going to let go because that would tell you who I really am and then I'd be too vulnerable,' " says Dr. Jackman. "This is based on the inability to be completely intimate. It represents fear of exposing ourselves, of losing control, fear that if you, my partner, find out my *real* secret, then you wouldn't love me anymore. If you found out how bad, or lustful, or sadistic, or foolish I really am, you would walk away. If a person, especially a woman, lets herself go and gives full vent to her sexuality, she feels that a man will judge her for it, that he will wonder where she learned such things. 'He'll think I'm promiscuous,' she says to herself, or 'He'll think I'm really a whore at heart.' People don't understand that all this exciting sexual stuff is in each of us *ready* to spew out, and that if we'd just relax we'd all learn how to learn what's in us already. It would come out naturally if we could get past the guilt, fear and self-doubt."

Singles' Sexual Fantasies as a Key to Singles' Sexual Experience

18. *What are your favorite sexual fantasies in masturbation and sexual intercourse? Please describe them in detail. What sexual acts and/or fantasies do you consider perverse?*

Approximately a fourth of the respondents reported that they neither fantasize nor masturbate. The other three fourths report a wide variety of erotic fantasies. As a general rule, men's fantasies include more forms of sexual variation than women's. They more commonly stress improbable sexual situations—wild scenes sometimes including "kink" or orgiastic encounters. Women's sexual fantasies are usually less lurid than men's. They tend to involve warm physical contact, petting, and straightforward sexual intercourse. Love is more often part of the fantasy for women than for men.

A representative sampling of fantasies include the following:

Woman: "Being hugged, kissed all over, stroked and loved by a wonderful man."

Man: "Having wild, free and euphoric love-making with a beautiful redhead. She places my thumb in her mouth and sucks on it, looking me straight in the eyes."

Woman: "I don't even think of direct love-making. I imagine being embraced and petted by various men I've liked and loved in the past. They whisper loving things to me. They hold and shelter me from the cruel world."

Man: "The woman is in a position on top. She is usually a blonde with long hair. I watch her breasts move up and down as we slide in and out. Sometimes I think of my girlfriend."

Woman: "The man is tall and rangy and he reaches out tenderly for me, but firmly and with passion. We embrace. The lights are very low and the room is filled with burning incense. We kiss through the night—we may or may not make love, depending on our mood."

Man: "A woman who I know I can trust and confide in. She wraps her legs around me tight as a vice-grip and squeezes as my juices come into her body. She wiggles around like a crazy woman while we fornicate wildly. She pants and sweats."

Woman: "I want a man who knows how to treat me like a woman, not too hard, not too soft, and who knows how to move when he's inside me. Give me a man who understands a woman's anatomy too. My fantasy man has taken a course at some fantasy school in how to please a woman sexually."

Man: "I am empowered with the ability to make love all night, and to have as many orgasms as I want. One after the other. The girl is beautiful, breathtaking body, honey lips, red cheeks, blonde hair in long braids. She is skilled at all the love-making arts and we make love for 24 hours straight, enjoying orgasm after orgasm. She makes love like a whore, and loves me like a mother."

There are numerous descriptions of more or less variant love-making.

Man: "Me a big brute but the woman clever, petite, yet the entire master of me. She subdues me physically and psychologically and makes me her slave. She carries a riding crop."

Woman: "Making love with rollerskates on, or while riding on a motorcycle. I also fantasize about making love with a weight-lifter doing bench presses."

Man: "Sex with another woman and another man. The woman I fuck while the man fucks me from behind. Then they reverse positions. A third woman strokes my forearms and nipples and a fourth sucks on the toes of my feet."

Woman: "Sex with a big black man who handles me roughly. He is an oriental slave from a harem who knows how to break a woman to his will but who also knows how to administer PLEASURE with his sexual skills."

Man: "I put a harness on my woman and ride her like a horse, dipping my spurs into her flanks while whipping her with a riding crop."

Woman: "Having sex with more than one man. Using objects inside of me like an artificial penis with feathers on the end. Letting semen get into my mouth and rubbing it over my body."

Man: "Tenderly spanking girls' bare asses. Just before sex, with her enjoying it. Beating a woman with a strap and her fingering herself while I do it. Thinking of innocent young girls reluctantly being forced into sex acts of all kinds."

Woman: "Having a complete full-course meal spread across my lover-partner, and myself devouring every piece of food while tasting his body at the same time."

Man: "I'm dreaming more of bondage lately—always with myself in charge of the situation. I've come to consider that pretty girls look prettier when tied, wrists crossed behind their backs or overhead—ensuring access to most tender spots, whether they are ticklish or not. Imagine a lady 15 years old stretched immobile on her bed, saying: 'I dare you . . .' and pretending she doesn't believe you will."

Women: "Being fettered while love is being made to me. Being blindfolded and kept immobile for long periods of time prior to intercourse."

The word "orgasm" appears more frequently in women's essays than men's. Many women talk of their climax as the crowning moment of their sexual fantasies, a reflection perhaps of the difficulty many women have in achieving orgasm.

Woman, Memphis, TN: In my fantasy my dream lover knows how to make me reach one unbelievable orgasm after the other, *ad infinitum.*

They come one after the other like waves on the sea. He is so skilled and good at love-making that he can bring me to orgasm with his tongue, his hips, his very look that burns into my soul!

Woman, Denver, CO: The most important part of the fantasy would be if the guy knew how to give me an orgasm. So far this kind of guy is just that, a fantasy!

Woman, Chicago, IL: "I see myself on the bed. A lean, marvelously formed man is on top of me. He is kissing my vagina, now he is licking it. I tighten all the muscles in my vagina and kind of force a wild tension in between my legs. His tongue moves faster and faster until *the* moment—when the stars and bombs explode and the whole world turns to color and inside me it's like an explosion."

Woman, Manhattan, NY: "I am masturbating alone in my bedroom. There is a knock at the door. Before I have time to get up the man is in my room, his finger to his lips. He assures me he is okay. He comforts me and takes me in his arms. Slowly he massages my hand with his over my vagina. I have the long-awaited orgasm that I have not had before. Then he leaves."

As part of their fantasy, men seem particularly fascinated by the notion of having sex with more than one woman at a time. At least one out of six or seven men speaks of it somewhere in his essay.

Man, San Antonio, TX: When I jack off I think mainly of getting it off with a bevy of show girls with long legs and long hair. They all crowd around me and I take care of them one after the other. I don't come in any of them, just keep on going down the lines satisfying one after the other. What a dream!

Man, Framingham, MA: When I do have fantasies, which is not that much, I think of sex with two girls at a time or of having a roomful of women I can choose from at random. Like Hefner's mansion in Chicago—girls all around and you can have your pick of who you want. They are all waiting and available. Free sex kind of thing. That appeals to me.

Also popular among men are artificial aids like dildos and vibrators. Women, on the other hand, are attracted to particular locales where the fantasy takes place—a cottage by the sea, for instance. Women also, as mentioned before, frequently require their fantasy to include some form of affection. Men are more prone to frame imaginary episodes in the context of a purely exotic and carnal encounter. Many male descriptions read like features from pornographic magazines.

Man, Hollywood, CA: Her two tits stick out like fleshy mountains against the horizon of her stomach. Her legs are long and perfectly formed; they wrap around me and squeeze while I shoot my hot gypsum into her waiting womanhood. "Fuck me! Fuck me!" she screams as we both writhe in an orgasmic explosion.

Here is a longer response that is particularly graphic:

Man: "Do you really want to know? Well, I'll tell you. It begins with a loud party in a smoked-filled room in NYC. I enter and someone hands me a joint. I take a short drag and pass it back. The scene is a total orgy, with men and women coupled up here and there, a couple of chicks strung up with ropes on either side of the room with a fat middle-aged faggot spanking them and forcing them to suck him, that kind of thing. Plenty of dope, of course. Music. Near the window a tall nonchalant woman is standing with black hair. She is involved in a conversation with a good friend of mine named Pete. I cross the room and encounter several party-goers in various stages of intoxication and undress. Stepping over my various friends, I meet Pete who introduces me to the raven-haired beauty— name of Carol. We find immediate rapport discussing the recorded works of Lou Reed. Anyone who can recite the words to 'Berlin' is an instant hit with me. The party swirls around us and we smoke a bit and drink a bit. She reveals that she has some psychedelic mushrooms and offers them. We divide up about 1½ grams each and we chew them and chase them with some freshly squeezed orange juice. In return I lead us to the bathroom where I set up 'the works,' a mirror, a razor blade and a blue plastic straw. Then I open up the glass vial containing the coke. I lay out six fat lines on the glass surface and hand the straw to Carol. She smiles and holding back her black hair, she snorts up a line. Then I do the same. We repeat until the glass is clear. She smiles broadly. It's been about 45 minutes since we chewed up, and the first tingles of the 'shrooms are mixing playfully with the coke buzz. 'Good coke,' she says. 'Great 'shrooms,' I reply. In a dreamy soft focus my enlarged head looms close to hers and we kiss very gently, very lightly. She runs her fingers lightly over my thighs and my crotch. I break out into a big smile. 'Let's get outside—I think someone wants to get in here to pee,' I say. We rejoin the party which due to the late hour and the chemicals racing through our bloodstreams, has become slightly surreal. Annie is dancing to some funky old Motown song, Stu is chugging a Guinness Stout, Carol and I smoke a bit more, but that is really unnecessary as the mushrooms have hit in full force and we are beyond the reach of the low-grade stimulants. The next hour is a blur of half-coherent conversation and loud music. Carol suggests a walk through the city streets to clear our fogged minds. We walk for a long time, sometimes laughing and speaking, but more often silent. We take another turn and find ourselves two blocks from Carol's apartment. She invites me in and once there we explore the domain of pure physical pleasure. With shudders of ecstasy we make love rubbing cocaine on vital spots such as cock, clitoris and nipples, then we take turns licking it off. We each climax several times in the pre-dawn New York City night with little variation in technique. The 'shrooms heighten our responses to the point of painful pleasure. I shoot semen on her breasts and she coos softly as I lick it off. We stop occasionally to snort some more coke. She devours my cock in her mouth, skillfully draining me. I get her screaming and leaping off the bed with a vibrator. As the sky begins to lighten and the first sounds of the city coming awake around us, we cuddle against each other and fall fast asleep."

Essays from men tend to involve a great deal of descriptive and visual data: The length of hair, the build, the shape of the breasts and so forth. Women are more inclined to speak of how the experience *feels*.

Man, San Diego, CA: I fantasize about sleeping with a beautiful tall Amazonian kind of woman like Irish McCalla who used to play *Sheena of the Jungle*. I think of her with green eyes, a few cute little freckles, very thin and wiry. She is very strong and lithe.

Woman, Sacramento, CA: We make love dreamily in the afternoon. I often have this fantasy and it is accompanied by a lazy kind of feeling. We both are happily exhausted and hold each other tightly. This man is warm and loving; he knows and understands my every thought. We make slow, slow, slow wonderful love and I feel like I am drifting away to the Promised Land. My whole body is softly on fire. We hold each other fondly and with tenderness. I feel alive and complete inside.

Women seem less willing than men to put their fantasies down on paper. The number of essays on the subject received from men is far in excess of those provided by women, and they are usually more detailed and revealing.

One of the predominant fantasies women do report, however, is that of being helpless or "taken advantage of." Women often talk about being used or abused against their will, of being forced into intercourse. Violent as these descriptions often are, they are usually qualified by the fact that the woman receives pleasure and even ecstasy from the aggressive act.

Woman, St. Louis, MO: I am held at gunpoint by a man with a mask. He makes me disrobe and forces me down on the bed. He pins my arms and I can't move while he makes love to me. Then another man takes his place and makes love to me again. Each time I have an orgasm with the man.

Woman, Seattle, WA: It's a dark night and I am walking home in the rain. I meet a dark stranger who invites me to his house. There he forces me to undress in front of him and then he uses me for his pleasure. Each time we make love he holds a gun at my temple. After a while I surrender and we make incredible sexual love together on the floor. Then he gets up and leaves. I dress and leave too and that's all. Until it happens again.

Woman, Newark, NJ: One fantasy is that I am a princess held for ransom by an older man in a castle. He comes in nightly and rapes me. He is very large and strong, and forces me to perform all kinds of sexual acts for him. I can in no way resist and am a helpless captive. Meanwhile my father is trying to get the ransom to free me from the castle. But he is a poor peasant and so far is not able to get the money. He is appealing to a knight to get the money and save me from the man. Sometimes the knight tries to save me when my older captor rapes me, but the older captor always beats him at the joust and the young knight is driven away until his next rescue attempt. Sometimes the older man rapes me in a chair. We do it in a large tub sometimes, and he submerges me for long periods of time against my will while we have sex. Or he makes me perform oral sex on him at knifepoint. I have many variations of this fantasy and have had it since I was a child.

"There are several interpretations about why women tend to have so many fantasies about being 'taken advantage of,'" says Dr. Seymour Fisher, Professor of Psychology, Department of Psychiatry at the State University of New York State Medical Center in Syracuse, New York. "No one really knows what causes them or why they are so popular. One interpretation is that there is so much guilt over having sex, especially in our society, that women tend to fantasize about its being done to them against their will. In this way it's not their fault. They don't have to feel guilty about it. Another interpretation is that women are taught a sort of masochistic role. They are taught to take blame, to assume that if something goes wrong it's their fault. A lot of women are socialized in this way. Thus in the sexual role it becomes a woman's part to be hurt, to be attacked. They must be the passive recipients of male aggressive and sometimes violent attentions. Hence the rape fantasies. It's one of *the* most common fantasies in women and is certainly *not* pathological. As a matter of fact, there are few fantasies I would actually term pathological. Some people enjoy or need fantasies even during intercourse, and that's fine. Men seem to need them more than women, but both have them."

As part of this same question on fantasy, we asked singles what sexual acts they consider perverse. Leading the list were the hard-core sadistic practices, bestiality, and any sexual act in which one of the partners is non-consenting. Fecal and urinary sexual acts are also thought to be perverse. Representative replies:

Woman: "Rape, engaging in sexual activities which you know won't be pleasing, anal sex (because it would hurt). Sex that has anything to do with children. And involvement with excreta of any kind."

Man: "Any sex that causes pain or injury, or adverse emotional trauma."

Woman: "Animals, dogs, gang rapes, sodomy, sex that is forced, chains, whips, ropes, gags, anal sex."

Woman: "My list would start off with sodomy. Other inclusions are group masturbation and group sex, and anal sex, heavy S&M, and sex in unusual places like the john or back of a bus or plane. I could never have sex with more than one person. Wouldn't want to spank or be spanked. Most sex is perverse, I feel, that does not lead to regular intercourse."

19. *What sexual variations, if any, do you indulge in?*

Because of growing insistence that the bedroom is a place where one invites neither preacher nor policeman, many erotic acts once considered perverse have risen in respectability; and today, as our survey shows, while most of these variations are still far from acceptable to the majority, they are *less* unacceptable than ever before, at least within the singles community.

Recently a new word has even been coined to describe these peripheral sex practices, which stand between the deviant and the normal. The word is "kink," and it can describe anything from nipple rouging, body painting, pornography, use of dildos and vibrators to voyeurism, anal sex, bondage, group sex, swinging, spanking, light S&M, and even further out activities. As can be seen from the answers below to question 19, kink—along with more standard sexual variations such as homosexuality—is not unanimously taboo among singles, but neither is it widely embraced:

Sexual variation indulged in	Men	Women
1. Homosexuality	3%	2%
2. Bisexuality	6%	3%
3. Group sex	11%	5%
4. Voyeurism	8%	3%
5. Bondage	5%	3%
6. S&M	2%	1%
7. Other	4%	1%

The placement of homosexuality under the category of sexual variation does not imply a value judgment but simply a statistical statement of fact. Though in some cities homosexuals account for a sizable part of the population, numerically speaking homosexuals still constitute a very small portion of the singles population, and homosexuals still remain a minority within the mainstream of American sexuality.

As to the question of bisexuality, we stand on less firm ground. Is a heterosexual man or woman with one or two homosexual encounters a bisexual? What about three or four? Five or six? How does one draw the line, especially when those in question are themselves unsure of where they stand?

Dr. Fred Klein is a psychiatrist in private practice in New York and author of the book *The Bisexual Option: A Concept of 100-Percent Intimacy.** In his dealings with patients and in his work as Director of the Institute of Sexual Behavior in New York City, he has observed bisexuality close up. He defines a bisexual as "a person who has sexual feelings, or experiences sexual behavior, for members of both sexes."

According to Dr. Klein, society has several fundamental misapprehensions about bisexuality. "The first is that the bisexual does not exist

* Arbor House, 1978.

at all, that a bisexual is really a homosexual. This is a very big misconception. Bisexuals are by no means homosexuals in disguise. The fact is that there is a category of men and women who receive genuine sexual satisfaction from contact with both sexes.

BONUS FINDINGS

- The longer a man is single, the greater the chances he will turn to bisexuality. However, the *older* a man gets, the less likely he is to become a confirmed homosexual.
- Men divorced twice or more are twice as apt to indulge in *group sex* as men divorced only once.
- Almost half of the lesbian population reports indulging in *group sex.* One out of five lesbians reports indulging in *voyeurism,* and almost a third report indulging in *bondage.* Among gay men, 30 percent report indulging in *group sex,* 30 percent say they have practiced *voyeurism,* and 7 percent have indulged in bondage.
- Twice as many men in their middle thirties indulge in *voyeurism* as do men in their early twenties.
- Practically *no* women over forty-five report indulging in *group sex.* Twice the number of higher-income women indulge in *group sex* as do lower-income women.
- If a woman is going to indulge in *any* sort of sexual variation, she usually does so in her middle twenties and early thirties. After thirty-five, female involvement in sexual variations diminishes significantly.
- Men divorced two times are more likely to indulge in *all* the sexual variations mentioned than any other status group.
- Bisexuality is highest among female students. Bisexuality among singles tends to show itself early—or not at all.

"The second myth is that if the bisexual does exist, he or she is by definition neurotic, sex-crazy, can't love deeply, can't make up his or her mind, is confused. Bisexuality *per se,* however, is not neurotic, and the same thing is true of homosexuals and heterosexuals. We have very neurotic heterosexuals and homosexuals, and we have very healthy ones."

What then about bisexuals as mates, even husbands and wives? "I would say it depends on how strong a person's attraction is toward members of his or her own sex. A man who dates only to fulfill the obligations of society and is predominantly homosexual is a horrible marriage or partnership risk. On the other hand, if he desires to have a family, to love a woman, if he is attracted to women, I believe that, despite his attraction to other men, he is still a good marriage risk. Of course you might ask 'How is a woman to know?' And all I can say is: How do you know if *anyone* is a good long-term risk? It depends on what the person does and says, how deeply she or he feels—the same as in any situation."

The next question will deepen our understanding of those who indulge in variant forms of sexuality.

20. *If you indulge in any sexual variation such as group sex, voyeurism (watching others have sex), bondage (tying or being tied up), S&M (giving or receiving pain), or any other, please tell about your involvements. Where do you contact partners? What takes place, and where? Please describe your feelings about the experience.*

Man, Syracuse, NY: I've enjoyed two group sex situations. Each of them I was with two lovers, one a woman I was carrying on a rather torrid affair with, the other an old friend. Two of us more or less seduced the third who was in the end an eager volunteer. We made love for easily four hours, and I was delighted about the sharing and openness we had together. Two features stand out in my memory (which was moderately clouded by the use of "controlled substances"): several times I found myself thinking that I was touching in some caring fashion one person and finding that it surprisingly was the other; and that it gave me a special good feeling to find how much delight the two women took in each other. This happened recently and the three of us intend to have many repeat performances. I would also like to try a foursome.

Woman, Louisville, KY: I have watched an orgy several times and participated. I was once at a very rich man's home where he had over 75 people involved in an orgy with free coke, pot, acid, mushrooms, poppers, everything you could imagine. The only thing that he didn't serve was liquor (he was a teetotaller). There was practically every kind of sex thing taking place. A woman was up in a tree and a man was on the ground trying to hit her with a long whip. People were standing around naked watching this. Love-making couples were around every part of the large house and a few were outside in the garden. There was loud rock music always playing. A man was riding a woman with a saddle on her, and then she rode him. There were other things too like a naked homosexual wrestling match. The master of ceremonies, the rich man, was a kind of gentleman type who was prominent in the business world. The word is on him he keeps women and several men on tap all the time at his mansion.

One of the alternate forms of sexuality most often mentioned is bondage. Figures from multiple choice question 19 show that 5 percent of men and 3 percent of women have actually indulged in this activity. Often associated with sado-masochistic practices, afficionados claim bondage to be a separate and—if practiced properly—safe sex game. Some agree with this assessment, some do not.

Man, Wilmington, DE: I've experienced bondage only once but it was with a woman I liked very much. The concept excited me, though in anticipation I had fears of freaking out in panic over what such a severe denial of freedom of movement would entail. Owing to the artificiality of our mechanical circumstances, there was an unduly heavy distinction between planning and execution, though we bludgeoned through it and humor prevailed. Since my lover had experience in bondage I was tied up first and she made magnificent love to me. To my surprise, I felt none of the fears I anticipated but a considerable amount of medium-level warmth and joy. However, the last 45 seconds before orgasm my entire body and soul were blindingly involved, and clearly the excitement was enhanced by the constraints on my limbs. In retrospect, perhaps it would have been better for my lover to be the first to be placed in bondage. In any event, it was a total delight to make love to her then tied up, though I found myself slipping into some of the standard nice things we do with each other. In a way it seems that bondage amplifies the excellent, but I sense that overdoing it would become counter-productive. In any event, a trusting, caring, rational lover would seem to be a necessary precondition for paranoid-free exercises in bondage.

Woman, Philadelphia, PA: I have participated in bondage. My partner was a single man I'd been dating for six months. He tied me up and tied me down to the bed. He rubbed my body with cooking oil, then squirted whipped cream all over me and licked it off. He tied me too tight and it cut the circulation in my wrists. As I was gagged, I couldn't say anything and he was so engrossed in his sex that he didn't seem to notice *me* anyway—I was worried about him for a couple of minutes when he seemed to be getting too rough. It was a painful experience. I'm somewhat glad I did it for experience but wouldn't do it again, or any of the far out things you mention again, unless the man was extremely gentle and understanding. Even then it's tricky, because if the guy is hung up on tying women then even a nice guy can get a little crazy when he's all sexed up.

"In every culture," remarks Dr. Fred Klein, "dominating or being dominated is an important aspect of relationships. And sexual relationships especially lend themselves to this interplay. In a sense it doesn't matter whether one person subdues the other with ropes, chains, or commands. The point is we are talking about power—submission and domination. And don't make the mistake that only men tie women up. A lot of times it's the other way around, men want to be tied up. In their daily lives men have more power than women, and they have control over women. But when it comes to a personal sexual relationship somehow or other it gives them a sexual thrill to be controlled, utterly and entirely controlled, by those they ordinarily have power over. It's almost as if they secretly don't want this power at all, and in the bedroom they can let go and give in.

"Bondage is as safe as the people participating in it," Dr. Klein tells us. "The act itself can be pure play or it can be pure pathology. It depends on the players. If for instance a couple willingly play-act at this game of bondage, and one of them is the dominant and the other is the submissive partner, as long as it gives them both enjoyment and they are able to realize that it *is* a play and a form of increased eroticism, I don't think there is anything wrong with it. Just watch out for danger signs. If anyone seems to be getting hurt or abused that's the sign that it's gone from erotic game to pathology."

Doctors Fisher and Jackson bring up the question of normal versus sick sexuality. The line is sometimes a hazy one, though not always. No respondents, for instance, mentioned engaging in fecal practices, child molestation, or the cutting or maiming of another human being.

We may assume that these and kindred practices belong to only an insignificant percentage of the singles population. At the same time, singles often mention sexual activities they personally consider to be psychopathic (we have read some in the previous section on fantasy), while others debate the question of what makes an act perverse:

Man, Los Angeles, CA: I consider myself fairly liberal about sexual matters. As far as the kinky kind of stuff you mention, it's all right in its rightful position. Stuff like anal sex, oral sex (yes, yes!), making a lot of noise when you fuck, rubbing jelly or chocolate sauce over the genitals and licking it off, weird sex positions, sex games, vibrators, watching X-rated movies together, is all great thinking. Orgies, though (I've been to one), are loveless and embarrassed events. Homosexuality is all right for the gays but not me, no—the trouble is once you start you can never return. I've seen it happen many times, the guy experiments and ends up being hooked on being gay. Bondage is something for you if you're not crazy. But can you really trust a person with ropes and gags and chains? The heavy scenes with those things are really sick in my notion.

Woman, Falmouth, MA: I would only indulge in a few things that others consider sick like oral sex, anal sex and maybe light bondage. This guy I know from Texas once told me about his experiences with group sex, and though he enjoyed it the description sounded like all the people there were emotional cripples. Which leads me to my point: the reason I would be so careful with sexual alternatives is because I think that the bottom line here is emotion, feeling; if sexual acts are based on aggression, hate, destruction, or even on domination and submission, then something important is missing. It doesn't have to be deep love that is present, but feelings must be there, and not just feelings of lust and anger. Perversion is any sexual act that is not based on mutual caring and concern.

"If psychological or physical damage is being done," says Dr. Jackman, "if somehow children are included, if people are involved who are not willing, then in my professional opinion this is pathological."

"During the years I've been a sex therapist," adds Dr. Klein, "I've come to the conclusion that people in general will consider any action or behavior that is different from their own as neurotic or pathological. What *they* like is of course perfectly fine. If they are voyeurs, voyeurism is fine. If they like group sex or S&M, then these are normal in their eyes. But just let a person *not* practice any of these and they are quick to label it 'sick.' "

Nonetheless, Dr. Klein does not believe the question of sexual pathology is entirely relative. "It all depends on the person. Say you have a voyeur, a man who likes to watch women get undressed. If he has a compulsion to do it, if he *must* do it every night, if he finds it difficult to function without it or to have normal sexual intercourse without such visual stimulation, I would say he is approaching pathology. The obsessive quality is a good way of measuring these things. But there is another way that is more important—intent. This is the real point I want to impress, that society should not necessarily label voyeurs pathological, or bisexuals pathological, or those practicing bondage pathological. What they categorically *should* label pathological is violence. When someone is hurt in a sexual act, when pain is inflicted and partners are unwilling, then that kind of practice is clearly beyond the bounds."

Leaving behind these alternate forms of sexuality, we return to the mainstream of singles' sexual practices and expectations.

SKILL AT SEX: SINGLES JUDGE SINGLES

21. *On the whole, how skilled have you found single men/women to be at making love?*	Men	Women
a. Skilled, imaginative, and caring	33%	31%
b. Mechanical, without much emotion	6%	9%
c. Repressed, afraid to really let go and enjoy	18%	7%
d. Anxious to please themselves but inattentive to a partner's needs	7%	21%
e. Only adequate	27%	18%
f. Unimaginative, habitual	4%	4%
g. Animalistic, harsh, sometimes cruel, inadequate	2%	1%
h. Don't know	3%	9%

Major Finding: Only about one third of men and women rate their lovers as skilled, imaginative, and caring.

BONUS FINDINGS

- The longer a man remains single the *less* likely he is to feel that a woman is skilled, imaginative and caring when making love.
- Men who are living with a woman are the *most* likely to view women as good lovers.
- One out of five men between the ages of twenty and forty-four feels that a majority of women he sleeps with are repressed and afraid to really let go. Only 10 percent of men in their late forties and early fifties feel the same way.
- Almost 40 percent of women in the thirty-five-to-forty-four-year-old range find their lovers to be *skilled and caring.* Only 21 percent of women in their late forties agree.
- The more money a woman makes the more she is inclined to say her lovers are *mechanical* and *without much emotion.* Women in white-collar jobs are the *most* likely to view men in this way, women in blue-collar jobs are the least likely.
- The older a woman gets the more likely she is to view a man's lovemaking as *unimaginative and habitual.*
- Low-income women tend to see men as anxious to please only themselves in a sexual affair.

Again we touch on the indictment that the sexes level so frequently against each other. Women are too passive, repressed, unimaginative, and uninterested, say men. Men are emotionally walled-in, selfish, hasty, eager for their own orgasm at the expense of the woman's fulfillment, counter women.

"As far as women go," comments Dr. Sandra Risa Leiblum, Associate Professor of Psychiatry and Director of the Sexual Counseling Service at the College of Medicine and Dentistry at Rutgers Medical School in New Jersey, "I think they frequently are leery of initiating different kinds of sexual activity from fear of appearing too knowledgeable or forward. It might cause a man to judge them as 'loose' or 'promiscuous,' some women reason."

In the opinion of Dr. Leiblum, the important thing for a woman is to understand her own responsiveness. "A lot of women assume that the man will arouse them and that somehow the right technique and method will magically be used. As a result, they offer the man little direct suggestion or advice. As women become better informed about their own ability to be aroused through reading sex manuals and other information, they should share this knowledge with the man. The man will feel like a good lover if he can be the instrument of exciting the woman. Women have a lot of information about their own sexuality but there is a discrepancy between what they know and what they will do. Though the woman's impulse may be to say nothing, it is better for both of them if she learns to tell the truth about how she feels and what she really wants. Women must know their needs and be willing to express them in a non-demanding and non-hostile way."

"Women are most interested in a loving relationship—everything follows from that," remarks Dr. Eli Feldman, psychologist and marriage counselor in Great Neck, Long Island, and author of *Peak Sex*.* "Women will hold back as long as they feel something is missing in the emotional relationship. They can only open up and, as you say, 'let go,' after they've first opened their hearts. This is not generally true of men.

"As to what makes a man a good lover," adds Dr. Feldman, "one of the biggest factors is *responsiveness.* By responsive I mean that the person responds to the *feelings* and *fantasies* of the partner. There does not have to be any verbal disclosure. One partner just feels the other's needs and reacts. If the woman has a romantic feeling, a secret wish, a need, and the man tunes into this, he opens the door for her and she melts. It's like finding the right key for the right lock. In *Peak Sex* we found to our surprise after interviewing a great number of people that the greatest sexual experience many people have ever had did not necessarily involve *intercourse.* I began to realize then that great sexual experiences are *experiences.* They are not performances. If you interview a group of women they'll tell you they don't really care *how* the man does it. They'll tell you they want something unusual to happen. They want a fantasy fulfilled. A surprise. The unexpected. A dream. An emotional experience. There's a man I'm working with now who is almost impotent. But he's been going out with many women who consider him a superb lover—because they have a great experience with him each time they're in his company. So you see, good love-making does not depend on biological skills. It depends on feelings, atmosphere, fantasy, and surprise."

Some 27 percent of men and 18 percent of women find their erotic partners only *adequate.* Interestingly, the positive assessment is a correlate of age and experience: the older a man and woman get the more

* Fawcett/World, 1976.

both tend to find their lovers *skilled, imaginative,* and *caring,* or at least *adequate.* Appreciation of lovers also increases with the number of times one has been married. Finally, the *least* satisfied among the different groups are the young, and especially those still in college or just starting out in their careers.

In other words, it seems clear that sexual satisfaction is a direct result of many years and many encounters: The wider one's range of contacts and sexual experiences, the greater one's chance of finding a pleasing lover.

What can be done to help men and women satisfy and excite each other more? "Men and women must become sexually educated," says Dr. Leiblum. "If a man hasn't read or learned about sex, then he may just want to have his orgasm and that's that. For a long time this was the attitude of many men.

"Education leads to experimenting with sexual technique. Men should heed their partner's verbal and non-verbal expressions and should not act simply on the basis of what they *think* or hope their partner likes. A lot of men assume that if they find one way that works to stimulate their partner, it will work every time, but that's not so. Nor will it work on every partner. Repetition in any activity becomes dull.

"Furthermore, there is the question of direct stimulation of the woman. I use the term 'over-vigorous clitoral stimulation.' The clitoris is an extremely sensitive organ. Too much stimulation becomes painful for a woman and turns off sensitivity and arousal. Men don't always know this.

"In this case the woman *must* say something. It doesn't have to be verbal. Showing the man where and how she wants to be touched by just taking his hand is all right. The clitoris has many thousands of sensitive erotic nerve endings, but direct stimulation along the shaft and glans is much more pleasurable to a woman then direct pressure on the head.

"Another thing about women's sexuality that all men should know: Women do not want a quick and mechanical roll in the hay. Women value stage setting. I do many workshops with women every year, and when I ask them to write a sexual script they always place an incredible emphasis on props, on a sensual environment—satins, silk, lace, fireplace, ocean, candlelight, wine, texture. Women grow up with this kind of romance—gazing into each other's eyes, the surrounding atmosphere, things like that. Men's masturbation fantasies, on the other hand, are more explicitly genital. Men should be aware that the place where sex occurs and the atmosphere the man is able to create go a long way toward arousing the woman. Finally, creativity in altering the time, the place, the when, how, and who-does-what of love-making can make for better lovers."

22. *How do you view yourself as a lover?*

As a check on the previous question we asked singles how they view their own sexual skill and expertise. Here's what they told us:

- Thirty-eight percent of men and 41 percent of women rank themselves as *very good lovers.*
- Thirty-one percent of men and 25 percent of women say they are *better with some men/women than with others.*
- Fifteen percent of men and half this number of women say they are *good on technique* but that they *avoid emotional involvement.* Five percent of men and 7 percent of women classed themselves as *inexperienced,* and another 6 percent men and 15 percent women said they were afraid to really break loose. Less than 2 percent of men and women believed they were *not entirely satisfying to my partners.* Finally, 2 percent of men and 1 percent of women say they thought they were *unusual and offbeat,* and 1 percent of men and 2 percent of women said they didn't know what sort of lovers they were.

Here is a curious paradox. We saw in the previous question that approximately half of single men and women express sexual dissatisfaction with a majority of their partners. Yet only two out of a hundred consider their *own* technique unsatisfying. Though many respondents qualified their confidence, totally negative self-judgments account for only a minor percent of singles, a fact that certainly says a good deal for the sexual self-image of the average single man and woman. Despite the many sexual doubts, insecurities, and question marks that appear throughout the survey, the single person ultimately considers herself or himself an adequate lover.

The majority who judge themselves good lovers are primarily the younger respondents. In fact, there is a definite cut-off point at forty-five. Past that age, one's estimation of one's sexual powers drops noticeably. Till this age, men and women share a positive attitude toward their sexual ability. As soon as the forty-five-year-old line is crossed, sexual self-image goes on the wane—and never regains its former standing.

BONUS FINDINGS

- Men who have been divorced twice are more likely to view themselves as *very good* lovers than men who have been divorced once. Many divorced men claim they are good on technique but try to avoid emotional involvement.
- The man living with a lover perceives himself to be a better lover than the man who lives with his family.
- Men with high incomes and college educations see themselves as better lovers than men with low incomes and a high-school education.
- Compared with college graduates, twice as many men with a high-school-only education say they are good on sexual technique but avoid emotional involvement.
- Forty percent of men from age twenty to forty-four rate themselves as *very good* lovers. From age forty-five on, however, only 33 percent put themselves in this category.
- Women who live with their family are more afraid to really break loose sexually than women who live alone or with a partner.
- Sixty-three percent of all high-wage-earning women view themselves as *very good* lovers. Only 38 percent of women in the low-income category make this same claim.
- Women view themselves at their sexual peak during their middle thirties. Younger women are much less likely to view themselves as good lovers.

PROFILE: The man who most commonly considers himself a good lover.

PROFILE SUMMARY: He has been divorced, probably twice. He can be any age from twenty to forty-four and is a high-wage-earner. He has a college education and is more or less committed to single life, having been unmarried now from three to ten years (and much longer if he was divorced at an early age). He is likely to live with a woman or by himself.

PROFILE: The woman who most commonly considers herself a good lover.

> PROFILE SUMMARY: She is very similar to her male counterpart. Like him, she has probably been divorced several times, has been single from three to ten years, is college educated, and most likely lives with a member of the opposite sex. She may hold either a professional or a white-collar job, and is well situated in the high-wage-earning range. She is also twice as likely to consider herself sexually competent as women in the lower-salaried jobs.

Once again, education, money and the privileges of the good life add up to sexual contentment. Or at least to sexual self-contentment.

23. *How has your sex life been as a single?*

- Thirty-nine percent of single men say their sex life is *good.* Fifteen percent say it is *better than married sex.*
- However, 21 percent term it *more exciting but ultimately less fulfilling than married sex.* Twelve percent call it *unsatisfactory.* And 6 percent say it is *inferior to married sex.* Finally, 8 percent say married sex and single sex are about the same.

Basically a positive, though not a completely delighted estimation. Women were slightly less enthusiastic:

- A quarter of single women (as opposed to 39 percent of single men) say their sex life is *good.* Sixteen percent say single sex is *better than married sex.*
- A quarter of women say sex is *more exciting but ultimately less fulfilling than married sex.* Some 7 percent say it is *unsatisfactory.* And one out of ten says it is *inferior to married sex.*
- Ten percent of women feel that it's the same as married sex, and 7 percent of women just don't know.

A few observations. Almost three-quarters of the women who have never married say their sex life is good. If they have been divorced once or more, they view it as far less satisfactory: Only 2 percent of female divorcees praise their sex lives.

The same goes for men. Again, we found that almost three-quarters of the men who have not married said their sex lives were good. As with the women, once they have been divorced, only 7 percent make the same claim. (This may account for the fact that statistically, divorced men tend to remarry within two years after divorce, and divorced women after three.)

Singles who live with a member of the opposite sex judge sex more positively than those who live alone, an interesting insight into the relative merits of casual and committed sex.

Finally, singles' enjoyment of sex drops radically as age increases. Seventy percent of men from twenty to twenty-four say their sex life is great. Forty-five percent in the twenty-five-to-thirty-four-year bracket make the same claim. During the late thirties and early forties only 20 percent say so. And a remarkably diminished 8 percent of men over age forty-five consider their sexual lives in a positive light.

Among women the dip is as precipitous and begins even earlier. Sixty-eight percent of women in their early twenties say sex is good. Only 29 percent in their late twenties and early thirties repeat this judgment. Among those aged thirty-five to forty-four, an astonishingly low 6 percent rank their sex life as good, and those over forty-five rate it even lower (3 percent).

To gain insight into why older singles are negative about their sexual life, we turn to answers from the following question:

24. *Have your feelings about sex changed over the past several years? Why? Do you find it as interesting and important as ever? Are you more adventurous about sex or have you become more conservative? Why?*

Perhaps the most important disclosure is that sexual life does not necessarily become more unpleasant as a single ages, but that it becomes less important, less a burning issue, less a focus of absorbed attention. The following responses are from singles in their thirties and forties.

Woman, Little Rock, AR: The way being single has changed the most for me is that I have relaxed more about the boy-girl part of it, and basically just don't give that fat a shit over whether or not I have a date, who I go out with, who I will sleep with. I have been single all my life and at one time that was the most important thing in the world to me. With age comes wisdom, I guess.

Man, Denver, CO: After being divorced many years with no marriage prospects in sight, the singles life seems bland and day-to-day. The original frenzy of chasing women has subsided. You have sex for the hundredth time and you realize it's just another thing, not that great. I feel like I've grown up a great deal by being single and alone, and one of these ways is to understand that sex is just a part of life and not even that big a part of it.

Woman, Sacramento, CA: After my divorce five years ago I was fairly free sexually mainly due to not being able to say "no" to anyone. I have since become more independent, less afraid of being rejected, and am enjoying sex more on account of it. I am less adventurous now with a stranger, more adventurous with a person I know well. I care less about sex now and more about being in love and being cared for. Sex and love are not the same no matter what people say. Being single these years has let me know that.

The essays divided into three categories. Those in the first group claim their feelings on sex have not significantly changed.

Woman, Baton Rouge, LA: Basically been the same over the past seven years. Enjoying dating as much, sleeping with a man I really like. Nothing too important that seems different.

Man, Albany, NY: My feelings haven't changed because of my personal influence and belief. Sex is always interesting—but only with the right person, a lawful wife. I have always felt this way; I always will.

Those in the second category feel that sex has become more of a gratification and adventure during their single years. Most in this group insist that this change has come about due to increased discrimination and sophistication in sexual matters. The essays emphasize the fact that sex, while becoming more of a pleasure, is simultaneously less important in their day-to-day existence. Most of the essays from older singles fall into this category:

Woman, Omaha, NB: I enjoy sex more now than I did when I was younger. I am more picky and choosy, and I don't let myself get used the way I used to. I can spot a louse a mile away. I know his smell. I don't swallow lines the way I did and I don't fall into bed with the traveling salesman. Sex really is no big deal anymore and I don't pay that much attention to the glamour hype that drives other women by the nose. I know what I like, what I want, how I want it—I feel good about myself, and I think a lot of women are feeling good about themselves—after having paid their dues.

Man, Birmingham, AL: Sex just keeps getting better and better as I get wiser and wiser. The more I learn 1) about what kind of woman I like and what kind I don't like; 2) the better I get at sexual technique, and the more I learn how to make truly caring and careful love; 3) the more I learn about women; 4) the more I learn about myself—the more wise I get in these fields, the better sex gets. In my early days screwing everything in sight diluted the pleasure. It was quantity but no quality. Now that I know who I am, I understand that quality is ALL and quantity means nothing. I have changed in that I make love better and I make love less.

Man, Jersey City, NJ: My feelings about sex have changed over the years. While married to my wife we had sex nearly every night of our twelve-year marriage. I found this very demanding on me and no doubt on her. I didn't talk to her about how the frequency was so draining and I couldn't talk to anyone else about it. I assumed that this sex was a duty or requirement for a healthy, happy marriage. After a while I used to become relieved when she would fall asleep on the couch while watching TV, and I would find excuses not to go to bed at the same time with her. It was not until we separated and I was going to counseling that I learned our sexual frequency was abnormal. Today I find sex more interesting and fulfilling. I have attended courses, labs, symposiums on sex. I have experimented with different partners. The outcome being, I am much more relaxed and open about discussing sex, and I know who I want to sleep with and who I don't.

Man, Ann Arbor, MI: While in college going out meant a beautiful girl, a bottle of champagne, and good music. Without any consideration towards emotional understanding. But today at the age of thirty-nine, I look for something more in a woman than just 36-24-36, i.e., a sense of humor, intelligence, imagination. I have lost the adventurous spirit of the playboy— good riddance! Today I have become very careful about the women I go out with and it's better this way.

Woman, Taos, NM: Sex is more important to me now. On the other side, I have become more conservative over *who* I have sex with. My tastes are sharper in what I like done to me by a man. My vagina seems more sensitive. This works both ways though, because I can't have vulgar, one-night stands anymore as I did occasionally when I was in college. They give me bad vibes. I want sex only with someone I care for and have a special feeling towards.

In the final category, accounting for about a third of the singles and including many older respondents, the essays report increased conservatism and skepticism about sex. This stems from emotional and sometimes physical injuries suffered during sexual encounters:

Woman, Troy, NY: My feelings have changed because of experiences with immature people and therefore a need to be more cautious about whose company I keep. My early sexual experiences included the follow:

- A man who beat me up and robbed me in a motel;
- A string of men who just used my body and left me;
- Two rapes;
- A man I loved deeply who ended up trying to kill himself and turning to use of dope.

After undergoing these things, I have become very unsure about my feelings for men. Don't get me wrong, I still like sex, but I only get involved now with a very special man (who is a rare thing). And only once in a while.

Woman, San Francisco, CA: My feelings about the "glamour" of single life are bitter. Too many innocent people have been hurt. I think it's all a false, insecure mask for immaturity and irresponsibility. All the sex is just a come-on. I rationalized my personal convictions and made excuses inside of me in order to please a selfish, insensitive lover. Now four years later, with plans of marriage within a year, I'm so glad to be getting away from the sexual animal rat-race.

Man, Jersey City, NJ: My attitude towards sex has become more dubious as I grow older and older. I have "O.D." written all over my sexual tombstone. After so many years of following the crowd and laying anything with two feet, I finally wised up and realized I was being used by dark forces for their own particular purposes. Sex is one of the devil's greatest tools if it is used in an incorrect way. If in a correct way it can be sublime. If incorrect, as today, as I observe all around me in this corrupt society, it becomes a way of making people lose all the things that should be important to them—deep caring, love of family, resoluteness, fidelity, stick-to-itness. My attitude towards sex is to realize that it is far more dangerous a thing than anyone ever told me, like a dangerous weapon handed to children. It can ruin you in a subtle way if it is misused, just as it can make you strong when used rightly. I sound old fashioned. But isn't it one of the devil's greatest ploys to make things that are good and wholesome seem "old fashioned," so that we will be thoroughly "modern" and keep up with the sexual Joneses? The things that people follow as fashion are what lead them astray. Sexual fashions say one should sleep around, not commit yourself, get into every kind of perversion. When young I believed this. Now I understand how terribly destructive this can become.

Man, Biloxi, MS: When I was a teen-ager I was "adopted" by an older, attractive woman. As it turned out, what she really wanted was a stud. She made me into her sexual servant. I was young, muscular, good-looking then, and I was just what she was looking for. To the neighbors we were just a happy family, the two of us. Inside I was her slave. She would force me to sleep with her every night, and she would take away my allowance if I didn't prolong her pleasures, sometimes for several hours. At school I was never allowed to have girlfriends, even though I was good looking and plenty of girls would have liked it. Why I didn't just tell the police of my plight I don't know. I lived with this woman for five years before getting wise and departing. The experience scarred me forever. Now I am in my late thirties, but I still cannot change my attitude toward sex and women, which is that it is dirty, painful and a chore. I have been to a psychiatrist but so far no help. I think he made it worse. Sometimes I consider doing away with myself. Sorry to get personal, but these things are sort of like the confessional in church, you get it all out of your system in an anonymous way.

FINAL CONCLUSIONS

Singles sex is a complicated, sensitive, and ambiguous experience. Singles, by their own report, while frequently the veterans of many sexual encounters, are yet guarded in their estimations of these encounters, turning an indifferent and at times even hostile shoulder to the many offerings which the sexual revolution has brought with it— easy, unusual or transient sex. Such relatively new freedoms are judged mostly in cautionary terms by singles, and this is true both for those who have not been directly privy to such encounters as well as for those who have intentionally sought them out.

Again, the portrait of the American single shows us a person with a healthy range of sexual experience but with a somewhat ambivalent and conservative estimation of its value, a person caught between the allurements of available sex and the realities that can result from its complications.

Singles, in the face of the sexual revolution, remain concerned with the benefits of sharing and caring, liking and loving. This message comes through over and over again. When these benefits are absent—as they are at an increasing rate—attitudes toward oneself, one's partner, and sex in general can become unpredictable if not directly critical.

At the same time, the increased allowances which the new sexuality has granted singles are also much appreciated; that is plain. And the new-found tolerances—freedom to speak openly about sex, to reevaluate roles and to question old norms, to experiment with sex, grow with it, relax into it, widen and savor its sweet pleasures as never before—are all far from wasted on the present singles generation.

Chapter 4

Living Alone ||||
Freedom vs. Loneliness

In this chapter on "Living Alone" we ask:

1. What effect has being single had on your ambition and achievement at your profession? Has it had any influence on job changes and choice, promotions, goal achievements? Please explain.

2. What do you consider the greatest disadvantage of being single?

3. How does being single influence your feelings about the place where you live? Do you consider it a temporary location to store your belongings or is it home? How do you deal with domestic necessities such as shopping, laundry, cooking, and cleaning? Describe how you feel and how you cope with such chores.

4. What are the major problems and pleasures of living alone? How do you deal with the loneliness, the sense of isolation, fear?

5. Describe how the following have helped you with problems of living alone and being single: family, religious or self-help programs, therapist, community-sponsored organizations, friends. In what ways have they not helped?

For some singles solitude is a pleasure and a goal. For others, finding oneself removed from one's family, or divorced from a long-term marriage, or forced to support a child alone, or thrown into the business world to fend for oneself, or having no one to depend on or call

217

for help—in short, the discovery of one's true *single-ness*—can be a rude and even traumatic experience.

In this chapter we deal with the day-to-day concerns of singles life: career and the place one lives; personal finances and friendships; the mental and emotional ups and downs one experiences; the social and psychological support people enlist in times of turmoil and during the course of daily affairs; and finally the methods singles develop to ensure that being alone is not necessarily being lonely.

SINGLENESS AND CAREER

1. What effect has being single had on your ambition and achievement at your profession? Has it had any influence on job changes and choice, promotions, goal achievements? Please explain.

Marital status has a profound effect on career and on attitude toward career. Approximately three quarters of respondents are highly motivated concerning their career, and many thank their single status for certain advantages. The other quarter falls within a spectrum of opinion that runs from ordinary discontent to horror at having to reenter the job market without skill, education, preparation, or the desire to go back to work in the first place. Rarely do the essayists say that their single status has no effect at all, and when they do the speaker is usually a student or young person fresh out of school.

Responses to this question fall into three general categories:

1. Singleness Helps Career

First are those who claim that being unmarried advances their careers. This group consists almost entirely of singles without children. Only one divorced mother writes of her career in a positive manner and she is independently wealthy.

Members of this group are positive for several reasons. First, because being single gives them more time to devote to their careers.

Woman, Syracuse, NY: I am more dedicated to my job because I can now put 100% into it. The top management prefers it that way—my hours are more adjustable, and it's easier for me to relocate if I have to. That's not so easy for one who is married. I can stay late hours and all my energy is channeled into my work, not like when I had to nurse my husband around. I was given this job in the first place because I'm un-attached and therefore flexible.

More time at the job means greater productivity and hence greater advancement.

Man, Boston, MA: Now I am able to travel more for my company. If I get a better job in another city I can take it too. Why? Because I'm free! I can work as many hours as needed without feeling guilty about coming home late. My work is better, and my boss is happier. I turn out twice the amount as before. Career opportunities are open to me, and I'm earning more than when I was married because I'm working harder.

Woman, Manhattan, NY: Being single has had *everything* to do with my success. It's opened my range (I can travel, I can quit tomorrow, I can get a better job, I can transfer to Pago Pago). It's certainly helped me advance rapidly—if I had a husband much less a family, I wouldn't have nearly enough energy on the job. I return too many nights exhausted and emotionally burned out to be sweet and loving to a man. My job is the core of my life. I firmly believe only the extraordinary woman manages both career and idyllic home life. *I am not that extraordinary woman!* I can't do both. Now comes the point where I say I'd chuck the presidency of the firm for the right man, eh? Forget it, Charley! I like my job!

For a few, however, even though increased time means greater promotion in work, dedication is motivated less by professional zeal than by a need to fill the emotional gap:

Man, Suffolk, NY: Being single has in fact made me more ambitious. My work now means more to me than before my divorce. Being realistic, it's the only thing I have left. So I apply myself more, work longer hours, and I like my work more than before. Work fills a space that was once filled by my wife, my two darling daughters, and my niece who lived with us. I'd rather have them back and not do so good at my job if given the choice.

2. The Pattern of Delayed Success for Newly Divorced Women

The second category, consisting mostly of female divorcees, describes specific stages in career life during and after divorce. Indeed, so many divorced women's essays tell of these stages that they suggest a common if previously unrecognized pattern.

The first stage consists of fear of failure and lack of confidence to function in the job market. These reactions occur primarily during marital separation when the woman begins to realize she is faced with the inevitability of returning to work.

Next come feelings of shock, mortification, and depression as one searches for a job, rejections pile up, and as one's limitations are highlighted by competition with others more qualified and self-assured. This sense of failure and embarrassment may continue even after a job has been secured, especially if the new career fails to meet one's expectations.

Third comes a time of suspended emotion. Some women speak of it as a period of "numbness," or as a "blank," a "blah." The respondent trudges off day after day. Somehow she manages, even if the job is difficult and associates are unsupportive. But for her the joy is out of things.

Next, the light begins to break. Having weathered the formative months, the respondent realizes not only that she is still holding together but that she is doing just fine. A sense of self-confidence and satisfaction begins to dawn slowly in some, rapidly in others. Eventually this new assurance becomes the realization that one can get the job accomplished after all; that, as a matter of fact, one can get it accomplished wisely and well. In many cases, this understanding leads to a permanent and committed career.

Woman, Aurora, IL: Since I have been single my ambitions have greatly enlarged. This is a great thing for me. After my divorce I was scared to death about going back to work. I was frightened as a mouse. Everyone seemed intimidating when I went looking, and I came home several times from job interviews crying like a baby, the whole thing was so demeaning. I got a job finally. Everyone seemed intimidating to me, my boss (a man), my co-workers (mostly women). Later I discovered they were all human like me, and that I could do many things better than most of those who had been there for years. I was always put down and told I couldn't further myself without a husband—now I know I can hack it alone.

Woman, Birmingham, AL: I've had to face the "real world" since I became single. But at times I'm surprised at the things I can handle that I never dreamed I'd even attempt. I'm still not doing the type of work I'd like to do but for my skills and the present job in Birmingham I'm doing better than a lot of my female friends. I am getting interested in my job now that I've been at it for a while, after a long fallow time when I just reported for duty and slugged through the day. It seems much more interesting to me now that I know I'm good at it, and even though it's not what I really want I'll try and advance as far as I can get.

Woman, Cleveland, OH: Presently my job in a management consulting firm is more important to me than dates or any man. I've worked my way up slowly and painfully, gotten past prejudice against women, leering male associates, whistling janitors in the halls, and jealous matrons guarding their sacred positions above me like they were 'the crown jewels. I feel like I've been in a battle for the six years since my divorce, but I'm flushed with victory too. I've come out on top: good salary, some of the best critiques in the office, a solid footing with great chance of promotion. I did this all myself. I struggled and fought. Sometimes I never thought I'd get past first base, especially in the beginning. Now I know I'm a home-run hitter and that this career is what I always wanted for myself.

Woman, Tulsa, OK: Being single has made *all* the difference. Without it I would never have the job I have now. No thanks to my ex, of course, who had me believing I could never get to first base on my own. I spent the first year at my desk thinking I would get the boot any minute. I didn't dare turn right or left, just eyes ahead and keep on going, Nancy, keep on going! It's all paid off now cause I make almost 50 thou a year and I'm the best in the business. All this thanks to my being single.

At first many female divorcees find returning to the job market so unpleasant that they stall for months until forced to take action. Those so forced, however, notice that while the new job is difficult it is invigorating as well, and the very challenge of the undertaking lifts them. As a result, many respondents return to college to begin or complete an education cut short by a prior marriage:

Woman, Washington, DC: The first few months of being separated from my husband were hell. He was a son of a bitch who taunted me with the fact that without him, the big deal stock option king, I'd never get work. He almost had me convinced. I had two years at Barnard and needed a bunch more credits to graduate. I had no particular skills and not much ambition to get them. A soft life for ten years had made *me* soft and unmotivated. Necessity is the mother of you know what though, and my urge to show my husband what-for gave me the will to rise off my fanny and get a job. I got a job all right, in a telephone answering service as operator (terrible), and started putting myself through business school at nights. After a year I switched to saleswoman at a film store which gave me lots of sales experience and taught me how to cope with a lot of different types. When I got out of school, a teacher of mine helped me land a job with an insurance firm, and I did more selling. Then I got a job working in the business office of the Department of Commerce where I am now. Having had a number of jobs, each one taught me something about the world and myself. I feel strong now and able to take care of myself and able to make a good, honest wage. I have several business skills which I intend to parley into profit during the next few years. What's even more important is that my self-esteem has grown and I feel proud of what I've accomplished.

3. Singleness as Harmful to a Career

Though a majority feel that being single has helped their careers, some don't, especially single mothers. For them the realities of going back to work are less than cheerful.

Woman, South Suburban, IL: I worked 7 years during my marriage until the baby came. I was a housewife then for a long time. Now I'm forced back on the job. Of course, you need to work to survive, but it's frightening to be responsible not only for yourself but for a kid. The difference from being married is it's only *you*. The pressures are tremendous right now and, to tell you the truth, I don't know if I'll be able to take them much longer.

Woman, Pompton Lakes, NJ: I have had to strive harder having two babies to support. One cannot rest complacently when survival is at stake. I find myself prey to fears, more insecure about the future. My life is a hard and unrewarding one. I get up at 6:00, feed the children, go off to work all day while the children are at day care, come back, feed the kids, fall into bed exhausted. I have only this to look forward to for the next ten years. It's the same thing night after night. The job is okay but just a job. Even if I wanted I couldn't get too involved in it because I don't have the time and left-over energy.

Other women report prejudice on the job:

Woman, Omaha, NB: It seems almost everyone is against the single person in some form. Added to taxes, insurance costs, etc. are the pressures of society and family. Companies frown on single people, especially women. After all—what happens if she becomes married or pregnant and has to leave her job? She can't really be serious—and she *is* a divorcee, you know!

Respondents complain of dull jobs, nasty employers, meaningless tasks, silly products—a kind of chronicle of dissatisfactions in our times:

Man, Queens, NY: I kept my job after we separated, and my wife got a job near me. Her job is okay but mine continues to be drudgery. Basically I turn a lot of knobs all day and dream about getting laid.

Woman, Providence, RI: I lost my job when I got divorced because my boss told me I was unreliable. Figure out the logic there. I can't. I'm working as a cook in a coffee shop out of desperation. The food is disgusting. My poor customers. I hate it but don't know what else to do. The pay is impossible as well, as are the waiters who keep trying to get dates, proposition, etc.

Woman, Baltimore, MD: Since my separation I've had to go to work at a plastics factory manufacturing incredibly stupid toys (the kind I used to picket in the 60s). The fumes are doing me in—the job is unhealthy. My co-workers are tired, depressed people with no meaning in their lives. I wish to God I hadn't been forced into this position.

Money and the Single Woman

In previous chapters we have seen that for singles, money is one of the truly significant determinants of the good life.

Statistics published by the U.S. Census Bureau reveal that even while singles are bringing home an increasing share of the national income, their earning capacity lags substantially behind that of married workers, as does the quality of jobs available to them. The higher-paying managerial, professional, and technical jobs are all filled with a greater percentage of marrieds than singles.

At the same time, entrepreneurs in many areas have learned that singles compose one of the largest pools of concentrated purchasing power in the nation. Over the past years a spate of products and services designed with singles in mind has come into being—single-portion soup cans, single real estate offerings, two-slice toasters with a switch to turn off one slot, and so on. Economically, singles are being exploited on both sides, squeezed by lower wages and lured into ever greater purchasing by billion-dollar campaigns.

Women are especially discriminated against in the job market. The following question, to which we will return in a later chapter for further analysis, shows to what extent money problems differ between the sexes:

2. What do you consider the greatest disadvantage of being single?	Men	Women
a. Loneliness	42%	44%
b. Fear due to living alone	4%	5%
c. Economic insecurity	2%	16%
d. Restricted sexual and social life	12%	10%
e. A tendency to become rigid, self-centered, selfish	14%	8%
f. The social stigma of not being married	7%	4%
g. The dating grind	14%	11%
h. Don't know	5%	3%

Among men only 2 percent checked economic insecurity, while among women 16 percent give it first rank, almost *eight times* the number. A 2 percent choice is just about a no-percent choice, compared to 16 percent, which accounts for almost a sixth of all female respondents.

PROFILE: The single woman most likely to have money problems.

PROFILE SUMMARY: Money problems are at their worst for the older, divorced, and less-educated female. Women who have been divorced once are twice as likely to have money problems as those never married. Women twice divorced are *three times* as likely to complain of finances as those never married. The main reason for this is no doubt the presence of children among divorcees. As revealed in the essays below, single mothers have by far the most difficult time, not only because they are forced to support a family on a single salary but because their many years as housewife-mother have often left them unprepared to undertake such a task.

Age is also a factor. In her early twenties a woman is half as likely to place money problems in the paramount position as a woman between twenty-five and thirty-four. For women in their thirties and forties, chances for financial turmoil climb even higher. White-collar female workers are more likely to cite money difficulties as their first problem than professional or blue-collar workers, exemplifying what has been termed "the middle-class money squeeze." Women who have finished college are less worried over finances than those who never attended.

Education and youth, however, are by no means foolproof protections against poverty. Even degree-holding women are often relegated to menial, low-paying jobs. Here is what women say about their financial plight and about how they cope with it:

Woman, Birmingham, AL: I am a factory worker and get a very low wage compared to what some people get (including women) in this country. It is the low wage that kills me. I never had an education and never wanted one when I was young. I figured why would I need one? Since I have been on my own, which is about six or seven years now, I have learned the reason why, slowly and painfully. I manage not to think about how poor I am by going out a lot, going to the movies with dates or alone sometimes if I'm in the mood, and generally not thinking about it. I can see all the nice clothes for sale in some of the shops at the mall near where I live and it is hard not to want to go in and steal some of these things. At least if I had some pretty clothes I might not feel so poor and alone all the time. I think that it would not take much to persuade me to become a criminal. Just look at what the oil companies make and then look around at the ordinary person. How can you call that fair?

Woman, Los Angeles, CA: As soon as I found myself a single mother in the world I realized that my education at Boston University plus a dime would buy me a cup of coffee. The first item on my list was learning a skill/trade, which I did at nights, studying hospital administration. After several tedious years and a lot of Mickey Mouse stuff at the school, I was qualified and now hold a good job that I like. I think that it's important for a single woman to have a trade/skill or business knowledge in these times. Women thinking about divorce should first go back to school and prepare in advance. Don't get stuck like I did with no talents. Especially if there are kids.

Woman, Providence, RI: I was one of the lucky women who was divorced at a later time in life. My children are grown and able to take care of themselves, and I had a degree in accounting which I earned while married. I had no trouble getting a job but my boss confided in me that because I was older, had no children at home to take me home on sick days, etc., no husband to demand I stay at home, etc., and was mature enough to handle a big job, he hired me. He said he wouldn't have taken on a younger woman for these reasons.

Women in the survey often offer pertinent financial warnings. Some of them, extracted from essay answers, include:

1. Have a Skill

"The most important thing I did after leaving my husband was to reenter the university and take my degree. That qualified me for hire in several different positions."

"Most of all—be prepared! Boyscouts! Girlscouts! Be career minded *before* setting out! Don't let men convince you you can't learn anything you want. I know a girlfriend of mine who became a carpenter and makes money at it today."

"I'm studying library science at night and holding down two part-time jobs by day. I wish I had learned a skill before because it would have saved me time and money!"

2. Learn as Much as You Can About Money

"I took two courses in money management at a school that offers adult education. It has stood me in good stead for taking care of my financial affairs."

"I finally got so tired of being screwed around by the government, my boss, men, big business, that I studied economics/accounting/stock market. No one can tell me what to do with my money now."

"The most important thing you can do as a single woman is learn how to handle your own money."

3. Make Use of Community Services

"I received some good financial help and information from a retail credit bureau . . ."

"I finally got so desperate . . . I used a legal aid society. I couldn't otherwise afford it. They gave me some counseling and referred me to a family service agency that helped me get my tangled family debts under control."

4. Learn to Keep a Budget

"I coped with not having money by keeping track of every penny I spent."

"Budgeting saved me . . ."

5. Don't Over-Extend on Credit

"I got myself tied up in knots by using too many credit cards. I still owe on them too much money."

"The biggest temptation was to run up my MasterCharge and Visa, which I did into the thousands, and then have been paying it all off through the nose since. It's so easy to do it and so hard to pay it off."

Woman, Manhattan, NY: Having a career since my divorce has taught me about something I really needed to know: money. I always let my husband worry about this previously. Thus I suffered when we were divorced. I think it behooves every woman *to know something about money*—investments, the stock market, prices, comparative shopping, how the system works, etc. There is too much ignorance on the subject among women and they pay for this ignorance if they find themselves divorced like me. There are plenty of courses around that a woman can take. Read books on the subject. Go back to school to learn. Read the financial section of the paper. When I first began I learned things like how to shop carefully, how to seek out the cheapest stores, how to budget, how to make up accounts for myself and keep them accurately. I took a course on money and money management, and got to know some money people. It helped.

"A lot of women are not aware that they surrender their power by giving up decisions about money," remarks Dr. Gail Barton, psychiatrist and Associate Professor of Psychiatry at University of Michigan, Ann Arbor, Michigan. "From an early age girls are shouldered out of the money picture. Girls can understand math just as well as boys, of course, but grade school textbooks often picture boys having money, and girls watching it being spent. Extend this a little further into maturity and you have the 'dumb broad' or 'dumb blonde' or 'helpless female' images so many women suffer from. If women learned from an early age how to use a checkbook, what a mortgage is, how to manipulate financial numbers and so forth, they wouldn't have the problems they often do when they find themselves alone in the world."

If a woman is single, claims Dr. Barton, she should make every possible attempt to gain financial savvy and control. Education is crucial. "There are adult education courses in many areas. There are dozens of new magazines with articles on women and money, banking, finances, and so on. Women must understand that this knowledge is necessary and that without it they are helpless. When you take control of your finances then you assume power over your life as well.

"If, say, you are going to live with a man and there's a mortgage on your home, then you should *both* sign it. If you've got stocks, it should be in *both* your names. Look into these things. Find out in advance what you must do. You must be absolutely straight and clear with each other *beforehand* about how the finances will be divided. Money is a difficult subject to talk about, primarily because it represents power. That's why nobody will tell you his or her salary. People will tell you their age, their sex life, but not their salary. Because that's giving *away* their power. If you can't talk about money before living together, you are going to have even greater problems with it once you are together.

"Women have often been encouraged to think of men as the breadwinners and women as the ones who eat the bread. The various consciousness-raising groups around the country do much to dispel this idea. These groups help women realize that they are *not* in a helpless position and that they *can* do something about their financial situation. You get to listen to other women's experiences and advice; you learn that a group process can be more helpful in getting practical things done. You learn that women can construct their *own* groups. There are a lot of women who are joining such groups today, and who are making their groups into networks with other groups—and this is one of the healthier signs."

THE HOME ALONE

Another important factor in living alone is the type of residence one inhabits. According to our demographic data, residential situations (i.e., whether singles live alone, in a group, with family, etc.) break down in the following way:

	Men	Women
Lives with member of the opposite sex	14%	11%
Lives with member of the same sex	11%	7%
Lives alone	47%	35%
Lives with family	23%	45%
Lives with group	5%	2%

About half of all single men and over a third of single women maintain their own dwelling, which could be anything from a mansion to a duplex condominium to a solitary hotel room.

The percentage of those who live alone is higher for those who have been divorced than for those who have never been married.

	MEN		
	Never married	One divorce	Two or more divorces
Lives alone	37%	58%	58%

	WOMEN		
	Never married	One divorce	Two or more divorces
Lives alone	33%	35%	41%

Here is how age affects one's living patterns:

	20–24	25–34	35–44	45–55
Age of single MEN living alone:	23%	46%	64%	64%
Age of single WOMEN living alone:	22%	35%	33%	45%

The fact that so many singles live alone indicates that a new lifestyle, one centered on the single household, has emerged.

3. How does being single influence your feelings about the place where you live? Do you consider it a temporary location to store your belongings or is it home? How do you deal with domestic necessities such as shopping, laundry, cooking, and cleaning? Describe how you feel and how you cope with such chores.

First, how does singleness influence one's place of residence?

Woman, Jacksonville, FL: I was living in a small town when I became divorced. I strongly wanted to raise my children in such a small place but since my ex was an important figure in the town, it was necessary for my peace of mind to move. We moved back to Jacksonville and it's now my home.

Man, Norfolk, VA: When my wife and I split, her fangs grew longer by the hour and her appetite for everything we had built *together* grew too. She had to have everything her eyes set on *including* the house that *I* had taken a year to build, partly with my own hands. She hired a fancy lawyer with money her father gave her, and he nailed me for about everything that meant anything. And the house with it along with most of my money. Today I live as far from San Jose as I can get and as far from her. I've started to build a new life and am presently living in a room at a downtown hotel, but hope to improve things when commissions from my new job come in.

Woman, Los Angeles, CA: I live more in the city than I'd like to for many reasons. Mainly because other available single people live here and that's an important thing for me. I've tried living alone in the country where I love it, but discovered that there are *no chances* of meeting people you have something in common with. It's a tough decision to make. Frankly, I chose the city to escape the loneliness of the country and the isolation. I hope that when I marry I can return to the beauty of small town country living.

Man, Kansas City, MO: I have always tried to select a residence in close contact with other singles. This means a) living in the city; b) living in a part of this city where other singles live; c) finding an apartment where other single people live. I've done all three and my social life is the better for it. Single people tend to seek each other out, and in every town there is a singles' "area." Even people who like their privacy eventually have to come out of their shell and go to bars, discos and places of entertainment. I save all that by being near the action where I live.

From these and similar answers, there's little doubt that a person's single status exerts much influence on choice of residence. Sometimes the situation is clear-cut, as in the case of respondents who choose their living area *specifically* to be near other singles. For instance, much media attention has been focused on the single condominiums and apartment complexes which have sprung up around the country, mostly in large urban areas on the West Coast and in Florida. These projects are complete mini-cities, self-sufficient and self-serving: They exist so singles can be near singles. Usually equipped with swimming pools, hot tubs, disco studios, and private after-hour clubs where singles can come for company and entertainment, some compounds have enough apartments to house ten thousand men and women, and as a rule few go unoccupied.

Among respondents only one mentions living in a singles complex. His report is a favorable one:

Man, Marina Del Rey, CA: I choose to live in a suburban apartment complex that caters to singles. Other people are allowed to live here, of course, but few other than singles do. The place is set up for singles only and would drive old people or people with kids crazy. There are more than 4,000 apartments in this complex and about the same number of single people. We have tennis courts, a pool in every district section, several common-interest clubs. I love it. It allows singles to get to know each other without the singles bar route. Everybody is very friendly and no one is uptight if you come up to them and say "Hi!" The fact that they choose to live in a singles village means they're interested in meeting new people and having new experiences.

"Singles complexes are growing," remarks Roger Libby, sociologist at the University of Massachusetts, Amherst. "But I don't think that this residential situation is the only one to look for in terms of how single people will live in the future. It will never, I believe, affect a majority of single people. For instance, you will rarely see single *parents* living in them, or *low-income* singles. You're only going to witness an affluent minority living there. The complexes will grow, all right, but only among the monied, upper-income classes."

Domestic Duties: A Male and Female View

Despite the proverbial lack of skill and motivation men have concerning household chores, almost *no* male essayist waxed bitter over household duties, and most—more than three quarters—admitted rather liking them.

Man, Philadelphia, PA: I realize it is not a macho thing to lay claims to liking household work. I am no domestic, but I have learned that I can do things mother never taught me. It is not that hard to iron and keep my rooms neat. I keep a whole five rooms neat now. I suppose the fact that I can decide the times I will do the work makes some difference. Those who are chained to a broom all the time have no choice, and it is a sense of choice in life that allows us to feel free. I am coming to like some of the around-the-house jobs and no longer feel that they are necessarily women's work. It's good exercise, and I get a feeling of achievement from conquering lots of those little skills like sewing and reweaving holes in pants.

Many male respondents derive pleasure from doing something new and different, especially if they have been married for a long time and have never learned household skills. A few say housework is "therapeutic." Most have their favorite chores plus a pet peeve. Cleaning is highest on the list of enjoyments. Many enjoy cooking, though most admit to a limited bill of fare (hamburgers, spaghetti, French toast, and so on). Ironing gets mixed reviews, sewing is by and large considered sissy, and laundry is the perennial male nemesis.

Behind all this good-natured willingness to scrub and boil, however, lie points more profound. Male respondents continually speak of "proving" themselves or of showing others that "I am capable of taking care of my own needs." Such phrases betray an underlying frustration. For younger males, the influence of mother is often apparent. It is she who has done all the scrubbing—to save her boy the trouble, no doubt, but in the process endowing her son with something of an inferiority complex concerning his ability to perform any household chore more complex than dropping a shirt in the hamper. Divorced men speak of ex-wives in the same way, complaining, as one man put it, that "emasculation can take place at the sink, over the stove, behind the vacuum cleaner, just as much as in bed." In most cases men feel that by performing basic household work and performing it well, they are somehow vindicating their blighted domestic honor. Men speak of their pride in being able to keep house as well as a woman, and—even more frequently—of relief in knowing *that they can do it at all.*

Man, Omaha, NB: The domestic necessities take up my time, but I do enjoy most of it. My friends tell me I keep a very clean house. I wish my ex-wife could hear them say it. Besides, it gives me a sense of independence, like, gosh, I did it all on my own. Gee!! PRIDE!!!

Man, Des Moines, IA: Over the years I have developed great pride in handling domestic necessities. This was hard when I first got my own place because I was used to my mom making the beds and doing the dishes. I had never even *tried* to iron a shirt. Accomplishing these things in the shortest amount of time has become a game with me and makes me feel good.

While men are occupied with the domestic arts, women are busy trying to forget them—unless of course there are children in the home. Brought up to be "good housekeeping machines," as a woman phrased it, many divorcees speak of their relief at no longer being responsible for providing husbands with tidy living rooms, delicious meals three times a day, spotless sinks, while never-marrieds talk of escaping parents who are "neatness freaks" or "little Napoleons." Some female respondents even take a kind of relieved and deliciously vengeful pleasure in letting the chores slide.

Woman, Glendale, AZ: Since I've been divorced I've opted for the easy short-cuts. I have no one but myself to please now. I have always liked to cook but on a tight schedule. I make use of TV dinners and microwave ovens, two things I would never have used when married and when my husband expected a home-cooked meal each night. I also let the work pile up out of sheer glee at not having to do it. There are no pressures from anyone including a live-in man! My house-cleaning just isn't so important anymore since my goals and interests have moved out of the house.

Woman, Tacoma, WA: As to chores . . . bah! I don't give much of a shit about them. After so many years cleaning, washing, ironing, sewing, cooking, starching, boiling, slaving for a husband who didn't appreciate it, I'm taking care of number one. This means I clean and dust when *I* want to, not when anyone else says so.

Children complicate the scene. Many mothers speak of the difficulties of keeping a house clean with kids about, or of determining how to teach children an awareness of policing their own messes.

Woman, Louisville, KY: When I went to work I lowered all standards for housekeeping. Initially I prefer to spend time with my kids rather than clean house but then things get out of hand and we all have to pitch in. The results of this are madness of a sort but in the end things do get clean. Finally though, I decided that the hell with it, let the kids do what they wanted. Now my house is still messy, kids are in teens and are slobs but they related well to others. Once I spent a weekend with six kids under 7 years old, four loaves of bread, and a jar of peanut butter—we survived but I no longer eat peanut butter.

Woman, Tacoma, WA: I'm a sloppy housekeeper and a lousy cook. I hate both but really feel I've accomplished something when I've managed to prepare something. I often put a roast in the oven or make either a humungus batch of chili or spaghetti sauce to cook all day on the stove top. Most of the stuff gets frozen and pulled out during the week as needed. It's usually in a casserole form and my son has it warming in the oven when I get home from work. I only clean once a week max, and it's an all-out war that I can never win and which I wish I didn't have to fight at all and which sometimes I don't. I hate the whole ordeal and have visions of tossing a match into the gas-soaked couch as I stroll out the door. My son shudders when he sees me gearing up for a house-cleaning, since he knows all too well that he's going to get tapped too and he doesn't like that much. It's "get this" and "do that" and "do it again till the job is finished the way I want." And by the time we're finished cleaning, my five trash cans are filled and I've got one or two boxes for Goodwill. I go to the dump, Goodwill, and the bar for a drink, and my son rests in peace. Two days later the house looks worse than it did before we cleaned.

The essay that follows outlines problems that are typical of young singles who live at home.

Man, Phoenix, AZ: I live at home with my family. I have several brothers and sisters. I love them all and care for them being around, but sometimes they take advantage of me and make me do more than my share of housework. It's hard to bring home dates because not only do they have to be liked by me but I seem to let my family influence my judgment of girls. They may not even say anything but their attitudes are revealed. I would like to have more romance with girls but find it difficult when there is nowhere to take them at the end of the night. There's always *someone* around the living room. I help with the shopping each week and also run out for things needed. I feel like an errand boy sometimes. I do my own laundry (mainly because my mother is unable, having suffered a stroke 7 years ago). I make dinner a few times a week and help with the dishes. I am not a bad cook. I don't mind any of it *too* much because I find it part of my duty of living with my family. Sometimes though I can't wait to get a place of my own.

Home, it thus seems, is indeed a high-priority item for singles and not just a place to stow one's belongings, but its importance stems from reasons different from those a married person or family member might consider. For singles there is less interest focused on home as a social center, more on it as a kind of haven where one does as one pleases. Though here and there reference is made to the residence as a showplace, seduction and ornamentation are secondary to the number-one requirement: the privacy to do as one wishes. In this sense the positive side of being alone is placed above all else, whatever variation on the theme of freedom each single person happens to favor—escape, mobility, peace and quiet, private indulgence, laissez-faire. This theme is continually brought up in both essays and multiple-choice questions:

Woman, St. Louis, MO: Home is an important place for me for lots of reasons. Of course I entertain often. I take pride in making my home a special and nice place for people to visit in, and much of my salary goes toward decorations, antiques, pillows, fabric, that sort of thing. Most of all, it's *my* very own special place. It does not belong to my parents, my ex-husbands, the State, or God. It is mine, to be with and do with as I like or dislike. It is hard to make clear to other people how much this means to me, especially to people who have never been married and have never had to share a place with another person on an intimate basis. Now I share the space intimately with *myself* and there is no one else to worry about. This is the best part of the unmarried life and I hope I can continue to enjoy it for many years to come.

Man, Tacoma, WA: When I first moved into my apartment I was living with a girl named Virginia. Virginia was a very beautiful woman, very caring and sweet. We had already lived together for several years in her apartment. This new one was to be *our* apartment. She had many precious things her grandfather had brought back with him on a ship from China, especially a collection of carved ivory statues and some jade snuff bottles. We built a special display stand for them in the middle of the room and that's when the trouble started. At first she wanted special lights put up on them. After that the stuff had to be under glass in expensive showcases. It started getting so that her collection was becoming the most important thing in the house and my stuff was getting squeezed out along with my boxer dog I have had since a kid. After a number of arguments about her Chinese goods we decided to give my furniture and antiques a place in the room too, but everywhere I put them she didn't like them because they "detracted from the Chinese ivory pieces." Arguments got worse and finally— there were other reasons behind it too—we split up and she moved out. Since then I feel like I have been reborn, I now have my own space without the intrusion of Virginia's possessions. Her things were like a marker that spelled: "This apartment is mine alone." Now that she's gone I feel that the house is my house and no one else's, and this is a very good sensation. I never realized before while we were living together just how much I really needed to be alone, surrounded by my own things, in my own private home. It has become a real high for me, and I feel better about myself as well.

LIVING ALONE: THE PROBLEMS AND THE PLEASURES

4. What are the major problems and pleasures of living alone? How do you deal with the loneliness, the sense of isolation, fear?

First the problems. They can be listed as follows:

1. Loneliness

Loneliness surpasses all rivals as the most persistent problem of single life. It is mentioned directly in the survey hundreds of times and via inference thousands of times. Almost 85 percent of subjects lament the wide-ranging difficulties that loneliness introduces into their lives. Here are just a few of the many things singles say concerning loneliness.

Man: "Eating alone, drinking alone, smoking alone, thinking alone, being alone. It's a bummer always being alone."

Man: "Since I lived with a girl for so many years the hardest part of being alone is coming home each night and finding no one waiting for me. The house is empty. Everything is exactly in the same place where I left it in the morning. That's spooky—nothing has changed—there's no life."

Woman: "My house is very big and I am very small. I wander through the rooms, always expecting someone will be there. But he never is. Only the silence. That is what it means to me to be single."

Woman: "Companionship, someone to know on a continuing basis, to have sex with, to help with repairs, someone to hug me now and then—I'm terribly lonely."

Man: "Being free is great but being lonely is bad news. I have learned the meaning of the term: 'To be with others but to be alone.' This is how I often feel on Saturday nights on a date or in a bar. Alone yet with hundreds of people. I find myself looking around the room and trying to find the location of at least one woman who is lonely and sensitive like myself. They all seem to be having such a good time and I wonder if I'm the only one who is so cut off like this."

2. Fear

This problem is mentioned second only to loneliness, mostly by women, and especially in reference to physical fears.

Woman: "The major problem of living alone is that every time I see a movie about some woman raped I get scared. I avoid these movies and am generally afraid."

Woman: "Fear is the problem. I carry mace and have a shotgun (loaded). I have eight phones in my house so I can cover myself and call the police. This is because of an actual threat I once got."

Woman: "My ex-husband just laughs at me when I tell him how frightened I sometimes get living alone, what with the rape, murder, robbery, etc. you find these days. But he doesn't understand how helpless a single woman can feel alone in her apartment at night."

Psychological fears are also mentioned:

Woman: "I am often afraid that I will remain single for an undisclosed number of years or that I will never meet anyone again, or will not find fulfillment with a man. I am also afraid that I will lose my ability to relate to a man in a real woman's way the way I once did many years ago with one special man."

Man, Phoenix, AZ: I find myself plagued by fear of a thousand different things, mostly a kind of spooky fear that just won't go away. An anxiety. I find myself worrying all the time about the future and what will happen to me. Where am I going, and what does life hold in store for me? Why did my marriage go wrong? What will my next marriage be like, and will there *be* a next marriage? At twelve o'clock at night, when I've come home from a movie or a date, or even from staying late at work, I find myself staring at the walls and wishing somebody was here to talk to. But on the other hand, I don't want anyone here living with me because that's a drag too. So I worry about both those things for a while, then I worry that I am worrying so much. About that time I start getting sleepy but when I get in bed I find my mind racing so fast thinking about love, marriage, sex, all that stuff. I suppose an amount of worrying is healthy but I feel that I am excessive on the subject.

3. Money

We have already heard respondents on this topic. Here are a few further comments.

Woman: "The major problem is you have only one income. No one takes care of you as in a marriage. Before my husband helped with the money and now I'm out of a job and am scared to death of the future."

Man: "How can anyone make ends meet as a single today? You have to live on one income and if it's low, forget it. I have to move out of my apartment soon and find a cheaper place. I need two salaries to get along."

Woman, Oklahoma City, OK: The greatest problem I had started when I moved out of my husband's house and went to work in a dry goods store. I suppose you could say that before that I had been supported by my husband and didn't really know the meaning of a dollar. Well, I learned! It's hard for a single woman to break into business. I started as a lowly salesperson but was given a salary so low that I had trouble buying groceries, and there was little chance of promotion. What a rude discovery that you are poor and that you just can't make ends meet. I would like to know how other single people manage to survive today. My parents have sent me a little, but my father has cancer now and most of the money at home is going toward his radiation treatment, which is very expensive and goes on for a long time. I have borrowed from a loan company in town and now find it terribly hard keeping up payments to return the loan. As a single woman it's been impossible to get credit. My ex-husband tried to help me but it didn't do any good, so I can't just whip out my handy-dandy MasterCharge in times of emergency. Those things help. It's lousy to have nothing in times of trouble to fall back on like that kind of credit. Once a man asked me to live with him and I was tempted not because I cared about him but because it would relieve money problems. That's what they do to a woman today, turn her into a paid prostitute.

4. Lack of Sexual Activity and/or Meaningful Personal Contacts

This is an aspect of loneliness, no doubt, but a variation meriting its own category. While sexual activity is one of the frequently praised benefits of living alone, lack of it is mentioned with almost equal regularity—lack of sexual opportunity or lack of *meaningful* sexual activity.

Woman: "The major problem for me is the absence of someone to come home to. To hold in bed at night and make calming love to. Sex is a major part of my life, and I'm finding it hard to find good sexual experiences and sometimes sex at all."

Man: "I do not believe in one-night stands and in slam-bam-thank-you-Mam kind of love-making. I am a very choosy person. Therefore I am almost a celibate person most of the time, and this is one of the hardest things."

Man, Washington, DC: When I first became single I, like so many others, figured I would be having a ball-and-a-half every night of the week with all those beautiful swinging single women out there. It didn't take long to get shot down my first try. That set the tone of things. Being single is a rush-rush to get nowhere. I've had a lot of dates where I've been turned off and down sexually, and that is a blow to the ego. "Swingers" are around but usually they're pigs and not too desirable. I find that I am still as sexually frustrated now as I was in a marriage with a woman who for the last nine months of our marriage wouldn't let me put a hand on her because she believed intercourse would give her a heart attack. Sexual availability of women is a problem that follows me around. Being a single man "on the loose" has not, to be honest with you, improved the situation at all and has made it worse. And I hate whorehouses!

Woman, Kansas City, MO: As a woman who treasures her virginity, I do not allow myself the liberty of sleeping around as do most other single people. Don't think that I do not have feelings though, or sexual longings because I do, many of them. I would very much like to have intercourse with many of the handsome and caring men I meet at work and even the ones I see at the stores. I long for marriage with the proper man but so far my dream has not come true, and in the meantime I must live with a constant desire and sexual urges that will go unfulfilled. Being single means being placed in jail and looking out the bars at all the handsome and available men out there who I could sleep with if I did not have high standards. This has been the hardest thing for me since I have graduated from college and gone to work and been in the adult world.

"Lack of sexual activity can affect different people in different ways," explains Dr. Jack Fitzpatrick, Staff Psychologist at the Lutheran Medical Center in Brooklyn, New York. "Recently in the papers some famous people have claimed that they are refraining from any sexuality because of a lack of meaningful relationships. One person I know stopped for two years and felt that removing the whole sexual pressure, plus the cynicism that goes with it, made him feel a lot better. Thus, there is at least a segment of the population that is withdrawing from sexual relationships because of negative experiences. Some people feel that if they refrain for a while and rejuvenate themselves emotionally, then they can return to the scene and be a little more cautious and watchful in their involvements.

"One of the things we've found about long-standing marriages is that a large percentage of family physicians report that their patients have stopped sexual activities entirely but are otherwise quite content. It's been my experience that the whole relationship-companionship aspect takes on greater meaning as people get older. And sex gets less important. This I'm sure is true with singles too. The point is that the old myth about needing to have sex all the time is indeed a myth. Many people can live without sex quite nicely."

5. Children

In another chapter we will examine the ambivalence single parents feel toward their offspring. Complaints, when they are listed here, are usually tempered with such phrases as "But I love my children very much," or "Despite the problems it's worth it."

6. Tendency to Become Selfish and Self-Centered

Living alone for an extended period, respondents say, tends to make one self-involved. It "promotes idiosyncrasies which could cause severe conflict with partners," as one single put it.

Man: "Lately I've started talking to myself and talking back to the commercials on television. When I'm alone I sometimes think there *is* no one out there and I feel like an isolated little ship in space, and get too in-turned and just please only myself and no one else."

Man: "I'm just scared that living alone is going to turn me into a hermit and make it hard for me comfortably to relate to other people and/or a woman in the future. You get stuck in your ways without realizing it."

Woman: "Watch out for getting too self-involved. It's a subtle trap for singles."

7. Social Pressures and Social Prejudices

Man: "The minute you live alone everyone thinks you're unhappy and lonely, and that it's their job to cheer you up, get you dates, get you married. Bullshit!"

Woman: "People try to take advantage or expect things from you because you are alone. Guys will come over and think because you invite them up and alone that they can stay the night."

Woman: "I've had trouble with landlords. They think because I'm a single woman alone I must be a hell-raiser. One landlord tried to have me evicted by making up phony charges against me. I had to take him to court. If you live alone there is a lot of prejudice against you from some people. If you're not married, they seem to say, you're an outcast."

Man: "People think you're weird or gay because you live alone. I'm over 35 and people *assume* I'm a homosexual when I'm far from it."

Woman: "I dislike the pressure to meet guys; and I like to stay at home. I like my own company and apparently everyone thinks this is very weird. I've gotten a reputation as a hermit. You feel you can't meet a man without seeing him as a potential bedmate."

Man: "I had trouble at the bank getting a loan when they learned I lived alone. At least I think this was the cause because my credit is great."

Though singles are much preoccupied with their problems, the emphasis in the essays nonetheless falls on the pleasures of the single life. Here is a list of these positive points.

1. Freedom

The first choice among practically all singles. The concept is described in a hundred different ways: "Not having responsibility for anyone but myself" is an especially popular phrase.

Woman: "You can do what you want, when and how *you* want. You don't have to stick to a meal schedule, share a bathroom, etc. If you want to be sloppy it's okay. If you're too lazy to wash the dishes, hang up clothes, no one will know. You plan your social life the way you like it. You have responsibility only for yourself. Whee!!"

Woman: "A pleasure is being my own boss and not having to answer to anyone. In my own home. I feel as if I could fly now that I am divorced, free as a bird with no responsibilities to anyone but myself."

Man: "I have remained single all my life because I love the freedom of it all. That is what being single is all about. That is the essence of being single: being free. All this other shit about sex and single bars is nothing compared to not having responsibility to another person."

2. Privacy

Related perhaps to freedom, but a particular aspect of it. Recently divorced singles especially tend to dwell on the pleasures of being left alone:

Woman: "My favorite indoor sport has become being private. No one to hit on me when I want to be alone like Greta Garbo. The right to close my door (and it's *my* door, not 'ours')."

Man: "I can have anyone over to my apartment that I choose since I live alone. No one to answer to. The right to be private with the person when I wish."

3. Chance to Make New Friends

Single residence means having a place to be with friends, give parties, be alone with a single partner. The home becomes a focus of social life, but on one's own terms.

Man: "My home is my castle and I have friends here now whenever I wish to, which is an important part of my single life. I can entertain or not, according to my feelings about the subject. In other words, in my house there is the chance to have friends in and out often."

Woman: "The most important part of my social life is my focus on friendships. As it was my friends who helped me through the difficult times when I first separated, so it is my friends who are now my greatest pleasure, and it makes me very happy to have them in my home and to serve them, to repay them for the kindnesses they showed me when I needed them."

Man: "When I was married my wife entertained our friends a great deal but it was always her show. I was sort of the odd-man-out and most people seemed to think she was a three-ring circus. She was very skilled at being a hostess but it seemed to me that she tried on purpose to always steal the limelight. This is why I enjoy having *my* friends to *my* house now."

Women essayists were far quicker to mention friends as an asset in single life than men. On this subject, Dr. Kenneth Solomon, Assistant Professor of Psychiatry at the University of Maryland School of Medicine, remarks, "Men avoid anything feminine in our society. To have friends you have to have feelings, and feelings are feminine. You have to be willing to share, to be intimate, to take chances. To really develop a friendship—I don't mean a drinking buddy—you have to give and be willing to receive emotionally, and men find this particularly threatening. We have a pervasive homophobia in this country by reason of which men somehow feel that if they are personally attracted to a man then they must be gay. This often keeps men from relating deeply with each other and is why men are not emphasizing friendships in the essays.

"To make new friends as a single you have first of all to be willing to take chances. You have both to open yourself up and at the same time to prepare yourself for possible rejection. You have to have the guts to try, and then if you're rebuffed, to say *they're* the ones who are losing out. The question behind it is always: How much are you willing to open yourself up and let another person in? The more willing you are, the more you will experience (a) being included; (b) being rejected. That's the price and that's the reward."

4. Increased Income

Approximately as many singles think living alone means financial delivery as think it causes financial burden. As some complain that they cannot "make it on a single's income," so others say, "I have only myself to pay for now."

Woman: "It's cheaper now. Sometimes I feel that I have almost twice as much spending money being single as I did when I was married. It all gets in a channel directly to me, and there is no sharing or dividing up anymore. No worrying either or feeling guilty about spending money on myself."

Woman: "Somehow there's just more money now, I'm not sure why that is. I make the same living but living alone is cheaper. Only one mouth to feed and only one body to groom makes a difference."

Man, St. Louis, MO: While I was married I don't think I ever realized just how many times more expensive it was to have a wife and children than it would be to be single and alone. They just eat up money in a hundred different ways that you never think of—until you're not paying for them anymore, then they become obvious. For instance, my wife would get her hair done once a week. For $22.50 a shot. She would purchase at least a few hundred dollars worth of clothes every few months, sometimes without consulting our budget. The kids would get toys all the time. My wife would give money each month to her mother. She also gave a lot to the church. All of these expenses add up at the end of the month until one day you look at the bankbook, you check and recheck it, and find you are broke! All the little expenses add up. When alone, as I am now, I can keep an eye on these "little" expenses and have cut them down greatly. While I pay child support and give my wife something each month, I am in control of the amounts and know where each penny is going. I feel much more on top of things financially and do have more money at my disposal.

5. Expanded Social Life

Woman: "I really enjoy going out a lot and attending different amusements. If you're living with someone you have to worry about whether you're making them mad, especially if they don't want to go out with you. My husband was the type that wanted to stay at home and he would feel neglected if I went out without him. Now I don't have to worry about that. My advice is that when you team with someone do it according to your tastes in entertainment, your patterns of going out or staying home."

6. Freedom from Housework and Cleaning Chores

We've already seen how important this can be for many single men and women. For some, release from the bondage of mop and pail is akin to flying.

Woman: "I feel like a person set free from prison. Not having to prepare dinner every night. Not having to sweep and sew on buttons. Staying away from the vacuum cleaner unless I feel like approaching it. Cleaning when *I* want to, and not having to worry so much about appearances. I am very joyful about all this."

7. Pleasures of Personal Creativity

Woman: "I like living alone. I enjoy decorating my own space, choosing the things I want and putting them there, i.e., shade of paint, furniture, rug, etc. I like creating my own environment without being told how and where."

Man: "Since becoming single and being alone a lot I have taken up pottery, read much more, thought thoughts I'd never considered before. None of this was possible when I was living with the same woman for so long a time. Living with someone takes away a lot of your creative energy."

8. Miscellaneous Pleasures

Man: "I like the flexibility of hours. I make my own clock and my own time."

Woman: "I feel living alone is better because I'm not always having to give in to male chauvinist ideas. I feel many times I'm being tested. Not by men but by Jesus! That's a wonderful thing to know, and it couldn't happen if I lived with someone else."

Woman: "Being able to read in bed when I want to . . ."

Woman: "You can walk around nude without worrying about anyone seeing you."

Man: "Being alone is not the negation of marriage. It is the natural condition of the evolved, aware human being. This is a pleasure. The pain is in the stereotyping."

Woman: "I love making my own rules and then not having to stick to them."

Man: "I can yell as loud as I want and no one can hear me. I can fart and no one will hold their nose. I can be stupid and no one will laugh. I can have pets and no one will complain. I like pets better than people anyway."

MORE ON LONELINESS

The greatest problem of being single is the problem of loneliness. In the essay question on the difficulties and pleasures of living alone, we asked singles how they deal with loneliness, isolation, and fear. The answers were lengthy, intelligent and sometimes profound. They reveal that:

1. Loneliness is indeed *the* monumental problem faced by people living alone;
2. Most people have in one way or another worked out their own personal method for dealing with this problem.

Here are a few solutions:

Man: "Whenever I feel particularly lonely I go to the mirror and start to talk to myself. Don't laugh, it's excellent therapy. I make faces at myself and joke with the reflection. After a while I start laughing at myself. I tell myself that I made the choice to be alone, and that loneliness is just a false idea bred by my own self-pity. Dig that it is myself telling myself this. Somehow this gets me out of the dithers."

Woman: "Whenever I start feeling that old sinking lonely feeling, like I'm never going to find someone nice, I force myself to get busy. I cook. I read. I go out for a walk or visit a friend. I do anything that keeps me busy and active. Soon it passes."

Woman: "Solution: Last week lunch with Shirley, John, Bob, Charles, Mary, Don. Twice dinner at my house with Don, John, Howard and Chris. Date every evening. Saturday afternoon, Sunday brunch. Cultivate neighbors, bridge partners. Swimming, bike riding. Beside this any one of my two jobs and one professional position would keep me out of trouble."

Woman: "I deal with loneliness with organizations such as Parents Without Partners, my close friends, and God. Also, by remembering you can be even lonelier in a marriage from neglect than from living alone."

Man: "Loneliness is a state of mind. I tell myself this. You can feel lonely in the midst of a party. I don't believe a healthy individual is any lonelier whether single or married."

Man: "Whenever I get lonely I eat a good meal and then go jogging to compensate for eating. Occasionally I take trips. I increase my involvement in my work—that helps. You have to face life as it comes and attempt to make the best for yourself."

Woman: "When I'm lonely I try to do something with my child. It makes me feel good to know that she's having a good time. I spend time with my family. Friends I can really talk to help get me out of depression. At night I watch TV and listen to the radio and read. I try to keep busy."

Woman: "The way to deal with loneliness is to be sure to make friends who you can call on the phone to chat with. The most miserable year of my life was spent when I relocated to a place where I had no friends. I wasted a year of my life there until I finally decided to give up my job and inexpensive apartment to move to a place where I had friends, even if my living expenses would be higher. You don't feel so desperate that way when you have friends to share your life with. Both male and female friends are important."

Man: "It's important to keep busy with anything—it doesn't matter what, as long as you are doing something. (I'm sitting in on grad school classes, but for no credit.) It's too easy to fall into a rut of watching TV every night. I like to do things that make me feel young like going to college. I go into depressions when I stay home alone too much."

Woman: "Loneliness must be realized to be a temporary state of mind. With all the tomorrows we know will come, surely we must realize there is something new and different. Be kind to yourself. Respect yourself. There is love to be found talking to an old lady in the park or watching the handicapped kids play. Or a Woody Allen movie. LISTEN to the world around you. One can be alone and not lonely. Be reserved in your nature and listen. Something will come along. Call a hotline. There are others who are in the same boat. You're never alone."

Man: "I realized early on in my life that the only way to really feel fulfilled is to search for something higher than myself. My spiritual adventure has taken me to books, meetings of all kinds, teachers. . . . I am never bored. It is the search alone (never mind what you find on it) that keeps me from feeling lonely. As to being alone, remember: You die alone."

"It is my firm belief that people are really not meant to be alone," states Dr. Arlene Heyman, psychiatrist and psychoanalyst in private practice in New York City, and member of the Affiliated Staff of the New York Psychoanalytic Institute. "The infant develops in close connection to a mother or a mothering figure, and that experience shapes the individual for all time. From the very start, then, there is a built-in need to relate in an intimate way to another person. This need continues throughout life. But it should not be confused with a very different, more pathological feeling—the inability to be alone, ever. People suffering that feeling experience panic and emptiness. It is as if they have no memories inside them of an early trustworthy relationship.

"All of us are lonely at one time or another. And some of us are driven to acts we wouldn't consider under happier circumstances. Much of the sex in the 'sexual revolution' is sex between strangers. Holding another body gives a transient illusion of intimacy; afterwards, one is often even more painfully alone. Some people go so far as to marry in order to escape loneliness. Extreme need overrides judgment and they give little thought to the suitability of their prospective mates.

"I believe that being alone should be a temporary state, not a lifelong proposition. After all, loving and being loved are very great pleasures in life. Perhaps they are the greatest pleasures."

"Loneliness is a feeling that one is without a source of emotional supply or support," claims Dr. Judd Marmor, psychiatrist at the University of Southern California in Los Angeles and past president of the

American Psychiatric Association. "Most people have this need for affection, and when they are bereft of that supply they get lonely and anxious. This is normal. We all want emotional ties—I think we place too much emphasis in our culture on being emotionally independent. We live in a society that places such emphasis on individualism and doesn't provide the kind of support system that other societies do. We are fragmented, with a tremendous emphasis both on independence and on being part of a couple. There is a terrible squeeze for the person caught in between—if individuals couple then they are not being independent; if they are independent then they are not coupling. Either way they can't win.

"There is also a pathological variety of loneliness," adds Dr. Marmor. "It is when one can never be alone *at all*. When one continually needs people around. When a person can't spend the weekend alone. This is pathological.

"I have found that generally women are more lonely than men. This is because men don't feel ashamed to go out with other men and do things as a group. Women often have built into them a sense that they don't want to be seen with other women, since this would be an admission that they don't have a boyfriend. I think too many single women act as though the lack of a steady man makes them failures. In my work with single women I try to have them appreciate the fact that they are persons first, and that they don't have to be an adjunct to a man to feel their lives are meaningful. Many women I see feel that if they are not attached to a man they are nothing, that a man is the only thing that counts in life. That's an attitude that I hope in time will lessen with women's new consciousness."

AIDS ALONG THE TRAIL: HELP AND SELF-HELP

5. Describe how the following have helped you with problems of living alone and being single: family, religious or self-help programs, therapist, community-sponsored organizations, friends. In what ways have they not helped?

Of all means of psychological and social support, the one most often mentioned is friends. Friends, especially friends who are single, are the best listeners, the best advice-givers, the ones with the smallest axe to grind. Most of all, friends are simply *there*.

Woman, Corpus Christi, TX: Friends who are also singles are of great help. We can share solutions and give support to one another. Married friends, and especially the kind that have not been single for a long time, don't seem to understand how any single person could possibly be happy. Even though they may have a very unhappy marriage themselves, they seem to "want company in their misery." Friends have helped by acting as a sounding-board and a sympathetic ear for my problems.

Woman, Addison, TX: Friends have been sympathetic when I've felt discouraged, which happens a lot when you live alone. They try to be objective and realistic when I am subjective and in a dream state. They expect me to be available to them as I expect them to be for me. As a "new" single, they admire my independence and give me "tips" on how to maintain a steady lifestyle. Most of all, my good friends understand my need for peace and calmness in life, and when they are in my environment, promote these vibes. My best friends were previously divorced. They helped me get myself together, and made me feel that in time I'll find someone else worth waiting for.

Man, Phoenix, AZ: The old saying that "friends are forever" is true, especially when you are single. You have no wife to depend on. You're too old for parental dependence or support. Most of these single "groups" are pretty Mickey Mouse about it all. What you really fall back on again and again are your friends, both men and women. They're the ones who get you through the long nights and the days that never end. When I broke up with my wife I was "flat broke." My best buddy took me in for a month until I could get a little money together. Then another buddy rented me a small trailer for six months till I could afford a better place.

The help provided by family is mentioned as frequently as help from friends, but with greater evidence of conflicted feelings. Family support is sometimes described as "help with strings attached." These strings are usually emotional, though sometimes they have a more substantive nature.

Man, Denver, CO: My parents have been of value in getting me on my feet economically. But we got in trouble over how much interest they want on the loans they give me. I felt anything over 4% was unreasonable (they want 6½%). My parents argued they'd be making far more if they had it in six-month bonds. They told me I was irresponsible and needed to learn what a dollar means. I think they are just stingy and are hiding behind self-righteousness. If I had a kid I certainly wouldn't charge *him* interest.

Some parents may disapprove of their child's divorce and may demonstrate this through a nonsupportive and even hostile manner. From the same impulse, parents may also exert impolitic pressures on their offspring to get married. Some respondents claim their mother and father are simply "emotionally unavailable."

Woman, New Orleans, LA: My parents offered me money, a roof over my head, etc., but failed to give me the one thing I really needed when I broke with Larry, which was emotional support. They just don't understand. They don't know how to feel.

The main emotion expressed by singles concerning family is *ambivalence.* In the same sentence subjects may extol their progenitors and then castigate them. An essay may continue for a paragraph describing the virtues of parental aid, then launch into a vituperative attack on family eccentricities.

Woman, Atlanta, GA: My poor father, until his death two years ago he always tried to find marriage partners for me! He did his best. The rest of the family has been little help except in one respect: one of my biggest problems has been as a single homeowner. My brother-in-law has been a jewel about helping me with the chores. My sister is a bitch but sometimes is okay.

Woman, Phoenix, AZ: My family is a close and religious one. But they have not helped by imposing their morals upon my lifestyle when at times I haven't wanted to know about it. I just need to be patted on the head, not lectured to. Of course, it's hard to bite the hand that feeds you too, and in so many ways they've helped.

Man, Darien, CT: Family has helped a bit but sometimes a family can be *too* helpful and pushy about not being single. I sometimes think my parents think I am "half a person" because I'm not married yet. Sometimes it seems they kill you with their good wishes.

Relatively few singles mention therapy as a means of coping with the problems of single life. Those who do, do so in a positive manner. Respondents report that psychological counseling has helped them to know themselves better, improve their self-image, and realize that their personal problems are rarely unique.

Man, Chicago, IL: Therapy helped me see myself as a whole and as a good person, it helped me deal with guilt feelings over divorce and to realize that others had many of the same kinds of feelings, it helped me feel I was not alone in the world. Lots of other people out there have similar mind sets.

Woman, Pittsburgh, PA: I used therapy very briefly after divorce to help make the initial transition from marriage to single life (about six visits). It helped me piece together the emotional reasons why I left my husband, to know it was okay. It helped me feel better about myself and understand why I do things. I intend to go back as soon as I have settled my life some more.

Woman, Manhattan, NY: A certain psychiatrist in downtown New York helped me screw my head back in place after it had been clubbed off by a certain young man I know. This guy was sweetness and light to the world, a demon at home and to me. His thing was sadism, sexual sadism. He would do all kinds of things to me, playing on my masochism, playing on my weaknesses as a woman. I don't want to mention them. I'll just give you one example. One day he came home with a large bag. "What do you think is in here?" he asked, and out of the bag took a black leather hood—before I had time to say anything he'd fitted it over my head—I'm many things but I've never been a "leather freak." These leather items impair your breathing but they have a gag built in and you can't talk. He locked it from behind and made me walk around the house naked with it on for hours at a time. Finally I was almost suffocating and even *he* could see that, and took it off my head. There were other crazy events like that that also happened. Otherwise he was okay. My shrink taught me to recognize that I invited masochistic treatment and he helped me deal with my own masochism as a woman. I was in deep analysis for a long time and I think that now I can at least approach the problem of having a non-neurotic sex life.

Religious groups receive a mixed billing. For some they are a source of inspiration, for others they prove rigid institutions where, as a man from Baltimore wrote, "It's not God that is dead but the people there."

God and religion are often mentioned as supports against alienation; and though some respondents believe that religious organizations are too dogmatic, the religious spirit itself is often claimed to be a profound comfort. Many times this distinction is drawn between organized religion and personal religious belief.

Woman, Toledo, OH: Religious groups have helped me realize that there's more than just me . . . that God's there ready to listen when I need a little support. The people at these places are a bit closed and moralizing. My belief carries me through. I take what is best from them and bring it home with me in my heart.

Man, Birmingham, AL: Religion gives me strength to face life and problems, and get over the rejection and depression of being single. The groups themselves are filled with some nice people and some sanctimonious, self-satisfied "Christians." The groups are still a good place to meet available Christian women, though they get a little goody-goody at times. When I feel myself becoming critical I remember that religion is about God Himself, not about personalities.

Parents Without Partners, a nationwide organization for divorced parents, is also frequently mentioned.

Woman, Baltimore, MD: Parents Without Partners has been the best help of all since I've become single. I have a two-year-old and a six-year-old. I bring my six-year-old to some of the affairs at PWP meetings, and there she can see that there are lots of other kids without fathers, and lots of other mothers without husbands. It's both a good place to learn about the latest methods of dealing with divorce child-raising stress (by talking to others, hearing lectures, participating in groups), and also meeting available men who have their own children and know the problems.

Few other organizations besides Parents Without Partners are mentioned specifically, though at least a quarter of all essays mention "social organizations" or "self-help groups," usually with mixed feelings.

Woman, Philadelphia, PA: Since my divorce I've gone to many of the so-called "self-help" meetings and they are much the same, peopled by earnest, well-meaning types who are also on the make due to their loneliness and despair. The groups are run well and professionally. Goodness, I don't want to sound like a snob. I think what I am trying to say is that the confusion and sadness of so many people here behind their smiles is too much for me at a time in my life when I feel so vulnerable anyway!

Man, Pittsburgh, PA: For the first several years I was a "groupie" kind of single, running off first to this self-help group, then to that self-help group. I attended lectures by psychiatrists on how to be your own best friend, cocktail parties for introducing single people to one another, seminars on being single, encounter weekends, all that stuff. It pretty much added up to the same few platitudes. A lot of these platitudes today I would even question. Like, "take care of yourself first and everything else will fall into place." "You have to take full responsibility for your life." "Feel good about yourself and everyone else will feel good about you too." These are just a few that I can remember. The notion of people getting together to do a thing in community spirit is good, I like it, but with singles groups people tend to be very selfish and self-involved, and these so-called groups are really just a collection of egomaniacs who don't care about anyone but themselves. Meanwhile the people who are running them are making money off our needs and vulnerabilities, and laughing all the way to the bank.

Woman, Washington, DC: I was helped enormously by my therapy group. The group was filled with other women, some of them parents in my same situation, who had been single for some time and who knew the ropes. We rapped and dialogued out lots of the troubles that single mothers run up against in daily life, and it's terrific to hear that others have the same problems as you. Misery loves company. But there's more to it also, because in these groups a lot of good, sound advice that comes from other people's experiences filters down, and it's the kind of stuff you can apply directly to your own life.

The consensus concerning social organizations that cater to singles is that they help, but only in a limited way. As one essay phrased it, they are "a relief from the pain of living alone but not a cure." In this same essay, it might be added, the respondent goes on to say that the final supports he found most useful were from his own "inner faculties." In this he sums up what so many other singles tell us concerning the fundamental problems of living alone: "I've had the best luck not depending on organizations or shrinks to fill the emptiness of living alone. I try to do that with my own interests and my concerns for people, especially my friendships and personal philosophical beliefs. After all, these organizations, all they can do for you is *help you help yourself,* get you accustomed to the difficulties of single life. I think the important thing is to take responsibility for your own emotional life. If you do this, everything else will fall into place."

Chapter 5

Living Together ||||

New Solution or New Problem

In this chapter on "Living Together" we ask:

1. Have you ever lived with a member of the opposite sex on an intimate, unmarried basis?

2. What would be the main reason why you might choose to live with a partner rather than marry him or her?

3. Is living together a step toward getting married or has it now become a separate lifestyle all its own? Could you see yourself living with someone indefinitely without marriage? Why or why not?

4. In your opinion, is sex better when married or when living together?

5. Do you think that living together is as personally fulfilling as marriage?

6. Would you live with a partner whom you didn't love?

7. What do you believe are the main problems and benefits of living together as opposed to being married? Which do you prefer and why?

8. In your opinion, should living together be an exclusive arrangement or should the partners have the right to date others? Why or why not? How would you react to infidelity by someone you were living with?

9. How would you handle infidelity on the part of someone you were living with?

An older single writes: "Although I've never had the nerve to live with a man out of wedlock, my daughter has done it several times. Secretly, I envy her. I wonder what it's like. I wonder what goes on. I wonder if it beats being married."

We wondered too. What is living together really all about? Do singles think of it as an alternative to marriage, or as a lifestyle all its own?

In the past thirty years the unmarried household has ceased to be either a refuge for rebellious bohemians or a social embarrassment, and has instead turned into an all-but-standard if slightly self-conscious social institution. Indeed, the trend toward living together has increased tenfold in the past decade, and estimates have it that anywhere from five to twenty million singles in the United States share lodgings on an intimate, unmarried basis. According to our findings, 5 percent of men and 8 percent of women are *currently* living with someone of the opposite sex, but many more have lived with someone at various times.

WHY SINGLES COHABIT

1. *Have you ever lived with a member of the opposite sex on an intimate, unmarried basis?*

Major Finding: Approximately half of all single men and a third of all single women have at one time or another lived with a member of the opposite sex.

> ### BONUS FINDINGS
> - Over half (51 percent) of men who have never been married have *not* lived with a woman.
> - A man divorced twice will live with a woman more readily than a man divorced once.
> - Twice as many high-income-earners as low report having lived with a woman.
> - Sixty percent of men in their early twenties have not lived with a woman. Only 37 percent in their late twenties and early thirties report the same.
> - More than half of never-married women have *not* lived with a man.
> - Women divorced twice are *three times* more apt to have lived with a man than women divorced once.

With these facts at hand, we asked respondents what seemed the sec-ond-most-important question:

2. *What would be the main reason you might choose to live with a partner rather than marry him or her?*

We wished to learn whether singles believe living together has become an independent lifestyle *unrelated to any matrimonial end,* or whether it is viewed as a stage in the modern marital process.

Respondents were split in their views. Almost half consider living together a preparation for marriage; the other half think it a substitute for marriage.

- Forty-three percent of single men and 48 percent of single women would live with someone because they wish to *test the depths of our compatibility before marriage.* This is the more traditional half of the group, partisans of what a decade ago was termed "trial marriage."
- About a quarter of men (26 percent) and a fifth of women (21 percent) would live with someone because *they would want the companionship but not the commitment.* This response reflects the general attitude of the anti-marriage contingent. Other answers along these lines include: *There would be no reason for the official formality of marriage* (9 percent men, 6 percent women), *living together offers a greater chance of compatibility than marriage* (6 percent men, 4 percent women), *I'd want to leave myself an escape hatch* (7 percent men, 8 percent women).
- Only 4 percent of men and women are overtly cynical about lasting relationships, claiming *I don't believe two people can make it over a long-term period of time.* Nine percent of women and 5 percent of men say they don't know.

We can identify two fundamental outlooks, the first constituted on the premise that marriage should be the aim of living together, the second that the value of living together lies in the fact that it helps people *avoid* marriage. These opposing views have a direct relationship to the age of the respondent. Note:

PROFILE: The single person who sees living together as preparation for marriage.

> PROFILE SUMMARY: Older male and female singles perceive living together as a *transitory experience* rather than a preliminary to wedlock. Young men and women, especially students, consider living together a trial marriage. The younger they are, the more likely they are to view things this way. Aside from age, few important characteristics differentiate the different groups. To an extent, college-educated persons are more likely to judge living together as a permanent relationship than those who attended high school only. Professionals are less prone to live together than white- and blue-collar singles. These differences, however, are not profound. What is profound is the fact that for the younger and hence statistically never-married single, cohabitation is thought to be part of the marriage process, while older, and hence statistically more frequently divorced singles see it as an escape from marriage.
>
> Detailed information on the two outlooks—living together as preparation for marriage, living together as an avoidance of marriage—is provided by answers to the next question.

3. *Is living together a step toward getting married or has it now become a separate lifestyle all its own? Could you see yourself living with someone indefinitely without marriage? Why or why not?*

The essays reveal four different groups, each with distinctly separate attitudes concerning the live together issue. They are as follows:

1. Those who sometimes live together.
2. Those who live together as an alternative to marriage.
3. Those who live together on a trial-marriage basis.
4. Those who live together for the sake of convenience.

1. Those Who Sometimes Live Together

Singles often share each other's living space without technically inhabiting it. Sometimes this setup is established before any kind of formal romantic promise has been made. Indeed, it is often of so casual a nature that it is considered an extension of the dating process and not a live-in situation at all. But it *is* living together, at least to the extent that sleeping together in the same bed each night can be considered living together.

Man, Burlington, VT: My girl and I date practically every night of the week. She sleeps at my place or I stay at her apartment over her garage. I don't know whether you would say we are living together.

In such situations the question of marriage has not arisen. Participants view themselves as free agents even though they spend most of their time together. Only the act of moving their belongings into a partner's space would establish the scene as official. The above essay continues:

At this point it's too soon for either of us, her or myself, to say if we're interested in marriage. We just groove on being together a lot. Her place or mine or whatever the place. If things get serious later on, then we'll discuss about getting "hitched."

Woman, Nassau, NY: Since I've been in college I have lived with three men. Though I spend my nights in a dorm I spend all the rest of the time with the man I love in his apartment and we cook together, I clean his house, etc. Living with a man has its problems but you can always check out the door if he gets too loud or obnoxious. Though I haven't really lived day after day with the same person, doing what I mentioned here is living together as far as I'm concerned.

Man, Syracuse, NY: My girlfriend and I don't really get along very well. That may sound like a strange admission. We just love being together for short periods of times, and we have great times in the bed. We are very well matched in a sexual way. I enjoy her body and she enjoys mine, and besides that we do like to bowl together, see movies, have long talks and go on canoe trips. But we get to a certain point where we just start to argue. It always happens. I spend a little time at her house and she spends a little time at mine, but we really couldn't make it full-time living together.

Of the four groups, those in this group are the least committed to each other. Those in the next category take things a step further, though here also commitment is qualified.

2. Marriage Alternatives

There are several reasons why singles may deny any close link between living together and marriage.

Some prefer living together because it allows them the intimacy of marriage without the responsibility. More than one respondent uses the phrase "having your cake and eating it too."

Woman, Ponchatoula, LA: Two people live together for the sake of happiness, convenient sex, convenient companionship, convenient financial security. Everything is and has always been designed for couples. Unless you have a companion, married or not, you're not complete. I personally like living together better than marriage because it has all the advantages of an easy escape route, mingled with the pleasures of intimacy. And none of the disadvantages.

Woman, Buffalo, NY: Since I've been living with someone for eight years, I can see it as a separate lifestyle. I feel as bound to this man as if we were married. Just living together is like having one less weight to carry. Not being legally bound offers a feeling of relief. And we love each other and enjoy all the advantages. I feel a freedom that flows into other aspects of my daily life.

Man, Sacramento, CA: Living together is better. It keeps both parties on their best behavior. In my own marriage I observed that we took each other for granted, my wife and I. We got so we would fart in front of each other or yell without thinking of the other's ears. She would look like a dog. I would neglect to take baths. In bed we took each other for granted. We got bored, too. There was no mystery any more and there was no special "mystique." I belonged to her legally, the state said so. She was my property too—the state said so. There was nothing to keep us alive, and I fear that many marriages are like that. Living together, on the other hand, forces a couple not to take each other for granted. Why, if one gets too forgetful of looking good or acting like a nice guy (or gal), the other can always up and leave. Living together makes it impossible for familiarity to breed contempt. You have to be on your best behavior all the time. This is why I prefer the live-together solution.

Other respondents mentioned that living together keeps sexual and romantic attraction alive in a way that marriage does not. This raises a separate though profoundly related issue, which we raised in the following question:

4. In your opinion, is sex better when married or when living together?

Major Finding: Approximately the same number of men claim that sex is better in marriage because it has time to grow and mature (30 percent), as believe that sex is different in both but equally fulfilling (29 percent).

However, only 10 percent of men and 6 percent of women say sex is *better when living together*. Here are the complete findings:

Is sex better when married or living together?	Men	Women
a. Better in marriage because it has time to grow and mature.	30%	38%
b. Better when living together because marriage makes sex boring.	10%	6%
c. Different in both but equally fulfilling.	29%	25%
d. There is no difference.	17%	16%
e. The very naughtiness of not being married makes sex better.	4%	2%
f. Live-togethers suffer a sexual guilt which can only be removed by marriage.	3%	4%
g. Don't know.	8%	9%

BONUS FINDINGS

- The younger a single man or woman, the more he or she is likely to claim that sex is better when living together because marriage makes sex boring. The older a single becomes the more likely he or she is to claim it's better in marriage because it has time to grow and expand.
- Blue-collar, high-school-educated men and women tend to think that sex is better when you are living together rather than in marriage, more than do college-educated professionals.
- The once-divorced male is more apt to prefer married sex than single sex. But the twice-divorced male does not agree. He prefers the liaisons formed in bachelorhood. Meanwhile, women divorced once or twice both prefer married sex.

Here are some essays on the subject of live-together sexuality.

Woman, Philadelphia, PA: I've never lived with a man but would imagine sex would be very stimulating that way because it would always be new and would not get static. Knowing you could leave any time makes both partners perform at their optimum and not just take sex for granted as people do (my husband did) in marriage.

Woman, Atlanta, GA: A question on the questionnaire asked if sex is better when you are living together. I don't think it is because when you are married you know the man's body and his physique very well. This is something that does not happen unless you are with someone a long while. You learn all the mutual tastes between you, sexually, and it takes perhaps many years to perfect the pleasure for each other. Only in marriage can this be achieved.

Man, Washington, DC: One of the biggest concerns these days is sex. What about sex? It's everywhere, it seems. If you live with a couple of girls through the years as I've done you get to be an authority on it. I have also been married. I prefer to be married but do not knock the other kinds of sex. Sex while married is better because it is the most intimate kind of sex. If you take two people who really know each other and keep them together nightly in the same bed they will get pretty good at it after a while. Sex is an art. It takes a long time before a woman learns the things that please a man and vice versa. Maybe a man likes certain things done to him. All personal preferences take a lot of time to learn. People are sometimes scared to tell them to each other and it takes years of marriage before they will come clean about it. Even when you live together people get very shy. They think: "I probably won't be with this person all my life. If I tell them certain of my secrets they will blab about them when we break up." You can see how this makes for mutual dishonesty and lack of sincerity. When married, partners know it is for keeps and they do not feel shy about divulging their innermost sexual wants and requirements. In all, I believe that though sex is nice it is best in a long-term, married situation.

There is a further variation under the category of marriage alternatives. This is the single who champions cohabitation as a statement of social philosophy. For this person marriage is a repressive institution that should be avoided at all costs:

Woman, Tampa, FL: I've been married and I've been single as a live-together person. By a million-to-one I prefer living together. Marriage is a deadening thing. It kills whatever it touches. It should be made illegal. I am a member of a society which stands up to the marriage laws and lobbies for better laws for people who want alternatives.

Man, Portland, OR: I am opposed to marriage on principle. For centuries it has handicapped men and women. Now the law is beginning to become a little enlightened and I say halalujah! At last we have the *legal right* to live with who we want. I say glory to the coming times. Down with marriage and up with the flag of sexual-personal-independent freedoms!

For some singles, living together has become something of a cause:

Woman, Cleveland, OH: It's time that married people woke up and realized that marriage doesn't work. People who are living together are a living proof of the fact that this is the coming trend. Marriage is outdated, moribund, unfair, unreasonable, and unsound. Marriage has kept people slaves for centuries. It is time to realize that social change is necessary. This is for everyone. Homosexuals have a right to live together too. What about disabled people? How long will we laugh at them? Don't they have rights? My boyfriend and I are committed to helping society help itself. We have started a commune where couples can come no matter what race, religion, creed, sexual persuasion, physical condition, and stay without benefit of clergy. We promote singles' rights, we don't just talk about them like you people which I call the "eggheads" of America. You talk, we act. A person has the right to do what they please. That's what the founding fathers started this whole thing for.

Such anti-matrimonial spirit, however, is rare among the essays. Only 4 percent of men and women said permanent relationships are impossible or outdated. Marriage itself is not generally attacked by those living together or lifetime singles, and even respondents who themselves dislike the institution usually admit it may be an acceptable convention for others.

3. Trial Marriages

Approximately half of singles believe that living together is a step toward marriage.

Man, Lansing, MI: Living together is a good test for marriage. I could not live with someone without any hope of first testing the relationship in the bedroom, and in the bathroom too. (By that I mean, does she leave the cap off the toothpaste, are our habits too different for compatibility?) Trial marriage is a great thing, and I'm pleased to be alive at a time when it's allowed. There would be fewer divorces if everybody did it.

The essays in this category convey the message that living together is a time for testing and sizing up, that it offers an effective means of avoiding big mistakes, that it permits a couple to learn their real feelings, and that such a test period is not only a smart idea but a mandatory precaution:

Woman, Winston-Salem, NC: Living together is *very* necessary. How can you tell if you're compatible or not? This is one of the best things to come out of the modern movements of our times. Why isn't *everyone* taking advantage of it?

Man, Seattle, WA: So many people get married without knowing how they'll do with each other's bodies. Living together informs you about the long-term benefits or drawbacks of your sexual life. Bad sex life, bad marriage; good sex life, good marriage. I firmly believe that.

Woman, Nashville, TN: By living together you are able to experience "marriage" in non-married status. That way you know if you share the same tastes, the same hobbies, the same kinds of friends, similar tastes in living arrangements. If your "trial" relationship endures adjustment problems then only should you take the final steps to marriage. This helps avoid bad marriages and divorces and hurt children.

Some respondents approach the question from a "scientific" viewpoint, offering a precise mathematics of trial matrimony:

Woman, Hackensack, NJ: Possibly if there were a prerequisite four to six months living-together time made for persons under the age of 25 there would be a lot fewer unhappy people.

Man, Grand Rapids, MI: I feel that if you are living together with another person for a year you should know then if it's going to work. You should let the first three months decide if your sexualities are meshed. The next three to see if your personalities are matched. The last six to see how your tastes towards the home match. Then put them all together for a complete picture. This is a terrific way of planning in advance!

5. *Do you think that living together is as personally fulfilling as marriage?*	Men	Women
a. It has all the advantages and few of the disadvantages.	18%	12%
b. Marriage is outdated; living together will replace it.	5%	2%
c. Partners don't take each other for granted the way they do in marriage.	18%	15%
d. Living together allows one to experience many meaningful relationships instead of just one via marriage.	14%	8%
e. The very lack of commitment stops it from being totally fulfilling.	35%	49%
f. Living together is a sin.	5%	8%
g. Don't know.	8%	7%

Traditionally more marriage-minded than men, women remain in favor of marriage even when offered the seemingly attractive alternative of cohabitation. Despite the assertions of some female respondents that marriage contracts are "only a piece of paper," marriage remains an important concern for a majority of single American women.

"If you take a whole group of women," claims Dr. Kenneth Solomon, Assistant Professor of Psychiatry at University of Maryland and coeditor of the book *Men in Transition: Changing Male Roles, Theory and Therapy,** "you are likely to find them reading the word 'love' into the word 'commitment.' Now living together, *per se,* does not necessarily imply commitment. And it's still part of the traditional feminine socialization pattern to have an affair *only* with someone whom one is committed to. On the whole, I think, men are still socialized in our country to avoid commitment, and women to *seek* it. All of this implies that men are more likely to support living together over marriage, and women to do the opposite.

"In our country men are not supposed to be dependent on others. That's part of the conventional masculine role, the pioneer man, the

* To be published by Plenum Press.

John Wayne image. Yet men do of course have very real needs for commitment. The way they satisfy these needs and at the same time maintain their autonomy is to live with a woman without marrying her. This meets their need for dependency yet gives the appearance to the outside world that they are still free. By living with a woman rather than marrying her, a man can have his cake and eat it too. It's a 'cool' thing for a man to live with a woman. If a man lives with a beautiful, desirable woman he gets macho points to his account, he makes other men envious, he beats them in competition. It becomes part of the male drive for success, part of the conventional masculine role."

Age and prior marital status also have much to do with response to this question of fulfillment in marriage and cohabitation. Almost a quarter of men between the ages of twenty-five and thirty-four think living together has all the advantages and few of the disadvantages of marriage. Only 15 percent over age forty-five agree. Far more men in middle-age say that by living together, the very lack of commitment stops it from being totally fulfilling.

For women the gap is even greater. A fifth under twenty-four say that living together has all the advantages of marriage. Only 4 percent in their forties come to the same conclusion.

"Young people are highly romantic," remarks Professor Joseph Garza, Associate Professor of Sociology at Georgia State University in Atlanta. "They believe they can have their cake and eat it too. But wait a few years and see what these same people say. People's attitudes to such questions change as they come to grips with the reality of *real* commitment. And as people get older they simply want more quality in a commitment, they want more real commitment, not just the quasi commitment offered when living together."

Subjects who support trial marriages have often lived alone for some years. Respondents who have recently been embroiled in painful divorce proceedings are more dubious about matrimony. Often their essays are punctuated with such statements as "My divorce taught me that marriage is an insane alternative," or "I was so hurt by our marriage that I'll never make the same mistake again."

Man, Detroit, MI: Marriage—it sucks! It stinks! I'd never let myself get roped in again by that fucking piece of paper that made me bleed my money, heartache. The only way I'd be with a girl now is to live with her, and I'd make damn sure we had a contract figured out beforehand so she couldn't act like Marvin's old lady and screw me!

Such wounds, though they leave scars, do apparently heal. We find subjects who, having suffered a difficult divorce and having been on their own for extended periods of time, are now once again in the marriage market. This time, however, they choose to take advantage of the protection a live-together arrangement supplies:

Man, Milwaukee, WI: I've come to believe that living together is the best way to get to know someone before marrying her. I wish I'd been able to do this with my first wife or I'd never have married her; and I wouldn't have been so poisoned against love for so many years due to our divorce.

Woman, Independence, MO: I never thought I'd say it again but after being single for a long time and trying out living with a man a few times, I think being married is all in all a better thing to do. Marriage was not fun for me. I think though that with the right man I could make it work (finding the right man is no easy thing). I promised myself I'd never marry again but that was when I was breaking up. It would not surprise me if most people who go through a divorce say they will never marry again and will only live with someone, if that. Living together is not the same as marriage.

Man, Toledo, OH: You have to be ready for marriage. Cindy and I are ready for it now because we both have been over the coals of the singles scene. Cindy has lived with men and I have lived with women. Cindy was jilted by one of them after he promised to marry her. She has a child. It was not easy for the child, you can be sure. Since then she has been against living with a man and wants to marry—me. And I her. I lived with a woman from Tennessee for a year and it was holy hell. Why I didn't leave sooner is beyond me. Both women and men need the security that marriage offers.

Though a large number of singles believe that living together offers a valuable testing time prior to marriage, some professionals question this idea. In a recent study conducted by the magazine *Medical Aspects of Human Sexuality,** several hundred psychiatrists were asked to respond to the question: "Does living together before marriage generally make for better marriages?" Only 14 percent said *frequently.* Sixteen percent said *usually.* Fifty-five percent said *sometimes.* Fifteen percent said *rarely.*

* December 1980.

Apropos of this question, Professor Garza recently presented a paper to the American Psychiatric Association entitled "Sex Roles Within Cohabiting Relationships." "In my own research," he tells us, "I learned that an overwhelming majority of subjects who live together do so on a trial-marriage basis. Preliminary analysis of my findings indicates that their experience does *not* turn out to be what they intend it to be.

"I was interested in the kinds of questions you are asking—why people cohabit, and does it really make a difference? I myself could find *no differences* whatsoever between the two types of married couples I studied, those who lived together before marriage and those who did not. I found no difference between them in terms of overall level of satisfaction. If a couple did not live together first they had the same chances of success as a couple that did live together, or maybe greater. In fact, the hypothesis that living together is a negative has a lot of plausibility. Being legally married, I believe, constitutes a kind of social incentive to *stay* married, to make it, to make the effort to remain a unit. Whereas people who live together say to each other, 'Well, we're not legally married, so it will be easier to get out of it.' And, of course, it becomes that way. This is why the conclusion I put forth in my paper to the American Psychiatric Association was that living together does not make any difference for a couple in terms of satisfaction, adjustment, and long-term working out. Logically it would seem very sound that living together helps. Empirically it doesn't work out that way."

A contrasting point of view is taken by Dr. David Viscott, California psychiatrist and author of such bestselling books as *The Language of Feelings, Making of a Psychiatrist,* and *How to Live with Another Person.** "I think," he tells us, "that living together is the healthiest thing that has come along for the individual in ages and probably in the long run is the healthiest thing for the institution of marriage. If you're going to have a marriage that works, it needs a trial period. It's been very common in Scandinavian countries. In the northern parts of Sweden people live together until the woman gets pregnant.

"Living together is not much different from being married. I know there are people who would fight me on that, but the commitment is either there or it isn't. It's not just marrying someone and having a legal commitment that makes a real commitment grow. The only commitment that matters is the one you make to unite your feelings with

* All: Arbor House,

the other person so that you are operating honestly and with as low a level of defenses between you as possible.

"One of the good things about living together is that you don't have to, and shouldn't have to, give up your individuality, the way people do in marriages. A lot of people enter marriages because they think they will be protected and taken care of. Isn't it better to enter knowing you have an escape hatch, and that you'll be earning your own bread, your own keep? This makes for a more realistic arrangement. If you're paying your way it's even better. I believe a man and woman should have their own separate expenses, that a woman should buy her own car, a man take separate vacations, etc. Everybody should be in a position where he or she respects the individuality of the other. That's made possible when you live together."

4. Marriages of Convenience

The final category of live-together arrangements is of course not really a marriage and in fact is often not a romance either. What the name implies is what one gets, a live-together situation based on totally practical concerns such as companionship, proximity, comfort, money, and general living expedience.

Man, Phoenix, AZ: I choose to live with a woman who I get along with, who has some money and doesn't live off me, and who's in the neighborhood. You all make such a big deal about living together in this survey! It's no big deal. It's just a good way to pool resources and enjoy each other. By mutual consent a man and woman understand that feelings *won't* be a part of the deal. By that I mean "love" is not necessary, just mutual agreement to share, enjoy and experience together and then, when the time comes, move on.

Woman, Newton, MA: I have lived together with many men. I specifically *do not want* a serious relationship! I want something mutual and warm. *I don't want to be ripped off!* I always spell out what I want with a man in a contract together so there is no problem when we split up. Living together does not have to be a "forever" deal. It can exist as necessary at the present time.

Man, Van Nuys, CA: Yes, if both of us were on the same socioeconomic level, and knew that all we wanted was temporary sex and companionship/support. No love, please! That's what causes people to hate so much! It confuses the issue!

Does love confuse the issue?

6. *Would you live with a partner*   **Men**   **Women**
whom you didn't love?

		Men	Women
a.	Yes, if the sex was good.	10%	3%
b.	Yes, if the relationship was convenient and friendly.	31%	16%
c.	Yes, if the partner took care of my personal and monetary needs.	4%	5%
d.	I wouldn't know if I loved him or her until we lived together.	10%	6%
e.	No, I would have to love the person first.	34%	48%
f.	No, I'd only live with someone to whom I was married.	7%	20%
g.	Don't know.	5%	3%

Major Finding: *Almost half of single men (45 percent), as opposed to a quarter of single women (24 percent), said they would live with a partner without loving her/him.*

BONUS FINDINGS

- The man *least* likely to live with a woman because the relationship is *convenient and friendly* is the blue-collar worker. The man *most* likely to live with a woman for this reason is the white-collar college graduate.
- Gay men and women are far more apt to say they would live with a partner *provided the sex was good.* Twelve percent of lesbian women claim they would live with someone if the sex was good—as opposed to 3 percent of heterosexual women. Twenty-six percent of gay men said the same—as opposed to 9 percent of heterosexual men.
- Women who have been single all their lives are *twice* as apt as all other single people to live with a man only if the relationship is *convenient and friendly.* Women never married are more likely to enter a live-together situation on these grounds than women who have been married. Women in their twenties are almost three times as likely to enter a relationship on these grounds than women in their forties.

For many singles, especially men, living together is not only devoid of romantic commitment, it is aromantic, placing friendship ahead of passionate emotions, and expediency before love. We must assume that the large number of singles who answered affirmatively to this question reflects the large number for whom living together is a kind of casual and even routine event.

"My guess," says Dr. Madeline Hartford, a Dallas psychiatrist, "is that people who live together without marriage or love have tremendous difficulty in making commitments in personal relationships. Perhaps they're the type more capable of making commitments in work, say, than in relationships. For them the advantage of living together would be in never having to go that one crucial step. These people really don't trust anybody enough to give up their autonomy, and in this sense living with someone you don't really care about is tailor-made for avoiding commitment. You're allowed to hold back your feelings all you want. That's the difference between living together and marriage. In marriage you must make a deep attachment and then make a constant effort to stay committed irrespective of what happens. I think people who live together feel they have a right to avoid this kind of effort."

THE QUESTION OF LEGAL CONTRACTS

Throughout the essays the term "contract" continually appears. In recent years the legal responsibilities of living together have been debated and occasionally defined in the courts, sometimes under the spotlight, as in the case of Marvin *vs.* Marvin. The result has been that today, prior to entering into such a relationship, many singles spell out their demands in legal documents. Sometimes these documents include a wide range of personal and monetary stipulations, as can be seen from our respondents:

Woman, Denver, CO: I learned in my last time living with a man that I should first sign an agreement. We decided who would spend what among our groceries, household goods, cleaning, and other shared expenses. Housework and chores were designated and separate bank accounts were preferred. In case of break-up it was told who got what and what belonged to who. This worked out fine when the time came for us to separate, as we both knew it would from the start (which is why we drew up the contract in the first place). The drawback to it was that it was cold and calculating. It did save a lot of time and heart-break, and a lot of money.

Those who prefer contracts have usually been hurt in a previous marriage or suspect that their present relationship will not last. They are often apologetic about the need for such contracts, but defend their choice by an appeal to past experience. "I've been hurt money-wise too much in the past," writes a single man. "So now if there's a rip-off I got a legal paper to protect myself."

Woman, Denver, CO: An important flash was that this time I should write up a contract with the man I lived with and have it legally sanctioned by a lawyer. I bought a book on the subject that suggested a contract, spelling out where we would live and who would be responsible for the rent; how we would split the housework; who owned what property and what we owned in common, to be divided by mutual agreement; food costs; laundry, dry cleaning, and utility costs, and how they are divided; entertainment costs and how they are split; credit cards and bank arrangements. I have tried this twice. The first time after I broke up with the man, he complied with all the things in the contract and it made separation easier. The second time it wasn't so easy. The man said he didn't care about the contract and said it held no legal weight. And after we had both consulted a lawyer together on it, I threatened to sue and got my lawyer to write a letter. In the end he came around because he learned the law has teeth!

Barbara Hirsch, an attorney from Chicago, Illinois, has dealt with such legal problems, and is the author of *Living Together: An Aid to the Law for Unmarried Couples.** The following dialogue with Ms. Hirsch throws light on many of the points raised in the essays:

Question: What are some of the legal points singles should be aware of if they are going to live with each other?

MS. HIRSCH: There are a number of things: The questions of adultery and divorce, of loss of custody of children if you are living together, of alteration of visitation rights by reason of living together. Questions of using a shared name, and what's implied if you use another person's name. Questions of property rights and obligations. How to hold property, how to incur credit on the part of the person you are living with. Questions of insurance, which relate to whether or not you can cover

* Houghton Mifflin, 1976.

the life, health, or property of the person you are living with (whom I call a "consort"). Then there are Social Security implications of living together, pension and death benefits, taxes, discrimination in employment, people losing their jobs because they are living together, military service, traveling with a non-spouse, consorts who are deported for not being moral in the eyes of the Immigration and Naturalization Service. Then there's a multitude of things covering such loose ends as whether you can testify against your consort in a criminal proceeding when you can't against your spouse, and so forth.

Question: When two people move in with each other, live together, then break up after a period of years, what claims does each have over the other person's possessions?

MS. HIRSCH: They say that possession is nine-tenths of the law, especially with personal property such as a couch or chair. People don't usually walk around with bills of sale for such things. If you have a piece of real estate then you have a deed and there's no legal question. But for personal items without a bill of sale, I'm afraid there really isn't very much you can do if the other person walks away with it.

Question: What about protecting your money? I heard of one case of a man who ran up a large number of bills on his live-in's credit card.

MS. HIRSCH: You should make it clear to the credit card company from the start that you are responsible *for your debts only,* and that no one else is authorized to charge.

Question: What if the woman assumes the man's name and they pose as a family? Then is he responsible for her debts even if they are not legally married?

MS. HIRSCH: Yes. And vice-versa. There is no sex distinction in this and there never has been. It has to do with what are called "family obligations" or "family expense obligations." You can't go out and borrow two hundred thousand dollars and start a business and then make someone else responsible for it. But with the ordinary personal necessities of living, each of you is each other's agent-for-purchase, and this includes clothing, food, and those things that are suitable to your standard of living.

Question: Do you recommend that live-together couples have contracts spelling out who owns what and other legal matters?

MS. HIRSCH: Sometimes. It depends on what the contract covers. Certain conditions are not really enforceable in a court of law. If the consideration of the contract is an illegal sexual relationship, this is something outside of the law and the court isn't going to enforce it.

However, if you have a regular *business relationship* together, or a lease together, and you want to make a contract in the event that one of you moves out, that's different. That is a straight business contract. There's no reason then why you can't have a fully enforceable contract on the business matters of living together.

Another expert on the subject of the legalities surrounding living together is Dr. Melvin Krantzler, a psychologist from San Raphael, California, Director of the Creative Divorce, Love, and Marriage Counseling Center, and author of several bestselling books including *Creative Divorce** and *Learning to Love Again.*†

"In many ways non-marital arrangements for living together are becoming legal arrangements," Dr. Krantzler observes. "The courts are making such situations quasi marital with a new body of laws relating to them. Now most people choose to live together in the first place because of what I call 'commitment anxiety,' which I think is a national epidemic. This is the fear that if one actually commits onself to someone else for life, you are going to be strangled or demeaned, and that eventually the relationship will break up anyway. People want a close relationship and at the same time they fear it. Finally they decide that the appropriate compromise would be some means of living together other than marriage.

"People opt for living together thinking there are no strings attached and later they find themselves strangled with strings. I think it's one of the reasons that more and more people these days are opting for marriage—because living together has become such a legal tangle.

"What I recommend is that people who are contemplating living together see a lawyer first and become informed about the laws that may affect their particular situation. It's a legal issue now where before it wasn't. Be especially careful about your separate property. Suppose you have an inheritance and then put it into a joint account. Later when things break up it's going to be difficult proving that it was your property. Technical things like that can raise enormous difficulties. Draw up a live-together agreement between you, paying close attention to the laws of your own particular state. Use a lawyer who knows the ins and outs. Understand what the differences are between 'separate property' and 'community property.' Learn the legalities of com-

* M. Evans, 1973.
† Thomas Y. Crowell, 1977.

mon-law marriages and all that it entails. Be informed of all of it *before* you get involved. It may save you a lot of money and heartache at a later date."

LIVING TOGETHER: PROS AND CONS AND FINAL EVALUATIONS

7. *What do you believe are the main problems and benefits of living together as opposed to being married? Which do you prefer, and why?*

First let's analyze the question of benefits. Here is a representative list from respondents. Many of the answers are drawn from divorcees who speak from experience.

Woman: "The divorce rate is so high that it may be the thing to do to live together. Marriage is not for everyone anymore but perhaps only for those who have a lot of patience."

Woman: "Living together benefits—everybody is on his or her best behavior. That really is the best part. Masks are kept on but that can be a good thing. When masks come off so does the illusion, and sometimes illusion is better."

Woman: "Living together has proved a lot cheaper because you put your money together and at the end of the month it adds up to a lot more than you could get yourself. This is true for a woman more than a man."

Man: "Because of the implied impermanence of living together it is a desirable lifestyle for those who are unable or unprepared to make a commitment to permanence."

Man: "Living together has been fun and broadening, in that it has exposed me to an alternate lifestyle that a few years ago I would not even have considered. I would have considered it too off-beat and avant garde."

Woman: " 'Roommates' tend to be more considerate of each other, I think."

Woman: "In living together certain stressful situations never arise, such as: Should we have (more) kids? What kind of lifestyle do we, as a family unit, share? What values do we wish to instill in our children? Does the macho man allow his woman to work? Thus, lack of stress makes living together easier."

Man: By live-together you are able to experience a 'marriage' situation with a non-marital status. If your relationship endures then if you want you can marry, being sure that it will work out for you and yours."

Woman: "The best thing of living together is the ease that you can separate if you want to. Marriage seals the issue. Divorce is a nightmare. It's costly for both. Living together lets you get on and off the train without paying too much for those tickets!"

Some essays claim that living together is a supportable institution *as long as children are not involved.*

Woman, St. Louis, MO: I lived with a man and my two sons for over a year. The whole time it was sheer hell. The boys (whose father is alive, well and living nearby) were confused about who this guy was. What his part was in our lives. Why he was there in the first place, and so on. The man I lived with resented the kids. They got in his way, never gave us any time together, didn't like him, were a discipline problem. We'd come down in the morning together and there would be silences and long faces greeting us. The boys ignored him completely. The whole thing got to be so bad a mess that we split up. We might have lived together happily but for the fact that children were there.

Man, Hollywood, CA: I support living together on principle but *de facto* it didn't work out well in my own life because of my kids. I have three of them and get them four days a week. I've lived with several women since being divorced and every time the kids scare away the woman, or the women try to get the kids out of the picture. You're basically taking a complex situation and stressing it to its limits.

A schoolteacher from Los Angeles, definitely pro live-together, warns that living together will work only if participants enter the affair with open eyes and the ground rules drawn. Many of her cautions appear in other essays as well:

Woman, Los Angeles, CA: I am divorced, twice married, and a teacher. Despite all the aches and pains men have handed me, I still believe in love. But not—repeat, *not*—in marriage. I've lived with several men on intimate terms in the previous several years. The main problem is that you're neither fish nor fowl, not committed to each other, not uncommitted. The main benefit is the same as the problem: you're uncommitted, you can leave any time. I think what's more important to realize is that living together must be handled in an adult fashion. It entails practically every part of life, especially concerns like money, possessions, housekeeping, emotions. Materially it's almost the same as being married. I suggest that, first, people who are going to live together know each other well before doing it. Don't come to this decision in a fit of passion or on impulse or when you're both drunk some night. You'll regret it later. In my opinion, it's best to move into a separate place together, not his or hers. Because then one person feels like the invader and the other person feels invaded. Stay as financially independent of each other as possible. Never do things like register under the same credit cards, or share a joint savings account. Don't legally change your name. Most people who live together break up. If you don't get your money affairs in independent order before, it will only make things impossible when that break comes. When it comes to chores around the house, make sure no one feels had. Agree beforehand who washes the dishes, makes the beds, or how important these things are. I have a friend who moved in with a man who's a neatness fiend. She's a slob. They solved it by making a contract agreeing that she would do a certain amount each day, and that he would pay for a maid to do the rest. Other expenses can be split 50-50 like food, rent, water, phone, garage space, garbage pickup, etc. Whatever you do, be certain you get the money part straight between you. If not before then soon after you move in. Many of the relationships I see breaking up are due to misunderstandings about that sad but necessary aspect of all our lives: money!

Respondents also mention that living together provides sexual intimacy without emotional commitment, which many consider an asset:

Woman, Indianapolis, IN: I married a man I lived with for two years. The time we lived together we had a lot better relationship based on *sex* rather than love. After a while we fell into love. During the two years I had no desire to go out with other men. When we finally got married, shortly after it I did go out with men.

Man, Newark, NJ: Living together allows me to enjoy the woman I'm living with on a sexual basis without committing myself the way you have to do when you get married. Also, the fact of not being married makes the sex juicier.

Some respondents praise living together because it defuses the question of adultery. Sex outside the relationship becomes a lesser issue, since the couple is not wholly committed in the first place. Others criticize living together for just the same reason. Without marriage, they claim, fidelity, and hence trust, can never be achieved.

8. *In your opinion, should living together be an exclusive arrangement, or should the partners have the right to date others? Why or why not? How would you react to infidelity by someone you were living with?*

Major Finding: Nine out of ten singles feel that living together must *be exclusive.*

Almost 90 percent of men and women alike claimed that living together *must* be exclusive, that infidelity will almost invariably cause a rift in the affair and will probably end it entirely. The passion that runs through these answers show that for many singles, living together is a veiled form of monogamy, a kind of temporary marriage:

Woman, Jamaica, NY: Exclusive! Infidelity is a situation that has nothing to do with marital status. It has to do with personal commitment and sharing of love. While lifestyles may have changed, we are still a one-on-one society with the morality that that entails.

Woman, Pittsburgh, PA: I would certainly not put up with infidelity. If he wants to see other women that is his right, but I don't care to be involved in such a situation. We would discuss our feelings about the matter and end our live-in arrangement.

Woman, Dallas, TX: I don't feel they should aggravate each other with separate dating. Why live together in the first place then? If my partner proved unfaithful, it would take a matter of hours to consummate the arrangement. I am very sensitive and can tell when being abused or used. There is a lot of fighting when couples cheat on each other. It never works.

Man, Louisville, KY: Forget it! Infidelity just proves lack of maturity. I don't feel a free and easy sex life must mean: "I fuck everything in sight." Animals do that—they have random sex. One of the things that separates man from the animals is that he is able to commit himself to one person, a single mate, and stay faithful to that person. If you're not going to follow that code then how much better are you than a monkey or a dog?

Only a few respondents espouse a relaxed attitude toward what one has termed "live-in adultery."

Man, Portland, OR: If you want to date others infrequently that's fine, because since you're not married, you haven't made the ultimate commitment. Infidelity would be acceptable if it was done, say, once or twice a year. More than that and it would be trouble.

Man, Syracuse, NY: Partners should have more than the right to be with others: they should view opening up to others by means of sex as an aid to growth. Infidelity is a concept that applies to marriage only. Open sexual relationships with lovers who care about each other contribute to rationality and civilization—and personal growth.

Woman, Nashville, TN: I think they should have the freedom to do as they please. Me and my lover do this. We just don't ever bring home someone unless we get into a threesome or foursome. As long as he doesn't smuggle someone in under my nose I don't really mind. It's okay as long as I don't know about it. If you get too many restrictions you might as well get married, right? And marriage is like living in prison.

Such answers constitute a tiny minority. The vast majority of those who live together, no matter what the arrangement—trial marriage, marriage alternative, marriage of convenience, sometime live-togethers, even those who say that love is not a desirable part of cohabitation—claim fidelity as the bottom line.

9. How would you handle infidelity on the part of someone you were living with?

Major Finding: Approximately three quarters of men and 80 percent of women said they would end a relationship on the grounds of infidelity.

- Forty percent of men and half of women (51 percent) claimed *I would insist that it stop. That we work it out. If my partner continued I'd leave.*
- A fifth of men and women alike (21 percent and 21 percent respectively) reported *I would leave no matter what.* Eleven percent of men and 9 percent of women said *I would put up with it if it happened occasionally. If it became a habit I'd leave.*
- Seven percent of men and 3 percent of women claimed *I'd be hurt but would not object.* Six percent of men and 4 percent of women said *my partner can have affairs as long as I don't find out.* Ten percent of men and 5 percent of women claimed *I wouldn't mind at all. I prefer an "open" sexual arrangement.* Finally, 5 percent of men and 7 percent of women said *I don't know.*

BONUS FINDINGS

- Men who have been divorced once are far less likely to tolerate infidelity in a live-in situation than men who have never been married.
- Homosexual and bisexual men and women are the *least* likely to leave on account of infidelity in a live-together situation. Among women, 22 percent of heterosexuals said *I would leave no matter what,* while only 15 percent of lesbians agreed. Among men, 23 percent of heterosexuals report they would leave *no matter what,* while only 8 percent of gays concur.
- Women who have been divorced once are *least* likely among heterosexual women to put up with infidelity in a live-together situation.
- Gays are more likely than all other groups to claim they would prefer an *open sexual relationship.* Among women, 4 percent of heterosexuals would prefer an open relationship; 37 percent of lesbians would prefer the same. Nine percent of heterosexual men prefer open relationships—as opposed to 17 percent of gays.
- The older a man or woman gets the more likely he or she would be to walk out in case of infidelity.

Sexual faithfulness is thus the *sine qua non* for most of those living together. Over and over the word "trust" comes up:

Woman, Chicago, IL: Even if you're not married, you have to have *trust* and *belief* in the person you live with. Trust is the stone that holds the whole building together. Forget about the piece of paper that says "marriage." Trust is what joins two people, and lack of trust is what drives them asunder.

Man, Atlanta, GA: Married or living together, it doesn't really matter. If you're going to make it over the long run you have to have love, trust, faithfulness. If these are there everything falls into place. If they're not things can just never hold together. Never.

We have heard how singles handle infidelity. Here they describe their attitudes toward other negative situations they may encounter when living together.

Woman: "Problems—legal problems—rights, fear of mate leaving whenever, financial responsibilities, family reactions."

Woman: "I have a young son and feel, due to family pressures, that a living-together situation with a man is an option I no longer have. I think it's fine for people without children."

Woman: "Very bad in event that one person is paying bills. Solution is—always have your own money."

Man: "I would always feel that the woman didn't love me enough if she just wanted to live with me but not marry."

Woman: "I take the old fashioned line that I don't want to be 'tried out' by some man before I'm married. Let him take me as I am without turning me into a guinea pig."

Man: "Most people choose a partner for idealistic or cosmetic reasons. Then most people quit as soon as things start going a little wrong. This fosters irresponsibility, a 'quitting' attitude toward things like the 'throw-away society' in which we live. It produces a nationwide belief that we can all just use people as we want and then dump them like plastic containers. We pass this idea on to the kids. Soon a whole new value system is in effect and everyone wonders how it got this way."

Essays are sometimes as relevant for their omissions as their commissions. Among the hundreds of essays concerning living together, only a handful mention the element of *social stigma*. Given the rigorous taboo against cohabitation that was in effect as little as twenty-five years ago, it is notable that whenever the subject does come up it is spoken of more in personal than community or legal terms. That is, *parents* are now the ones to disapprove, not Miss Grundy or the corner butcher and baker. It is *family* that will not understand, not preacher or policeman or President.

The large exception to the above is the concern that living with someone will harm one's professional life, though this springs more from a fear of appearing unconventional than of being viewed as immoral:

Woman, Omaha, NB: I don't think it's anybody's business whether I choose to live with my boyfriend or not. My kids and I and my boyfriend share a comfortable apartment, and at night I'm the mother-lover-housewife-jack-of-all-trades to my "family." During the day I work at a straight job as an airline sales ticket person. On the job they have *no*(!) idea that I (shocking!) live with a man! If they did my boss would think I was one of "them" and probably fire me. I've heard him talk like that about those "hippie girls." He's a little paranoid, I think. I like my job and want to keep it, so I keep my mouth shut.

A frequent grievance against living together pertains to the fact that it is not legally binding. "That's what's good about marriage and being married," writes one of our subjects. "It's legally official. You have the law assuring you that the other person can't leave so easily. Don't knock that. It gives you a lot of peace and security, two things I've found missing in the single bonanza population." Another respondent: "Baby, there just ain't no way living together keeps you together. You need that nasty piece of paper called a marriage license with all its do's and don'ts." In other words, the strictures of marriage that so many singles complain of are at the same time the very supports that make for stability between mates:

Woman, San Francisco, CA: I lived with a man (unmarried) for five years, and I will not do it again. It's too vague, too unclear—and it's very hard to make it clear unless you have a contract or a plan—verbal, preferably written. If you go to the trouble of making a contract, you might as well be married, right? If there is no contract, I think it's very hard to grow together. I think the tendency is more to grow separately but also apart unless something like marriage unifies you. There's always that vagueness—are you a couple or not? I think it's natural to avoid that vagueness by marrying. It never gets cleared up while you live together.

"Vague" and "unclear"—two words that commonly turn up. People speak of existing in a "vacuum." If living together is a test, all right—but when exactly is the verdict delivered? No one is quite sure. Often singles talk of a live together situation dragging on for years with neither partner able to take a next step.

Man, Detroit, MI: Living together makes it so you never fish or cut bait. It's always the future, the future. Someday in the future you will get married—maybe. Or maybe you'll split up because, as the boys say, "the ass is always greener on the other side." You live in a state of fear about two things: 1) having to get married; 2) having to separate. You never do know where you stand.

Finally, if a couple lives together rather than marries, many respondents say, it is an overt admission that love and steadfastness are missing. "Living together is like saying I love you, but I don't love you enough to fully commit," explains one single. "Whatever way you look at it, it's a slap in the face."

Woman, Passaic, NJ: I've been living with someone for eight years, but only as a temporary thing. I have felt bound to this man, but not as much as in marriage. We simply don't have that special bond that marriage provides, and so we don't have that special trust. I have gone off on my own periodically, for other men or various experiences, yet this man accepted me. It was painful for him, I know. Still in all, we both look at each other sometimes and know in our hearts that we are fearful of commitment and deep love, and that's what keeps us from marrying.

CONCLUSION

In a phrase that singles themselves often use, you can't have your cake and eat it too. A person, it would seem, cannot experience the freedom that living together provides and at the same time enjoy the securities of matrimony. The two are mutually exclusive: What one gains by the first, one loses by the second.

This is the abiding judgment of singles. Marriage entails a commitment and closeness that can rarely be achieved by merely living together. Yet it is this very commitment that frightens many people, especially those who have witnessed prior marriages crumble. What is seen as the greatest benefit by one single is viewed by the next as the greatest drawback.

Implicit in this response is the judgment that living together is no panacea for the relationships between men and women, that it cannot shield a person from the entanglements that romance and attraction invariably breed. The bond of living together has its own benefits, its own freedoms, and its own drawbacks.

What then is the final verdict?

A split decision, singles tell us. Living together is judged neither as the ultimate answer to relationships nor as a desperate alternative, but as one choice among several, a choice determined by individual circumstances, value systems, wants, and, perhaps above all, by a single's individual needs.

Chapter **6**

The Single Parent ||||

Making It Alone

In this chapter, "The Single Parent," we ask:

1. How do most of the men/women you date feel about the fact that you have a child/children?

2. How do your children usually react to your dates?

3. How would you feel about living with a single man or woman who had a child/children? What would be the greatest problems and greatest pleasures?

4. If you are a single parent, how do you handle romance in front of your child/children? What advice would you give on the subject?

5. Would you ever consider having children even if you were not married?

6. What aspects of the single household are the most difficult for your child/children?

7. How do you feel about remaining a single parent?

8. If you are a single parent, what have you done to ensure the psychological and emotional health of your child? How has she or he reacted to the one-parent household situation? What have been the major pleasures and problems of being a single parent?

According to a 1980 bulletin of the United States Census Bureau, 12.2 million children in this country (one of every five) live with only one parent. This number is more than *twice* that of the 1960 figure.

Moreover, the Bureau projects that at least *one-half* of all those born in 1980 will live part of their lives with a single parent.

Single parenthood stands apart from all other aspects of single life. It is clear from the essay and multiple-choice questions that single parents are subject to a variety of social, monetary, and emotional complications that do not touch childless singles, and that the presence of a child in a single's home exacerbates the difficulties already inherent in the fact of being single.

At the same time, however, though a child brings an array of problems, his or her capacity to love and be loved is usually considered more than a compensating fact. For the lion's share of single fathers and mothers, a child is both the most frustrating *and* the most rewarding part of being single.

Our emphasis throughout this study has been on the social, psychological, and sexual aspects of singleness. It is these factors vis-à-vis the life of the single parent that we addressed in this chapter—for instance, the question of children and the courting process. Some parents, we learn, take it for granted that dates will be scared off by a child, and they thus attempt to hide their progeny until that moment when the "unveiling" will, they believe, cause the least difficulty. Others take the opposite view, believing that their children will be psychologically harmed by the presence of an invading male or female; and as a consequence they go to considerable lengths to keep all trysts clandestine and all suitors far from the door. From answers to the following question, we learn that neither fear is entirely realistic.* Concerning how dates feel about children:

1. *How do most of the men/women you date feel about the fact that you have a child/children?*	Men	Women
a. It frightens them off.	5%	7%
b. It has frightened some, others respond positively.	19%	26%
c. It's of secondary importance to them.	29%	22%
d. It has ruined my romantic life.	3%	1%
e. Most men/women like it.	17%	10%
f. Most men/women don't care.	28%	32%
g. Don't know.	1%	2%

* Questions in this section were answered only by single parents.

Major Finding: Most single parents report that their dates do not mind the fact that they have children.

The presence of a child is *not* a principal factor in determining how a date reacts to a single parent. Single men are a bit cooler toward children than single women, but on the whole neither sex considers them much of a liability and some welcome them.

Still, a small group of single parents, especially women, report troubles because of their children. Who are these women?

PROFILE: The single mother who reports having the most trouble with dates because of her children.

> PROFILE SUMMARY: By a rather remarkable margin, this woman is from a blue-collar, high-school-educated, low-income stratum of society. Women who are in the lowest income bracket are more than *five times* as likely to have trouble with men on account of their children than those in the highest bracket. Women blue-collar workers are almost twice as likely to have trouble on this score as professionals, and five times more likely than white-collar workers. If the woman is college-educated the men she dates will object much less than if she has attended high school only.

BONUS FINDINGS

- An insignificant percentage of males between the ages of thirty-five and forty-four feels that having a child frightens women off. Younger men, however, are less sanguine. Twenty-seven percent of them feel that in fact the presence of children *does* scare away dates.
- Forty-one percent of women divorced twice or more feel that most men don't care about the fact that they have children. Far fewer once-divorced women feel the same way.
- Not a single woman in the thirty-five-to-forty-four-year-old bracket claimed that children had ruined her romantic life. And only 7 percent of those in their early twenties feel this way.

Among men, approximately one-quarter of those twenty-four or younger claim that most of their dates *are* frightened off by children, while fewer than 9 percent of men over twenty-five say the same, and *no* men in the survey between thirty-five and forty-four complain of this problem. Almost 40 percent of men over thirty say *most women don't care,* while only 20 percent of men in their early twenties offer the same response. With women, 15 percent in their early twenties claim children are a deterrent. Only 4 percent of those over thirty-five say the same. Forty percent of women over forty-five report *most men don't care,* while only 22 percent in their early twenties agree.

"We live in a world where divorce is very common," remarks Dr. Susan Wheelan, Associate Professor of Psycho-Emotional Processes at Temple University, Philadelphia, and co-author (along with Melvin Silberman) of *How to Discipline Without Feeling Guilty.** "People are putting off marriage until later in life or are going through several marriages. A man of thirty-five, when he looks around for dates, sees many more single women in his age bracket *with* kids than without. It's become a part of the cultural pattern. This is why so many singles are indifferent to the fact of children. I think, however, this may not be true for all singles. I think that in the case of *younger* singles, children might in fact be viewed as a deterrent."

So much for the parents and their dates. What of the child? How upset are children likely to be at the arrival of what some young minds see as a potential competitor, others as a potential parent?

2. How do your children usually react to your dates?	Men	Women
a. With resentment, aggressive anger.	3%	9%
b. With indifference.	14%	11%
c. With reserve.	14%	17%
d. They try to make each into a substitute parent.	3%	3%
e. I rarely bring dates home.	15%	12%
f. They seem to have no hang-ups about it.	45%	45%
g. Don't know.	7%	4%

* Susan Wheelan and Melvin Silberman, Hawthorn-Dutton, 1980.

Major Finding: Almost half of single parents say their children have no problems or hangups about their dates.

By and large the estimations are similar for men and women. Exactly 45 percent tell us that their children have no problems with visiting dates. Nor can we really term acting with "reserve" or "indifference" as problems, and these account for a generous percentage of the other responses.

When difficulties do arise they center on a mutual sense of intrusion: The child feels invaded by the date, the date feels put off because of the child. The situation crops up in different essays:

Man, Los Angeles, CA: One problem I've had being single is dealing with my girlfriend's child. This child seems to think I'm about the worst stinker in the world, because every time I walk in he runs away to the bathroom and sulks the entire time. I plead innocence about having ever harmed the kid or even done anything to hurt it. I tried arriving at the house with presents. The child would just grab the toy and run off and do the same thing.

Woman, Santa Fe, NM: Have you ever tried to please a lover and your own child at the same time? Take my advice and *don't.* Especially if the child is a spoiled brat and the lover is a spoiled brat. I feel like being in the middle is the hardest of all places to be. Both of them are just stubborn males, neither of whom will give an inch. The only thing that I am waiting for is time to pass, and hoping that eventually both will give a little, and realize that both are here to stay.

"I just finished running a workshop on assertion with kids," reports Dr. Wheelan. "One of the things we discussed is how the arrival of a new boyfriend can create problems at home. The child in such a situation often sees the parent directing attention toward the new date, whereas before all the energy went to the child. The child feels he or she will be displaced by the boyfriend—which to an extent is often the fact. The child has already gone through one breakup in his or her parents' divorce and now senses the same will happen again. This makes for problems.

"On the other hand, if the date feels that he doesn't have the right to intervene with the kids, or to act as disciplinarian, this can be grating on his side, especially if the child is a problem. The date must sit by and let the child act like a monster and is not allowed to do or say anything—a terrible situation. The problems that arise on both sides have to do primarily, I believe, with improper communication about roles.

"The way to clear the air when this happens is with *direct communication between adults*. It's best not to treat children as adults or to lay adult-like problems on their heads. Rather than that, open up communications between parent and date. You have to talk about matters that happen daily, discuss things clearly as they come up, and come to resolutions about them. Then when you've arrived at a solution between you, the parent has to tell the child about it. You should let the child know that you are fond of this person and that you will be going out with him regularly, and that we'll all see how it works out."

"I think the single parent should expect *some* type of negative acting-out by a child when the parent starts dating," says Dr. R. John La Manna, Senior Child Psychologist at Coney Island Hospital, Brooklyn, New York, and Adjunct Professor at Brooklyn College. "There are two factors involved. One is the fantasy of the child, that his or her parents will get back together again. Outside dating interferes with this fantasy, and causes a reaction on the child's part. Second, there is fear of losing the parent, fear that the date will take the parent away, that any security or stability the child had is going to be removed.

"Now, how to deal with it. Acting-out is a kind of code. There is a hidden message to it; it is not just nastiness for its own sake. The parent must respond from an understanding that the child is *communicating* something by acting unpleasantly. For example, if the parent is aware that the child is particularly bothered by a 'getting-back-together' fantasy, and if he or she knows this is at the root of the acting-out, then the parent should respond to the problem and not just react to the child's provocations. If you respond to the child's provocations, then she or he will become more angry. Discipline will have the same effect. It reinforces the child's abandonment fears and so the child acts-out all the more. By being sensitive to the real messages implicit in a child's behavior, by going past the symptoms and straight to the problem itself, a lot of difficulties can be better handled."

CHILDREN AND THE LIVE-IN LOVER

How do singles feel about actually *living* with a man or woman who has a child? Now the child no longer has a casual once-a-week dater to put up with but is faced with a full-time surrogate parent. And the adult? Gone are the few minutes of banter with a child in the living room before leaving for a date. Instead comes full-fledged, day-to-day parenthood. Now considerations become complex and definitions blur. What part must the newcomer play in the child's life? Who is responsible for the discipline of the child? The new live-in does not even warrant the title "step" parent. Society has not yet coined a term to describe his or her difficult role. Who exactly is he or she? The child wonders, too. So does the ex-spouse. Even if this newcomer has previously maintained a good relationship with the child, his or her arrival on a permanent basis is bound to make waves.

3. _How would you feel about living with a single man or woman who had a child/children? What would be the greatest problems and greatest pleasures?_

Major Finding: Most singles would not want to live with a single parent on an unmarried basis.

Woman, Cleveland, OH: I'd be worried about how the child would be affected. Especially if the child is unstable. Unstable children are not unusual in houses with single parents. I would have-to be certain the child was good and sane, and even then I'd probably not do it.

Man, Grand Rapids, MI: I don't think I could. Too much tension from the child. They'd get used to you and then you might leave. Where would that leave the poor child? Think if this happened over and over, what a mixed-up view the child would get of relationships.

Woman, Cleveland, OH: I would be worried about how the child would be affected. If I felt the child would benefit, I would not hesitate. However, if the child was unstable, I would not do it. It would be very hard to discipline the child. What if you broke up with the man and the child had learned to love you by then? What would you say to the child and how would you explain it to them? I don't think I could.

Woman, Denver, CO: The pleasure would be fulfilling the loneliness and needs of a child. The problems would be being afraid of becoming too attached to your partner's child for fear of losing them if you should break up. Also, interference from the natural parent would be a problem. There really are a lot of problems, in fact, too many for me at this time in my life.

A sizable portion of respondents take offense on *moral* grounds. The objection is twofold:

1. Living together out of wedlock is wrong.
2. Living together with a single parent conveys a dangerous and unethical message to the child.

Woman, Omaha, NB: I'm not sure I could unless the children were small. If they were older (teenagers) I don't think I could, as the double-standard would bother me. I feel with kids you have to practice what you preach. I preach wholesome relationships between the sexes and virginity before marriage.

Man, Toledo, OH: Living out of wedlock with children is extremely hard on the kids, especially if they are over five years of age. Society is still not accepting of this type of arrangement, and the kids are the ones who get caught in the cross-fire. The kids at school will make fun of them, call them "bastards." Furthermore, I am not convinced that the sloppy morality today—"you live with me for a while, I'll live with you, and we'll see if it works out" kind of thing—is healthy. Add to this the presence of a child and I'm *sure* it's not. What is this saying to the child? Remember that a child needs a sense of permanence in its life. Not a fleet of passing ships in the night, or a mother who plays house with one man after the next. The future of our country depends on the values we give our kids today.

Among the high percentage who said they would not want to live with a child, the majority were men, though a plurality of women also said they would avoid living with someone if children were involved. As to the small percentage of respondents who told us they would live with a single parent, most said yes out of a strong parental impulse.

Woman, Des Moines, IA: I love children. Naturally if a man I was living with had them I would want to treat them as if they were my own. Children are part of God's creation and are really what makes a home sparkle. Without them life is only half complete. If I never have my own children, which I hope to, I would enjoy sharing them with a partner, married or not.

Man, Newark, NJ: If I loved the woman totally I would also love her child. If I could handle it financially I'm sure I could handle it emotionally. The fact that I like children helps a lot. Even if a kid is a pain, just having one around peps things up. A definite yes!

Those who have lived with an unmarried parent tell us about their experiences.

Woman, Sacramento, CA: I could go on for pages about this from having had three kids and several men living with me in my house. First the problems, of which there are plenty. A) Does the child like the man? B) Does the man like the child? C) Where are you going to live, in his house or in yours? If in his, the child has to make the adjustment. If yours, the man has to make the adjustment. D) What about discipline? The guy tries to step in and the child hates him for it. Or the woman expects the man to be a strict disciplinarian and the guy doesn't want to be bothered. Say the man tries to be Mr. Nice Guy and not say anything when the child annoys him. Then one day he blows his stack and totally *freaks out* the kid. That's a nice one. E) The other parent—if the father is in the picture (or mother) all kinds of jealousies take place. The live-in guy is jealous of the father, the father of the guy, the child of the guy, the mother of the father, the guy of the child, and on and on. I believe from my own go-rounds of not having my husband here (I'm a widow), that it's easier this way, no father at all, and is less complicated. F) When you break up it's another lolapalooza! The kids are attached to the guy, and then he up and leaves. Not nice at all! My kid had tantrums when a sweet heel I had living here for three years took off one day with a floozy, and he (my son) still hasn't forgotten or forgiven the betrayal/rejection. My advice to any single parent thinking about having a man live with you is to think twice about it, then three times, then four, then five, then six, then seven. . . .

The problems most often mentioned include jealousy (between children and live-in, both ways), run-ins with the ex-spouse, confusion, money worries (how much does the live-in contribute to the children's welfare?), and the impermanence children sense from a live-in situation. The pleasures spring from a sense of "household," and, for the in-coming partner, from the satisfaction of helping to raise and guide a small life:

Man, Danbury, CT: By far the best pleasure of living with my woman is watching her child grow up and taking a helping hand in the process. It makes me feel good to know that the child loves me, appreciates what I've done now that she is old enough to understand. We have become fast friends and that counts for a lot.

Woman, Denver, CO: I'd say the biggest problem has been how to explain the relationship to the child (especially my school-age ones—how do *they* explain it to their friends' questions and taunts in school?). My children have already been through one divorce. Then I put them through several others of a sort with men who came and went. This made me feel terribly guilty and still does. Also, how to handle sex and explain it to the kids? They *do* have ears and eyes. The pleasures are: 1) Having a man around to help with the children; 2) Watching the children respond positively to the man, when it happens, and knowing that they are getting at least some kind of fatherly attention; 3) A feeling that we have a "family" around us again.

Woman, Royal Oak, MI: Being a single parent I feel the question should first take into consideration the child himself/herself. Their age and mental state. If they *could* accept a parent's new partner into their life. I'm divided on the question because of the children's welfare. The greatest problem would be to handle fears and jealousies. The greatest pleasures would be to be accepted by the child as a person and not as a threat to their homelife. You'd have to show the child a lot of attention and let them know you care. I feel the adults should care enough to eventually marry, as it would be so damaging to the child if the parent lived with someone out of convenience—a mother figure or father figure—a housecleaner or a pay check—sexual reasons. The parent that moved in out of convenience would gain no respect at all. In conclusion, I feel from experience that if children are involved it would be better to wait before living together, to make *sure*. And if you *are* sure, why not get married then?

Several pieces of advice pertaining to singles' living together consistently appear in essays from single fathers and mothers.

1. Allow a Transition Period between Divorce and Living with Another Person

This is stressed many times. Respondents urge single parents not to jump into a live-in situation immediately after divorce even if the children claim they want it. "Allow some time after the separation," warns one essay writer; "let the kids adjust to the absence of their parent. To suddenly replace daddy or mommie with a stranger without allowing any breathing room was a disaster for us." "If you must live with someone," writes another respondent, "for God's sake wait a while. Get your head together. Let the kids get used to the fact that their life is going to be different. Everybody is always saying how 'flexible' kids are. Well, in my book they're flexible because they *have no choice in the matter,* but inside it's breaking them up to see all these sudden changes!"

2. Let the Child Know She or He Is Number One

We know from many studies that a principal reason children react negatively toward a live-in mate is that they feel their parent's love will be taken away and given to the newcomer. Respondents stress children be *continually* assured that this is not the case. "Give them plenty of love, as much as you can," writes a single parent. "Let them know they are the *most* important, and that the person living with you comes *second.* All they really want is to be reassured you're not going to abandon them."

Respondents also urge spending time with children, being careful not to make them feel left out. "It's very important that you include the child in things, not make him or her feel that your live-in is more important. Let them know how much you love them. Do it as often as you can. When you're with them be *with* them and don't daydream or give vague answers and responses."

3. Do Not Let Discipline Lapse Because of Guilt over Separation

Single parents almost universally experience guilt feelings toward their child over divorce. When the extra guilt of having a live-in mate is added, many try to compensate by allowing the child to do whatever she or he wishes. The child in turn becomes unmanageable. "Don't let your guilt let you stop putting the child in its place," writes a single mother. "Children scream for discipline. I felt so badly about having Paul in my house at the beginning that I let the kids run around like wild Indians and never scolded them no matter what! After a few months I had two brats on my hands and it was my fault because I let them take advantage of my guilt feelings. I got stricter and after a while they got better."

4. Don't Try to Force a Relationship Between Your Partner and the Child

Respondents promise that the inevitable friction which arises between the new arrival and the child will eventually slacken. But do not try to force the issue. "There is no way you can make someone love another person," advises a single mother. "My daughter took more than two years before she would accept Mac, my boyfriend. After that they became very tight." "Allow things to follow their own course between children and dates," writes another. "Things will happen the way they will and you can't 'help them along' by trying to play matchmaker. The problem is, after all, *between them*. There's nothing you can do to improve the situation but wait."

5. Don't Try to Become a Substitute Parent

Those who have moved in with a single parent warn against playing surrogate mother or father. They suggest becoming a friend instead. "The biggest mistake I made," writes a man who lived with a woman and her three daughters, "was to try and become the father-figure around the house. They'd have none of it because their own father was alive and well and living about ten miles down the road. Eventually I settled for being their friend and that is far better for everyone." "When I first came to live with Dick," tells another woman, "I thought I should move into the mother role for his child. But his kid would not listen to me when I tried. He would not accept my discipline or my love. He would not accept *me* and the efforts I made to make a home life and family. Eventually I gave up on this and tried to just help out as well as I was able."

"I have clients who are parents and are living with someone," remarks Dr. Ann Ruben, a family and child therapist and President of Marriage and Family Therapist Society in North Miami, Florida. "I encourage them to be open. To tell the child *why* you do not choose to marry, or that you will be marrying six months from now if things work out, whatever the case. Tell them you are living together as though you were husband and wife, but that you are *not* really married. The most important guideline that has to be set is *what kind of authority does this live-in person have over them*. Is the person going to be able to set any of the rules for the family or be involved in the decisions that affect their lives? That must all be spelled out for the kids. If it's left vague and murky there's sure to be trouble.

"Sometimes I think our child orientation gets in the way of our good judgment," adds Dr. Ruben. "And our good sense. It's my belief that adult relationships do not have to be blessed by a five-year-old's sanction. Children may be going through all kinds of things, and they are changing emotionally and psychologically all the time. One day they like you and the next they don't. For you to base your decisions about a relationship on these fickle reactions is ludicrous. It gives the child too much power, and they're not ready for that. It's *our* job to decide what's best for the child, and not vice versa."

Breaking Up

When a couple remains together for a long time, the children often become attached to the girlfriend or boyfriend. When the couple separates, the children may undergo a mini-crisis similar to the one they passed through at the time of their parents' divorce. Parents in turn suffer their own emotional traumas, and these are also sensed by the child and contribute to its dilemma.

Descriptions of such breakups or similar situations are often poignant.

Woman, Oklahoma City, OK: After a few years of living together Jim left my daughters and me and went to live with another female. I was so sick of him I didn't care. I'd only kept the thing going because my girls got on with him. When Jim left they screamed and made a big scene. They called him on the phone over and over, so that he got so he wouldn't return the calls. One of my girls talked about "blowing his head off with a sawed-off shotgun of her boyfriend's," which wasn't like her to talk at all. They still mention Jim today even if it's been over seven months.

Woman, St. Louis, MO: My son has tried to make the two men I lived with into fathers. He has a tendency along those lines because his real father deserted us and never calls. When the men live here and then leave he has had a real difficult time adjusting. I am thinking now about keeping *all* my dating times outside the house and not having anyone live here again.

Man, Houston, TX: I have one son, a seven-year-old who is blond, husky, and quick on the draw. Three years ago I fell in love with a wealthy, warm and beautiful debutante. She had a large modern home and wanted my son and me to live with her, which we did. She became a second mother to him. His real mother had left us and gone to live in some oriental monastery outside New York City. My son only hears from her by cards. Never a call or letter. So this woman became his mother. They went everywhere and enjoyed a mother-son type of situation. She encouraged him calling her "Mom," and he did it. She changed her will and made him and I the heirs. Last year she was in an automobile accident and after a period of suffering she died. My son took it very badly and I did also. We live in the house now, but since the accident my son has become very quiet and sullen. The money and house mean nothing. Her "ghost" haunts this place, and me, and my son.

"Often after a breakup," says Dr. La Manna, "children will start acting up. Then, when the parent comes down hard on them for misbehaving, the problem intensifies, and so you have a vicious circle. The child should have an opportunity to express herself or himself in these cases. The child is probably thinking that two have now left, the parent and the lover. Maybe the remaining parent, the mommy or daddy, is thinking of doing the same thing. As a result the child acts in a way that demands attention. In fact he or she is looking for assurance.

"Also, it's very important to *explain* why things did not work out, and to remove any possible feelings of guilt on the child's part that she or he was somehow *responsible* for the breakup. This is a very common thing—the child takes the responsibility for separation on him-/or herself, thinking he/she was too naughty, or whatever. The parent should tell the child quite clearly that it was *not* the child's fault. They should be very specific and concrete on this fact. 'Look,' they should say, 'this was just between me and so-and-so. Things just didn't work out and it has *nothing to do with you.* This does not change my feelings toward you. Nor does it change so-and-so's feeling toward you.' "

SEX AND THE SINGLE PARENT

Some parents report feeling resentment toward their offspring because of the crimp children put in sexual freedom. Others show concern that the child will get "wrong ideas" or become "permanently damaged" should he or she discover what goes on behind closed doors.

Man, Memphis, TN: Problems include how to have the woman live with you and have good sex and not have the kids jealous over it. I have a small house, and when my four-year-old daughter stays over she can hear every little sound. One night I found her standing in the hall near my door listening to me "going at it" with a girl who was staying with me for a few months. In the morning she asked what we were doing and why we made such "jerky" noises. I tried to explain it to her and ended up giving a "birds and bees" lecture, which I really didn't want to do. When I got to the part about a man putting his penis in a woman's vagina she asked me if she had a penis or a vagina, and if she could do it to herself. I realized how little kids understand at this age and how hard it is to make them aware of certain things.

Woman, Baltimore, MD: Single parenting has been very good except for certain problems. My daughter likes my fellow a lot, and he her. Think about this though. My daughter is very young and she keeps asking me what we do when we get into bed at night. She has also asked me why I sleep with my fellow rather than with Walter (her father who visits and takes her Tuesdays and Thursdays). She asked me if we "fucked together." I have no idea where this got into her vocabulary—she is very young to know such words! She often asks us questions about how men and women make babies. She only started asking these questions when my fellow and I started seriously dating.

As we have seen (question 2), some parents rarely bring their dates or lovers home at all. Most who do, do it carefully. Many times respondents make a distinction in their essays between "affection" and "sex." Affection is permissible in front of children if one is "serious" about a person. It includes hand-holding, kissing, embraces. Overt sexual displays or verbal allusions are almost universally decried, even among those who may be casual concerning other aspects of sex.

4. If you are a single parent, how do you handle romance in front of your child/children? What advice would you give on the subject?

Woman, Jacksonville, FL: I try to expose them to as few different men as possible, like when you are dating one man more than others, let them pick you up at home. But meet the others away from home. Keep the physical closeness to a minimum. Always tell them where you are going. Try never to lie, but on the other hand no need to go into long explanations, and it is certainly permissible to leave a lot out. Just give them the "bare facts." But keep in mind, "mothers must go by a whole separate code than most people" (direct quote from one of my boys). I try very hard not to let them know I get lonely sometimes, even though they are around. I try to make them feel needed and loved and wanted.

Man, Tampa, FL: Children do not think of their parents having sex. All children, no matter what effort is put forth, resent a second household. Women, who usually have the custody of children, should be very discreet about their relationships with men, *never* alluding to sex; and, they should confer with their children, convincing them that their mother *needs* companionship, male and female—assuring them, no matter their conjecture, that mom's interest in males is purely social and innocuous, and not intimate. Children must be made to feel that mom's dates or her "special fellow" in no way detracts from her love for them.

Woman, Omaha, NB: The children do not seem to resent a man touching or kissing me, but I can tell when they don't like someone. So far we have been able to handle these times with a talk between ourselves. My kids want me to be happy, and in this I know I am very lucky. My advice would be for the parent to go slow and not force anyone on the kids. At the same time, don't let the kids decide who you will like or be with. I don't believe a parent should have many "friends" sleep over. I don't feel I could let anyone else stay overnight, simply because I do care about what the kids think. I feel sorry for any child who never knows who will be in mom's bed on Sunday morning.

Dr. Ruben believes that the amount of affection that can be displayed in front of children depends on how the children feel toward the lover in question. "If the children like this person," she says, "they'll be much more accepting of that person's affection. If they can't stand the person, then they'll find *any* kind of affection between parent and lover abhorrent."

"The way one handles sex in front of children," remarks Dr. La Manna, "depends on the age of the child. As a general rule of thumb, the younger the child, the more she or he needs consistency and stability in the environment. So, for example, if a parent has many boyfriends or girlfriends coming and going, this would probably do more harm than good to the child because of the implied impermanency. In fact, after witnessing a chain of lovers coming in and out of the parent's bed, the child viewing all this may come to feel that heterosexual relationships are kind of scary. Parental relationships, remember, serve as a model for a child's own dating and subsequent marital relationship. What they witness at an early age will serve as a standard that they will follow for the rest of their lives."

Woman, Chicago, IL: I don't let men stay overnight at my house when the children are home. I am always home by the time the kids get up in the morning. I will show affection in front of them such as a kiss or hug, holding hands, but nothing more involved. I must really like a man before I'll bring my children into the relationship.

Man, Dallas, TX: When I took my children out with another girl and her kids, my ex would question them about it, and there was hell to pay. The kids were punished and I was not allowed to see them for weeks and months on end. It became more prudent to date and keep things secret. The advice I'd give is to play it by ear. Each person behaves differently, but do try and protect the kids if you can. If anything over-protect them from knowledge of sexual activity instead of under-protect them.

Woman, Indianapolis, IN: I am very relaxed about it. I answer any questions fully and honestly, but wait for the questions. I have had the beautiful experience of very good relationships which my children have had no cause to resent. Be open. Be honest. Answer all questions directly and without lies.

There are many theories concerning the kind of information parents should impart to their offspring concerning sex. Recently some psychologists have urged parents to be as honest as possible in describing sexual activity. Several children's books have been published in the last few years, illustrating the sexual act in vivid, if whimsical, terms. Many other psychologists and educators stress that children are not equipped to deal with sexually sophisticated information, and that exposing them at an early age is confusing at best. For the single parent this question is especially pertinent:

Woman, Providence, RI: When my son turned seven the question of sex reared its ugly head. He had heard the word "fuck" at school and had been told it meant that a man and woman go to the bathroom together and have a baby. Even at seven this didn't make much sense to him so he came to me one puzzled afternoon for an explanation. Ah, that inevitable moment! When I was a child that moment didn't arrive until I was eleven. I never heard dirty words till I was in fifth grade. How to explain it without lying but without going overboard and becoming too prolific and explicit? Well, I decided that I would give an explanation in a hundred words or less. This was a challenge and, it turned out, a good idea. I ended up succinctly explaining the rudiments of the "birds and the bees" but without getting too specific. I don't really think he *wanted* to hear anything too specific because he seemed perfectly satisfied. The question of sex did not come up again until he became a teenager, so from my standpoint the talk was a success. I have always tried to run a moral household since my marriage ended, and have never let my son see me with men here in the house. For all he knows, his dear old mother is nothing but a virgin, tra la, tra la.

Man, Milwaukee, WI: Being alone with my daughter, the problem of sex does come up. Once in a while I'll try to "smuggle" a date in after she's gone to sleep, but once that backfired and I haven't tried since. My daughter got up in the middle of the night and came into my room asking for a drink. It was a bad scene and I think it shook her up a whole lot when she saw a naked stranger lying next to me. She asked me a hundred times to explain what we were doing. I decided to stretch the truth and not give a real explanation. I just said we were friends and liked each other a lot, and that's what a couple does when they like each other a lot. I don't know how good an answer it was.

"There are some things that I explain to single parents concerning sex," says Dr. Ruben. "If they are going to demand appropriate sexual behavior from their children then *they* must act as proper models themselves. I encourage them *not* to bring men and women home and sleep with them with children in the house. I stress that single parents must keep their sexual relationships separate from their children. I see children get hurt time after time by people who make this mistake.

"I know single people all need sex, and that it's a natural thing. But I encourage them to use a motel or to go to an apartment where they will have privacy, to keep the whole thing separate from the children, especially so the children don't see them in bed together. What a single parent does sexually is privileged information. I don't think they ought to disclose it to their children at whatever age."

SINGLES AND THE OUT-OF-WEDLOCK CHILD

With recent social changes and the advent of a new sexual ethic, a certain portion of singles have chosen to *raise* their out-of-wedlock children rather than give them up for adoption. Though this sentiment is far from average, it is more liberally sanctioned than might be supposed. In fact, according to 1979 U.S. Government Census Bureau figures, births among unwed women have increased 50 percent in the last decade, and today at least one of every six babies in the United States is born out of wedlock. Thus we asked:

5. *Would you ever consider having children even if you were not married?*

Major Finding: **Almost a quarter of men and almost a fifth of women said they would consider having children out of wedlock.**

- Twenty-three percent of men and 19 percent of women said an outright *yes.* Three percent of men and women alike have done it and said *it turned out well.* Another 3 percent of both sexes have done it and say *I wouldn't advise it for others.*
- Thirteen percent of men, and 12 percent of women, are on the line, claiming: *I'd like to but believe it would be too hard on the child.* Fewer than 2 percent of each sex claim *I'd be worried about what others would think.* Fifty-five percent of men and 59 percent of women said *I would never do it.*
- Two percent of men and 3 percent of women said they didn't know.

PROFILE: What man is most willing to have and raise a child out of wedlock?

PROFILE SUMMARY: He is quite young, usually in his early twenties (the older a single gets, the less inclined he is to have a child out of wedlock; those in their forties and fifties are only *half* as willing as singles in their early twenties). He has never been married (the more marriages, the less willing). He has had some college and has a low income.

PROFILE: What woman is most willing to have and raise a child out of wedlock?

PROFILE SUMMARY: The female profile is practically the

same as the male. She is in her early twenties, is a student or a white-collar worker, earns a low income and has never been married. In both cases, male and female, the idea of having a child out-of-wedlock is the notion of the young, liberal, inexperienced and experimental single. As single people grow older, as they learn the realities of child-rearing and perhaps raise a child themselves, enthusiasm becomes far less evident.

BONUS FINDINGS

- Never-married men are far more apt to say they would have a child out of wedlock than those who have been married and divorced. This is even more true for women.
- Men and women who have been single all their lives are more likely to want a child out of wedlock than singles who have been unmarried for under ten years.
- Among both men and women, those who *tried* having a child out of wedlock were almost invariably divorced twice or more.
- Twenty-eight percent of men in their twenties and 24 percent of women in their twenties say they would consider having children if not married. However, willingness declines with age: only 14 percent of men and 8 percent of women over forty-five say they would do the same.

Among the essays, only two subjects actually revealed that they have borne and kept children out of wedlock. Both were obviously dedicated to parenthood.

Woman, Omaha, NB: I am approximately 4 months pregnant and have no intention of getting married in the near future. I found it difficult to tell older people that I'm pregnant. Most ask if I'm getting married. Some even go so far as to suggest abortion. For some people I think that it's the best move, but for myself, I'd rather have the baby and see it grow up.

Woman, Nashville, TN: I have been living with a man for ten years, and we share a child between us, a beautiful young son. Though there have been times when trouble has come, and we've been asked to show marriage licenses, the going has been smooth. We do not pretend to be married, and our son knows we are not. Perhaps it is a source of worry for him that we will separate some day, but with all the divorce around I should think he would have no more to worry about than anyone else. At school occasionally they call him a "bastard," but he beats their ears back when they do, and then feels pretty proud of himself. People ask why we don't get married. I say "because our son wouldn't understand." They laugh, but I'm not so sure I'm kidding.

"One thing clear from the findings here," remarks Dr. Melvin Silberman, family therapist and professor, Department of Psychoeducational Processes, Temple University, Philadelphia, speaking of the relatively high percentage of singles who would consider raising a child out of wedlock, "is that the taboo against single parenting and bastard children is obviously less in force than in the past. There are several reasons for this. First, people are saying that it's such a hassle to try and work out parenting with someone else that they think they can do it better themselves. Second, having children no matter under *what* circumstances is something that makes single people feel a little more legitimate. There is still something shaky about the status of being single, you see. It is still not quite okay. This is why, especially in the lower-class cultures, there are so many pregnancies among teenagers, because having a child for them is a measure of their self-worth. It just may be that the same process is at work for single people too."

DIFFERENT AGES, DIFFERENT PROBLEMS

According to single parents, very young children—those between ages four and six—and youngsters in their teens are the most difficult to deal with concerning sex. Several essays mention the negative reactions children pass through during their fours and fives, and how after they reach latency, antagonism fades. Teenagers are often undisguisedly angry at the parent and the lover alike. Again, this antagonism tends to abate during the later teenage years when the young persons begin moving off on their own:

Man, St. Paul, MN: When my children were in their teens this question was at its worst. Every time I had a date both my daughter and son, both teens, would make hostile comments *in front of* the dates. My son, then fifteen, asked one woman if she was sleeping with me! It was very hard not to blow my top. I took both of them aside and had a very long talk about my rights, their rights, everybody's rights. Not that the talk did much good but it did cool things down a bit. After they got a little older the problems tended to decline. They got involved in their own romantic lives and forgot about mine, I suppose.

Woman, New Orleans, LA: My five-year-old hates the man I go out with. He often spends the night. Next mornings, like clockwork, my son has a tantrum when he sees this man. My son will bite, scratch, scream and just can't be controlled until the man leaves. The tantrums don't begin again until the man returns.

Anna Sue, a widow from Boston in her late forties, has a nineteen-year-old son named Jason. Anna was widowed more than fifteen years ago, and though her marriage was, as she describes it, "tolerable usually, and ecstatic every now and then," she has never seriously considered remarrying.

"I never wanted to remarry," she tells us. "Because it's too good being on my own. Even with a son all these years, the feeling of freedom has been too good to sacrifice."

Anna Sue's compromise was to live with her lovers rather than marry them. "I've had three men I've lived with. The first one was a fast job based on sexual attraction. The second two I deeply loved. And still do."

What stages did Jason pass through during these years? "I think he did quite well, considering that his father was taken away when he was so young, and that he never had a permanent role model to fixate on."

The most difficult times were the early times: "When Jason was five and *very* Oedipal, a lovely man named Markos moved into our small apartment in Providence. Markos came from a large Greek family of nine children, and he knew all about kids. Ray, my husband, had been dead a few years now, and Jason was terribly clingy and pesty. I could never go out of the room without him screaming for me. I had the belief that when Markos made the scene he would relieve the situation. Keep dreaming! Jason got worse! I think he channeled all his hostility on this poor man. Markos was patient as could be, but my God, how patient can you get? Jason wouldn't talk to him for the first few weeks, even though Markos did everything. I remember he brought him home this terrific toy called 'Rock-em Sock-em Robot' which cost a fortune and which Jason had been dying for for ages. Don't you know that Jason wouldn't look at it. When both of us were in the room he picked it up, carried it to the window and threw it out the window of our third-story apartment! That time he *did* get a spanking.

"After a few months finally, Jason allowed that Markos wasn't the devil anyway, and he acknowledged some of his efforts. Grudgingly! Never was there a breath of affection or trust between them though at this time."

Time passed, however. Markos and Anna Sue lived together for five years. "The first two years were hell as far as Jason went. The kind of thing I've told you about went on all the time. Jason would get coy sometimes, like the time he took all the shoelaces out of Markos' shoes and hid them. He told us he was 'only kidding.'

"Then, almost to the day Jason turned seven, something changed. He began to overtly show affection for Markos. The two quickly became friends. From then on until Markos left they were like father and son. Jason was devastated when Markos moved out finally—it had been coming a long time, and in fact Markos' relationship with Jason was one of the reasons he didn't leave sooner. Jason was devastated. To this day they're still in contact."

Jason's antagonism increased once again toward his mother's lovers when he was in his early teens. "I was, and am now, living with a man named Victor. If I ever marry it will be to him. Victor was in the beginning a substitute for Markos. Jason accepted him after a short 'trial period,' and they liked to do things together, like go to the baseball game or do archery, at which Victor is a champion. Then came the good old teenage years. When Jason was twelve or thirteen he started to go into long periods of silence. He wouldn't talk to *either* of us. He seemed equally angry at me and at Victor. His marks got worse and he quit the soccer team, even though soccer had been his be-all and end-all up to that time. When I asked what was wrong he would just hang his head and look down and say 'nothing.'

"What I finally got him to tell me after many agonized hours of trying, was that he felt Victor was being unfair to him at home, that Victor didn't like him, that Victor and I spent too much time at the movies, that Victor this and Victor that—in other words, he now had decided Victor was Simon Legree.

"I said there was nothing I could do about it, that I loved him (Jason) more than Victor, and that he (Jason) was still the dearest thing of all to me. In this I did not lie. I understood what he was feeling, but Victor and I were in love and cared very much about each other. I said other things too, but I'm not sure I handled it in the right way. Perhaps I should have had help.

"This sulky period lasted too long. But it kind of evaporated when Jason was about sixteen. He and Victor were friends again and they've been friendly since. I don't understand how it works or what makes it work. But there definitely seem to have been phases in my boy's life in which acceptance of a male figure was at its most difficult."

HELP FOR THE SINGLE MOTHER

6. What aspects of the single household are the most difficult for your child/children? (Choose as many answers as are appropriate.)	Men	Women
a. My involvements with other women/men	17%	19%
b. My ex-spouse's involvements with other men/women	15%	9%
c. Lowered standard of living	14%	29%
d. My depression, worry, and self-concern	12%	34%
e. My absence during the day due to work	20%	30%
f. Being shunted around from home to home	11%	5%
g. Don't know	24%	13%

BONUS FINDINGS

- With women, earning capacity proves to be a direct determinant of happiness and well-being. Women who did not attend college and who are in the lowest income group are approximately *twice* as likely to cite depression as *the* problem of child raising as those who are educated and hold high-paying, professional jobs. Blue-collar women earning low incomes are three times more apt to complain of *lowered standards of living* than those in the higher bracket. High wage-earners, on the other hand, have a different problem. Almost a third of them claim that their *involvements with members of the opposite sex* are the most trying part of single parenting.

For males, the findings support what essays have already suggested, that there is no single outstanding problem among single parents, that all concerns mentioned so far—discipline, guilt, insecurity, ex-spouses, and so on—demand their price. With women, however, certain factors are definitely more problematic than others. Common grievances among single parents center on "lowered standard of living," "absence during the day," and "depression, worry, and self-concern." In all three a far higher number of women express concern than men, perhaps because in 90 percent of divorces women receive custody of the child.

Thus a pattern emerges here that has followed us throughout the survey, that of the single mother forced into the world to make a living, support her children, arrange her social and psychological life, all under conditions that are harrowing at best. She must bear the brunt of child-rearing while going into the marketplace to survive—and this may lead to emotional overload and even despair:

Woman, Memphis, TN: I didn't realize how divorce affected children. It took at least three years before I realized what was happening to my sons. I hardly had a chance to make a decent living. My children had many problems between them, and I was taking any job to make ends meet. Child support came in only at unpredictable times. Women get cheated all over in car repairs. I worked all year to keep a car in condition, at $2.75 per hour. Even $3.00 an hour didn't prove enough to eat decently, and as my sons grow older clothes are more expensive. My children went through a period of wanting you to marry anyone just so they can have a father to provide for them. At times they would get so bad that they'd *ask* me to marry someone, or even propose to dates themselves! Being a single parent and woman involves double responsibility and a tough job. When a couple gets a divorce the courts should make it a definite responsibility that the father pay child support. A woman is always under the threat of child support being taken away. If support is sent late there is hardship. Some women's husbands skip or don't pay anything, so children have to suffer for it. The mother goes to work all the time and the children get lost or go wild, most of them, or get influenced by bad company. The man has much resentment paying child support, and takes it out by causing problems for the woman. If the parent has a hard time adjusting to the new situation, and working all the time, never being home, imagine how the child feels? If you are an older woman in her fifties what chance is there to get a decent job paying decent wages? If you are divorced in a prejudiced town, people know both of you—and talk about you sure spoils your chances for a decent job. Women, children, men need education before a divorce to know what is ahead for them and to be prepared. Women especially have to be told what hardships are awaiting them out in the cold, cruel world.

"We find depression to be particularly common right after the divorce period," claims Dr. Silberman. "There is a mourning period at this time, even if the person didn't want the marriage in the first place. There is the fear of having to shoulder things by oneself, of having to face life alone.

"One of the main things that happens to people just after divorce is that they realize there are a lot of ultimate kinds of questions that they haven't thought out yet. Back during the time when they were considering divorce they said to themselves: 'I don't know, I can't foresee the future. But I *know* my marriage is crazy and I want out!' Once you make a decision as big as this you have to get very hard and determined inside yourself. I've noticed people, especially women, will have a kind of grim resolution written all over them. But a few months after the divorce is over and this resolution has served its purpose, there begins to creep in this very scary thing: 'I haven't figured out certain problems yet. Like custody. Child support. Where will I live? Where will my husband live? How will I make ends meet?' All of this. Suddenly concerns that were once vague become frighteningly real. Depression can be the result.

"However, many single parents are not as trapped as they think they are. They are psychologically trapped, perhaps, but this can be a way of not coping with the adjustment to single parenthood. That's part of the reason for their depression. A single parent will sometimes exaggerate her immobility as a way of not having to cope with change. She may almost revel in her lethargy. In cases like this the *worst* thing you can do is let that person cry on your shoulder. A real friend would try to offer concrete guidance instead. Like: 'Look, you really need to get out of the house.' Or 'You should stay home once in a while and learn to be by yourself.' Whatever. The sort of advice that will produce concrete action. A woman must realize that she may indeed have options, but that they are worthless unless she acts on them. Just this realization may help."

"Most single parents know what they can do to help themselves get over depression," asserts Helen DeRosis, M.D., editor of *The American*

Journal of Psychoanalysis, Clinical Professor of Psychiatry at New York University School of Medicine, and author of the bestselling *Women and Anxiety.** "But the question is 'Why don't they do it?' They don't because they feel they need someone else to help them. They feel they can't do it themselves. They really don't feel up to it at this time, even though deep inside they know they were quite capable of the task in the past. As a result the efforts they make are without enthusiasm, very often inconsistent, and usually too short to be of much use.

"One mistake single parents make is to look at their situation as a whole, a totality. If they teased apart the elements of the problem—the child, the job, their love life, the neighbors, the income—and took part of one problem at a time and said okay, I'm having trouble at work, or my boss is giving me a hard time, or I run the risk of losing my job, then they might be able to tackle one of these things. For instance, approach your boss and explain to him why you are late: that the children are sick, perhaps. Then tell him you are trying to manage this problem better. Perhaps the situation will then be somewhat eased. And if you can resolve just that one problem you will feel better. But of course that's only one detail in life. From here you would go on to another detail and treat it in the same way. And another, and another. You get a whole different view that way. Instead of waking in the morning and saying 'I can't manage anything,' you learn that you can handle item number one, and then you can handle item number two, and three, and so on.

"The single parent has to decide if she needs professional help, or if she can help herself. She must learn to structure her time and space. She must set aside time not only for the family but for herself. Just four hours a week—someplace. She has to have time set aside *specifically* for her own pleasure. And that doesn't mean she has to run off with a lover or anything like that. She needs a place where she can be alone, a place off-limits to children. It can even be in the house, but if it is she should have somebody to stay with the children and keep them away. During this time she gives herself a chance to pull her life together without having a half dozen items that have to be attended to immediately.

"Further, a single parent must not neglect his or her social life. By social life I don't mean parties, I mean people, being with people. Sin-

* Helen DeRosis, Delta paperback.

gle women always seem to be looking for some perfect fellow. They aren't usually aware of it, but they have a fantasy image in their minds, and so they reject many opportunities because they are waiting for the fantasy person to appear. If a woman should meet her ideal person, however, he may not have had *her* in mind. Thus she's spent her time waiting for someone to come along and hasn't made good use of her own time in building up a more flexible social support system. Furthermore, when we speak of social life, we are not talking just about males, but about anybody: old people, young people, men, women, girls, boys, parents, singles. Anybody. Human beings are what make up the social system and it is human beings who ultimately will help when a person is depressed."

Specialists also warn against another cardinal problem not brought up directly in the survey, that of *over-investment in one's child.* "There are these myths concerning the 'super-powers' of perception children are supposed to have," remarks Dr. Silberman. "Someone always tells me that his or her child 'really sees into me,' or, 'My kid understands all my moods.' I think a lot of this is projection, the notion that children have kind of a magical radar screen for adult emotions. I'm not entirely discounting it, but people tend to exaggerate what kids' powers and perceptions and emotions really are. This is one reason that we feel hesitant about how to deal with our children—because we are worried that the tiniest false move will be picked up by them and will turn them into neurotics.

"The point is that single parents are far more preoccupied with their children than married parents usually are. That's one of the real dangers of single parenting, that the children become too much the center of your life because maybe that's all you have. When parents who are too child-dependent come to me for therapy I see if I can find some strategy to help them develop a separate life of their own."

HOW SINGLE PARENTS COPE

7. *How do you feel about remaining a single parent?*	Men	Women
a. Both my child/children and I like it better this way.	13%	15%
b. My child wants me to remarry but I have no desire to do so.	5%	9%

c. I would live with someone but not
   marry them. 9% 5%
d. I don't want to remarry but probably
   will for the sake of my children. 3% 4%
e. I'd like to marry again. 43% 42%
f. At first I wanted to remarry quickly.
   Now that I see I can swing it on my
   own I'm in no hurry. 18% 20%
g. Don't know. 10% 5%

Major Finding: Approximately one third of all single parents prefer to remain without a spouse.

In spite of the burdens that visit the one-parent home, approximately a third of all single parents prefer to remain unmarried. Older single mothers feel this way especially. Forty-eight percent of single mothers under thirty-five said they would like to marry again, while only 37 percent of those over forty-five said the same. This attitude is of course influenced by the mother's relationship with the child—we often notice that mothers of older children seem less interested in remarriage than mothers with children who are very young. The opposite is true of men. Though 46 percent of men under thirty-five want to remarry, almost 50 percent of those over forty-five would like to marry again.

Woman, Little Rock, AR: The biggest problems were when Gil was young, in her early stages. I wanted to remarry then but, you know, now that she's older I don't care as much. She is such a big girl, over fourteen, and has done okay without a father. We can be friends and I don't worry about wiping her mouth after she eats and about whether she'll miss a daddy. When they get older it's less a chore to keep them happy. You can settle back and enjoy their company and it's a lot different.

Man, Newark, NJ: If I had it to do all over again as a single parent I would import a wife for the first seven years of child-raising, then give her her walking papers. After seven it's all downhill. You get so that you can behave with them like young adults, and things get a lot simpler because all you have to do is get through the first part, but that's not easy!

Parents' answers consistently demonstrate a sense of dedication and responsibility toward the welfare of their children. The very fact that a parent *is* single, respondents tell us, causes the parent to work harder at parenting. In this way single parents often prove superior parents, even if their actions occasionally fall short of their aspirations. "The very adversity of being single and a father," writes a respondent, "has stretched me and made me into a father 100 times better than I was when we were a family together, and this is at least one advantage of divorce."

"Actually," says Dr. Silberman, "it *is* possible for a single parent to be two parents. The usual problem of single parents is that they get caught between the nurturing role and the director role—what we might call the 'executive role.' We normally think of a mother in the nurturing part and a father in the executive part. These things are difficult to merge because they seem so contradictory. Often what happens is that the single parent must learn to be a loving, caring person, *and* at the same time achieve what we think of as 'executive distance.' This distance involves the ability to make decisions even if the decisions are not popular with the kids. Some ability to be the bad guy, too, and that's terribly hard for a single parent. Although parents should be loving and should communicate with their kids, I think it's necessary for parents to learn the other, harder disciplinarian part too. And many single parents today are pulling this off beautifully."

We were curious to know how single parents create the proper conditions for a child's healthy home life:

8. *If you are a single parent, what have you done to ensure the psychological and emotional health of your child? How has she or he reacted to the one-parent household situation? What have been the major pleasures and problems of being a single parent?*

Single parents often advise making wise use of "resources,"—day-care centers, family, babysitters, counseling services, friends. One of the most commonly mentioned resources are grandparents:

Woman, Pittsburgh, PA: We have lived near or with my parents who provide more security for my child. I have been very selective in choosing child care when I'm working. My child was very small when I divorced so she did not suffer the same type of trauma as an older child. But still she has missed her father (or "a" father) and the grandparents have tried to substitute. I also have tried to instill in my child that God is her father and that if I am not around or her grandparents, she can call on Him.

On the whole, parents report that children do eventually adjust to the one-parent home no matter how painful the process. Whether this adjustment is rapid or slow depends on the child, the parent, and the situation:

Woman, Kansas City, KS: My teenage daughter has responded very well to a one-parent household. She needed counseling at the early stage because her father had brought in a younger lover who had a young child of her own. Also, the rules and regulations this new woman placed on her were severe. However, after counseling my daughter accepts the situation with her father. In our own home we are very honest and open. She is an excellent student, active in church, and has many friends.

Woman, Tacoma, WA: My son blossomed when we split up. He is happier and doing better in school. He doesn't whine like before. He appears to respect me. When he has chores to do he still hates them but does them with fewer complaints and he does a better job. His whole attitude has changed. It's as if he had been waiting for us to split. It makes me wonder if a broken home isn't better than an unhappy one.

Woman, Cleveland, OH: My son did not at all take well to being part of a divided family. My ex-husband would tell him that I was to blame for our divorce, and he would come home angry at me, and tell me the awful things my husband had said. My son hated school at this time and scared away all his friends. It was truly awful. He seems a little better now after two years, but his father continues to poison him. My son has also developed several tics that I believe are from the breakup, plus a slight stuttering problem.

Respondents frequently mention that the ex-spouse can be a source of trouble or—and this is more common—a source of genuine support.

Woman, Omaha, NB: When we first were divorced, I went to great pains to tell the children that *they* were not at fault, and I explained that Daddy just didn't like me anymore and he wanted a divorce (which was the truth). Both seem to have confidence that I told the truth, especially my daughter who lives with me. My son who lives with his father has had to rationalize his behavior and lays the blame entirely on me. However, my son is asking a lot of questions so he evidently doesn't entirely believe his father. Both seem to be better off emotionally now that we are divorced because both parents are more at peace. My son has grown away from me because he lives 200 miles away and my ex doesn't want me to come there so I can't see his football games or any of his projects. I see him maybe twice a year or maybe three times. We'd talk on the phone and I'd send him the sports section from the *Omaha World Herald* because he lives in a small town and doesn't have access to the information. My ex just won't relent and try to keep things clean and in harmony between us. He insists on being at odds.

Woman, Cleveland, OH: I have bitten my tongue so many times it should be a stub by now. The one time I began to tell my son (11 years old) what I really disliked about his father he ran out of the room and said he didn't want to hear such things about a person he loved. I didn't say anything particularly nasty about his father, but my son really didn't want the information he asked for. At his age he identifies very strongly with his father, which is important, so I have refrained from saying any explicit or implicit negative comments. I think the emotional health of my children is due to their individual strengths and the concerted effort of my ex-husband who, whatever I may feel about him, has been a real mainstay for the kids and a good parent. I limit our differences to ourselves and assure the children they are loved by each of us, although we could no longer love each other. I live about 2 miles from their father, so they have frequent visits.

The very fact that divorce has become so prevalent in this country has had an interesting effect on the relationship between ex-mates. In an earlier time overt hostility was the norm following divorce. In fact, any connection continuing after marriage was considered "oddball" and was frowned upon. Today, with divorce almost as common as marriage and with the single household a widespread phenomenon, amiable relationships between ex-husband and -wife are more acceptable than in the past. In fact for many single parents, the ex-mate represents a resource rather than a liability:

Man, Indianapolis, IN: I still maintain a lot of respect for my wife and think she is doing a terrific job bringing up our kids. We sometimes try to schedule joint activities. The kids now know we will never get back together, but it just makes them happy to see us all together again for a few hours. My wife never nags me if I am late on child support and I try to keep up my end of things too.

Man, Burlington, VT: Since divorced, wife (ex-wife) still remains good mother. We both agree that since we are sharing in the duties of raising the child it is necessary to keep lines of communications open. This is hard sometimes but after the first few years you get the routine of it and things get easy after that and you just keep at it. My ex-wife has a fairly decent live-in guy who serves as friend but not father, and ex-wife makes sure it's kept this way. I am grateful to her for that, as I want my child to be raised knowing I am the father, not the live-in friend. It is very important to let child know you and ex-wife are still friends and not always spatting, etc.

Here are some comments on how single parents go about ensuring the health and adjustment of their offspring:

Woman, Cleveland, OH: "They (the children) see a mother who cares for them; has a life of her own which they must respect; they see a mother who cannot provide them with the extras that their Dad does, but who works and does the best she can. We all do household chores and it gives us a sense of accomplishment and pride. We are working together to make it *our house.* We have free time to do fun things together—like sitting in front of the fire after dinner with hot chocolate and telling stories.

Woman, New Orleans, LA: My son is my number one priority and I insure his emotional health by trying to keep in tune with him. He takes a part in most of the decisions I make, especially major ones, and I respect his personal opinions and make sure he knows that. I try to raise him to be independent and responsible, to believe in himself. That's the most important thing.

Woman, Albuquerque, NM: I believe that the psychological and emotional attitudes of my daughter depend a lot on my own. Being a single parent takes a lot of everything! Giving 100% because there is no one else. My daughter is well adjusted, but my attitude has to be positive to assure her happiness. I take her many places with me and include her in my life. She knows she is important to me. I don't push her to grow up too fast. I try to surround her with beauty; her room is hung with interesting pictures from all over the world, and I choose her toys very carefully, being sure not to give her anything that is grotesque or frightening. As much as possible I try to keep her away from overstimulating media like TV and cinema. I have a good relationship with her father and often praise him to my daughter. I try to keep a tight hand on discipline. I'll give her plenty of leeway, but then the clamp comes down, and when I say *no* I mean it. I never renege on my demands as I believe *consistency* is one of the fundamentals in rearing a child, especially when there is only one parent. Above all I am extremely honest with her. I make it a point never to lie. That doesn't mean I tell her everything that is going on in my life. That's something else entirely. Children usually sense when you're lying, even if they don't say anything about it. It's in this way that dishonest and crooked people get started in life, through the lies and dishonesty of their parents. On the other hand, I never tell the child my woes or troubles. I try to keep the world a bright, happy place for her even though I am sometimes ready to throw the rope across the rafters and put the noose over my neck. I bring my daughter up with a sense of God and a respect for the Divine Creation. I have never known this attitude to hurt anybody, and I have known its absence to make the heart cold and remote. I teach her about living things, and help her to love animals and nature. But I try not to sentimentalize it either, and to make her know (mostly through fairy and myth stories and games) that there *is* a dark side to this world. I could go on, but you can get the gist of how I cope with this difficult but beautifully rewarding situation.

"There are some very specific things that singles can do to help their children and themselves," remarks Dr. DeRosis. "The single parent has to get across to the children that family life at home is a cooperative unit, and that everybody pulls his or her own weight. Mommy does not service children—period!

"If you give a child important but simple family responsibilities and make the child feel part of the family unit, it doesn't matter so much anymore if he or she has trouble outside of the home. The child remains important within the family, and that's where it counts most.

"As far as the housework goes, I don't feel you should burden the children with tasks that are beyond their ability. Children from four to five can learn simple repetitious household chores. They can set table, make salads, clear tables. They can even do the dishes sometimes or put them in the dishwasher. They can separate clothes, put clothing in the washing machine, fold them, dust, pick up things. By the time they are eight they can do practically all the things you do in the house. It's good for everyone's esteem that way and good for the house too. If they grumble tell them it's their job. Don't take their labors for granted, but don't over-praise them either. If you assign tasks to children, do so without grading them or comparing them to other children. Just make them feel they are a helpful, important part of the unit as a whole, and that you appreciate their cooperation. Keep in mind that children really want to please you."

Finally, single parents speak about themselves. And here is their final message, as expressed by a single father: "Single parenting is a difficult road, though at the end you're glad you saw it through because the real rewards are having a happy healthy kid and being a better person for it."

Woman, North Suburban, IL: I have custody of three kids, a boy 12, and two girls, 9 and 7. As a single parent I've had to make *all* the adjustments. There are *changes,* and changes are difficult. As a single parent I've forced myself to reassess who I am, where I'm going, what I want, what I'm about. I've confronted practically every problem a single parent can—baby sitters, daycare centers, poverty, men on the make, hostile ex-husband, no place to live, ferrying kids to activities, maintaining a home and a yard, shopping, clothing, making a living, you name it. My challenges have been learning to live an adult life—and to do it without a man to support me. I miss the ready availability of sex, and believe me, it's a drag to have to slink around your own house at night like a guilty child if you want to make love to someone. I delight in seeing my kids grow up and myself with them. We help each other. We try to be kind and loving in my household, and that works miracles, really! I trust that my kids are better able to exist in today's world than many from a "normal" two-parent family. If they're not, oh well, you try, you know what I mean? I believe that in the end it all works out as it should, and as it must.

Chapter 7

The Single Life:||||
An Evaluation by
Singles

**Questions asked in "The Single Life: An
Evaluation by Singles" include:**

1. Why are you single?

2. Do you plan to stay single indefinitely or would you like to
   marry? Why? If previously married, which lifestyle do you
   prefer, single or married? Why?

3. Are you unmarried by choice or because of circumstances
   beyond your control? Do you think marriage is a surrender
   to social pressures or is it a basic human need? Why?

4. As a single do you ever feel pressures to get married?

5. Please rate how important each of these circumstances is
   in making you happy:

   a. Good health

   b. Being in love

   c. Personal inner growth

   d. Job or career advancement

   e. A good sex life

   f. Financial security

   g. Social and family life

6. In your opinion, who has a more difficult time being single, a
   man or a woman? What are the reasons for your opinion?

7. Describe the differences between your expectations and/or fantasies about single life and the reality of single life you have experienced. In your opinion, is single life accurately pictured by the press, by glamour magazines, by popular attitudes, and among married people? Why or why not?

8. What do you consider the greatest disadvantage of being single?

9. What do you consider the greatest advantage of being single?

10. On the whole, has being single been a pleasant or unpleasant experience for you?

WHY ARE SINGLES SINGLE?

After all is said and done, what do singles think of being single?

In this section we zeroed in on the specifics of why respondents recommend or do not recommend being single. We wondered if the growing population of unmarried people in America defines itself as a separate community committed to a particular "singles lifestyle," or if most singles see themselves as ordinary men and women who simply happen at the moment to be unmarried. We were looking for appraisals and value judgments, warnings and recommendations, advice and self-help.

1. *Why are you single?*	Men	Women
a. Marriage entails too much commitment and responsibility.	11%	7%
b. I haven't found the right person to marry.	34%	35%
c. I prefer the lifestyle.	10%	8%
d. I liked being married but my marriage failed; I'll marry again when the chance comes.	28%	37%
e. I prefer members of my own sex.	2%	1%
f. Why get married when people can live together?	5%	3%
g. I don't want to be tied to the same person for life.	4%	3%
h. Don't know.	7%	7%

Major Finding: *Only one-third of single men and one fifth of single women are single specifically because they like or desire the single lifestyle, or because they do not wish to be married. The rest are single for personal reasons, or because they have not yet found a suitable mate.*

BONUS FINDINGS

- Forty percent of widowed men say they are single because they like the lifestyle. Only 6 percent of men who have been divorced once feel the same way.
- The longer a man is single, the more likely he is to feel that he's unmarried because he hasn't met the right woman.
- Over half of men who have been divorced say they plan to remarry again and that they like being married.
- Twenty-six percent of high-income bachelors say they are single because they haven't found the right person to marry. Forty-five percent of low-wage-earners make the same claim.
- Almost one-fourth of men in the twenty-five-to-thirty-four-year-old age bracket would remarry if given the chance. Fifty-five percent of men over forty-five say the same.
- Almost two-thirds of divorced women say they like being married and will marry again if given the opportunity.
- The highly educated woman has the most difficult time finding the proper mate. Forty-five percent of college-educated women say they haven't found the right man yet, as compared to 29 percent of women who attended high school only.

Those who checked answers a, c, f, and g make up the approximate one-third of men and one-fifth of women who are pro-single lifestyle *or* anti-marriage, and who in either case are committed "lifers," people who wish to maintain their single status. This means that more than two-thirds of the singles population perceive marriage as a desirable goal. Singleness as a permanent way of life gets relatively few votes (see option c above), and marriage comes out surprisingly well. Even among men and women divorced two times, more than half claim they enjoy marriage and would try it again if the opportunity presented itself.

Men Earning High Wages Are Most Likely to Praise Marriage

High-wage-earning men, we discover, are almost *twice* as prone to like marriage as those who make thirteen thousand dollars or less a year. And the high-wage-earner is almost *four times* as likely to marry or remarry as those who are in the low-income brackets. This figure seems even more significant when compared to the figures for women, among whom there is practically *no* difference in preference among income groups.

Are we to conclude that low-wage-earning men have a greater chance of remaining single after divorce than men with large incomes? And if so, does this mean that in the future the singles community will be predominantly populated by the low-wage-earning male? If such is the case then money proves a factor not only in determining the quality of life while single but in deciding whether or not one will stay single at all.

"Part of the reason men with low incomes hesitate about getting remarried," says Dr. Barry McCarthy, clinical psychologist and sex therapist in Washington, DC, Professor of Psychology at American University, Washington, and author of *What You Still Don't Know About Male Sexuality,** "is that many of the things that traditionally attract men to marriage, things like children and family life, now appear adverse. This man may presently be fighting expensive court battles and alimony support payments. He may not be allowed to see his children. He's really turned off by the whole institution, and certainly he's not anxious to plunge back in, especially if he makes little money and has to pay for all these things.

"Even if he did want to remarry, so many of the available women have children, he might not want to pick up that responsibility. It would just cost him *more* money.

"Within the lower income groups there's a certain harshness and bitterness that goes into male-female relationships. The singles scene is very different in this community from that of the well-off. There is a certain kind of toughness and jadedness here. I'm struck in my own practice by the differences in sex problems that exist between the mid-

* Thomas Y. Crowell, 1977.

dle class and the lower class. A significant proportion of the lower-class women are into humiliating their men. Sort of like 'Listen, we had this bargain and you're supposed to come through. You're not a man.'

"All this means that you will probably start seeing a predominance of lower-class single men in the singles world, especially as you go up the age scale. If a middle-class man divorces he takes it hard, but it does not necessarily ruin his self-image. If a lower-class man gets divorced he tends to take it harder. He will feel especially ridiculed and humiliated. This man is not as likely to remarry as the average member of the middle class."

Further amplification on the matter of matrimony:

2. Do you plan to stay single indefinitely or would you like to marry? Why? If previously married, which lifestyle do you prefer, single or married? Why?

Major Finding: *Most singles plan to marry again.*

Approximately three quarters of men and women speak positively of marriage. The remaining quarter speak of it disparagingly and intend to stay unmarried. Those in the second category usually have had unhappy previous marriages (only a tiny percent of those who have never married intend to remain single for life). First let's listen to the 25 percent who, for various reasons, wish to stay single:

Woman, St. Louis, MO: Right now I am completely happy with being unmarried. I am proving myself and my career, and as an individual. After living for 20 years in a traditional marriage and realizing how much of myself was devastated by my husband's ego and business image, I doubt if that type of marriage would be tolerable for me again. Besides, I'm enjoying myself too much. I come and go as I please, I have sex with whom I please and enjoy the variety. True, it does get to be a rat race, but so does marriage.

Woman, Spring Green, WI: I definitely prefer the single life as compared to married. It never gets boring. If something goes wrong with one boyfriend you can always amuse yourself with another—being

happy and single has a lot to do with physical attractiveness. I never
have any problems meeting guys. Marriage allowed me no freedom
and a boring day-to-day routine, although our sex life was great until
the last day of marriage.

Enjoyment of the lifestyle is the positive reason some singles speak
up for singlehood. Others prefer it simply by contrast. These criticize
the institution of marriage in and of itself, or, relatedly, they report
having experienced a disastrous coupling and wish not to commit the
same error twice.

Man, Albuquerque, NM: In my last marriage I found that I could
not meet my wife's needs nor could she meet mine. We "took" from
each other's resources but never replenished the supply by giving.
The reason I could never marry again is because I learned how tremendous my needs are and how little I can give of myself. Before I
"inflict" myself on anyone again I must mature, and that will take a
lifetime.

Woman, Kansas City, MO: I would really have to know and love the
person over a long period of time before I would marry again. My second marriage was a mistake (less than a year after a divorce from a 15-
year marriage). I knew the man six weeks and didn't find out until
after the marriage that he was a real con artist. He had lied to me about
everything including his love and loyalty. He had been married five
times—not once. He was a cook in the army, not an officer. He was a
high school drop-out, not the holder of an M.A. degree from Harvard
University. He was deeply in debt, not wealthy with a "lucrative" business in Hawaii. After four weeks and many disclosures from him I
kicked him out and got the marriage annulled. This mistake cost me a
lot of money but worse, it cost me my oldest daughter. She hated this
man so much that she moved in with her Dad, and has been living with
him ever since.

As we have seen in an earlier chapter, some prefer to remain single
because of their careers.

Woman, Corpus Christi, TX: Since my divorce I've been promoted two
times and have become really interested in the retailing side of my

work. Marriage sat on my skills and thwarted my career. I now choose career over marriage.

Woman, Indianapolis, IN: I'm interested in my career future and refuse to allow my career to be overshadowed by a man's. I've seen too many bad marriages come to this, including my own. A married woman doesn't have that good a chance in the business world.

Another reason for remaining single is based on a kind of interpersonal claustrophobia. "Fear of getting trapped" is the most common phrase used to describe it. "Marriage means walls closing in on you," writes a young single. "Marriage is like being a rat in a trap." And several more: "When I was married it was a no-exit relationship." "Marriage is like being in jail." "Anything but that 'closed-door' kind of feeling!"

A third reason is the availability of romance and sex: "When you're married you have to sleep with the same person all the time." "I like being single because I can date whom I like. Marriage ties you down." "Since being single I've enjoyed the sex most, having who you want when you want them. No guilt. It feels good!"

There are other causes too. Most of them are mentioned in the following essay by a female respondent. Her list comes close to being all-inclusive.

Woman, Burlington, VT: Why do I want to remain single?

1. I can't see myself tied to one person forever. I'd feel trapped and cornered.
2. Being single gives me freedom. That's the big one; to come and go as I want and please, see who I want; it represents liberation.
3. I like being private and alone. If I was married I could never have this. Another person cramps my style.
4. I have no wish to have children. So why marry?
5. I like sex but prefer it with a variety of men, not one only. That gets boring. Variety is the spice of love as well as of life.
6. Being single lets me follow my career. And my career's doing great. A husband would end all that.
7. Being single means I can make more money and spend it on what I want, not on what *he* or *they* want.
8. I consider my home to be my castle. I don't want anyone coming in and changing it, or announcing we're moving to *his* place. I like to have things the way my taste tells me.

Fear of being "trapped," having "the right to go where I will," love of privacy, need for sexual variety, the "excitement of meeting new people," the mobility and "freedom of being alone," these phrases come up consistently among the one fourth of respondents who prefer being single.

Whatever reasons singles may give for maintaining their status, however, behind these reasons invariably lies the notion of free choice. That is, an unmarried person in the United States today is almost totally in charge of his or her own marital destiny. Unlike the custom that prevailed in America a century ago, unlike the custom that is found in many other parts of the world, the decision to marry is currently a matter of personal choice and inclination. And this is a significant change.

"Ours is the first generation," claims Dr. Warren Farrell, author of the book *The Liberated Man** and national lecturer on male-female relations, who currently resides in San Diego, "that can really make the conscious choice of whether to be single or whether to be married. This is the first generation that is not being pressured into matrimony, the first that is looking at the quality of their life and making choices based on that quality, not on social pressures. Today people can be single because they prefer it that way, not because they are undesirable or unwanted. To be single no longer means to be rejected. In fact, it may have quite the opposite meaning—it may mean that the person has enough personal security to discriminate; or that exposure to so many options creates the dilemma between continuing the dating smorgasbord or settling on a single intimate relationship. Many among the new singles breed, then, are choosing between two desirable options, rather than trying to prove to parents they are 'mature' by 'settling down' and getting married. There never has been a group exactly like this group, and it remains to be seen how they will grow and change."

Many Respondents Object to Being Labeled a "Single"

Many respondents cited a distaste for being categorized as "singles." They remarked that unmarried people are not "singles," as in the phrase "singles bar" or the "singles scene," but simply people who are at present not married. More than once, both here and in other essay sections, respondents took umbrage at such a label, complaining that

* Bantam Books, 1975.

such classifications tend to stereotype them and force assumptions that do not apply universally. "I am not presently married," writes a woman from Manhattan. "But I am not 'single' either. I do not look upon myself as being in some special 'cage,' nor do my friends. I am not part of some abandoned group of hell-raisers nor am I a lonely spinster. I plan to marry someday and until then prefer only to be known as a 'me.' " Another single appended the following comment onto an essay question: "I don't consider myself a 'single' or part of that lifestyle. Singles are people who read *Apartment Life,* go to bars to drink fashionable drinks, buy Pablo Cruse records, read Kurt Vonnegut and are 'heavily into running.' I'm just not married."

Man, Bethel Park, PA: First off, I think "singles life" is the most overplayed, blown-over bit of hot air I have ever come across. Singles life is made out to be like some sort of disease or an elixir of good fortune. The singles life, singles bars, singles apartments, singles hangouts, singles this and singles that. Look, I'm just an ordinary guy. My being single is just as natural to me as my skin color. I know nothing else. I am what I am. Don't make out that my way of life is something to be gawked at.

Singles Who Wish to Remarry Do Not Usually Look on Their Single Life as Unpleasant or Undesirable

Most respondents who plan to marry or remarry are not critical of the single condition. They simply look upon it as a temporary state of affairs. Respondents who have previously been married especially view their single years as a pleasant if sometimes trying interim: a period of time in which they can pause, recollect, grow, enjoy, experience a wide range of romance, plan for the future—and move on. Many wish for marriage, but not now, not so fast, not until the time is ripe:

Woman, Nashville, TN: Sure I want to get married. You think I'm mad? But on my own terms. In my own time—to a guy who is *super* and nothing less. Otherwise I'll stay single. I have to go out in the world and taste a lot of men and learn a lot of things. There's so much to know, so many places to go, and so many people who are fascinating. When I finally give my soul to a man I want to say to myself: "I'm sure of this man. Because I've known many men, many experiences and many places, and now I can be certain."

Woman, Atlanta, GA: I do plan to marry eventually, but as long as I am single I hope to remain happy, busy and fulfilled as possible. I don't view marriage as the most important thing, but I do intend to marry someone who will be compatible and keep life interesting. When he comes along, fine. Till then I'm having a good time on my own.

A sizable group of respondents disliked the "singles scene" in general, and perceived marriage as a kind of escape from this way of life. Approximately half of the women and a third of the men claimed to be marriage-minded, often for this reason.

Woman, St. Louis, MO: I would like to marry—to end loneliness—for companionship—to share vacations, or simply a TV program and a bag of popcorn. For security, not only in expenses shared but knowing someone you care for is there. I'm tired! I'm worn out meeting men and going together awhile with one man or another. I'll feel better also about sex—having it with only one—one I deeply care for—I will like myself better. I don't care anymore to share this most intimate of relationships with someone simply out of needing "to be touched" sometimes.

Man, Santa Fe, NM: I would like to remarry if the right woman comes along. Single life is lonely and empty. I prefer married life to single because I want to share. I hate being alone. It's been okay being single, I've learned a lot. But enough is enough. In my opinion being single for too long makes a person selfish. It drives one into themselves. They forget about giving.

Single by Choice or by Chance

3. *Are you unmarried by choice or because of circumstances beyond your control? Do you think marriage is a surrender to social pressures or is it a basic human need? Why?*

Answers overlapped those from the previous question ("Do you plan to stay single indefinitely or would you like to remarry?"). Marriage was again applauded and was frequently mentioned as the ultimate goal. As before, most said they were unmarried because they hadn't met the right mate:

Woman, San Antonio, TX: I'd marry if there was the right guy. Don't think I haven't tried. I've stooped so low as to go to a meat market dating dance club. How badly I've wanted to get married! I met two men there. The first one was very handsome and very dumb. He took me home and we spent hours looking at his collection of tropical fish. That was all he cared about. He never hinted at anything personal. When he took me home he was the perfect gentleman and asked me to come back some time because I was one of the few women who liked his fish! The second screwball I met there was into running. He was a sexy guy and we ended up spending the night together. I really wanted to get closer to him as I got to know him but, though this may sound not believable, he wouldn't get serious because I wasn't a good enough runner. I mean it. We would go out on a track and we'd run for, you know, twenty minutes until my stomach was about to split open. He was having a ball and when I complained he told me he was *just warming up!* If I got tired out and stopped he'd look at me in a critical way and I just *knew* I was losing points. These are just two of the experiences I've had out of many with men, including one serious relationship. Of course marriage is a basic need. I've been needing it for years!

Most respondents feel that marriage is a basic need and not simply conformity to social pressure. Some support this view on moral and religious grounds:

Man, Little Rock, AR: To me marriage is as basic as soap and water. Why? Because of basic moral values. A man's good name is his most precious possession. When he bestows his name on the woman he loves it becomes her crown and she is his queen—for all the world to know and see.

Other respondents feel marriage is basic because of the nature of men and women. "Men and women are as much part of nature as day and night," a woman remarks. Similes of this type commonly turn up: "Man and woman are like Adam and Eve all over again; it's God's law they be wed." "The positive and negative poles of the world are like man and woman married together and united in one cosmic whole." "A man and a woman are as natural for each other as bread and butter."

Man, Dayton, OH: Could man and woman have chosen marriage over the past 5,000 years simply out of social pressure? I don't think so. Social pressure is an element of human behavior but somewhere behind it all there has to be an urge and a will. Nothing lasts *that* long without having a universal basis of fact. Feminists and modernists can go on all they like about marriage being societal coercion and that we are "brainwashed" into it. But a little real thinking shows differently. Anything that has been around for so long a time, has satisfied so many people, been at the heart and soul of every human society, the very *center* of all family life on this planet, just can't be a "deviation," as a bright date I once had told me. Perhaps it is *we* who are deviated today with our moral anarchy.

Woman, Brooklyn, NY: Marriage is a logical consequence of two people being in love. It's a way of assuring each other of loyalty, responsibility, commitment that forces one to become serious towards their life. People who shy away from marriage are usually frightened or immature people who run from the very things that might center them and bring them into balance with their better side.

A few disagree:

Woman, Chicago, IL: I don't believe marriage is a basic human need. It certainly isn't mine except on very dark, dreary evenings when it's raining and I've had too much to drink. When my sanity returns so does my confidence and self-reliance. In the marriages I've seen, I'd say 3 out of 4 were instances of succumbing to social pressure. I have a terrible tendency to sneer at marriage and regard it as an indication of personal weakness.

Man, Danbury, CT: People get married because they're told they should. If there were no laws, no social pressures, and no Puritanical "sick" hangups in society, we wouldn't need an institution as warped as the one we have, mainly marriage. I've never done it and I never will.

A majority of those who are unmarried say they are unmarried out of choice. Those who claim "circumstances beyond their control" describe these circumstances in a variety of ways, some poignant, a few bizarre:

Pompton Lakes, NJ: I am unmarried because my husband died of cancer in January. We had a beautiful marriage—deep with joy and love. I think marriage is a basic human need—to give oneself totally and receive another totally is the greatest of human happiness.

Woman, San Diego, CA: I am unmarried because of circumstances. In my case a fifty-five-year-old grandfather (my husband) chose to leave his family and marry a twenty-year-old girl. This certain grandfather has grown children and has been called by all his friends a "responsible citizen." Of course this is his choice for whatever reason. I felt used emotionally and financially . . . my domestic rug was pulled right from under me . . . and after thirty-six years of marriage . . . it's tough going into the working market again, wouldn't you say?

Woman, Atlanta, GA: I left my husband because of an extreme drinking problem, and he committed suicide. I enjoyed marriage but not *that* marriage. I sought to get out because the relationship had become dangerous both emotionally and physically.

Woman, Des Moines, IA: Right now I am unmarried, but the reasons why are varied. I have a serious relationship with someone I want to marry. But he isn't ready. Because he can't decide if he is AC or DC. I have gone through much pain waiting for him to decide, even to the point of surprising him when he has been with another man. Yet he does love me, I can tell, and our sex life together has been fantastic. I suggest therapy for him but he keeps claiming nothing is wrong, that it's perfectly normal to "go both ways." He wants a marriage on these grounds. He wants to have men occasionally and still be married. I cannot accept this so I remain in waiting.

4. As a single do you ever feel pressures to get married? (Choose as many answers as are appropriate.)	Men	Women
a. Never	44%	46%
b. Yes, from my parents	13%	19%
c. Yes, at my job	7%	6%
d. Yes, from my own personal feelings	25%	28%
e. Yes, from the people I date	17%	8%
f. Yes, from my children	3%	9%
g. Yes, because I feel guilty about not being married	5%	5%
h. Don't know	2%	2%

Major Finding: At least half of all singles feel pressured to get married.

BONUS FINDINGS

- Men living with a woman out of wedlock are more likely to be pressured into marriage *at their job* than men who are either living alone or living with a roommate.
- Men who have been divorced twice feel much *more* pressure from their dates to be married than those married once or not at all. Men who have never married feel the *least* pressure from their dates to be married.
- The older a man gets, the more he is likely to feel pressure for marriage from the women he dates.
- When a woman has been divorced twice or more she feels more pressure than other women to remarry *from the people she dates,* and from *herself.* If she is a parent, she also feels more guilt about not being married, and indicates that she receives a good deal of pressure from her children.
- Women living with men out of wedlock receive the *same* amount of pressure from their parents to marry as women living with a roommate of the same sex. Women living with a group receive the *most* pressure to marry.
- Women divorced once say they get the *least* amount of pressure from their employers to marry. Women who have never married and those divorced twice or more get the *most*.

Leading the list of responses chosen is "My own personal feelings." Both sexes agree on this, though women feel this pressure slightly more than men. Next comes pressure from dates (i.e., pressure from lovers pushing for the resolution to an affair). Here men feel the pressure more than twice as much as women.

The findings, moreover, reveal that many singles experience *some* kind of pressure over being unmarried, but that this pressure comes almost as much from psychological sources ("My own personal feelings," "I feel guilty about not being married") as from external ones. Though the stigma attached to being unmarried has not been removed, its source has shifted. It now apparently derives as much from inner compulsion as from social mandate.

WHAT MAKES SINGLES HAPPY?

In order to probe more deeply into what it is like to be single, we posed a list of items usually thought to be productive of happiness:

a. Good health
b. Being in love
c. Personal inner growth
d. Job or career
e. A good sex life
f. Financial security
g. Social and family life

We requested singles to rate these items on the following scale:

1. Very important
2. Somewhat important
3. Neither important nor unimportant
4. Somewhat unimportant
5. Very unimportant

The question requested respondents to:

5. Using the scale, please rate how important each of these circumstances is in making you happy.

a. Good Health

Almost nine out of ten men and women thought good health either *very important* or *somewhat important*. The puzzle perhaps is the 10 percent who think it *very* or *somewhat unimportant*. One might guess this response comes from younger singles who, statistically, have not yet encountered many health problems. But no, quite the opposite. Twice the number of older men as younger ones, and three times the number of older women, declare good health to be *unimportant*.

b. Being in Love

About two thirds of men and four out of five women say that love is *very* or *somewhat important* to their happiness. It is worth noting that singles of both sexes who have been divorced twice put a greater premium on being in love than those who have never been married.

c. Personal Growth

While singles depend on romance for much of their happiness, an even greater source of fulfillment comes from the development of personal skills, values, ideals, and potential. Three quarters of men and 84 percent of women say personal growth is *very* or *somewhat important.* This answer, then, received the largest percentage of responses. Singles search for their satisfaction as much from private interests as from social or romantic ones, and the life of the single is made pleasurable as much from interior as from external concerns.

BONUS FINDINGS

- Personal growth is *most* important to the man who has never married, and *least* to the man who has been divorced twice or more. Also, the older a man gets the less important personal growth is for him.
- Almost half of high-wage-earning men say their jobs and career are very important to them. Only a third of middle-income men say the same.
- A good sex life is more important to a man when he is in his middle thirties than when he is in his early twenties.
- Almost 60 percent of low-income-earning women claim that being in love is important for them. The more money a woman makes, the less important being in love becomes. (Only 40 percent of middle-income women make the same claim.)
- The woman who deems her career *most* important tends to be in her early twenties. Women in their middle forties and early fifties find career *least* important.
- Almost 45 percent of twice-divorced women say a good sex life is important for them. A little more than a third of never-married women say the same.
- The more education a woman has, the more she is likely to rank personal growth as important.
- A good sex life is *most* important to women between the ages of twenty-five and forty-four. It is *least* important to women in their very early twenties and to women over forty-five.
- The more education a woman has, the less importance she places on a good sex life.
- Social and family life are more important to older women (forty-five to fifty-five) than to younger women.

"I have to ask each person what he or she means when saying personal growth is a goal," remarks Dr. Louise Sonnenberg, psychiatrist in private practice in Philadelphia, Pennsylvania, and Clinical Assistant Professor of Psychiatry at Thomas Jefferson University. "The phrase implies a variety of things to a variety of people. Some people who need a whole lot of structure think of it as going to school, taking courses. Others who are a little less structured see it as cultivating abilities and challenges in themselves, making personal changes, focusing on interests they've never before had time to focus on. In fact personal growth is defined largely by the person who is involved in it.

"It's interesting to me," Dr. Sonnenberg adds, "that women deem personal growth so important, since for many years women weren't supposed to *have* personal growth. A woman got married, raised her children, kept her house, and always put family above personal needs. Now things are changing—you can see it in your statistics: Women are becoming more aware of their inner requirements, more assertive, more insistent about fulfillment outside the family. And part of all this includes greater demands for space to develop inner resources. All of this puts pressure on both partners in any relationship, since when two people are involved in separate interests the two interests can clash. Women have traditionally been at home at the service of men. Now women are out in the world attending to personal and career interests. These take time away from the man. So the big question remains to be answered: How can two people realize themselves in a relationship without threatening each other, and without stepping on each other's toes? This is a problem people are just beginning to face, and just beginning to find solutions to."

d. Job or Career

Seventy-two percent of men rank their career as a main source of happiness, calling it *very* or *somewhat important*. Seventy-five percent of women answer in the same way. We have seen in Chapter 4 ("Living Alone") that when a person is single he or she is apt to sublimate the energy that might otherwise be invested in a marriage into a passion for work. We also saw that the cultivation of a profession, though often toilsome in the beginning, can turn out to be a permanent source of satisfaction.

"There's certainly a sign here," states Dr. Sonnenberg, "that a greater shift is taking place among women toward autonomy, a trend that is not characteristic of the traditional female. All in all it looks as if women are definitely expanding themselves out of the role of home-maker and home, and are now placing themselves in the business world and job market in a way that never used to be the case. In the future we will see more and more women involved with jobs, less and less at home or in motherhood."

e. A Good Sex Life

Among men, about half said it was *very important* and a third said *somewhat important*. Few—less than one out of ten—were indifferent. Among women, almost 40 percent said *very important* and a third said *somewhat important*. Taking this and the related question above, it is obvious that romance and sex are high on the list. Yet they are not on top.

f. Financial Security

Seventy-two percent of men and 83 percent of women declare financial security to be *very* or *somewhat important*.

g. Social and Family Life

About 70 percent of men and 83 percent of women speak of these as *very* or *somewhat important*. Women are more enthusiastic than men but both are affirmative.

The image that emerges from these responses is one of relatively balanced pleasures drawn from both inner and outer resources.

WHICH SEX HAS A HARDER TIME BEING SINGLE?

6. *In your opinion, who has a more difficult time being single, a man or a woman? What are the reasons for your opinion?*

Major Finding: *Women have a far more difficult time being single than men.*

By an overwhelming plurality, respondents of both sexes agree: It's harder for a woman to be single than for a man. Almost 90 percent of male essays and 80 percent of female essays agree that the problems of being single weigh more heavily on women. Here are some male respondents on the subject:

Man, Louisville, KY: I think women have a tougher time, because of the double standard. A woman can't go or do what a man does, or she is considered a slut. She can't go alone where a man can go without being sexually in jeopardy, psychologically and even physically sometimes.

Man, Manhattan, NY: A woman has a more difficult time—because there are about ten single women to every single man. And men like younger women as a rule, so that makes the odds worse.

Man, Los Angeles, CA: Traditionally it has been and will continue to be easier economically for the single man. His income is greater. This is unfortunate because money is power, and the one with the power is on top whether it is a possessive husband or a capitalist male-dominated nation.

Man, St. Louis, MO: Most guys are single because they want it that way. But to me a woman who grows up an old maid would feel ugly and rejected, and this makes it hard for her not to be married. It's considered cool for a man to be single in our society. But if a woman is single and let us say over thirty-five years old, people think something is wrong with her.

Now the women's answers:

Woman, Louisville, KY: Women! More social pressure for a woman to be married; more social restrictions on women's dating and sexual behavior. If a woman is divorced she has a "reputation" automatically—even among "enlightened" people. Divorced women with children have a very hard time dealing with social-family pressures and dating at the same time.

Woman, Phoenix, AZ: A woman. She's left with the family and supporting kids—while her ex is running around having a ball. Young children make it fifty times harder. Try having a boyfriend and keeping the children happy too sometime.

Woman, Milwaukee, WI: Women have so many things to be frightened of. Men don't know about being raped, used. Being alone is harder for women because they are family-oriented. We need life and fun around us, as well as children and song!

Sifting through the reasons women give as to why their position in the single world is so difficult, the following points appear with the most frequency and authority.

1. Women have less sexual and social freedom than men. It is still the man who makes the dates, still the woman who must sit and wait. "Women are still passive in this society; we've got to rest at home in a lady-like way till the man contacts us. Bah!" "As much as I may want to, society says it's the man who makes the dating rules."

2. Divorced mothers usually end up with the burdens of running the family. "Imagine taking care of two kids still in diapers and doing it all on your own—then if you're a man thank God you're not a woman!"

3. A woman alone is far more vulnerable to (and frightened of) physical abuse than a man. Rape fears are real fears for many single women (recall that approximately a third of single women have suffered some form of abuse at singles bars). "The hardest thing is being scared," writes one single female.

4. Age is a more profound liability for the single woman than it is for the man. This is, of course, an ancient refrain but still a relevant one. "If a woman is gray she's considered over the hill. If a man is gray he's thought to be dignified and distinguished." "In this world if you're past thirty-five and have a few wrinkles they turn you out to pasture. At that age a man is sometimes just coming into his own, looks-wise."

5. Single women earn less than men, suffer more job discrimination, and have fewer career opportunities. This problem is especially hard for the recently divorced mother who is catapulted into the labor market, often without the appropriate skills. (We have discussed this problem in Chapter 6, The Single Parent.) "Setting out to get some money is so hard if you ask for a job because you're a woman." "To put it mildly, women have less of a chance of economic survival than men!"

6. Single women have less social mobility than men; i.e., it is more difficult for women to travel alone, eat alone, enter a bar without an escort, live alone. "I'm hampered, because if I go anywhere without a date all the men in the room take this as an invitation for sex." "Women can't move around as freely as men because of social strictures and old-fashioned taboos."

Here are further essays on this subject by women:

Woman, Syracuse, NY: In this sexist society the single woman is a target for every kind of rip-off, money scam, sex come-on, or whatever. A single man is defined as a bachelor. But a single woman—oh no, she's got to be either an old maid or a loose woman! It's very sad, but still very true.

Woman, San Diego, CA: A woman has a more difficult time. If she's a divorcee she's more than likely to have children. She probably hasn't been working before, and all of a sudden has to go back to work. This is not easy. Single women who work don't earn the same as men, and this represents a financial burden. Most men aren't as materialistic as women and their needs are minimum. There's always the danger of being overpowered physically by horny men, and believe me, many is the rape that goes unreported. I was raped once on a first date by a minister's son who I met at a block dance. He's known as the "nice boy" of the neighborhood, so of course I trusted him when he asked me back to his condominium apartment. There he wasted no time in stripping me against my will and having his fun. Of course I didn't say anything because I didn't want trouble. That's one of the hazards of being a single woman.

Woman, Los Angeles, CA: A woman definitely, because women are not raised to be as independent and achievement-oriented as men. A single woman, as myself, is confronted with daily situations of being assertive and aggressive in certain confrontations that do not come easily. Women are often conned by men and looked upon as mere sexual objects both in their jobs and socially. Single women are confronted with a great many stereotypes rigidly placed in persons' minds. Certain biases exist in different realms of society such as insurance companies, bank loans, real estate, and in certain jobs. Single women, more than men, are continuously exposed to being outcasted and condemned because they don't happen at this particular time to have a husband.

Woman, Des Moines, IA: Frankly, single life is lonely, expensive, and not worth the headache. Men don't understand what it is to be a woman alone. You're uprooted, unprotected, unloved, discriminated against, vulnerable to physical molestation, a regular sex object for most men, just one more face at the dance hall.

Woman, Nashville, KY: A woman. Especially if the ex-husband is an ass like mine, who does not give any support. Where then does a woman get the money to live on? Maybe she has no profession, has not worked in 10 years or longer. I went to visit a girlfriend of mine in Tennessee for a week when I was married. I had $50.00 on me. I called my husband in three days because I loved him and missed him so much. I asked him to send me my money so I could get a ticket home at the end of the week. He said, "No, I don't want you to come home, I like being free and doing as I please," which was, I might add, drinking to excess, gambling, and sleeping with other women to prove himself attractive. He was 375 pounds, lost down to 198 pounds. To me he was beautiful at 375. I worshipped him. My love was enough. He was very self-centered and demanding, so the psychiatrists say. Anyway, I was in Tennessee, no money, no home, no job. What happened? I collapsed mental and physical. I ended up in Central State Mental Hospital for 5 months. Try getting a job when they find out you have been in a mental institution. I *lied.* I got a job in breathing therapy at a hospital. My work is good and I stayed. The church gave me money for my utilities and a down payment on a car. The more I try the harder it becomes for me. I believe many women have these problems. Men don't care or respect a woman's feelings (though some women do deserve what they get).

Only a small percentage of respondents think men have a tougher time than women. Women tend to feel more sympathy toward the male position than men themselves do. Perhaps sympathy is not the correct word. Women most commonly cite the fact that "men are not trained to take care of themselves," or that they are "helpless" when faced with keeping a home, cooking, getting the dirty collars scrubbed—evaluations that are colored by mixed emotions:

Woman, Tulsa, OK: A man has it more difficult. He's been in the habit of being waited on and cared for when he was brought up. He was never taught household skills. When he leaves home and is not married the care is missing and he doesn't know what to do with himself. Let's face it, if a man doesn't have someone to take care of him he's like a helpless baby!

Woman, San Diego, CA: Right now I'd say guys—because it's up to the women to have the power of accepting or rejecting the gentleman's offer to dance, go to the movies, etc. She can nip a relationship in the bud or wait till she comes across a guy she's interested in and can start the conversation. All right, all right, but if you really want to know what I think it's that men have it hard because they can't take care of themselves. My ex-boyfriend and I broke up last year. As a rule I had cleaned his house for him once a week and cooked dinner. When we broke up he went to pieces, and his house became a pigsty. He called me up, and asked if he could "hire" me to clean his house once a week!

Woman, Baltimore, MD: A man. Men are usually stunted emotionally, are locked into male stereotype images, are threatened by the women's movement, and are not into exploring and growing within themselves. Men in general are letting the world pass them by and waiting for someone to take care of them. They are just little boys playing King of the Mountain. Women, on the other hand, are taking care of themselves and don't have too much left over for the dependent male. Switcharoonie, uh! Reasons for my opinions? Simple? My experience.

"Basically, people can live more economically when they are married," says Dr. Joseph Pleck, Director of Wellesley College Center for Research on Women, Wellesley, Massachusetts. "And of course in our society women have less earning power than men. That's the big reason why women may have a more difficult time being single.

"However, from a psychological point of view many studies indicate that women are basically the *maintainers* of all social networks. Men are more socially and emotionally isolated than women following a breakup. Men have fewer skills for initiating new relationships. In seminars that have been run for people just divorced, women tend to take the leadership and make more appropriate use of the resources that are available to them. So we see two trends in two different directions. Economically, there is no question that it is the woman who suffers. But socially, emotionally, psychologically, I think you'll find men less equipped to deal with the unmarried life."

EXPECTATIONS VERSUS REALITY: WHAT SINGLES WANT —AND WHAT THEY GET

7. Describe the differences between your expectations and/or fantasies about single life and the reality of single life you have experienced. In your opinion, is single life accurately pictured by the press, by glamour magazines, by popular attitudes, and among married people? Why or why not?

Woman, Syracuse, NY: Singles life is not accurately pictured by the press, etc. The concept of a singles lifestyle is the invention of the "free market" of the U.S., purely in order to sell more useless products, for example, "natural makeups," hair blow-dryers, deodorants, singles clubs, singles vacations, bar life and so on, ad nauseum.

Woman, Pittsburgh, PA: The way single life is portrayed is that no one seems to work. They are always on some exotic vacation or weekend getaway. They have very expensive apartments and very beautiful friends. But in reality most singles live in a one- or two-room apartment, often with their parents' old furniture or something from the Goodwill shops. At best they get their two-week vacation, and then they have only enough money saved for a week at the beach, probably Ocean City, Md., not the Bahamas. They drive their old model car to this "heavenly" vacation, hoping it doesn't break down until they get back. That's the reality versus the bullshit.

Woman, Medford, OR: Single life is put across as being exciting, glamorous, fun, fulfilling and safe. It's none of these things. Out of all my many, many single friends, no one leads a glamorous, exciting or fulfilling life. They just live like any of us, day to day, taking things as they come. TV, the press, books, magazines, have brainwashed women right out of the home and the side of their children. We have been used, abused, lied to, cheated (I do not think "murdered" is too strong a word) into thinking that if we are only unmarried then we will be free, happy, carefree, and live the perfect life. Look around. Do the single people you know seem happier than anyone else?

Plainly disillusioned by unfulfilled media promises, singles stress the fact that being single is by no means an escape or dodge from the difficulties of living. In this sense, many claim, the media are culpable. "Being unwed and living alone," says one woman, "for me is just having one set of troubles instead of another. It's certainly not the steady fun and thrills which what I call the 'Good News People' are always talking about in their hype."

From all the essays received in this section, only a handful found that the realities of single life fit with popular media mythology.

Woman, Portland, OR: I'd say the way the press handles single life is fair. It's been a good time for me, better than I thought it would be (or fantasized, as you put it). Perhaps the press overplays it a bit but not that much and I've had lots of good times.

Man, Manhattan, NY: I am definitely a "swinging single." I am the kind of single the magazines write about. I'm out every night with a different person, most of whom I score with. I have no intentions of settling down. I prefer single life above all. If the papers show single life as all glamorous I believe it is my duty to live up to their image. And I do.

Most of the answers, however, form a kind of irate litany.

Man, Queens, NY: The singles life is pictured by the press as all glamour. It portrays singles life as one big party time, with sex orgies every night and affairs in an unending chain. The reality of the singles life is the same reality as married, with bills to pay, obligations to meet and children to raise. The only additional reality is that the single has to make all decisions alone and has no one to blame for errors.

Woman, Chicago, IL: I thought single life meant 'life in the fast lane.' Many times I feel lonely, bored and insecure. I need the feeling of being loved.

Woman, Hollywood, CA: Many TV shows and other media promote the lives of single actors and actresses that are gorgeous people. The majority of us are plain and semi-pretty people who get lonely and the blues.

Man, Dayton, OH: I had hoped for fun and excitement but I find it rather dull—as far as the dating goes. The swinging-single life according to the press is a lot of hooey! I think it confuses and distracts married couples and misdirects a lot of singles.

"Fantasies bred through the media can be very misleading," remarks Dr. McCarthy, Professor of Psychology at American University in Washington. "I've had clients who have gone away to singles' weekends. People in their surroundings, especially married people, leer at them—'God, that must have been great!' The reality, it turns out, was that there were plenty of lonely parts to the experience, or that it didn't go well at all, or that the person got caught up in some sort of social-sexual situation and then felt lousy about it. All of this produces the feeling of 'Gee, I should have done better,' or a version of that— 'Everybody else is doing great except me, nobody else is lonely except me.'

"The images that people compare themselves with are entirely unrealistic—and the result is that the person's self-esteem is lowered by comparing himself or herself to these fantasies. Very little of the programming in the media, especially television, is on target psychologically, in terms of how life really works. This is because it really doesn't make good entertainment to describe the mundane realities of life, the ordinary ups and downs. To make a good program you have to have plenty of drama and glamour. This is fine from the standpoint of making successful television, but from the viewer's standpoint it gives him or her a lot of incorrect notions of what life is about. This kind of thing is particularly harmful to people in the middle years of marriages. It creates pressures to break out and divorce."

Many Singles Blame the Media for a False Picture of Single Life

Respondents frequently claim that there are three misleading notions concerning the single life that occur again and again in films, TV, and the popular press. The first of these is that being single is tantamount to an endless sexual party:

Man, New Orleans, LA: To a certain degree single life is pictured by the press to be sex, sex and more sex. They don't consider that some people just date for pleasure. They dwell too much on sexual performance and phony romance. Being single has sex difficulties just as being married has sex difficulties. There may be more chances to have sex if you're single, but remember, this means more chance of complications and VD too.

Second, singles complain that much of the promo given single life portrays it as a round of disco dancing, vacation-going, and festivities of different kinds. But who is to pay for it all?

Woman, Albuquerque, NM: Glamour magazines perpetuate a warped image of single life. They display single life as constantly romantic, never indicating the lack of warmth one can feel from a date. They display singles as all beautiful, rich, free, irresponsible, able to do whatever they want when they want to. Isn't this just playing on people's wish fulfillment? Life is portrayed as a game in which the partners lure one another into a phony, fabricated world in which the real traits of the person, be they selfishness, conceit, vanity, temper, are covered up by plush apartment settings, contrived dating plans, sexy lingerie, expensive nights on the town, make-up, etc. Nothing is mentioned of the boring nights. Or the roach-filled, paint-peeled-off apartments. And especially of the fact that all these pleasures cost *money!* I said *money!* Did you hear? All you little boys and girls out there in Dreamland reading about love and sex in singletown—did you hear? It all costs a bundle, more than most of us could *ever* afford. You'll be lucky if you can pay your rent on time, let alone have all that fun. The whole thing is hype, my friends, and all it does is confuse people, lure a lot of happily married people into divorce.

Man, Winston-Salem, NC: The most difficult part of being single is being broke. And who isn't broke these days? The most difficult part of being broke is being told that single life is just one big blast and why aren't you out there having fun? Well, Officer, it's because my pockets are empty. See. No cash, Nash.

Lastly, there's the notion of freedom, that much used and much misused term. In singles' language, freedom means freedom to "come and go," to "do as I wish," "to be what I want." This is one of the most important and constant themes in the survey, that being unmarried provides a degree of social and psychological independence that is not possible in a permanent situation.

And in fact, respondents bear out the validity of this claim. The message we receive is that being single *does* provide individuals with the personal space and self-determination they had hoped for. Autonomy is especially valued among the ranks of the recently divorced, and almost invariably this new sensation of freedom is the headiest part of being unattached.

However—and the "however" is a major one here—though the independence of single life is a real asset, it is far from a cure-all for the woes of the human condition. For freedom casts its inevitable shadow, and this is *loneliness*. The essay that follows speaks for many respondents:

Man, Los Angeles, CA: The best part about being single is being free and left alone. That's the part all the glamour media emphasize. What they don't show us is the terrible loneliness of single life. Or if they do show it they gloss over it, with some banal tripe about how to "cure" loneliness in three easy steps. As if loneliness could be overcome by some mechanical formula, like pimples or a cold. Nonsense! There is no cure for loneliness other than the warmth of love. That's the truth. Let's make this definite—getting laid sixteen times a week is not love and is not a cure either, as the mash-line might imply if not state. In fact, promiscuity works the opposite way, making alienation even greater. Sex and love are not the same thing. One of the really stupid errors of our time is this error. The word love and sex have become practically the same. Loneliness is the price one pays for freedom. If you're going to be alone and free, better expect to be alone and lonely too. You can't have your cake and eat it too. One more time, folks: loneliness is the price you pay for freedom.

Freedom vs. Loneliness

"Loneliness is the price you pay for freedom." Emphatic words. As commonly expressed, however, is the opposite sentiment. In the words of one single: "The cost of losing my singleness would be, I feel, losing my freedom." So the bind. Almost all singles agree: To be unattached means to feel alone, but to commit oneself to another is to sacrifice the intoxicating sensation of being footloose and unengaged.

Further evidence concerning this dichotomy between loneliness and freedom is offered in answers to two multiple-choice questions:

8. What do you consider the greatest disadvantage of being single?

9. What do you consider the greatest advantage of being single?	Men	Women
Greatest disadvantage		
a. Loneliness	42%	44%
b. Fear due to living alone	4%	5%
c. Economic insecurity	2%	16%
d. Restricted sexual and social life	12%	10%
e. A tendency to become rigid, self-centered, selfish	14%	8%
f. The social stigma of not being married	7%	4%
g. The dating grind	14%	11%
h. Don't know	5%	3%
Greatest advantage	**Men**	**Women**
a. Mobility and freedom	49%	49%
b. Availability of romantic partners	6%	3%
c. Time to pursue personal interests	17%	21%

d. Economic security and independence	3%	4%
e. Privacy	8%	10%
f. Social life in general: dating, entertainment, excitement	15%	12%
g. Don't know	2%	2%

BONUS FINDINGS (QUESTION 8)

- Men who suffer least from loneliness are in the middle-income bracket. Those who feel it the most are the ones who earn least.
- Never-married women do not fear economic insecurity as much as women who have been divorced once or twice.
- The longer a woman is single the *less* likely she is to consider loneliness a problem.
- Women who have never married suffer *most* from the dating grind.
- The woman who suffers most from loneliness tends to be a high school graduate, earns under thirteen thousand dollars a year, works at a blue-collar job, and has been divorced. The man who suffers most from loneliness has had some college, makes a low salary, and works in a white-collar position.
- The older a woman gets the more likely she is to cite economic insecurity as the greatest disadvantage of being single.
- The women who feel *most* restricted sexually and socially are the very young (twenty to twenty-four) and those in the oldest age group (forty-five to fifty-five).

Loneliness in one column and freedom in the other—both number one, and both picked almost three times more often than any other choice. Anyone who wishes to understand what it means to be single in America must realize that for most people these extremes are an integral part of single life. As often as singles complain of alienation and loneliness, they praise freedom and lack of commitment. The situation offers a kind of scale, freedom on one side, loneliness on the other. The balance is decided by the circumstances of the person's particular life. If these circumstances are cheerful and fulfilled, freedom will predominate; if circumstances are difficult, loneliness will prevail.

"The crucial question that I face over and over again with single people," claims Dr. Warren Farrell, "is whether one wants stability or freedom.

BONUS FINDINGS (QUESTION 9)

- A man who has been married and divorced tends to place less of a premium on freedom than the man who has never married.
- Twice as many widowed men (as compared to men made single by divorce) cite the pursuit of personal interests as the greatest advantage of single life.
- Men who support mobility and freedom as the greatest advantage of single life tend to be in their twenties and early thirties. Older men (forty-five to fifty-five) appreciate it the least.
- Older men tend to appreciate the availability of romantic partners more than younger men. However, for men over forty-five enthusiasm for this option diminishes dramatically.
- Mobility and freedom are *most* appreciated by women in their middle twenties and early thirties. Appreciation declines in importance among older women.

"Marriage is biased toward stability, singleness toward freedom. The problem is, of course, that most of us want both. Society, however, tells people they must be either single or married. All or nothing. Thus, single people yearn for a long-term stable relationship, and married people want to be free."

We asked Dr. Farrell for his opinion on how best to resolve this difficult choice. "The key question one must ask oneself," he claims, "is: 'At this time in my life, what do I need and want more, security or independence? Stability or freedom? Or some balance between the two?'

"The answer then determines whether one enters a relationship in which most energy is devoted to each other (high stability—and this usually includes marriage), or a relationship (sometimes a marriage) in which more energy is devoted toward other people, outside projects, careers; or a sexually open marriage; or singleness itself.

"There is, in brief, no right or wrong structure—only asking internally honest questions of oneself, and then finding a partner or partners who match one's internal needs. This, of course, is a much different process from automatically marrying a person simply to appear mature to the world.

"For example, in my own life a while back I took an entire year and promised myself that during this year I would not date any one person consistently. Never before had I been without a primary relationship to depend on, and now I felt I needed to experience a whole year learning to live by myself: spending nights alone, not having someone meet me after work, not sleeping with another person. I felt that until I could do this, I would never do a woman justice. That is, I would never be sure whether I was living with a woman to fill those vacuums, or whether I was living with that woman because I truly cherished her for herself."

In the long run, singles life *is* life. It is neither an escape from personal problems nor a fall into endless turmoil, but simply one kind of arrangement among others with its associated losses and gains. To expect the single condition in and of itself to make one happy, or for that matter unhappy, is, as essay after essay stress, to nurture futile expectations:

Man, Cleveland, OH: It's hard to say if being single is better or worse than being married. Single life isn't all fun and games, of course, loose women and high living. In reality it has the advantage of being free and not tied down to one person or way of life. But it means not having a loving companion to share the world with, not being able to experience the good things with someone you love, and doing such boring tasks as washing and cooking, all lonely and tiresome pursuits. I think the truth of it is, "The grass is always greener." If you talk to marrieds, they will wish they weren't married. If you talk to singles, vice versa. The grass is always greener—until you jump over the fence.

Woman, Jacksonville, FL: It's nice not to worry about dinner, and I can prepare whatever my child and I want. You come and go as you like, your own chief and your own Indian. The single life is painted glamorous but it is anything but that, as one finds herself juggling to make house payments, utilities, food. All the important decisions are on your shoulders. When you're alone the nights are long.

The Overall Experience

10. On the whole, has being single been a pleasant or unpleasant experience for you?	Men	Women
a. It's been wonderful.	23%	12%
b. I've been married and I've been single and I prefer being single.	10%	8%
c. I've been married and I've been single and I prefer being married.	20%	24%
d. It's been an unpleasant experience.	3%	5%
e. Anything would be better than being single.	1%	1%
f. It's fine for a while. Then one gets tired of it.	14%	16%
g. There have been plenty of problems but basically it's been fine.	27%	33%
h. Don't know.	2%	1%

While slightly more than half of the respondents (60 percent of men and more than 50 percent of women) indicate that they enjoy aspects of being single, the other half said they do not enjoy being single. The reasons for liking or disliking being unmarried have been counted and recounted throughout the study. What is important here is the split itself, 50-percent pro, almost 50-percent con. This split mirrors the general attitude of singles throughout the questionnaire: The pros and cons are both part of the basic experience.

"We tend to go from one extreme to the other in this life," states Dr. Farrell, "saying that marriage is the answer or singleness is the answer. What we have to do is look at our own personality and find out what stage we're at in our lives, what psychological needs we have, and then decide what structure best suits our needs. Thinking in terms of one as all good and the other as all bad, marriage as great and singleness as terrible, that sort of thing is to miss the point. Asking what I can and should do for myself at this time in life is more important, and more helpful too."

The very ambiguity of singles about singleness shows there *is* no final definitive opinion about whether it is good, bad, or indifferent to be unmarried in America, other than that which the individual concludes from his or her own experience. Singleness is as problematic as any other condition, and as in most any department of life, this rela-

BONUS FINDINGS

- Almost 40 percent of men who haven't married as yet say that being single is wonderful. However, after two or more divorces only 7 percent of men feel the same.
- Men who live with a group are the first to tire of the single life. Those living with a woman are the least likely to tire of it.
- Widowed men tend to adjust better to the single life than divorced men. Almost 40 percent of widowers say that, despite problems, the single life is going well. About half that number of divorced men agree.
- The older a man gets, the less likely he is to say that the single life is pleasant.
- The divorced male who is most anxious to remarry tends to be older (between forty-five and fifty-five years old), in the high-income bracket, and either a professional or a white-collar worker.
- Men who have been married but prefer the single life tend to be blue-collar workers, between thirty-five and forty-five years old, have only a high-school education, and earn less than thirteen thousand dollars a year.
- A quarter of women who have never married say that being single is wonderful. Only 6 percent of women who have been divorced once say the same.
- Twice as many widowed women would like to remarry as would those who have been divorced.
- Almost half of the women who have never been married say they have been able to handle the problems of being single. Only a quarter of divorced or widowed women say the same.
- The woman who most enjoys being single is young (between twenty and twenty-four years of age), has never been married, is a college graduate, and is in the high-income bracket.
- Women who are most likely to say they prefer being married have been divorced twice or more, have a high-school education, and are in the low-income bracket.

tively new and admittedly complex phenomenon is ultimately what one is willing to make of it.

Woman, Cincinnati, OH: Singles can be exciting or dull, happy or sad. It depends on many things, such as your temperament, your finances, whether you have children, where you live, your friends, your intimates, your interests, how much you like or dislike living alone, support you get from others, your sex needs, your appearance, your religious beliefs, how nice or not nice you are to others, how safe you feel, how healthy you are in head and body. All these count. If you have more gold stars than Xs on your report card it will be okay for you. You know the cliché—life is as pleasant as the person who is living it.

Chapter 8

The Future of Singles ||||
Life in America—
As Predicted by
Singles

**Questions asked in "The Future of Singles
Life" include:**

1. Do you feel the expansion of the singles lifestyle in modern society is a healthy or unhealthy event?

2. Which of the following, if any, do you find an attractive substitute or alternative for marriage?

   a. Polygamy

   b. Trial marriage

   c. Polyandry

   d. Serial marriage

   e. Abandonment of all sexual conventions and establishment of free-love society

   f. Group or communal marriage

   g. Open marriage

3. If you were given absolute political power, what laws, changes, and reforms would you institute for relationships between men and women? Would you make sex more avail-

354

able or less? Would you alter the institution of marriage? What alternatives would you introduce, if any? Would you allow free love, or would you tighten the laws that already govern sex? How would you treat homosexuality, bisexuality, promiscuity, S&M, prostitution, group sex, and so forth? Describe the society you would create.

4. What do you think is the future of the single lifestyle in modern society?

Today's singles find themselves caught between past norms and present change, between traditional values and modern redefinition of these values. In response to such tensions some individuals lean toward custom, others toward change, and still others—in fact the majority— do a bit of both. All, however, are subject to this seesaw between old and new. Herein is where so many of the conflicts *and* the pleasures associated with being single originate.

Singles life, consequently, is a movement still in the transitional stage, still in process of developing. Despite the insistence of some social scientists that we have already reached an era of completed social-sexual reform and that singleness has now emerged as a wholly new lifestyle, the message learned from this survey is that sentiments are still in flux and that no one is really clear about where the institution of singleness is actually headed.

SINGLES ARE STILL AMBIVALENT ABOUT SEXUAL PERMISSIVENESS

We have seen in many places, for instance in the first sections of the "Mating" chapter, that sexuality is more available in America than in the past, that sexual liberty is not uncommon among singles, and that sexual "experimentation" is on the increase. We have also seen that a strain of conservatism affects sexual issues and that the sexual revolution, while bringing the full range of human eroticism into the open, has by no means made easy, transient, or unusual sex an undisputed standard of behavior. In fact, we have witnessed that a majority of singles, even those who have experienced a wide range of sexual activity, often express negative feelings toward promiscuity, cheating, one-night stands, group sex, kinky sex—and that if given the choice, the majority would still prefer intimate, permanent, one-on-one relationships. Indeed, many would still prefer marriage.

SINGLE LIFE IS GENERALLY MISREPRESENTED

Respondents' verdict on the single life informs us that it is neither the wild spree advertised by sensationalists nor the dour state of loneliness many fear it to be. Though it contains elements of both, the majority of respondents reveal that its main ingredients are more or less those that accompany most any lifestyle today. In this sense singleness is just one mode out of many, neither more nor less productive of happiness than any other. It is this fact that causes many respondents to insist that they are not "singles" at all but people like you and me who, for whatever reason, are simply not married at the present time.

DIFFERENT SOCIAL GROUPS EXPERIENCE SINGLENESS IN DIFFERENT WAYS

We have observed that there are differences in the way various groups participate in the single world. Blue-collar, white-collar, and professional single groups each inhabit separate social areas and have independent value systems which, while they may occasionally overlap and cross in interesting configurations, rarely correspond. The high-earning, educated single has substantially different likes and prejudices from the low-earning, non–college-educated single; a young person's experience of singleness is different from a middle-aged person's; never-marrieds differ basically from divorced singles; women's experience of singleness is unlike men's, and so on. This means that before coming to conclusions about singleness *per se* it is best to learn who the single in question really is—his or her age, sex, income, etc.

MOST SINGLES STILL APPROVE OF MARRIAGE, BUT FOR MANY DIFFERENT REASONS

Even though the single population is expanding in this country, it is not necessarily because Americans seek the single lifestyle *per se* but because *they find it so difficult either to stay married or to find an acceptable marriage partner.* This is a fundamental distinction and cannot be stressed strongly enough. We learn that while most singles basically enjoy being single, a majority prefer matrimony, and that when given the hypothetical choice between the two, most choose the latter. The single community is composed of no more than 20 to 25 percent of committed "lifers," while the remainder in one way or another view themselves as candidates for future marriage. We learn that though the novelty of having many mates provides contentment for a period of time, after a while most singles begin a serious hunt for a permanent partner. Moreover, respondents select marriage even when offered seemingly attractive alternatives such as a live-together arrangement. Finally, when questioned directly most singles advise married people who are considering becoming single to remain married. In plain terms, most singles are single not because they wish to be partnerless but because they have found that marriage *as it presently exists* does not meet their psychological and social requirements.

MARITAL NORMS: PRESENT AND FUTURE

Will singleness become the marital norm of American men and women? Will it replace marriage? Or is it simply a transitional condition, one that exists as a result of the fact that marriage itself has recently undergone such change? What do singles predict about the matter? This is the last aspect of singles life we wished to examine, the future of singles life as perceived by singles themselves. We posed several questions to respondents.

	Men	Women
1. *Do you feel the expansion of the singles lifestyle in modern society is a healthy or unhealthy event?*		
a. Generally healthy.	30%	18%
b. Very healthy—it is a step toward sexual freedom and the replacement of marriage.	6%	2%
c. Healthy—it offers attractive alternatives to marriage and provides people freedom of choice.	24%	27%
d. Unhealthy—it is a sign of the breakup of the social structure and family unit.	15%	23%
e. Profoundly unhealthy—it marks the disintegration of norms and values that have kept society intact for centuries.	3%	6%

f. It is impossible to tell at this time.	13%	15%
g. It is probably not important one way or another.	7%	6%
h. Don't know.	2%	3%

Almost twice as many men as women call the movement *generally healthy,* while approximately a third more women than men deem it *unhealthy.* Throughout we have offered reasons why women might come to this judgment—job prejudice, physical fears of living alone, the hardships of custody, money problems. Women who feel this way are predominantly over forty and have been married once or twice. Younger, never-married women—and hence less experienced women—are prone to think the singles movement healthy and to judge it as a positive social benefit.

"Younger women will naturally enjoy being single more," remarks Dr. Warren Farrell. "In her early twenties she is freer than she will ever be again. First, she's away from home for the first time and has the freedom to be single in the way she *wants* to be—as opposed to being single under the pressure of parental expectations or college dorm restrictions. She's probably earning her own income, which allows her to be her own boss. Further, it's still an acceptable thing from society's standards for a woman to *be* single at this age; pressures for marriage haven't begun in earnest, and a person can enjoy their independence at this age without feeling too much guilt because they haven't settled down. Finally, according to society's standards, a woman's looks are at their best in her early twenties.

"In these findings men seem to perceive singleness as more healthy than women. This is because most men are not so tied to societal norms that center on issues of relationships. Men are tied to norms concerning financial achievement—that's how a man learns to define himself. But a man's not as conditioned as a woman into feeling an intimate relationship is the most important of all things. Women learn much stricter societal patterns of what's right and what's wrong. One of these lessons is: marriage is right. This is drummed into them from an early age, and it's not easy for a woman to get it out of herself. Thus she is generally less likely to think of her single status as a 'healthy' condition until she has been married once and seen for herself that, first, marriage is no panacea and, second, that *until she knows how to be single happily she will hold on to a poor marriage for fear of entering a vacuum.* That, in my opinion, is not marriage out of love, but marriage out of

BONUS FINDINGS

- Men who have never married feel the single life is generally healthy. However, once a man has been married and divorced, his feelings about the health of single life lessen substantially.
- Men living with a roommate of the same sex are *most* likely to see the expansion of single life as a healthy sign. Men living at home with their families are *least* likely to see it this way. Men living alone or with a family are twice as likely as those living with a member of the opposite sex to label single life "unhealthy," feeling it is a sign of the breakup of the social and family structure.
- The older a man gets the more he feels that the singles life is generally healthy—until he reaches the age of forty-five. At this point a man tends to look at single life in a generally *unfavorable* light. (One in four men in the forty-five to fifty-five-year-old bracket cite the single lifestyle as a force that is breaking up the family structure.)
- The more education a man has, the more money he makes, the more likely he is to label the expansion of single life a healthy sign.
- Thirteen percent of bisexual and lesbian women feel that the expansion of the single lifestyle is a step toward sexual freedom and replacement of marriage. Only 1 percent of heterosexual women agree.
- One out of five widowed women are emphatic concerning the unhealthy implications of single life, stating that it marks the disintegration of social norms and values. Only 5 percent of other groups feel the same way.
- Eight percent of high-income, career women believe the expansion of singles life is very healthy, and that it represents a step toward sexual freedom and the replacement of marriage. Only 1 percent of the women in the middle- and low-income range agree.
- The older a woman gets, the less likely she is to view the growth of single life as a healthy sign. About a third of women over forty-five cite single life as leading to the breakup of social and family structure (while only 17 percent of women in their early twenties agree).

fear. Prior to the women's movement I would say most women were married more out of fear than love. Independent women are the biggest boon to love in marriage."

ALTERNATIVES TO MARRIAGE—AND SINGLENESS: WHO WANTS THEM AND WHY?

Few men or women thought singleness to be a benefit on the grounds that it would replace the institution of marriage. Rather, their positive attitude stems from the fact that singleness offers *alternatives* to traditional marriage. What precisely are these alternatives?

2. Which of the following, if any, do you find an attractive substitute or alternative for marriage? (Choose as many answers as are appropriate.)	Men	Women
a. Polygamy (more than one wife)	8%	1%
b. Trial marriage	44%	39%
c. Polyandry (more than one husband)	2%	5%
d. Serial marriage (a different marriage every certain number of years)	6%	5%
e. Abandonment of all sexual conventions and establishment of free-love society	5%	2%
f. Group or communal marriage	2%	2%
g. Open marriage	8%	6%
h. None of these	34%	45%
i. Don't know	2%	3%

BONUS FINDINGS

- Three times the number of men who have been divorced twice opt for polygamy than those men who have been divorced once.
- Trial marriages are of the least interest to widowed men. Of all subgroups, however, this same segment is the *most* interested in open marriages.
- Seventeen percent of male homosexuals and bisexuals opt for abandonment of all sexual conventions

and establishment of a free-love society. Only 5 percent of heterosexual men wish the same.

- The man least interested in open marriage now lives with a woman. The man most interested is living with a group.
- Trial marriages are of greatest interest to men in the twenty-to-thirty-four-year-old bracket, with almost half of them citing this idea as an attractive alternative to marriage. Older men thirty-five to forty-four feel less strongly concerning its desirability (only 39 percent marked this choice).
- Polygamy is *most* attractive to low-wage-earning men. The more money a man makes the *less* attractive he finds the possibility of having more than one wife.
- The older a man becomes the more likely he is to wish for the abandonment of all sexual conventions. When he reaches forty-five, however, this wish declines, and the percentage of those over forty who support sexual anarchy lessens substantially.
- Professional men have four times greater interest in serial marriage than blue-collar men.
- Women most interested in trial marriage have been divorced twice or more, are living with a man, make a very low salary, and are in their early twenties. Women not interested in trial marriages have been divorced once, are high wage-earners, and live at home with their family.
- Almost 10 percent of women divorced twice or more opt for polyandry (having more than one husband). Only 3 percent of women never married agree. We also found greater interest in polygamy among women presently living with a man than among those who live alone. If a woman is living with a roommate of the same sex her interest is minimal.
- Five times as many women who live in a group want serial marriage as do those women who live alone.
- Scarcely a single widow opts for open marriage. An average of 9 percent of women divorced twice or more, however, consider open marriage an attractive alternative.
- The older a woman becomes the *less* likely she is to express interest in trial marriage.

Singles Are Conservative Concerning Marriage Alternatives

What strikes us concerning answers from both sexes is how restrained and nonexperimental most of them are. Such choices as polygamy and polyandry receive extremely low ratings. *Open marriage* or *communal/group marriage*, both of which have received wide coverage in the press and have been touted by more than one influential thinker, receive less than 10 percent, and in some cases less than 5 percent, acceptance. As a collectivity singles are *not* in support of drastic social change or unorthodox lifestyles.

The one option that is broadly supported is trial marriage, the arrangement based on the understanding that if the relationship works marriage will be the next step. Of all alternatives to marriage, this is the only one that singles look at with a serious eye.

Indeed, some state legislatures are considering the legal recognition of trial marriage. In a 1966 issue of *Redbook,* Margaret Mead, famous anthropologist, suggested that marriage be a two-stage affair. In the first stage would come "individual marriage," where the bond is "ethical" rather than "economic," and where contraception insures a childless first few years. The second stage, "parental marriage," follows when the first stage has proven successful. Only at that point would mates commit themselves to a lifetime of partnership and parenting.

Mead's system is one of several suggested in the past years, the point being that the anxiousness of singles to accept new formulas for marriage is mirrored in the recent proliferation of such formulas by many thinkers.

IF SINGLES RULED THE WORLD

3. *If you were given absolute political power, what laws, changes, and reforms would you institute for relationships between men and women? Would you make sex more available or less? Would you alter the institution of marriage? What alternatives would you introduce, if any? Would you allow free love, or would you tighten the laws that already govern sex? How would you treat homosexuality, bisexuality, promiscuity, S&M, prostitution, group sex, and so forth? Describe the society you would create.*

Almost 30 percent of subjects said they would make no changes at all. Those who in their answers endorsed the status quo did so because, as was often said, "Things are just fine as they are now."

Most Singles Would Alter Marriage Rather Than Replace It

The 70 percent who desired change offered a range of suggestions, most of them centering on methods of altering or improving marriage. A majority supported marriage but wished to amend it in different ways. Some spoke of making divorce less difficult to attain.

Woman, Grand Rapids, MI: I think marriage has been far too easy to get into, and far, far too difficult to get out of. Hence I am of the thought that I would change the law and make divorce as easy as one, two, three! This would mean that people could slip into and out of marriage as easily as into and out of an old coat. It would diffuse many of the emotional problems surrounding marriage. However, if there were children involved it should be made more difficult. In my kingdom I'd have two kinds of marriage, without children and with. The first you could get a divorce just for the asking. The second would take you many years (if you had kids), lots of time, and money and difficulty.

Man, Boston, MA: Why not make divorce easier to obtain? It would solve a lot of problems. If I had absolute power I'd make divorce as easy as marriage and cut the heads off anyone who made people feel guilty about it. Off with this one's head! Off with that one's! Guilt-mongers all! It's time we were allowed to be free from the past, and get on with it!

Conversely, others said that divorce should be more difficult to attain.

Man, Buffalo, NY: In my magical kingdom I'd make marriage something very strong and permanent. People could get out of it only with effort. First, I'd make marriage a privilege. Only certain people could qualify. They'd have to make enough money, have a good record with the police, show evidence of sound moral character, explain to an impartial jury how they would profit each other and why they are compatible. Marriage should be made a great privilege and something to be earned. Then it wouldn't make any difference if divorce was hard or easy, because most people would want to stay married even when things got hard.

Woman, Boston, MA: I would alter the institution of marriage. There should be new rules for divorce, for instance. There should be a fair way of divorce without making *lawyers rich*. Lawyers have done everything in their power to exploit people getting divorced. I've known several divorces that started out amiably but where the lawyers turned the people into rank enemies. I would make divorce a difficult thing but would have the individuals do all the work and not lawyers. They would do all the filing, paper work, etc. The cost should be minimal and should be paid to the *state,* not to a lawyer. But divorce itself should be granted in some cases and not in others, depending on how valid the reason be. Not like today where if a marriage doesn't work out ideally in five minutes people are screaming SEPARATION! In my world I would make lawyers illegal, because it's they who have created many of the problems which they then charge us to remedy.

Man, Atlanta, GA: I think marriage is imperfect but the basic idea is good. So I would keep it, I guess. One thing I'd do as king is make it hard to get married and hard to get divorced. Couples should live with each other for a set number of months or years. Then they should *apply* to get married and have to pass a test.

More than a few suggested unconventional plans for rewriting marriage law:

Man, Chicago, IL: First, I would not do away with marriage because people are monogamous by nature (or at least they need to channel their feelings into one person and one family at a time). What I would do I would do in this order:

1) Only people of the same race could marry each other.

2) Only people of the same religion could be married (or atheists with atheists, agnostics with agnostics).

3) Only people who are gainfully employed could be married. A prerequisite for marriage would be a job. Anyone who is unemployed over a year or on welfare does not qualify. They must go out and get themselves steady work, and have proof that they've been at it over two years.

4) Only people with the approximate same education level can be married. That is, those who never graduated from high school cannot marry college graduates. Illiterates can only marry illiterates and so forth.

5) Only people within a certain age of each other could be married. Men would have to be at least five, and preferably seven years older than women. No one under age 25 could be married.

6) No one would be allowed to have children for the first three years of their marriage. If they then wanted children they would have to apply to a special bureau and undergo a series of psychological tests to see if they qualify mentally and emotionally. It is a big undertaking to raise a child and many people do not have the emotional and psychological equipment to do it properly. If parents were screened better before they had children there would be less child abuse, desertion, etc.

7) If a married couple had no children, divorce would be easy to attain. Once children come no divorce would be possible except under the most dire circumstances. Any couple divorcing with children would have to pay heavy fines.

8) People who stay married ten years without filing for divorce would receive huge tax breaks from the government. Every five years thereafter the break would get better.

9) If someone does get a divorce there would be a mandatory time, like two or three years, during which he would have to stay single. He could live with someone but not marry them. Single people would receive more support from society than they do now, and prejudice against them would be illegal.

Woman, San Antonio, TX: I would initiate a long dating period or courtship, and make it mandatory before marriage. I would not allow free love as it is today but would let people live together—no, make it a *law* that they live together for a special amount of time before marriage. It should be mandatory that everyone get a checkup before being allowed to have sex of any kind—stamp out VD! Anyone not getting this checkup I'd arrest. Also, before living together a sound sex education should be mandatory. Sex education is what will help all problems in our society.

Woman, Los Angeles, CA: There should be all kinds of different types of marriages open to the individual. Open marriage and traditional marriage, according to taste. A man should not be allowed to rape his wife legally. There should be condoned homosexual marriage, of course. And also three-way marriages of mixed sexes. Everyone would remain very true this way because it's something they specifically want. Also, how about a group of people all marrying each other at once, like fifty people, twenty-five men and twenty-five women, all married to each other legally? The children belong to the group communally. Another thing is marriage that lasts only a month and is renewable at that time.

Woman, Brooklyn, NY: One thing I would do if I could—every single person (unmarried) over eighteen would be put on a computer dating machine. Finding compatible people is entirely too haphazard, especially for someone like me who is not active in sports, won't go to a bar, and has weird religious beliefs. People should not be allowed to marry until they check out for compatibility on the computer. Lots of people moan about these compatibility services, but I think they are great. Why not let technology work for us in a positive way? Do a computer check on each person based on EVERYTHING about that person, a two hundred–page report that covers their life. They must match up before they can marry.

Woman, Salamandra, NY: For myself, I would like to live in polyandry. I cannot see any reason in the world that a woman shouldn't have as many committed husbands as she wants, provided everyone is willing. Another concept I like is Robert Heinlein's chain marriages where boy marries girl, who marries another boy, who marries another girl, *ad infinitum.* That way there would be one united world (I think? Gulp!).

The following essay, though tongue-in-cheek, makes its point concerning these subjects:

Man, Queens, NY: U.S. Government Department of Sex, or, what's right and wrong, and how to tell.

1. Prostitution is decreed the new substitute for meaningful marriage, as it is new, fast, quick, cheap, shiny, sexy, pretty, easy, fresh, light, efficient, a taste treat, saves gas, cuts time, makes cleaning fun, has a modern scientific formula, and no one, that's right, no one, has to take any responsibilities for anything anymore including their own feelings. Those taking responsibility for their own feelings and even having real feelings that go beyond their genitals will be castrated in public ceremony.

2. Promiscuity is mandatory.

a) Men *not* being promiscuous will be punished with Spanish fly treatments (length based on degree of offense). Any man who does not exploit every woman he can get his hands on, screw anything with legs, break every promise he makes, use women for his own gratification, lie and hand out phony lines, fake feelings of love and affection to gain sex, boast in intimate detail to his friends about how many women he has ravaged and abandoned, impregnated women and left them to abort, gain his sense of masculinity from how thoroughly he can fool women and make them trust him, will be subject to heavy fines and/or three years in prison.

b) Any women found *not* being promiscuous will be punished with hormone injections to increase her sexual capabilities. Any woman reported *not* frequenting singles bars each night and throwing herself at men, looking for a man on the grounds of how rich, good looking, and sexy he is and how well he skis rather than how good his heart is, getting sucked in by the most obvious kinds of flattery and sexual come-ons, spending 95 percent of her time in front of the mirror and the rest of the time at Bloomingdale's, changing her mind each time someone better looking comes into the room, getting drunk and turning on, getting pregnant right and left and then aborting as she pleases (it is "her body" after all), losing all sense of shame and trying to prove she can do anything a man can do including *becoming* a man, will be subject to heavy fines and/or three years of enforced motherhood.

As to how singles would deal with homosexuality, bisexuality, promiscuity, and so forth, the phrase that comes up consistently is "Anything is all right if it doesn't hurt anyone and is done by consenting adults."

Man, San Francisco, CA: If I had political power I would make sex more available. I would allow free love, legalize prostitution (as long as they were checked every so often for VD). I would treat homosexuals and bisexuals fairly and allow them equal rights along with everyone else. However, I would insist that straights have *their* rights too and not let them be bothered by militant gays who insist on carrying their platform *everywhere!* I am very broad-minded and feel that if a person is into unusual sex acts it's okay as long as they're done in the proper place with another consenting adult.

Singles Are Open-Minded about Morals—Except in Cases of Personal Harassment

While approximately a quarter of respondents in their "rulerships" take a hard line on sexual-moral issues, most are fairly tolerant. Many singles, however, say that public displays of sex, flagrant prostitution, pornography on public display, sexual violation of children, and anything that harasses the individual without his or her consent should be controlled.

Man, Van Nuys, CA: Whatever people do at home is their business. I would only change the punishments for sex offenders, especially rape, and make castration a punishment for it. Also, there is too much pornography forced down our throats these days, and I include all those jeans ads especially. Sex is a fine and healthy thing, but Jesus, it can be overdone! I don't want it shoved down my throat anymore. I believe the government has been lax on this question and has allowed big business to exploit the public with sex so it can make a profit.

Woman, Marina Del Rey, CA: The important thing I would do if I had any say in things was make it safe for people to meet people. Not bars, a turnoff for many, but an alternative. The singles sex thing is okay but it forces people to always be on the make. Marriage is fine the way it is—I wouldn't tax married people. Free love is a fallacy—there are no free rides. If in my role as queen mother I had full power, I'd let people have complete free love one day a year. Get it out of their systems, then return to controls. Also, what you do in your own bed is your own business, but when gays, or leather-jacket boys, or dikes, or whores, or anyone starts to crowd me on the street and hang their wares in the window and tell me *I'm* the perverted one for not doing what they do, then I say, "Hold it, wait a minute! Slow down! Something's wrong!" Keep it private, that's all. And leave me alone.

4. What do you think is the future of the single lifestyle in modern society?	Men	Women
a. It will become a significant alternative to marriage but will never replace it.	39%	37%
b. It will be just one of the many new alternatives to marriage that will arise in the next few years.	15%	14%
c. It is just a fad—marriage and traditional values will ultimately return.	13%	18%
d. It is the beginning of a new trend that will finally do away with marriage and become the foundation for a society based on complete sexual freedom.	7%	4%

e. It will probably remain the way it is today, neither growing nor declining.   22%   24%

f. Don't know.   4%   3%

BONUS FINDINGS

- Almost a third of never-married men believe the single lifestyle will remain as it is, neither growing nor declining. Men who have been divorced twice or more are not so sure—only 7 percent echoed this same sentiment.
- Men in the highest income bracket feel that single life will become a significant alternative to marriage but will not replace it. Almost 50 percent give this answer. Bachelors in the low-wage-earning category do not have such strong convictions; a little over a third checked this option.
- Women living at home with their families are *most* likely to feel that the single lifestyle is just a fad, and that marriage and traditional values will ultimately return. Women least likely to feel this way live in a group.
- High-wage-earning women with a college education are *most* likely to believe the singles lifestyle will become just one of many new alternatives. Less-educated and lower-paid women feel that the singles lifestyle is just a fad. Also, the older a woman becomes, the more likely she is to agree.
- Widows and widowers consider singleness more of a fad than do divorced or never-married men and women.
- The older a man and woman become the more they judge the spread of the single lifestyle to be just a fad.

The majority of both sexes feel that the singles life is here to stay, that in and of itself it is a perfectly acceptable way of life, that it may in fact expand to larger dimensions than it knows today, but—that it will not replace marriage and should not replace marriage, and that it is just one of many new social changes and alternatives that will arise.

On this relatively optimistic and open-ended note the survey ends. Singleness is fine, respondents say, and marriage is fine too. Both will be around for a while, and neither is the ultimate solution to those most ancient problems, man and woman, happiness and human contentment. "Singleness," writes a respondent, "is sometimes shown to us like it is a separate movement apart from all other movements that are going on today. But it is not separate. It is just a fragment of the whole, and a part of something much greater and larger. Where this greater part is headed, furthermore, is more than anybody's guess. Certainly not backwards though, certainly not backwards."

The First-Year Syndrome: A Separate Survey on the First Twelve Months After Divorce

Singles and professionals alike generally acknowledge that the first year after divorce is the most disorienting, turbulent, and uncertain time in a single's life. This turbulence is not entirely adverse, however. In fact, divorced respondents frequently say that feelings of frightening disorientation and giddy independence—and thus of depression and euphoria—often come side-by-side in surprising juxtaposition.

We were interested in learning about the changes, shocks, and revelations that a single might expect in his or her initial year of being alone. We were concerned not only with psychological and sociological reactions to the first year of divorce, but with physical reactions as well—decrease or increase in sex drive, development or loss of nervous symptoms, changes in sleep and weight patterns, and so forth.

To do this we devised a separate questionnaire designed to reveal what we have termed the "First-Year Syndrome." This separate questionnaire was addressed solely to singles who had been divorced one or more times.

Among the 3,000 subjects involved in the original survey, 367 responded to this separate questionnaire. One hundred and thirty-two of the newly single subjects were male, 235 were female. All subsequent percentages are taken from findings within this specific group.

Results from this separate survey demonstrate that there are indeed identifiable trends native to the period after divorce, and that these trends can be isolated and in certain cases predicted. We divided questions into four categories: physical responses to the first year of being single, psychological responses, sexual responses, and social responses.

CATEGORY I: PHYSICAL AND BODILY RESPONSES TO THE FIRST YEAR OF SINGLE LIFE

1. Drinking: Amount indulged in since single

Major Finding: In most cases, first-year single men and women drink considerably more than when married.

Though drinking could as easily have been considered a social or psychological phenomenon, we placed it in the category of physical response, perhaps because it is on the physical level that its results are most apparent.

Men

- One percent *started* drinking for the first time in their first year of being single.
- One percent *stopped* drinking entirely.
- Thirty-four percent *increased* drinking.
- One percent *decreased.*
- Forty-seven percent showed *no change.*
- One percent of men in this sample *do not drink at all.*
- Fifteen percent answered *"Don't know."*

Women

- Six percent *started* drinking for the first time in their first year of being single.
- Less than 1 percent *stopped* drinking entirely.
- Twenty-four percent *increased* drinking.
- Four percent *decreased.*
- Fifty percent showed *no change.*
- Fourteen percent of women in this sample *do not drink at all.*
- One percent answered *"Don't know."*

Most newly divorced men and women show a tendency toward greater alcohol consumption, no doubt for several reasons. First, both sexes tend to socialize more often when single than when married, and both are more prone than previously to visit bars, dances, cocktail parties, singles' spots, and other places where drinking is encouraged. For some unmarried people, drinking is a way of handling the anxieties of first-year syndrome, a method of dealing with fears and pressures. It should be noted that among newly single men, 99 percent *are already* drinkers, while among women one out of about six or seven does not drink at all.

"It's a shame that we can't tell from these answers whether the increase in drinking is solitary or in bars," comments Dr. Jack Chernus, Life Fellow of the American Psychiatric Association and formerly Assistant Professor of Psychiatry at Mt. Sinai Medical School in New York City. "Social drinking is due mostly to the need to circulate and let go. Private drinking stems from anxiety and depression and is thus much more serious. If singles find themselves drinking out of social motives, it may be perfectly natural, at least for a while. Drinking alone, at home, however, may be a sign that professional help is required, especially if the drinking is excessive.

2. Smoking

Major Finding: *In most cases, first-year single men and women smoke more than when married.*

Men

- Less than 1 percent *started* smoking during the first year of being single.
- Less than 1 percent *stopped.*
- Twelve percent *increased* smoking.
- One percent *decreased.*
- Thirty-five percent continued to smoke approximately the *same amount* as when married.
- Forty-two percent of newly single men *do not smoke.*
- Eight percent answered *"Don't know."*

Women

- Six percent of women *started* smoking in the first year of being single.
- Four percent *stopped*.
- Seventeen percent of women *increased* smoking.
- Three percent *decreased*.
- Thirty-five percent continued to smoke approximately the *same amount* as when married.
- Thirty-six percent of newly single women *do not smoke*.

Smoking, like drinking, can be both a social habit and a response to psychological pressures. And, like drinking, first-year singles who do smoke tend to increase rather than decrease their intake.

3. Narcotic Drug Use

Major Finding: **Most newly single men and women do not take drugs.**

There is little indication to show that divorce either encourages or discourages singles' narcotic usage.

Men

- One percent of newly single men *started* taking drugs.
- One percent *stopped*.
- Eight percent *increased* drug consumption.
- Three percent *decreased*.
- Fourteen percent *neither decreased nor increased*.
- Seventy-two percent of newly single men *do not use* narcotic drugs.
- Two percent answered *"Don't know."*

Women

- One percent of newly single women *started* taking drugs.
- One percent *stopped*.
- One percent *increased* drug consumption.
- Less than 1 percent *decreased*.

- Sixteen percent *neither increased nor decreased.*
- Sixty-eight percent of newly single women *do not use* narcotic drugs.
- Twelve percent answered *"Don't know."*

Among both sexes, the number of drug users is a minority, about 20 percent for women and 26 percent for men. Note also that the designation "narcotic drugs" includes not only such substances as cocaine and heroin, but the milder marijuana as well. This indicates that the percent of hard drugs used by recently divorced people is even smaller than the percentages recorded here.

4. Ability to Sleep

Major Finding: *One out of four men and a third of women experience sleep problems during the first year of being single.*

Men

- Sixteen percent of men reported *improved* ability to sleep.
- Twenty-five percent of men reported *sleeping problems.*
- Fifty-nine percent of men reported *no change.*

Women

- Thirty-three percent of women reported *improved* ability to sleep.
- Thirty-three percent of women reported *sleeping problems.*
- Thirty-four percent of women reported *no change.*

The significant point here is that there *is* so much alteration of sleep patterns among newly divorced singles. Sixty-six percent of the women reported some kind of change, as did 40 percent of the men. Apparently the fundamental physiological processes of both sexes are affected by the shock of separation, especially a function as delicate as sleep.

According to Dr. Chernus, "Many of those who report *improved* sleep after divorce may have had fairly severe sexual disharmony during marriage. With these demands, fears, and sexual frustrations now gone, these individuals sleep better. For those with worsened sleep, it may be the other way around. The person who is newly divorced worries about whether he or she will be able to function efficiently with new partners.

"Sexual problems often work in an individual's unconsciousness," adds Dr. Chernus, "even if he or she is not aware of them; and from my experience such unconscious fears are often the cause of insomnia and disturbed rest."

5. Energy Level

Major Finding: Energy level tends to increase during the first year of being single, especially for women.

Men

- Thirty-five percent of men reported *increased* energy level after marital separation.
- Twenty-one percent reported *decreased* energy level.
- Forty-four percent reported *no change*.

Women

- Fifty-three percent of women reported *increased* energy level after marital separation.
- Twenty-eight percent reported *decreased* energy level.
- Twenty percent reported *no change*.

Increased energy level is usually viewed as a correlate of psychological enthusiasm and optimism. Despite the fact that depression is a common feature of first-year syndrome, the vitality level of singles during the initial period of being alone often increases.

"During the first year of divorce," remarks Dr. Chernus, "a person is past the agonies of indecision concerning whether he or she should make the marital break. With indecision often comes depression. People who can't make up their minds are paralyzed and listless, trapped in their own inertia. When they do choose, whatever their choice may be, a feeling of freedom and happiness often replaces the lack of energy—and with happiness comes energy, at least in the initial period after the choice has been made. Choosing, making up one's mind, seems to unblock our energy channels; indecision acts like a dam.

"Furthermore, the social excitement of the first months of being single tends to get the juices flowing. The new impressions that single life affords breathe life into a person who may have felt smothered in a bad marriage. But beware of this—the high doesn't go on forever. It can sometimes turn into a big low. It's not unusual to see a newly single person's energy level go up and down like a yo-yo in the first year, as his or her moods swing from elation at being free to depression about being alone."

6. Weight Change

Major Finding: In most cases, some kind of weight change takes place among new singles. In the majority of cases, singles lose weight.

Men

- Twenty-five percent of newly single men reported weight *gain.*
- Thirty-seven percent reported weight *loss.*
- Thirty-seven percent reported *no change.*
- One percent answered *"Don't know."*

Women

- Twenty percent of women reported weight *gain.*
- Forty-four percent reported weight *loss.*
- Twenty-nine percent reported *no change.*
- Seven percent answered *"Don't know."*

"Divorce produces unbelievable tension," remarks Dr. Selma Miller, marriage counselor in private practice in New York City and past president of the New York Association for Marriage and Family Therapy. "People tend to react to it in two ways: Either they try to take away the pain by eating too much, or they deal with the pain by not eating at all. In the latter case, weight loss becomes part of the whole depression syndrome, and may be just one of several symptoms. People react differently. Some say 'As soon as I get upset I lose weight.' Others say 'I just can't stop eating when I feel badly.' However, don't forget that many of the singles who lose weight have done so purely for cosmetic reasons, to improve their physical appearance. Not all those who report weight loss are necessarily thinner for psychological reasons."

7. Overall Health

Major Finding: *The health of newly single people improves more often than it declines.*

Men

- Twenty-seven percent of men reported an *improved* state of health in the first year of being single.
- Nineteen percent reported *worsened* health.
- *Fifty-four* percent reported *no change.*

Women

- Thirty-two percent of women reported an *improved* state of health in the first year of divorce.
- Twenty-one percent reported *worsened* health.
- Forty-seven percent reported *no change.*

"Although the time before divorce is tremendously tense, the very act of making a decision," comments Dr. Miller, "produces relief from stress. Thus, many of the stress-related ailments like insomnia, headaches, and so forth are alleviated."

"The process that takes place" continues Dr. Miller, "is not strictly physical or strictly mental. Whenever you have large psychological changes, such as during a divorce, and you have corresponding physiological changes taking place, *both* forces are at work. Psychological upset brings on bad health; bad health brings on mental depression; and so forth. Since after divorce health tends to improve, this suggests that for most the gains made through the sense of relief at separation outweigh the losses—and this is registered in the body."

CATEGORY II—PSYCHOLOGICAL RESPONSES TO THE FIRST YEAR OF BEING SINGLE

8. Happiness and Well-Being

Major Finding: Happiness and well-being improve substantially during the first year of divorce.

Men

- Fifty percent of men reported that their happiness and well-being *improved* during the first year.
- Thirty-three percent reported a *decreased* level of happiness.
- Seventeen percent reported *no change.*

Women

- Sixty percent of women reported that their happiness and well-being *improved* during the first year.
- Thirty-two percent reported a *decreased* level of happiness.
- Eight percent reported *no change.*

Dr. Marvin Lifschitz, a New York psychologist, adds a note of warning to these findings. "In many ways divorce is akin to death," says Dr. Lifschitz. "People who claim they are much happier during this time may be saying this as a defense against feeling pain; they haven't yet let themselves experience the mourning and the loss of the relationship, which should be a natural part of any traumatic personal rupture. Many people try to deaden feelings that are unpleasant. It is a form of running away. Since the termination of any real relationship invariably results in real feelings, those who try to mask them behind a false front or who lie to themselves about such things are getting in the way of the natural process of mourning. Thus the situation is not what it may seem. Those who claim to be 'up' all the time just after a divorce are, I would suggest, hiding some basic facts from themselves."

9. Feelings of Self-Respect

Major Finding: Feelings of self-respect increase measurably during the first year for singles.

Men

- Forty-nine percent of men reported *increased* feelings of self-respect.
- Fifteen percent reported *decreased* feelings.
- Thirty-six percent reported *no change.*

Women

- Sixty-four percent reported *increased* feelings of self-respect.
- Seventeen percent reported *decreased* feelings.
- Nineteen percent reported *no change.*

"There are people who stay in bad marriages simply because they don't have the courage to face up to the truth," claims Dr. Lifschitz. "Those who finally admit to themselves the futility of such situations, and who terminate such relationships, often experience an increase in self-respect because of these decisive moves. In a bad marriage one of the partners is usually the victim. This victim takes it and takes it and takes it, often for years, without fighting back. When the victim does at last take a stand and make a decisive move, this can be incredibly nourishing to his or her long-battered ego. While these persons may have a sense of loss from breaking the marital bond, they will at the same time have a heightened feeling of inner strength, and a new belief that they are okay after all."

10. Sense of Personal Growth

Major Finding: Most singles experience an increased sense of personal growth. More women than men report increased growth.

Men

- Fifty-nine percent reported an *increased* sense of personal growth.
- Eleven percent reported a *decreased* sense.
- Thirty percent reported *no change.*

Women

- Seventy-six percent reported an *increased* sense of personal growth.
- Twelve percent reported a *decreased* sense of growth.
- Twelve percent reported *no change.*

"It's a lot easier to stay in a relationship that doesn't work than to go out into the world and start again," remarks Dr. Lifschitz. "At first people think they can't go it alone. Then, as time passes and they survive on their own, they realize they can take care of themselves, and that they won't fall to pieces. They realize they can survive without the nurturing from the opposite sex.

"Women are especially enthusiastic in responding to questions about self-growth. In many cases they are learning they can survive without a man, that they can take care of themselves, make a living, support the kids, dig a garden, plant trees, drive the car, pay the bills, all without a male. This builds confidence and makes for good feelings about oneself. With men it can be the same thing. They discover they can cook and clean and sew and take care of their private needs. Some women have made a practice of buffaloing husbands into thinking they can't tie their shoelaces without 'mama's help. Once single, these men learn that so-called 'women's work' is not so arcane or complicated a thing, and certainly not so difficult. All these are the kinds of discoveries that would be made by a single person in, say, the first six to eight months after the marital cord has been severed. So it doesn't surprise me to learn that a sense of personal growth increases. I would, however, like to see the statistics on *depression* during the first year also, since I have an idea that these may show that the post-divorce period isn't all psychic roses either."

11. Depression

Major Finding: Depression is common among first-year singles.

Men

- Thirty-four percent of men reported *increased* depression during the first year of being single.
- Seventeen percent reported *decreased* depression.
- Seven percent reported depression *started* for them upon becoming single.
- Four percent reported depression *stopped* for them upon becoming single.
- Thirty-nine percent reported *no change*.

Women

- Forty-five percent of women reported *increased* depression during the first year of being single.
- Twenty-four percent reported *decreased* depression.
- Six percent reported depression *started* for them.
- Six percent reported depression *stopped* for them.
- Twenty percent reported *no change*.

"When you're speaking of depression," remarks Dr. Howard Glazer, Senior Research Scientist at the Post-Graduate Center for Mental Health in New York City and Clinical Assistant Professor of Psychology at Cornell University Medical Center, "there are many misconceptions that arise, the most important being that depression is an intensification of feeling down or blue. In fact, people can experience clinical depression without *any* particular sensations of being down. Instead they may experience what we call 'neuro-vegetative' symptoms, physiological symptoms such as early morning awakening, changes in appetite, changes in weight, changes in sexual interest, and so forth. I see a number of depressed people who have *no idea they are depressed.* There are probably many more people than have shown up in your statistics who are depressed and simply don't realize it.

"When dealing with depression it's necessary to understand that the most fundamental cause at work is the feeling of *loss,* especially loss of a thing that has a long history behind it and which is, or has been, somehow associated with comfort and, perhaps more importantly, habit. Even if a person suffered for many years in a painful marriage and initiated the divorce, these many years of association have fashioned habits and connections. When these connections are broken, when they are lost, depression often follows, though not necessarily in the guise of melancholy."

"Of course," adds Dr. Glazer, "a person will not inevitably react to divorce by becoming classically depressed. Everyone has a unique set of defenses, everyone behaves in his or her own special way, depending on their psychological mechanisms. A person may become compensatory and throw themselves into another area of work. They may be compulsive and become workaholics. They may be addictive personalities and overindulge in food, drugs, or drinking. Everybody goes through some kind of reaction, depending on his or her tendencies. These reactions usually take a while to resolve themselves—at least a year will have to pass after divorce before one can return to normality. Moreover, even if a person feels nothing peculiar is going on inside him or her, most likely something *is* going on, and others may notice it in that person in the form of unusual or even bizarre behavior. It's very easy to fool oneself during this sensitive and delicate period of time.

"Everybody experiences some kind of upheaval after divorce—or at least *should* experience it. If a person automatically represses or denies the experience of great loss, then this repressed material has to come out at a later date, often as a form of neurosis. Thus, I think that to deal with the loss that takes place in divorce one must realize: (1) that the pain is a natural and inevitable thing; (2) that it *will* take time to heal; and (3) that there are few shortcuts around the pain and no panaceas—but that if one participates properly in the mourning process, this process can be productive of inner psychological growth and health."

12. Tendency Toward Suicide

Major Finding: During the first year approximately one out of five singles occasionally considers suicide.

Men

- Seventeen percent of men *occasionally* considered suicide.
- Two percent of men *often* considered it.
- Two percent of men *attempted* it.
- Seventy-eight percent of men *never* considered suicide during their first year of being single.
- One percent answered *"Don't know."*

Women

- Twenty-nine percent of women *occasionally* considered it.
- Three percent *often* considered it.
- Four percent *attempted* it.
- Sixty-four percent of women in their first year of being single *never* considered suicide.

"It is a difficult thing," remarks Dr. Glazer, "to interpret what a person is really saying when they speak of suicide. For one person it will mean an active plan—jumping off the bridge next Wednesday. For another it can be just a fleeting thought—'Is life worth it?'

"The second category occurs to all of us at one time or another. It is a kind of magical thinking, a search for force beyond ourselves to take away our problems. Certainly it does not represent a serious pathological condition. Indeed, the suicidal part of such thinking is often incidental to the escapist part.

"In the first category, however, a person who thinks specifics concerning his or her suicide can be in real trouble. Such thinking is dangerous not only because it takes things a step further than passive idealization, but because repetition of it can prepare the ground for actual suicide.

"It is possible that a divorce can trigger a suicide, even with someone who has tolerated all other kinds of pressures in life. People who place a high premium on marriage and require a happy domestic life for their self-image and self-respect, may especially be in a position to go under when faced with the trauma of divorce. Whatever the situation, however, I would certainly advise anyone who has active thoughts of suicide to look for trained professional aid as quickly as possible."

In looking over the statistics in the suicide columns, we note that women are more prone to think of suicide than men. "The fact that divorced women think of suicide more often than men does not surprise me," claims Dr. Glazer. "If you look at the records you'll find that a certain kind of psychopathology is higher among women than among men. And there is very little biological basis for it. Such a phenomenon is largely cultural in basis. Women are *expected* to respond to stress with affective disorders, with highly emotional and perhaps self-destructive responses. These can be anything from depression to hysteria. On the other hand, men are expected to react to loss with obsessive-compulsive disorders, by becoming workaholics, say. This is culturally the traditional division between the sexes in time of stress—men compulsively throw themselves into things, women become more emotional."

CATEGORY III—SEXUAL REACTION AND RESPONSIVENESS DURING THE FIRST YEAR OF BEING SINGLE

13. Sexual Responsiveness

Major Finding: Sexual responsiveness increases during the first year of single life.

Men

- Fifty-nine percent of men reported *increased* sexual responsiveness in the first year of being single.
- Ten percent of men reported *decreased* sexual responsiveness.
- Twenty-six percent reported *no change.*
- Five percent answered *"Don't know."*

Women

- Fifty-five percent of women reported *increased* sexual responsiveness in the first year of being single.
- Thirteen percent of women reported *decreased* sexual responsiveness.
- Twenty-seven percent reported *no change.*
- Five percent answered *"Don't know."*

"There are two factors at work in singles' increased sexual responsiveness," remarks Dr. Glazer. "First, anxiety and depression are contrary to good sexual functioning—and if a marriage is shaky the stress that accumulates dampens both partners' sexuality. On the other hand, you have here a classic example of compensatory behavior that takes the form of promiscuity. This is a fairly natural reaction among those who are recently freed from a bad marriage. Divorced people, it seems, bounce back and forth in the early stages, experiencing a great deal of release on the one hand, a great deal of loneliness on the other. The release is expressed by a period of post-divorce indulgence, with reports of greater enjoyment and greater experimentation. The fact that men and women are having more sex, with a wider range of people, some of it good and some of it bad, but all of it involving new experience, in itself may account for increased reports of responsiveness."

14. Sexual Activity After Divorce as Compared with Activity During Marriage

Major Finding: Sexual activity increases during the first year of being single.

Here sexual activity is measured against sexual frequency during marriage.

Men

- Fifty-four percent of men reported *increased* sexual activity in the first year of being single.
- Twenty-seven percent reported *decreased* activity.
- Nineteen percent reported *no change.*

Women

- Forty-four percent of women reported *increased* sexual activity in the first year of being single.
- Thirty-six percent report *decreased* sexual activity.
- Twenty percent report *no change.*

However, more than a quarter of men and a third of women reported *decreased* sexual activity during their first single year—a departure from the norm associated with new-found sexual freedom.

"Women are more likely to report less sexual activity than men," remarks Dr. Glazer, "because of cultural expectations. In our culture men are *expected* to pursue a path of aggressive sexuality, especially after divorce when they are free once again to prove their manhood. It's an appropriately macho thing to do. Women who do it, however, are often labeled promiscuous. Thus, while these figures do express a statistical reality, they may have little to do with the *psychological* wishes of the individual and the individual's sexual capabilities in terms of enjoyment.

"Many of the people sampled in this part are probably individuals who've been married for five to ten years, and who are probably now in their mid-thirties or older. These were people still brought up in a generation where the mores and values were traditional, and where it was still largely unacceptable for a woman not only to seek a wide scope of sexual experience but even to *want* such a thing. Women of this generation thus still perceive frequent sexual encounters with a number of people as a very negative thing. They may be very sophisticated women, and very grown-up, but certain values that one has been brought up with just don't change."

15. Sense of Being Desirable to the Opposite Sex

Major Finding: **Most singles experience an increase in the sense of sexual attractiveness.**

Men

- Fifty-eight percent of men reported feeling an *increased* sense of sexual desirability.
- Thirteen percent reported a *decreased* sense.
- Twenty-nine percent reported *no change.*

Women

- Sixty-one percent reported an *increased* sense of sexual desirability.
- Fifteen percent reported a *decreased* sense.
- Twenty-four percent reported *no change.*

Questions 13, 14, and 15 constitute a kind of trio showing to what extent singles vary in their response to the sexual opportunities offered during the First-Year Syndrome. While responsiveness and activity may be increased, it is difficult to tell from these statistics how altered the *qualitative* side of the experiences becomes. Can we read between the lines of these statistics to comprehend what the experience of post-divorce sexuality really *feels* like?

"After five or ten years of marriage," Dr. Glazer observes, "a person loses the social skills required in dating—meeting people, starting conversations, playing the games required for contact. Even if a marriage has been unhappy, there has still been a lot of comfort and mutual knowledge attached to it. Suddenly none of this can be assumed when dating strangers. It now becomes a matter of redeveloping a series of social skills, which for many of us were never developed in the first place. That's why it is often so hard to break back into the sexual ritual and to make it work happily.

"All in all, divorced persons can expect to go through *phases* in their sexual experience before becoming comfortable with it. The initial experiences of sexual encounter rarely will be all pleasant or all painful. In fact, patients often describe the first romantic encounters as being accompanied by feelings of deep loss—a kind of existential loneliness, a kind of sensation of 'Is this what it's going to be like now?' Usually, however, these feelings are just a phase in the process; they tend to diminish as sexual experience becomes more gratifying, and as a person learns to be more sexually discriminating and careful. At first a newly divorced person, especially a man, is apt to pursue sexual fantasies, and this accounts for much of the ambivalent experiences reported during the early months. There is usually very little concern with the interpersonal meaning of sex. It is just sex for sex's sake. However, patients often tell me that these experiences are so disappointing, so unfulfilling, that they catapult one into the realization that for sex to be good, *real* feelings have to be connected with it.

"I remember one person, for instance, a man who right after his divorce acted out one of his fantasies. He was thirty-five, and after his divorce he found himself a gorgeous eighteen-year-old girl. He told himself that now he was free to act out his greatest fantasy, and he did—and the next morning he woke up, opened his eyes, and couldn't begin to describe the feelings of emptiness and depression that followed. That's a fairly common experience, first because the person becomes acutely aware of the loss they have experienced, and second because, since this is a compensatory rather than a meaningful encounter, the person feels emotionally empty and barren. As my thirty-five-year-old patient said about the eighteen-year-old, 'I couldn't relate to her—there was just no relationship there.' As with much else in life, sexual fantasies are overly built up. And when people pursue them, and find them to be empty, depression may result.

"My impression of newly single people," adds Dr. Glazer, "is that most of them genuinely want another relationship. There may be a passing phase of promiscuity and elation and excitation and freedom—but still, most people are married within three years after their first divorce, and that has to say something. So the question is not just how to enter the sexual scene, but what to expect in terms of one's own ups and downs, one's own psychological reactions to the strangeness of these sudden new encounters. The way in which this occurs will be as varied as the people who are involved."

16. Masturbation

Major Finding: Masturbation tends to increase among newly divorced men and women.

Men

- Twenty-five percent of men reported an *increase* in masturbation during the first year of being single.
- Seven percent of men reported a *decrease*.
- Three percent reported *starting* masturbation for the first time.
- Two percent reported *stopping* entirely.
- Thirty-one percent reported *no change*.
- Thirty-one percent reported they *never masturbate*.
- One percent answered *"Don't know."*

Women

- Twenty percent of women reported an *increase* in masturbation during the first year of being single.
- Five percent reported a *decrease*.
- Five percent reported *starting* masturbation for the first time.

- Less than one percent reported *stopping* entirely.
- Twenty-eight percent reported *no change.*
- Forty-one percent reported they *never masturbate.*

While social and sexual contact among most singles increases immediately after divorce, so does the solitary practice of masturbation. Is this a contradiction of fact, or simply another aspect of the sexual picture during First-Year Syndrome? "Masturbation," claims Dr. Glazer, "is not necessarily an idle form of self-pleasure. Nor is it necessarily a substitute for intercourse. It may even be a complement to it."

Many individuals, according to Dr. Glazer, use masturbation in the first few months of divorce as an antidote to their loneliness and alienation. "It is a self-medicating process for some people," he claims. "Especially among those who show addictive personality structure. We know from studies that the classic addictive types, who are reliant on drugs, alcohol, etcetera, are essentially trying in an unconscious way to protect themselves against depression. In this sense masturbation may also be a form of self-medication, an attempt to stem off the pain of loss by use of autoeroticism as a kind of antidepressant."

"For some people," adds Dr. Glazer, "the sexual aspects of the post-divorce period have a kind of compulsive quality. It is as if these people are avoiding their loneliness or depression by increasing their sexual activity, by using it as a kind of screen. This activity does not have to be heterosexual, either. It can be autosexuality, any kind of sexuality, in fact, as long as it deadens the feelings of pain."

17. Sexual Dysfunction

Major Finding: *Singles in their first year complain of a variety of sexual dysfunctions. Lack of sexual desire is the most common.*

Men

- Twenty percent experienced *lack of desire* during their first year of being single.
- Eleven percent reported *impotence.*
- Thirteen percent reported developing an *inability to have an orgasm.*

- Eight percent reported *premature orgasm.*
- Three percent reported acquiring a *venereal disease.*
- Forty-eight percent reported *no type of sexual dysfunction.*

Women

- Forty-five percent of women reported *lack of desire* during their first year of being single.
- Twenty percent reported an *inability to have an orgasm.*
- One percent reported developing *frigidity.*
- One percent reported acquiring a *venereal disease.*
- Thirty-five percent reported *no type of sexual dysfunction.*

It is interesting to compare the relatively high percentage of reports of people experiencing lack of sexual desire, with the earlier findings among the same group which report *increased sexual responsiveness.* Though these two findings do not necessarily contradict each other entirely, since different individuals may be responding to different aspects of the question, the results do reflect the somewhat "schizophrenic" mentality we have found among men and women experiencing first year syndrome.

Despite the wide number of sexual opportunities offered to the new single, one out of five men and almost one out of two women report experiencing lack of sexual desire at some point in the first year of being single. This phenomenon, though not often mentioned in popular discussions of sexual dysfunction, has been termed by one doctor as "the sex problem nobody talks about."* We have learned from the responses to the questionnaire and from other medical sources that in fact low sexual desire is a common and for some an agonizing reaction to stress.† "Libidinal loss is one of the classic signs of depression," remarks Dr. Glazer. "Women are more apt to report it than men because sexual interest for women is more tied to the notion of relationships and romance in general. Men tend to be genitally oriented. A man may work out his depression by having a lot of sex. A woman does so by abstaining from it. However, in either case, when the person discovers that they simply have no sexual drive, that they are not interested, a

* Interview with Dr. Helen Singer Kaplan, "The Sex Problem Nobody Talks About," *Family Circle,* November 15, 1977.
† "Absence of Sexual Desire in Men," *Medical Aspects of Human Sexuality,* August 1973. "Low Sexual Drive in Men," *Medical Aspects of Human Sexuality,* March 1974.

majority of the time, I believe, you will find depression at the bottom of things."

We also know that though impotence is the perennial fear of many men, and has received, as it were, heavy press over the past few years, there are other dysfunctions that are equally widespread, namely inability to have orgasm and premature ejaculation. "Both of these stem primarily from the same root," claims Dr. Glazer, "specifically anxiety and problems of self-esteem. Each individual manifests his or her sexual dysfunction in his or her own peculiar way. The basis of many of them is the same, however: The person is passing through a difficult time, is depressed and frightened, and feels that he or she must perform sexually in a perfect manner, or they will not be considered desirable. Each new potential mate represents a threat. Whatever the particular cause, the stress, fear, and, in some cases, hostility involved brings on the dysfunction. It is my experience, however, that these dysfunctions are quite transient, and that as a person's living conditions and psychological conditions improve, the dysfunction lessens as well."

18. Relationship with Family (Parents, Siblings, and So On)

Major Finding: Relationships with family tend to improve during the first year, or to remain the same.

Men

- Thirty-eight percent reported *improved* relationships with family.
- Twenty-six percent reported *worsened* relationships.
- Thirty-six percent reported *no change.*

Women

- Fifty percent reported *improved* relationships with family.
- Thirteen percent reported *worsened* relationships.
- Thirty-seven percent reported *no change.*

More than half of the respondents of both genders reported some kind of change in their relationships with their family due to their divorce. For both sexes the change is predominantly for the better. Women experience a somewhat greater feeling of family reunion and closeness than men in a time of separation, divorce, and aloneness. This is true for the next query as well.

19. Relationship with Children

Major Finding: **Relationships with one's children tend to improve during the first year or tend to remain the same.**

Men

- Thirty-nine percent reported *improved* relationships with their children.
- Eighteen percent reported *worsened* relationships.
- Forty-three percent reported *no change.*

Women

- Fifty-four percent reported *improved* relationships with their children.
- Twelve percent reported *worsened* relationships.
- Thirty-four percent reported *no change.*

As in the previous question, 18, both sexes reported domestic improvement. However, women led men in their positive response to both questions. "The obvious reason for this," remarks Dr. Jonathan Weiss, clinical assistant professor of psychiatry at New York Hospital, Cornell University Medical Center, "is that women are the ones who get custody of the children. When they speak of improved familial relations they are thus speaking of improved relationships with their children and not, say, with their parents. Children are the direct recipients of whatever it is the woman is going through. In a bad marriage women often vent their negative feelings on their children. When the marriage is dissolved, once the separation takes place and the tension lessens, women may find themselves more relaxed and thus better parents. Men, on the other hand, are often aloof from children in marriage. They are at the office all day, and generally tend to hide their feelings around children more than women. After the divorce, however, they may find themselves called upon to take the children more and be with them more, and this may at first cause a strain on the relationships, especially if the children blame the father for the breakup."

20. Commitment to Profession

Major Finding: Commitment to profession increases in the first year following divorce.

Men

- Forty percent reported *increased* commitment to profession.
- Ten percent reported *decreased* commitment.
- Twelve percent reported *changing their profession* because of becoming single.
- Thirty-eight percent reported *no change.*

Women

- Forty-four percent reported *increased* commitment to profession.
- Five percent reported *decreased* commitment.
- Twenty-one percent reported *changing their profession* because of becoming single.
- Thirty percent reported *no change.*

21. Earning Capacity

Major Finding: Earning capacity increases among new singles.

Men

- Forty-two percent reported *increased* earning capacity.
- Twelve percent reported *decreased* earning capacity.
- Forty-six percent reported *no change.*

Women

- Forty-seven percent reported *increased* earning capacity.
- Twenty-four percent reported *decreased* capacity.
- Twenty-nine percent reported *no change.*

Men and women both express increased interest and involvement in their jobs, and greater salaries. Reasons for these improvements are discussed in Chapter 4 (Living Alone). Briefly, they include more time to invest in the job, less demands at home, more available energy, and greater job mobility. As to higher earning capacity, this is a tricky statistic, especially in the case of divorced women. Some divorced women may not have held a job at all while married, so that *whatever* their new job may pay it is higher than before. In a situation where both married partners were working, there may now be greater earnings registered by the individual separated mates, yet even this increase fails to provide the same real individual purchasing power experienced when the two salaries were pooled. In any case, indications are still generally positive concerning a new single's chance for financial and occupational success.

The Essay Question

For a final perspective on the first year of separation we added an essay question to the questionnaire: What were the greatest problems and pleasures you faced when first becoming single?

Woman, Chicago, IL: "The greatest problem I faced was my self-esteem. I thought very low of myself and thought no guy would ever be interested in me again. I was very young but felt like I had aged ten years. When I told others I was divorced I would get a bad reaction, so I have quit trying to tell others."

Man, Queens, NY: "Problems—financial insecurity, feelings of being alone, feeling unneeded, confusion about knowing what will happen to me in the future. *Pleasures*—freedom, ability to think, learn, do, follow research of my own."

Man, Boston, MA: "My greatest problem was adjusting to the fact that my wife left me for a man she hardly knew, for money. She left me with our three-year-old son, and he has been a problem to raise alone because he misses his mother. It has been hard to accept the fact that she did not feel the same toward me as I did her. The only pleasures I have are a deepening relationship with my son, and the chance to learn a new career."

Woman, Los Angeles, CA: "Fear of being rejected by the opposite sex and fear of failing at self-actualization. Pleasures—ability to do and act as freely as I want without worrying about my husband's disapproval. A calmness comes over me that has made all the difference."

Woman, Philadelphia, PA: "No problems. Just pleasures and freedom. Greatest pleasure knowing I was out of a most unpleasant situation. That my life would once again be my own. That I was three thousand miles away from that son-of-a-bitch-bastard-shit!"

Man, Brooklyn, NY: "Paying child support. Loneliness. Everyone else is married, me alone. Can't communicate your problems. Meeting my ex everywhere. Finding a woman. Pleasures? Few and far between."

Woman, San Francisco, CA: "Problems are lack of security, loss of friends. Filling spare time. Telling my parents about divorce, being alone. Not enough sex (you get used to it). Difficulty meeting decent men. Men expecting sex as payment for a date. No sex, didn't call again. Sleeping alone in a cold bed. Talking to men on a personal basis is hard. Most don't care about you. Learning to trust again. The hard, cruel world out there, buster! I got married at fifteen and divorced at twenty-four, so am rather mixed up about men. Sometimes people need professional help after divorce."

Man, Hollywood, CA: "Learning to live alone after having a wife and three children. Also my eating habits changed, and I started drinking more than normal. I got tired of moving around. I had five different addresses within the first year. Some of my greatest pleasures were that I could come and go without getting yelled at. I enjoyed dating at first. I enjoyed making new friends and meeting new people. I still like meeting people, but dating gets to be a bore and a drag."

Woman, Tampa, FL: "Getting used to the decrease in sexual activity has been difficult. I was scared of the fact that I would not be able to support myself and my son. Thank goodness my mom took me in. This may sound dumb, but I depended on my husband to wake me up for work in the morning because I can't hear alarms. I was so confused and nervous that I really wasn't thinking straight."

Man, Queens, NY: "Greatest problem was getting over constantly talking about my former wife to everyone I meet, and the absence of my children. I liked being able to say good morning to a partner and mean it. Freedom to experiment sexually and socially. I wondered if I could make it with another woman in a reasonable time because it had taken me years to reach a sexual rapport with my ex-wife. Trouble accepting the fact that I was a single and not part of a pair—using the words 'I' and 'me,' and dropping the use of 'us.' "

Woman, Jersey City, NJ: "Greatest problem was dealing with and raising my children alone, and being responsible for supporting them alone, and myself. But I feel the ideal of knowing I'm doing it on my own. I find that a lot of tension is gone, and I get along better with my children, and I respect myself again."

Man, Omaha, NB: "Problems: loneliness, lack sexual arousal because unable to have orgasms (recurs periodically). Fear of rejection. Pleasure: feeling of freedom without having to answer to any woman for my actions. Responsible to myself. Freedom to be open with women and men. Doing things I never had time to do before. I especially like freedom from my old wife."

Woman, Des Moines, IA: "The only real problem is financial now. I had never had money worries before and now cannot make ends meet. The relaxed atmosphere at home has improved for my children as well as myself. My children are very important to me, and seeing them so much happier makes me happy. I don't have much time evenings to go out but do make it a point to meet with adults at least one night a week, and most of my social activity is with the Singles Club in which I am a member."

Man, Pompton Lakes, NJ: "Facing the fact that my life (as I knew it) was irretrievably altered, and I could not put it back together as it was. Problems with feelings of inadequacy and that I had failed. Pleasures were getting out of debt. Increased feelings of self-sufficiency."

Woman, Buffalo, NY: "The greatest problems that I faced were loneliness and no sex life. But now I realize that one can be happier living alone than with the wrong person. One of the advantages of being single is that you can do as you please. However, if I were married to the right person I would be even happier than I am now."

Man, St. Louis, MO: "Loneliness, a feeling of being isolated from life's meaningful values. I missed *belonging* so very much. When I found myself facing the world alone, with nobody to share life's experiences and emotional needs, it was tough. It was a 'traumatic tragedy' despite the ramifications that marriages inevitably present. Man was not meant to live alone. All of life is a challenge that fosters growth; as individuals we grow by experiences of adversity; but personal growth doesn't supplant two people growing in togetherness, love requited. The pleasures of being single are few, and somehow meaningless."

Woman, Manhattan, NY: "Hard was dealing with the good memories and wondering if I made the right choice in leaving. Growth is painful and leaving one who has not grown with you is very tragic. Wondering how he's doing and knowing that to pick up the phone is wrong for both of you. Pleasures are freedom, right to grow and expand. Fresh air and sunshine. Life and love."

SUMMARY

The predominant attitude that emerges from this special survey is in agreement with the attitude toward singleness that pervades and indeed dominates the survey as a whole: ambivalence.

During their early days of singleness, divorced people seem to inhabit a kind of schizophrenic world. Respondents almost invariably report dips and rises, highs and lows; few speak of their first year after divorce in entirely positive *or* negative terms.

Specifically, *both* increases and decreases in somatic disorders are experienced, as are ups and downs in self-esteem and personal happiness. Though one's path may be troubled by nervous reactions, bouts of anxiety, and general malaise, one can also expect increased energy, well-being, and sometimes even euphoria. Divorce is both an emancipating and an inhibiting event. On the one hand, the divorced individual is now freed from what was almost invariably an untenable personal relationship. With this freedom naturally comes a decrease in mental and, hence, physical stress. At the same time, the disorientation and sense of loss that follows a breakup, even when the marriage itself was hopeless, brings an almost equal though different kind of psychic and psychological pain.

Many people who have undergone First-Year Syndrome were singularly unprepared for the experience. Though on the one hand there is little one can do to really prepare for the shock of divorce, it is nonetheless significant to observe how many respondents seemed genuinely amazed at the conflicting emotions they encountered in the first year, so certain were they that by ending their marriage they would end the problems attached to it. But as we have seen throughout, "divorce just means giving up one set of problems for another."

Equally, however, respondents told of being surprised to find that once the plunge had been made, divorce was far from the solitary nightmare they had envisioned. Others were affected by the power of the emotions unleashed by divorce; in many cases these feelings, so long pent up or ignored, became the singles' first real encounter with the potency of their own unconscious drives—and with self-knowledge as well.

Whatever the nature of one's experience immediately after divorce, there is little doubt that the more one is prepared for its intense eruptions and for the life-changing psychological perspectives that ensue, the better one will weather the storm. In this sense, for a person about to terminate a marriage, simply reviewing the data from a survey of this kind can be an aid both in preparation and in understanding.